Microsoft

EXCEL 97

The Cram Sheet

This Cram Sheet contains the distilled, key facts you'll need for the Excel 97 Proficiency exam. Review this information right before you enter the test room, paying special attention to those areas where you feel you need the most review. You can transfer any of these facts from your head onto a blank sheet of paper before beginning the exam.

Excel 97 Proficiency Cram Sheet

CREATING WORKBOOKS

1. Know how to work with multiple sheets in a workbook. Click a sheet tab to make a worksheet active.
2. Use the vertical and horizontal scroll bars to scroll up and down and left and right in a large worksheet. Click the scroll arrows to make small jumps. Click on a scroll bar to make large jumps. Drag a scroll box to get to the cell, column, or row you want to work on.
3. It's important to know how to select a cell and range of cells when entering a formula, copying a formula, formatting column headings, and creating a chart with the ChartWizard. Click on a single cell to select it. Click in the first cell and drag over a group of cells to select a range.
4. There are 3 types of data you can enter: text, numbers, and formulas. Click on the cell where you want to enter data, type the data, and press Enter.
5. To create a multiplication formula that calculates a percent of increase, you need to multiply the value by the percentage of increase. As an example, multiply a salary of $40,000 in cell E4 by a 20% increase (for example, =E4*1.20).
6. To save a workbook and retain the original name, click the Save button on the Standard toolbar.
7. To close a workbook, click the Workbook Window Close (X) button in the upper right corner of the Workbook window.

MODIFYING WORKBOOKS

8. To insert a new sheet, click the sheet tab where you want to insert a new sheet. Select Insert|Worksheet.
9. To change an existing worksheet name, double-click on the sheet tab, type the new name, and press Enter.
10. To center column headings horizontally and vertically, select the range you want to format, and select Format|Cells. Click the Alignment tab. In the Horizontal list, choose Center. In the Vertical list, choose Center. Click OK.
11. To rotate column headings at 60°, select the column headings, and select Format|Cells. Click the Alignment tab. In the Degrees box, type 60. Click OK.
12. Copy a formula down through a column by using the Copy button on the Standard toolbar. Or you could use the mouse by pointing to the fill handle in the cell that contains the formula and drag the fill hand to copy the formula into the cells you want.
13. Insert a new row by clicking on the row header number where you want the new row to appear. Remember that the new row will appear above the row you selected. Select Insert|Row.

14. Make sure you understand absolute cell referencing. To enter an absolute formula, enter the formula and use the F4 (Absolute) key to make a cell reference absolute (for example, =A4/$B$9).

USING FUNCTIONS

15. Always use the Sum tool on the Standard toolbar to quickly create a sum function to add numbers in a column. The sum formula looks like this: =SUM(B5:B10).
16. Use the **MAX** function to calculate and find the maximum number in a range [for example, =MAX(B5:B10)].
17. Use the **MIN** function to calculate and find the minimum number in a range, such as =MIN(B5:B10).
18. Use the **AVERAGE** function to calculate the average for numbers in a range, such as =AVERAGE(B5:B10).

FORMATTING WORKSHEETS

19. Know how to change the font, font size, and font color for text in worksheets. Select the cell or range you want to format. Use the Font, Font Size, and Font Color buttons on the Formatting toolbar to quickly make changes to a font.
20. Alter a border by removing the left and right border and leave the top and bottom border. To do this, choose the Format|Cells command, click the Borders tab, and take a look at the sample outline border. Click on the left and right border to deselect them and you'll be left with the top and bottom border. Click OK.

WORKING WITH RANGES

21. To go to a named range, press F5, double-click on the range name.

USING DRAWING TOOLS

22. To change a logo created with WordArt, select the WordArt logo so that you can make changes to it. When you select the logo, Excel displays the WordArt toolbar.
23. To change the font and font size for a WordArt title in a worksheet, click the Edit Text button on the WordArt toolbar. Choose a font and font size, and click OK.
24. To format the WordArt text by changing its color, click the Format WordArt button on the WordArt toolbar. Choose a color, and click OK.
25. After you're finished using the WordArt tools on the toolbar to make the necessary changes, just click any cell outside the logo, and Excel will hide the WordArt toolbar.

PRINTING WORKBOOKS

26. Switch to Page Break Preview by selecting View|Page Break Preview. To return to Normal view, select View|Normal.
27. To exclude a column while in Page Break Preview, drag the right blue border to the left.
28. When you want to print directly from Page Break Preview, click the Print button on the Standard toolbar.
29. To find a range name, press F5 (Go To), and double-click on range name in the list. To print a range name, press Ctrl+P, choose Selection in the Print What Area, and click OK.

CREATING CHARTS

30. Create a chart using the Chart Wizard. Select the data you want to chart. Click the Chart Wizard button on the Standard toolbar. Choose an area chart with series in rows, enter a chart title, a category X-axis title, a value Y-axis title, and no legend. Insert the chart as an object just below the worksheet that contains the data you're charting. The Chart toolbar will appear after you create the chart.
31. To move a chart, click on it to select it, and drag it to the new location.
32. To resize the chart to fit it into a specified range, drag a selection handle to stretch or shrink the chart.
33. To display and print your worksheet and chart using Page Break Preview, choose View|Page Break Preview, and click the Print button on the Standard toolbar.

CREATING INTERNET AND INTRANET DOCUMENTS

34. Save a named range as an HTML file by going to the range name with the F5 (Go To) key. Double-click on the range name in the list. Select File|Save as HTML. Accept all the default settings in each Internet Assistant Wizard dialog box and click Finish.

Microsoft Office User Specialist Program

Application	Proficiency	Expert
Microsoft Word 97	Proves your ability to handle a wide range of everyday tasks. This exam will not qualify for Office Integration Expert.	Proves your ability to do all everyday tasks, plus more complex assignments.
Microsoft Excel 97	Proves your ability to handle a wide range of everyday tasks. This exam will not qualify you for Office Integration Expert.	Proves your ability to do all everyday tasks, plus more complex assignments.
Microsoft Access 97	There will be no Proficiency exam.	Proves your ability to do all everyday tasks, plus more complex assignments.
Microsoft Outlook 97	There will be no Proficiency exam.	Proves your ability to do all everyday tasks, plus more complex assignments.
Microsoft PowerPoint 97	There will be no Proficiency exam.	Proves your ability to do all everyday tasks, plus more complex assignments.
Microsoft Office Integration	There will be no Proficiency exam.	Has attained Expert status in each of the 5 core Office 97 applications. Demonstrates an ability to synthesize the various applications within the Office Suite.

The **Microsoft Office User Specialist** program will be expanded to include Microsoft applications outside the Office Suite, such as Microsoft FrontPage 97 and Microsoft Project.

Proficiency and Expert level tests are also available for Microsoft Word 7 and Microsoft Excel 7 (Office 95).

Microsoft Office User Specialist Program

Microsoft EXCEL 97

MICROSOFT OFFICE USER SPECIALIST

Trudi Reisner

Microsoft Excel 97 Exam Cram

The Coriolis Group, Inc.
An International Thomson Publishing Company
14455 N. Hayden Road, Suite 220
Scottsdale, Arizona 85260

602/483-0192
FAX 602/483-0193
http://www.coriolis.com

Library of Congress Cataloging-in-Publication Data
Reisner, Trudi
Microsoft Excel 97 Exam Cram / by Trudi Reisner.
p. cm.
Includes index.
ISBN 1-57610-221-1
1. Microsoft Excel for Windows 2. Electronic spreadsheets.
I. Title.
HF5548.4.M523R454 1999
005.369--dc21 98-11496
CIP

Printed in the United States of America
10 9 8 7 6 5 4 3 2 1

Publisher
Keith Weiskamp

Acquisitions Editor
Shari Jo Hehr

Marketing Specialist
Cynthia Caldwell

Project Editor
Ann Waggoner Aken

Technical Reviewer
John Nicholson

Production Coordinator
Kim Eoff

Cover Design
Anthony Stock

Layout Design
April Nielsen

CD-ROM Developer
Robert Clarfield

an International Thomson Publishing company

Albany, NY • Belmont, CA • Bonn • Boston • Cincinnati • Detroit • Johannesburg • London • Madrid
Melbourne • Mexico City • New York • Paris • Singapore • Tokyo • Toronto • Washington

14455 North Hayden, Suite 220 • Scottsdale, Arizona 85260

The Smart Way To Get Certified™

Thank you for purchasing one of our innovative certification study guides, just one of the many members of the Coriolis family of certification products.

Certification Insider Press™ was created in late 1997 by The Coriolis Group to help professionals like you obtain certification and advance your career. Achieving certification involves a major commitment and a great deal of hard work. To help you reach your goals, we've listened to others like you and have designed our entire product line around you and the way you like to study, learn, and master challenging subjects. Our approach is the *Smart Way to Get Certified.*

In less than a year, Coriolis has published over one million copies of our highly popular *Exam Cram*, *Exam Prep*, and *On Site* guides. Our *Exam Cram* series, specifically written to help you pass an exam, is the number one certification self-study guide in the industry. *Exam Crams* are the perfect complement to any study plan you have, as well as to the rest of the Certification Insider Press series: *Exam Prep*, comprehensive study guides designed to help you thoroughly learn and master certification topics, and *On Site,* guides that really show you how to apply your skills and knowledge on the job.

Our commitment to you is to ensure that all of the certification study guides we develop help you save time and frustration. Each one provides unique study tips and techniques, memory joggers, custom quizzes, insight about test taking, practical problems to solve, real-world examples, and much more.

We'd like to hear from you. Help us continue to provide the very best certification study materials possible. Write us or email us at **craminfo@coriolis.com** and let us know how our books have helped you study, or tell us about new features that you'd like us to add. If you send us a story about how an *Exam Cram, Exam Prep, or On Site* guide has helped you and we use it in one of our books, we'll send you an official Coriolis shirt for your efforts.

Good luck with your certification exam and your career. Thank you for allowing us to help you achieve your goals.

Keith Weiskamp
Publisher, Certification Insider Press

To Frederick E. Levine, in gratitude for keeping me sane during the life of this project.

❧

About The Author

Trudi Reisner is a computer technical writer specializing in software technical writing and courseware development. Trudi is both a Microsoft Office Proficient Specialist and a Microsoft Office Expert Specialist in Microsoft Excel 97. Trudi has written numerous books including *10 Minute Guide to Excel 5, 10 Minute Guide to Windows 95, Easy Excel 5 for Windows, Easy Microsoft Office 97, Easy Word 6 for Windows, Outlook 97 One Step at a Time,* and *Word 97 One Step at a Time.* Trudi has also written software documentation manuals on insurance, manufacturing, clinical, financial, and font creation software.

Acknowledgments

Many thanks to David Fugate, my agent, for acquiring this project for me. Special thanks to Shari Jo Hehr, acquisitions editor, who gave me the opportunity to write this book; Ann Waggoner Aken, my project editor, who tirelessly got the entire project into shape and gave excellent suggestions; and Mary Millhollon and John R. Nicholson, who copyedited and technically reviewed the manuscript with great efficiency, thereby preventing any embarrassment. Many thanks to Kim Eoff, my production coordinator, for producing the entire book. Finally, thanks to Cynthia Caldwell, marketing specialist; Robert Clarfield, CD-ROM developer; April Nielsen, interior design; and Anthony Stock, cover design, all of Coriolis, for their work on the book and disk.

Contents At A Glance

Table Of Contents

Introduction

Welcome to *Microsoft Excel 97 Exam Cram*. This book aims to help you get ready to take—and pass—the Microsoft Excel Proficiency and the Microsoft Excel Expert exams. In this introduction, I introduce the Microsoft Office User Specialist program in general and talk about how the *Exam Cram* series can help you prepare for the Microsoft Office User Specialist exams.

Exam Cram books help you understand and appreciate the subjects and skills you need to pass Microsoft Office User Specialist exams. The books are aimed strictly at test preparation and review. They do not teach you everything you need to know about an application. Instead, I (the author) present and dissect the questions and problems that you're likely to encounter on a test. I've worked from Microsoft's proficiency guidelines, the exams, and third-party test preparation tools. My aim is to bring together as much information as possible about the Microsoft Office User Specialist exams.

Nevertheless, to completely prepare yourself for any Microsoft test, I recommend that you begin your studies with some classroom training or that you pick up and read one of the many study guides available. We recommend *Exam Preps* from Certification Insider Press—a complete learning and test preparation system when used in conjunction with the Exam Cram you have in hand. Exam Preps feature a practice environment that simulates the application you are learning on the companion CD. If you choose another study guide, I strongly recommend that you install, configure, and fool around with the software or environment that you'll be tested on, because nothing beats hands-on experience and familiarity when it comes to understanding the questions you're likely to encounter on a certification test. Book learning is essential, but hands-on experience is the best teacher of all. The tests are designed to validate your skill level for a specific Microsoft Office application. They accomplish this by testing you on real-world problems within the application on which you are being tested. The Microsoft Office User Specialist certification sets you apart from candidates with whom you are competing for job openings in all areas of business and industry. It proves to a potential employer that you have the skills that are in demand.

The Microsoft Office User Specialist program currently offers certification for Word, Excel, PowerPoint, and Access. Exams are available for Word and Excel in '95 versions, Word 97, Excel 97, and PowerPoint 97; Access 97 is due shortly. FrontPage, Outlook, and Office Integration Expert will follow over the next several months.

There are two certification skill levels for Word and Excel: Proficient and Expert. Only the Expert level is offered for all other applications at this time. Proficient Specialists are able to perform a wide range of daily tasks. Expert Specialists are able to handle more complex tasks in addition to the daily tasks.

The most prestigious certification is that of the Microsoft Office Expert. In order to obtain the Microsoft Office Expert certification, users must obtain Expert Specialist status on all five core Office 97 applications and then pass the Office 97 Integration exam. Passing this exam guarantees that you are not only skilled in each application, but also that you possess integration skills between the Office 97 applications.

Taking A Certification Exam

All Microsoft Office User Specialist exams are offered by Authorized Client Testing (ACT) Centers. Although exams are currently available only in English, exams in Japanese and other languages will be offered as soon as courseware exists. Each computer-based exam costs between $50.00 and $100.00, and if you do not pass, you may retest for an additional $50.00 or more each time. Although most centers require that you pre-register, you may be able to walk in and test. Don't be afraid to ask. You may register by calling 800-933-4493, or contact a local ACT Center directly. If you dial the 800 number, you will be asked for your ZIP code. You will then be given the contact information for one or more centers located near you. Each ACT Center has policies that cover cancelling an appointment, missing a scheduled appointment, and arriving late (e.g., you may not be able to get a refund for a missed appointment). Be sure to find out about your responsibilities and your options. Visit one of these Web sites for more information about the program, the exams, and what people are saying about their test experience before you schedule your exam: **www.officecert.com** or **www.microsoft.com/office/train_cert**.

All exams are timed; you will have one hour or less for each one. The tests measure productivity and efficiency; that means that both speed and accuracy are important in order to pass! You will be asked to perform approximately 40 tasks within about 60 minutes.

Be sure to arrive early enough to complete the registration that you began on the phone. Many centers require you to appear within a specific time interval before the test begins. For example, you might have to arrive 30 minutes prior to your test appointment time. When you call to schedule your exam, ask when you need to be there. You must provide two valid forms of identification at the test center. The tests are monitored and you may not use any test aids (books, notes, etc.). A blank sheet of paper and pencil or a wipe-off board and marker will be provided on which you can take notes. If there is a task with which you are unfamiliar or one that will take more time than you feel you have to complete it, answer it anyway. You have to answer the questions in the order in which they appear. You must complete all parts of a question if you are to receive credit for any of it. Office Help screens are available to you, but you won't have time to use them *and* complete the exam within the time allowed. You must surrender the paper or wipe-off board on which your notes are written when you leave the test room.

Test results are shown on the computer screen when the exam ends, so you will know immediately if you passed or failed. On most exams, you will pass if you perform all but two tasks correctly, so there's not much room for error. If you do not pass, the screen will display a wide range of skill areas that you need to practice before you attempt to take the test again.

Tracking MOUS Status

If you pass your exam, a certificate will be sent to you by mail within one to two weeks. Exam results are reported only to you and to Microsoft. If you pass the Excel 97 Proficiency level exam, your certificate will affirm that you are a "Microsoft Excel 97 Proficient Specialist." If you pass the Excel Expert level exam, your certificate will affirm that you are a "Microsoft Excel 97 Expert Specialist." You will have the proof you need to substantiate the level of expertise you include on your resume.

How To Prepare For An Exam

At a minimum, preparing for an Excel 97 test requires that you obtain and study additional materials. We highly recommend the *Microsoft Office User Specialist Microsoft Excel 97 Exam Prep,* also from Certification Insider Press. This comprehensive, Microsoft-approved study guide provides step-by-step coverage of all of the topics included on the exam. There's a lot of practice, too—end-of-chapter review questions and projects in the book, plus the award winning Excel 97 tutorial simulator on the companion CD-ROM. This interactive tutorial guides you every step of the way through all of the Excel 97 basics and then tests your skill mastery. The CD-ROM also includes the practice documents you'll need in order to perform all of the exercises in the book, saving you hours of valuable study time.

If you can't find the *Microsoft Excel 97 Exam Prep* on the shelf at your favorite bookstore, please visit our Web site at **www.certificationinsider.com** or ask your local bookstore to order a copy for you.

If you know that you need more practice or if you like to study by using a variety of resources, then please refer to the "Need to Know More" sections at the end of each chapter. These Web sites also offer suggestions for further study: **www.officecert.com** or **www.microsoft.com/office/train_cert**.

About This Book

Each topical *Exam Cram* chapter follows a similar structure, along with graphical cues about especially important or useful material. Here's the structure of a typical chapter:

- **Opening hotlists** Each chapter begins with lists of the terms, tools, and skills that you must learn and understand before you can be fully conversant with the chapter's subject matter.
- **Tasks** After the opening hotlists, each chapter gives you a series of tasks to complete related to the topics.
- **Study Alerts** I will highlight information helpful for the test using a special Study Alert layout, like this:

This is what a Study Alert looks like. Normally, a Study Alert stresses concepts, terms, or activities that will most likely appear in one or more certification test questions. For that reason, I think any information found offset in Study Alert format is worthy of unusual attentiveness on your part. Indeed, most of the facts appearing in The Cram Sheet (inside the front cover of this book) appear as Study Alerts within the text.

I have also provided tips that will help build a better foundation of knowledge about the Office application on which you'll test. Although the information may not be on the exam, it is highly relevant and will help you become a better test taker.

This is how tips are formatted. Keep your eyes open for these, and you'll become a test guru in no time.

You will also find items called "Hold That Skill." Consider these as necessary skills you should practice over and over again until you can do them without thinking. They are essential for you to pass the exam.

HOLD That Skill!

Look to Hold That Skill as something for you to practice so you can ace the test.

- **Practice Exercise** This section presents a series of mock test exercises and solutions.

- **Details and resources** Every chapter ends with a section titled "Need To Know More?" That section provides direct pointers to Microsoft and third-party resources that offer further details on the chapter's subject. In addition, this section tries to rate the quality and thoroughness of the topic's coverage by each resource. If you find a resource you like in this collection, use it, but don't feel compelled to use all the resources. On the other hand, I recommend only resources I use on a regular basis, so none of my recommendations will be a waste of your time or money.

The bulk of the book follows this chapter structure slavishly, but there are a few other elements that I'd like to point out: the sample tests and the answer keys to the sample tests that appear in Chapters 12, 13, 24, and 25, and a reasonably exhaustive glossary of terms. Finally, look for The Cram Sheet, which appears inside the front cover of this *Exam Cram* book. It is a valuable tool that represents a condensed and compiled collection of facts, figures, and tips that I think you should memorize before taking the test. Because you can dump this information out of your head and onto a piece of paper before answering any exam questions, you can master this information by brute force—you need to remember it only long enough to write it down when you walk into the test room. You might even want to look at it in the car or in the lobby of the testing center just before you walk in to take the test.

How To Use This Book

This book is designed to be read in sequence and the tasks and skills practice questions allow you to build on what you've learned. I encourage you to do yourself a favor and go for a complete review. However, if you already know Excel 97 and are just brushing up before the exam or if you have taken the exam and failed, you can take the practice exam at the end of the book to reveal any skill weaknesses you need to work on. You can then focus on practicing the skills that you need to work on (the one challenge in this approach is that the practice documents that are provided on the companion disk may build on earlier practice questions).

We'd like to hear from you! If you have comments about our *Microsoft Office User Specialist Exam Crams,* please email us at craminfo@coriolis.com or email them directly to me at trudir@aol.com.

Thanks, and enjoy the book!

Microsoft Office User Specialist Tests

Terms you'll need to understand:

- √ Exercise
- √ Task
- √ Testing strategy
- √ Testing environment
- √ Careful reading
- √ Process of elimination

Skills you'll need to master:

- √ Preparing to take a Microsoft Office User Specialist exam
- √ Practicing (to make perfect)
- √ Making the best use of the testing software
- √ Budgeting your time
- √ Guessing (as a last resort)

You've probably taken literally hundreds of tests in your life by now: multiple-choice, essay questions, fill-ins, and the kind where you have to show your work. Microsoft Office User Specialist tests focus on accomplishing real-world requirements through the use of documents and tasks. You've probably already performed many of these tasks during your training or day-to-day work, so your job is to learn how they are formatted for the test.

The concept behind testing is that if you pass, you know the material and are proficient at it. However, as we all know, some folks are better test-takers than others. This leads to the notion that someone who is very good at doing the actual work could still fail the test, while someone who is only mediocre could pass the exam with flying colors.

In fact, even the most carefully designed test cannot perfectly predict on-the-job performance. Be that as it may, most people would agree that a well-constructed test is better than no test at all. What other objective measure can employers use to tell the difference between those who claim they're knowledgeable and those who really are? Therefore, it's up to you to learn the skills and strategies you need to do well on the test.

Understanding the exam-taking particulars (how much time to spend on questions, the setting you'll be in, and so on) and the testing software will help you concentrate on the material rather than on the environment. Likewise, mastering a few basic test-taking skills should help you recognize (and hopefully overcome) the tricks and traps you're bound to find in the Microsoft test exercises.

In this chapter, we'll explain the testing environment and software, as well as describe some proven test-taking strategies you can use to your advantage. The entire Exam Cram Team has compiled this information based on the many Microsoft Office User Specialist and other Microsoft certification exams we have taken ourselves, and we've also drawn on the advice of our friends and colleagues, some of whom have taken quite a number of Microsoft tests themselves!

The Testing Situation

When you arrive at the center (see the introduction for more information on how to find a test center near you) where you scheduled your test, you'll need to sign in with a test coordinator. He or she will ask you to produce two forms of identification, one of which must be a photo ID. Once you've signed in and your time slot arrives, you'll be asked to deposit any books, bags, or other items you brought with you, and you'll be escorted into a closed room. Typically, that room will be furnished with anywhere from one to half a dozen computers, and each workstation is separated from the others by dividers designed to keep you from seeing what's happening on someone else's computer.

You'll be furnished with a pen or pencil and a blank sheet of paper, or in some cases, an erasable plastic sheet and an erasable felt-tip pen. You're allowed to write down any information you want, and you can write stuff on both sides of the page. We suggest that you memorize as much as possible of the material that appears on The Cram Sheet (inside the front cover of this book) and then write that information down on the blank sheet as soon as you sit down in front of the test machine. You can refer to it anytime you like during the test, but you'll have to surrender the sheet when you leave the room.

There are several techniques you can use to memorize important facts and figures for the exam. One is to associate a list of facts with an easily remembered phrase. For instance, Microsoft Excel 97 order of mathematical operations: Multiplication, Division, Addition, and Subtraction. You could make up a phrase to recall these, such as: My Dear Aunt Sally. Corny, but it works!

Most test rooms are designed to permit the test coordinator to monitor the room, to prevent test-takers from talking to one another, and to observe anything out of the ordinary that might go on. The test coordinator will have preloaded the Microsoft certification test you've signed up for (for this book, that's Microsoft Excel 97 Proficiency or Expert) and you'll be permitted to start as soon as you're seated in front of the machine.

All Microsoft Office User Specialist exams let you to take up to a certain maximum amount of time to complete the test. The Microsoft Excel 97 Proficiency and Expert exams each consist of approximately 40 tasks, randomly selected from a pool of tasks. You're permitted to take up to 60 minutes to complete each exam. All the Microsoft Office User Specialist exams are Pass/Fail. The system will calculate your score and let you know right away (in less than an hour) whether you've passed or failed, but it takes a couple of weeks to get your certificate in the mail.

All Microsoft Office User Specialist exams are computer-generated and use a document (exercise) format. The exercise format means that there will be perhaps nine to ten tasks in each exercise, each task being a one-or-two-sentence instruction.

Although this might sound easy, the exercises are constructed not just to check your mastery of basic facts and figures about Microsoft Excel 97, but they also require you to evaluate one or more sets of circumstances or requirements. There will probably be several technically correct ways to accomplish the objective, but you need to use the most efficient method, or the best or most effective solution to a problem. To get an idea of what Microsoft considers the best method for doing a task, try consulting the Help system within the application (remember, you'll have to do this before the test, because there won't be enough time to consult Help during the test).

In any case, taking the test is quite an adventure, and it involves real thinking. This book will show you what to expect and how to deal with the problems, puzzles, and predicaments you're likely to find on the test.

Test Layout And Design

A typical test exercise and ten tasks are depicted in Exercise 1. It's an exercise that requires you to use a simple worksheet with a preloaded selection of data, then enter text and numbers, enter formulas, format the worksheet, save the workbook, and close the workbook. Following the exercise is a brief summary of each potential technique for performing the tasks and an explanation of why it was either the optimum solution or not. Also, we've included a few examples of how the exercise objectives might have been misinterpreted.

Exercise 1

You work for a small company that stores its employee records in an Excel spreadsheet. The spreadsheet information is in the form of rows and columns of data, and there are now 15 employees, 3 of whom have a last name of Smith. Using the spreadsheet file Employees.xls, build on the spreadsheet named Employees.

1. Open the workbook
2. Enter a new employee named Karen Fishell
3. Give the new employee a salary increase of 10%
4. Calculate the new salary based on the increase
5. Calculate the total original salaries
6. Calculate the total current salaries
7. Right-align the column headings
8. Format the totals with currency and 0 decimal places
9. Save the spreadsheet as Compensation
10. Close the spreadsheet

The fastest way to open a workbook file is to use the Open tool on the Standard toolbar. For Task 2 you'll need to insert a new row by clicking on the row header where you want to insert the row, and then selecting Insert|Rows. The correct way to enter data in an Excel worksheet is to click on the cell where you want to enter the data, type the data, and press Enter. You must be familiar with the process of opening workbook files, inserting rows, and entering text and numbers in order to complete the first three tasks.

For Tasks 4, 5, and 6, you must be familiar with entering the **SUM** function (notice that the tasks don't come out and tell you specifically that this must be done, but it definitely has to happen for the exercise to be correctly completed). For Tasks 7 and 8, you must understand how to format cells using the alignment commands and number formatting. You must also be familiar with saving and closing workbooks.

This sample exercise corresponds closely to those you'll see on Microsoft Office User Specialist tests. To correctly complete the tasks during the test, you would read the document, perform each task in order according to the instructions, and indicate when you are done. The only difference between the Microsoft Office User Specialist exam and this exercise is that the real exercises are not immediately followed by the answers.

For these exercises, one or more solutions to the tasks may exist, and, as far as we can tell (and Microsoft won't comment), such exercises are scored as wrong unless the best solution is chosen. In other words, a technically correct but less than optimum answer does not result in partial credit when the test is scored. In addition, if you make the wrong choice when you solve the first task, don't worry about it because each task is independent of the next one.

Make sure you are familiar with how to navigate using the mouse or the keyboard throughout the application. When the test starts, the application will be present on your screen, as well as the task instruction box. The instruction is repeated at the bottom of the screen, and therefore, you don't need two sets of instructions. As soon as each task instruction box appears, you can just click anywhere on the worksheet to remove the box. Then, all you have to do is read the task instructions at the bottom of the screen. Also, be familiar with the menu choices for using tools such as Find and Go To. With Microsoft Office User Specialist exams, speed counts.

If there are any data files you need to complete an exercise, they will be provided. Occasionally, you will be asked to enter data, create a chart, and so on, but the application should contain most of the objects and data required.

Using Microsoft's Test Software Effectively

One of the first things to check for when you begin your testing experience is to make sure everything is working properly. Is the monitor large enough to use easily? Does the software seem to be functioning smoothly, and are all the required controls present (such as OK and Cancel buttons)? If anything unusual is occurring or something doesn't seem right, make sure the test administrator is aware of it.

If a Quit button displays at any time during the test, do not click it. It will stop the test and there will be no warning dialog box or other option to cancel the Quit command.

There should be an opening message on your screen when you first sit down at the workstation. After reading the message, click the Go to Test button. Don't worry; it doesn't start the test. A warning box will display (read it and click OK), then the Instruction window opens.

The Instruction window contains instructions for taking the test. Read through them all before clicking the Start Test button. The timer doesn't start until you click the Start Test button.

Do not use the numeric keypad to enter numbers on a worksheet. Make sure you use only the numbers on the top row of the keyboard.

Keep working on the tasks until you are absolutely sure of all your answers or until you know you'll run out of time. It's a good idea to solve as many tasks as you can, even if you guess. No answer guarantees no credit for a task, and a guess has at least a chance of being correct. This strategy only works because Microsoft counts blank answers and incorrect answers as equally wrong.

During your test period, you're better off guessing than leaving tasks blank or unsolved.

Taking Testing Seriously

The most important advice we can give you about taking any Microsoft exam is this: Read each exercise carefully! Some exercises are deliberately ambiguous; some use double negatives; others use terminology in incredibly precise ways. We've taken numerous practice exams and real exams ourselves, and in nearly every test, we've gotten at least one task wrong because we didn't read it closely or carefully enough.

Here are some suggestions on how to deal with the tendency to jump to an answer too quickly:

- Make sure you read every word in the task. If you find yourself jumping ahead impatiently, go back and start over.
- As you read, try to restate the task in your own terms. If you can do this, you should be able to perform the task much more easily.
- When returning to a task after your initial read-through, reread every word again—otherwise, the mind falls quickly into a rut. Sometimes, seeing a task afresh after turning your attention elsewhere lets you see something you missed before, but the strong tendency is to see what you've seen before. Try to avoid that tendency at all costs.
- Forget the task for a moment and try to write down, in one phrase, the exact thing you don't understand about the task, or what appears to be missing. If you chew on the subject for a while, your subconscious might provide the details that are lacking, or you might notice a "trick" that will point to the right solution.

Above all, try to deal with each question by thinking through what you know about the Microsoft Office application utilities, characteristics, behaviors, facts, and figures involved. By reviewing what you know (and what you've written down on your information sheet), you'll often recall or understand things sufficiently to determine the best solution to the task.

Task-Handling Strategies

Based on the tests we've taken, a couple of interesting trends in the solutions have become apparent. Many of the tasks have only a single correct solution, but usually there will be several workable methods that seem to be suggested by the text of the task. Unless the correct solution leaps out at you (and if it does, reread the task to look for a trick—sometimes those are the ones you're most likely to get wrong), begin the process of arriving at the correct solution by eliminating those methods that are obviously incorrect.

To identify whether or not your solution will work, you must be aware of each requirement for a given scenario. If you need to use awkward data types, strange calculations, too many extra fields or tables, or nonexistent functions, there's a good chance you're on the wrong track. Also, if a button or an option in a dialog box is unavailable (grayed out) or the exam displays an information message, then you know you're doing something wrong. If you've done your homework for an exam, no invalid or unwieldy methods should be necessary to complete a task. As long as you are sure what's right, it's easy to eliminate what's wrong.

Numerous tasks assume that the default behavior of a particular Office application is in effect. It's essential, therefore, to know and understand the default settings for Microsoft Excel. If you know the defaults and understand what they mean, this knowledge will help you untangle many complex situations.

Likewise, when dealing with tasks that require multiple steps, you must know and perform all the correct steps to get credit. This, too, qualifies as an example of why "careful reading" is so important.

As you work your way through the test, another counter that Microsoft thankfully provides will come in handy—the number of tasks completed and tasks outstanding. Budget your time by making sure that you've completed one-fourth of the tasks one-quarter of the way through the test period. Check again three-quarters of the way through.

If you're not through with the test after 60 minutes, use the last 5 minutes to guess your way through the remaining tasks. Remember, guesses are potentially more valuable than blank answers, because blanks are always wrong, but a guess might turn out to be right. If you haven't a clue about any of the remaining tasks, use whatever solutions come to mind, even if you're pretty sure they're wrong. The important thing is to submit a test for scoring that has a solution for every task. By the way, it appears to us that as little as three wrong choices can cause you to fail the test, so be careful.

Strategies For Success

The most important single factor in passing the test is a thorough understanding of the material coupled with extensive practice. As the saying goes, practice makes perfect, and practicing the demonstration of knowledge on simulated exams is just the ticket. If you study the materials in this book carefully and review all of the practice projects at the end of each chapter, you shouldn't have any trouble identifying those areas where additional preparation and practice are required.

Next, follow up by reading some or all of the materials recommended in the "Need To Know More?" section at the end of each chapter. The idea is to become familiar enough with the concepts and situations you find in the sample tasks to be able to reason your way through similar situations on a real exam. If you know the material and have practiced extensively, you have every right to be confident that you can pass the test.

Once you've worked your way through the book, take the Proficiency practice test in Chapter 12 and the Expert practice test in Chapter 24. This will provide a reality check and additional help in identifying areas that need more work. Make sure you follow up and review materials related to the questions you miss before scheduling a real test. Only when you've covered all the ground and feel comfortable with the whole scope of the practice test, should you take a real test.

If you take our practice test and don't score at least 75 percent correct, you'll want to practice further. At a minimum, check to see if there are Personal Exam Prep (PEP) tests and the self-assessment tests available at the Microsoft Training And Certification Web site's download page (its location appears in the next section). If you're more ambitious or better funded, you might want to purchase a practice test from one of the third-party vendors, although none were yet available at press time.

Armed with the information in this book, and with the determination to augment your knowledge, you should be able to pass the Microsoft Office User Specialist exam. Considering the fee for taking the test (pass or fail) each time may be from $50 to $100, it's definitely worth the effort to work hard at preparation. By the way, you may want to price-check several test centers before scheduling an appointment for an exam because the prices vary from center to center. The test may even be free with enrollment in a class at training centers. If you prepare seriously, the exam should go flawlessly. Good luck!

Additional Resources

We've distilled all the best Microsoft Office User Specialist exam information into this book, but if you want to delve into great detail, an excellent source of information is maintained by the Microsoft Corporation itself. Because its products and technologies—and the tests that go with them—change frequently, the most up-to-date place to go for exam-related information is online.

If you haven't already visited the Microsoft Training And Certification pages, do so right now. As we're writing this chapter, the Training And Certification home page resides at **www.microsoft.com/train_cert/ie30.htm** (see Figure 1.1). Another Web Site devoted exclusively to Microsoft Office User Specialist certification is officecert.com (no www in the URL), and New Horizons, a Microsoft Independent Courseware Vendor with offices around the country, maintains a succinct Web Site detailing the Microsoft Office User Specialist program at www.newhorizons.com.

> ***Note:*** *They might not be there by the time you read this, or they may have been replaced by something new and different, because things change regularly on the Microsoft site. Should this happen, please read the section titled "Coping With Change On The Web," later in this chapter.*

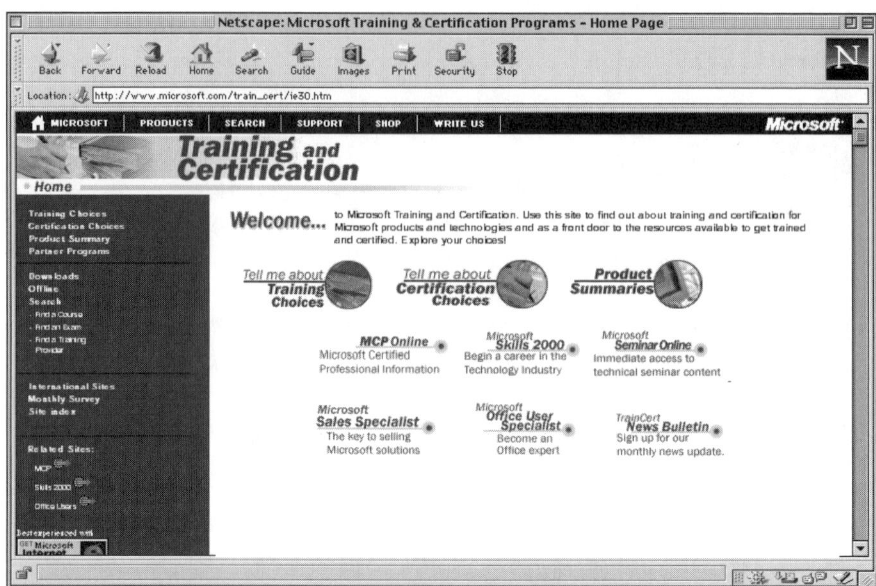

Figure 1.1 The Microsoft Training And Certification home page should be your starting point for further investigation of the most current exam and preparation information.

The menu options in the left column of the home page point to the most important sources of information in the Microsoft Training And Certification pages. Here's what to check out:

- **Training Choices/Certification Choices/Product Summary** Use these to jump to product-based summaries of all classroom education materials, training materials, study guides, and other information for specific products. Under the heading of Microsoft Windows/Excel 97 you'll find an entire page of information about Microsoft Office User Specialist for Excel 97 training and certification. This tells you a lot about your training and preparation options, and it mentions all the tests that relate to Excel 97.

- **Downloads** Here, you'll find a list of the files and practice tests that Microsoft makes available to the public. These include several items worth downloading, especially the Certification Update, the Personal Exam Prep (PEP) tests, various assessment exams, and a general Exam Study Guide. At press time, Microsoft still had not provided these aids for the Office User Specialist courses, but we hope they will be there by the time you read this. Try to make time to peruse these materials before taking your first test.

- **Search/Find a Course/Find an Exam/Find a Training Provider** This pulls up a search tool that lets you list all Microsoft courses, exams, and training providers. You can find information about any course offered by Microsoft, all exams pertinent to any Microsoft certification (MCSE, MCSD, MCT, Microsoft Office User Specialist, and so on) as well as those exams that cover a particular product, and links and phone numbers for Microsoft Independent Courseware Vendors (ICVs). This tool is quite useful not only to review the options, but also to obtain specific test preparation information, because each exam has its own associated preparation guide. For this test, be sure to grab the one for Microsoft Excel 97 Expert.

Of course, these are just the high points of what's available in the Microsoft Training And Certification pages. As you browse through them—and we strongly recommend that you do—you'll probably find other things we didn't mention here that are every bit as interesting and compelling.

Coping With Change On The Web

Sooner or later, all the specifics we've shared with you about the Microsoft Training And Certification pages, and all the other Web-based resources we mention throughout the rest of this book, will go stale or be replaced by newer information. In some cases, the URLs you find here might lead you to their replacements; in other cases, the URLs will go nowhere, leaving you with the dreaded "404 File not found" error message.

When that happens, please don't give up! There's always a way to find what you want on the Web—if you're willing to invest some time and energy. To begin with, most large or complex Web sites—and Microsoft's qualifies on both counts—offer a search engine. Looking at Figure 1.1, you'll see that a Search button appears along the top edge of the page. As long as you can get to the site itself (and we're pretty sure that it will stay at www.microsoft.com for a long while yet), you can use this tool to help you find what you need.

The more particular or focused you can make a search request, the more likely it is that the results will include information you can use. For instance, you can search the string "training and certification" to produce a lot of data about the subject in general, but if you're looking for the Proficiency Guidelines for the Excel 97 Exam, then the search phrase "Microsoft Office User Specialist for Excel 97" will be more likely to get you there quickly.

Likewise, if you want to find the Training and Certification downloads, try a search string with Boolean operators (AND, OR, NOR, and so on) such as this one:

```
training and certification AND download page
```

Finally, don't be afraid to use general search tools such as **www.search.com**, **www.altavista.com**, **www.webcrawler.com**, or **www.excite.com** to search for related information. Even though Microsoft offers the best information about its certification exams online, there are plenty of third-party sources of information, training, and assistance in this area that do not have to follow the corporate line (like Microsoft does). Essentially, if you can't find something where the book says it is, start looking around. If worse comes to worst, you can always email us! We just might have a clue.

2

Brushing Up On Excel Basics

Terms you'll need to understand:

- √ Menu bar
- √ Toolbar
- √ Scroll bars
- √ Select

Skills you'll need to master:

- √ Selecting a menu command
- √ Using toolbars
- √ Moving around workbooks
- √ Moving around worksheets
- √ Selecting cells

Excel Overview

Excel makes managing information easier, letting you create worksheets, databases, charts, and macros. Specifically, you can use Excel to lay out a worksheet, calculate numbers, make editing changes, undo mistakes, check spelling, and make formatting changes. Excel also lets you change how data is printed, preview your print job, and chart numeric data. With more advanced Excel features, you can audit worksheets, import and export data from other applications, create lists, work with multiple workbooks, and use templates. You can also share Excel information with other people using Excel's workgroup functions. In this chapter, you learn how to start Excel, how Excel is arranged, what commands each menu has, and how to get around in Excel. This chapter serves as a memory jogger and organizer for Excel as a whole.

Excel Basics

You start Excel as you would any Microsoft Office program, by using your Windows Start button. When you open Excel, the application displays an empty workbook containing three empty worksheets.

A *worksheet* is a grid of columns and rows. The intersection of any column and row is called a *cell.* Each cell in a worksheet has a unique cell reference. A *cell reference* is a designation formed by combining the row and column headings. For example, A3 refers to the cell located at the intersection of column A and row 3. A worksheet contains 256 columns identified by the letters A through Z and then AA through IV. A worksheet contains 65,536 rows identified by the numbers 1 through 65536. The total number of cells on a worksheet is 16,777,216.

Task 1 Starting Excel.

1. Click the Start button on the Windows taskbar.
2. From the Start menu, choose Programs.
3. From the Programs menu, choose Microsoft Excel.

The Excel window should open, and you should see the screen shown in Figure 2.1. Excel displays a blank workbook. The workbook is a file in which you store your data, similar to a three-ring binder. Within a workbook, you have sheets, such as worksheets, chart sheets, and macro sheets. A new workbook contains three sheets, named Sheet1 through Sheet3. You can have up to 255 worksheets per workbook, depending on your computer's available memory.

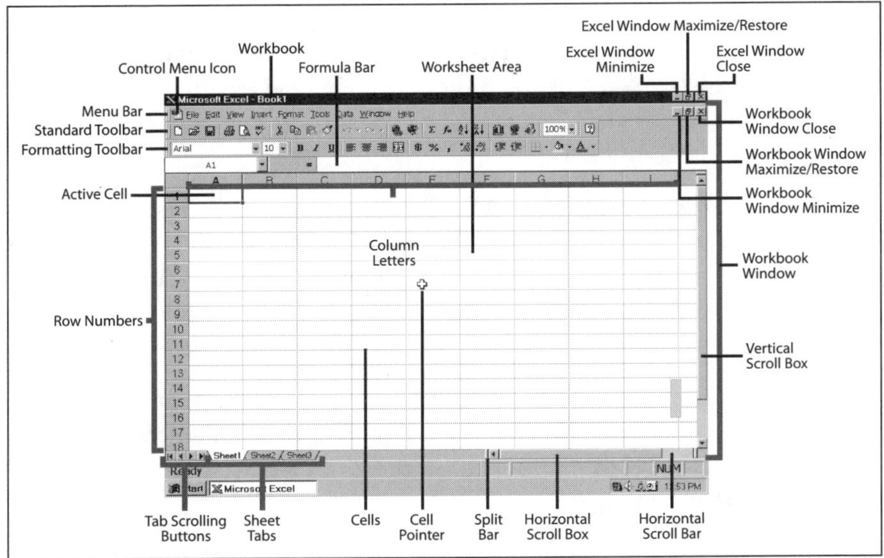

Figure 2.1 The Excel window.

Quick Brushup

The main characteristics of the Excel window consist of the following:

- **Menu Bar** The menu bar is just below the title bar. The menu bar displays Excel's main menu names. You select a menu command to perform operations such as saving a file, formatting numbers, or printing a worksheet.
- **Standard Toolbar** The Standard toolbar contains buttons that execute many common Excel commands, such as save and print.
- **Formatting Toolbar** The Formatting toolbar contains lists and buttons that implement the most common formatting features, such as bold and currency style. Clicking a button on a toolbar is a shortcut for selecting a menu command.
- **Tab Scrolling Buttons** You can move from sheet to sheet in a workbook to find the sheet you want to view or change by using the tab scrolling buttons. The tab scrolling buttons are the four buttons that appear to the left of the sheet tabs at the bottom of the Excel window. After you use the tab scrolling buttons to display the appropriate tab, you must click on the tab to select and display the sheet. Once the sheet you want to work on is displayed, you need some way of moving to various cells on the worksheet. Keep in mind that the part of the worksheet displayed on screen is only a small part of the worksheet. The

split bar is a gray vertical bar that appears at the beginning of the horizontal scroll bar. You can use the split bar to display more or fewer sheet tabs. When you display more sheet tabs, you see more of the horizontal scroll bar. When you show fewer sheet tabs, you see less of the horizontal scroll bar.

- **Horizontal and Vertical Scroll Bars** The worksheet is much larger than one screen can display. To place data in the many cells that make up the worksheet, you must be able to move to the desired locations. You can use your mouse, the vertical and horizontal scroll bars, or the navigation keys on your keyboard to move around a worksheet.
- **Cell Pointer** The *cell pointer* is a cross-shaped pointer that appears over cells in the worksheet. You use the cell pointer to select any cell in the worksheet. The selected cell is called the *active cell.* At least one cell is selected at all times.

A *range* is a specified group of cells. A range can be a single cell, column, row, or any combination of cells, columns, and rows. *Range coordinates* identify a range. The first element in a range coordinate is the reference of the uppermost left cell in the range. The second element is the reference of the lowermost right cell. A colon (:) separates these two elements. For example, the range A1:C3 includes the cells A1, A2, A3, B1, B2, B3, C1, C2, and C3.

In Task 2 you'll be using the File Open command to open a workbook. This chapter's workbook is set up for you to use when you go through the rest of the tasks in this chapter. There are 10 sheets in the workbook. With these multiple worksheets, you'll be able to practice moving around the workbook and the worksheets in Tasks 4 and 5.

Task 2 Selecting a menu command.

1. Point to the File command in the menu bar.
2. Click the left mouse button.
3. Point to the Open command in the File menu.
4. Click the left mouse button.

   You should see the Open dialog box.
5. In the Look In list, find the file named Ch2 Task.xls on the companion disk.

   Note: If you haven't already done so, copy and unzip the files from the companion disk and place them on your hard drive. See the readme file on the disk for futher instructions.

6. Double-click on Ch2 Task.xls.

Now you should see the Ch2 Task workbook on your screen.

To close a menu without making a selection, press Esc.

When you select a menu command, Excel displays a drop-down menu, which contains a list of commands. Figures 2.2 through 2.10 show each Excel menu in the menu bar.

Task 3 Using toolbars.

1. Point to the New button on the toolbar, and leave the mouse pointer on the button.

   Notice that Excel displays the button's name in a light yellow box near the button. This is called a *ScreenTip*.

2. Click the New button.

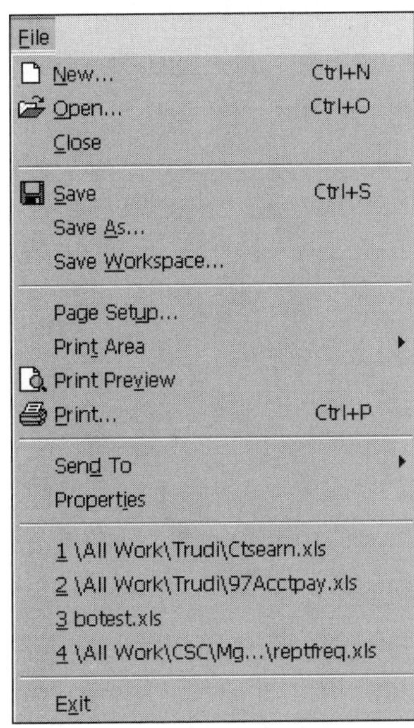

Figure 2.2 The File menu.

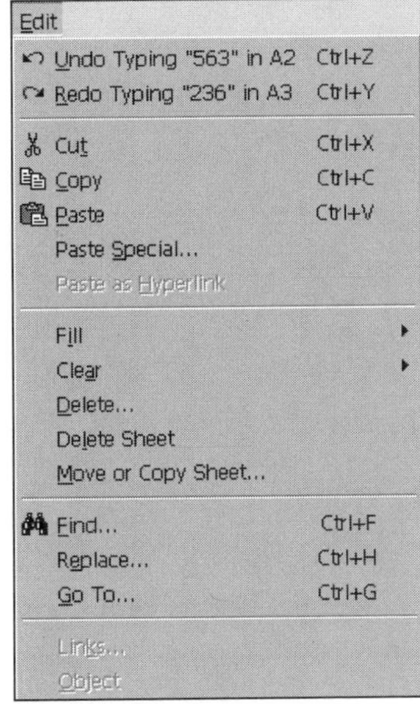

Figure 2.3 The Edit menu.

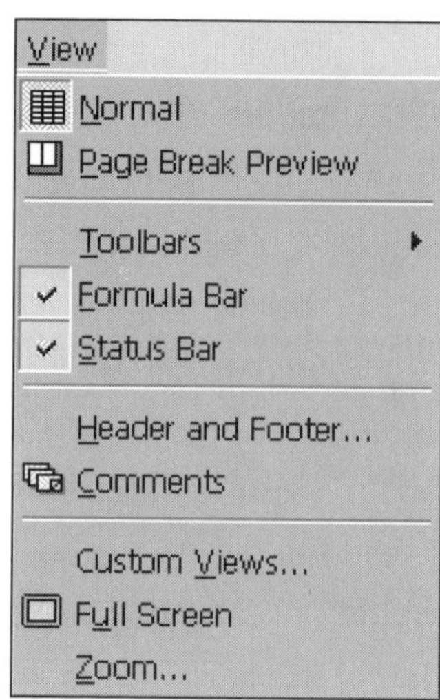

Figure 2.4 The View menu.

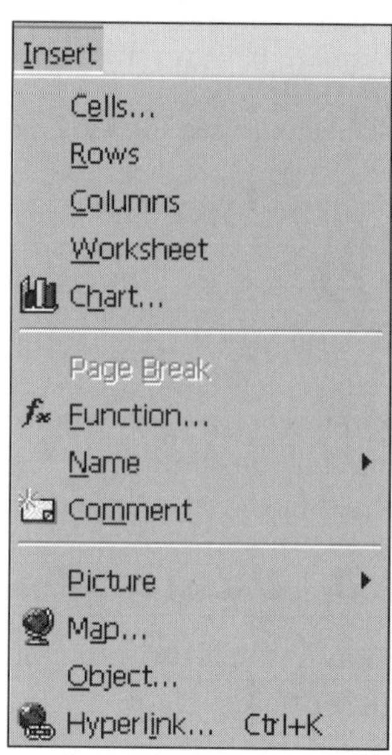

Figure 2.5 The Insert menu.

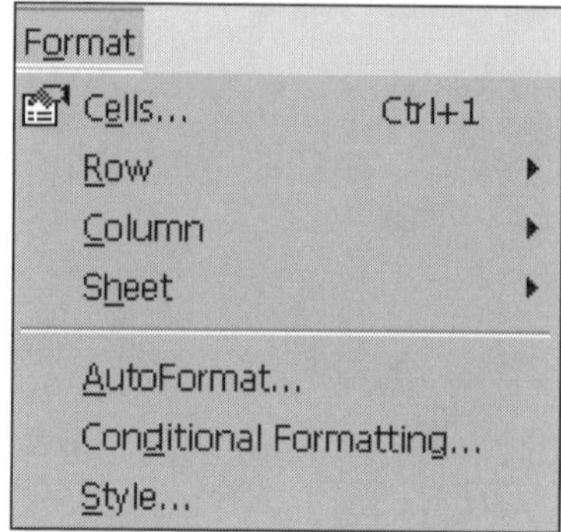

Figure 2.6 The Format menu.

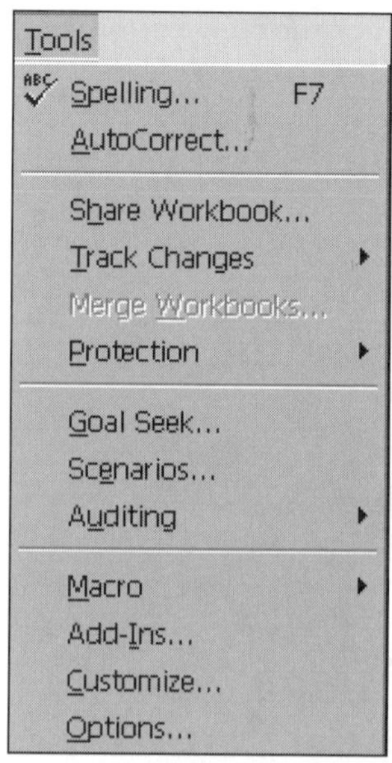

Figure 2.7 The Tools menu.

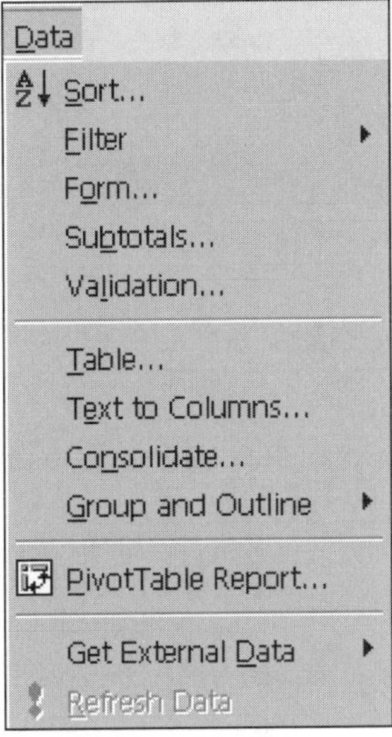

Figure 2.8 The Data menu.

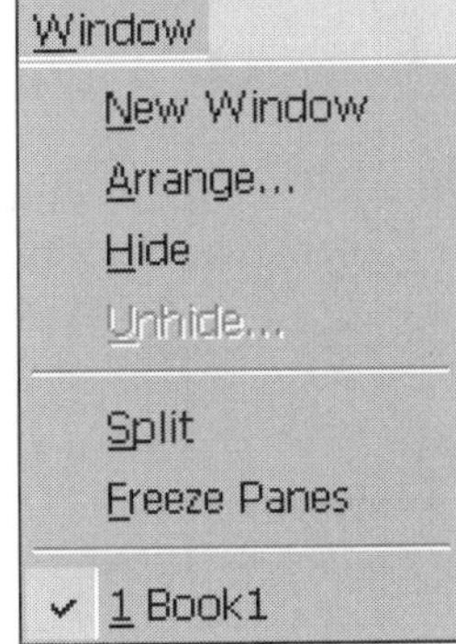

Figure 2.9 The Window menu.

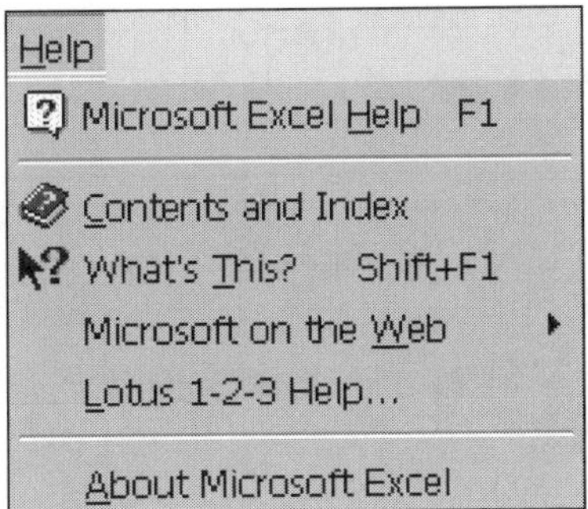

Figure 2.10 The Help menu.

When you click on a toolbar button, Excel performs the command you selected. In this exercise, a new, blank workbook is created (named Book2).

3. Click the Workbook Close (X) button in the upper-right corner of the document window.

You have closed the new workbook. You should see the Ch2 Task workbook on your screen.

Figure 2.11 shows the buttons on the Standard toolbar.

Figure 2.12 shows the buttons on the Formatting toolbar.

Figure 2.11 Standard toolbar buttons.

Figure 2.12 Formatting toolbar buttons.

Task 4 Moving around workbooks.

1. In the Ch2 Task workbook, click the Next tab scrolling button (see Figure 2.13). Excel scrolls the sheets to display the next sheet tab on the right.

   Note: When you create a new workbook, you will have three default sheet tabs showing. When you click on the tab scrolling buttons, nothing is going to happen. When you insert additional worksheets in a workbook, you will be able to scroll around the workbook to display the sheets you want to view.

2. Click the Previous tab scrolling button. Excel scrolls the sheets to display the preceding sheet tab on the left.

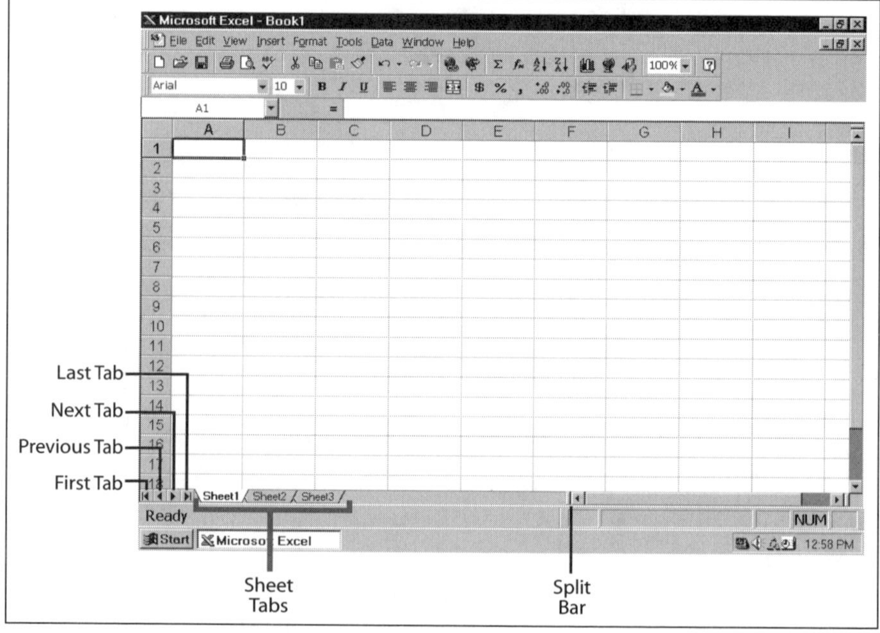

Figure 2.13 The tab scrolling arrows.

3. Click the Last tab scrolling button. Excel displays the last sheet tab in the workbook.
4. Click the First tab scrolling button. Excel displays the first sheet tab in the workbook.
5. Drag the split bar to the right to display more sheet tabs and less of the horizontal scroll bar.
6. Click any of the sheet tabs to make a sheet active.

It's important to understand how to work with multiple sheets within a workbook. You must know how to select a sheet tab to make a worksheet active.

Task 5 Moving around worksheets.

1. In the Ch2 Task workbook, click on an arrow at the end of a scroll bar. Excel moves the worksheet incrementally in the direction of the arrow (see Figure 2.14).
2. Point to the up, down, left, or right scroll arrow, then click and hold down the mouse button to scroll continuously in the particular direction.

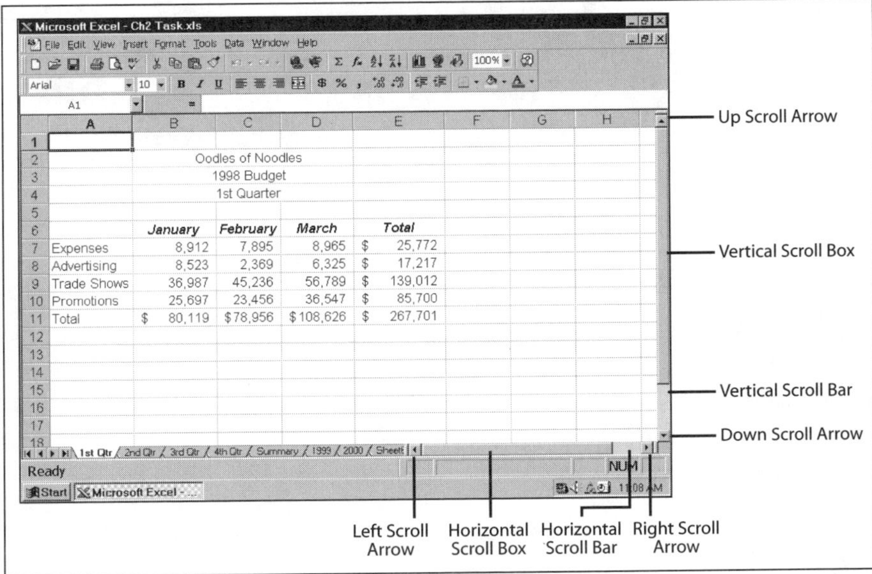

Figure 2.14 The vertical and horizontal scroll bars.

3. Drag the scroll box inside the scroll bar to the area of the worksheet you want to view. Excel moves the worksheet quickly to a new location in the direction you drag the scroll box.

4. Click once inside the scroll bar, on either side of the scroll box. Excel moves the worksheet one screen display at a time.

Be ready to scroll up and down and left and right in a large worksheet. You'll need to know how to make small and large jumps using the vertical and horizontal scroll bars to get to that cell, column, or row you want to work on.

Task 6 Selecting cells.

1. Click any cell to make it the active cell (you should still be in the Ch2 Task workbook).

2. Click and hold down the mouse button, and drag across several cells to select a range of cells.

3. Press and hold down Ctrl, and drag across several cells to select another range of cells (see Figure 2.15).

4. Click any cell to deselect a range of selected cells.

Microsoft Excel - Ch2 Task.xls

	A	B	C	D	E
1					
2			Oodles of Noodles		
3			1998 Budget		
4			1st Quarter		
5					
6		January	February	March	Total
7	Expenses	8,912	7,895	8,965	$ 25,772
8	Advertising	8,523	2,369	6,325	$ 17,217
9	Trade Shows	36,987	45,236	56,789	$ 139,012
10	Promotions	25,697	23,456	36,547	$ 85,700
11	Total	$ 80,119	$78,956	$108,626	$ 267,701

Figure 2.15 Selected ranges in a worksheet.

5. Click any cell to make it the active cell.
6. Press and hold down Ctrl, and click any cell to select a noncontiguous range of cells (a range of cells that are not next to each other).
7. Click any cell to deselect a range of selected cells.
8. Click the Workbook Close (X) button in the upper-right corner of the workbook window and close the workbook without saving the changes.

You have closed the Ch2 Task workbook.

Prepare yourself for selecting a cell, noncontiguous cells, and a range of cells over and over again. You'll be expected to select cells when entering a formula, copying a formula, formatting data, and creating a chart with the ChartWizard. In some tasks, you will not be instructed to deselect a range of cells. If a range of cells remains selected after you finish a task and if you're unsure whether to deselect the range of cells, you should just leave the cells selected and proceed to the next task.

Practice Exercise

The Information Systems Department at the Sandy Shores Company has just installed Excel 97 for Windows on all its desktop computers. As one of the Excel users, you will need to look at a Sandy Shores sales report for the first quarter. No changes will be made to the report at this time. This exercise will just help you get your feet wet by using Excel basics.

Figure 2.16 shows what the worksheet contains before you work through the instructions in this exercise.

1. Open the Chapter 2 Prac Ex workbook file located on the companion disk.
2. Point to a menu command and open the menu.
3. Close the menu without selecting a command.
4. Create a new workbook using the Standard toolbar.
5. Close the new workbook.
6. Select Sheet2 to make it active.
7. Now make Sheet1 active.

	January	February	March	Total
Flip Flops	5,000	5,000	5,000	$ 15,000
Sun Shields	3,256	3,157	3,794	$ 10,207
Castle Builders	5,698	6,981	2,354	$ 15,033
Sand Chairs	6,791	5,482	6,741	$ 19,014
Total	$ 20,745	$ 20,620	$ 17,889	$ 59,254

Figure 2.16 The Practice Exercise before you begin.

8. Use the vertical and horizontal scroll bars to practice moving around the worksheet.
9. Select cell C2.
10. Select the range B6:E6.
11. Select another range without deselecting the first range A7:A11.
12. Deselect the selected ranges.
13. Save the workbook with the same name.
14. Close the workbook.

Answers To Practice Exercise

1. Click the Open tool on the Standard toolbar; double-click on the file called Chapter 2 Prac Ex.xls.
2. Point to any command in the menu bar, and click on the command to open the menu.
3. Press Esc to close the menu.
4. Click the New tool on the Standard toolbar. A blank workbook appears.
5. Click the Close (X) button in the upper-right corner of the new workbook window.
6. Click the Sheet2 tab to make Sheet2 active.
7. Click the Sheet1 tab to make Sheet1 active.
8. Click an arrow at the end of a scroll bar to move the worksheet incrementally in the direction of the arrow. Point to the up, down, left, or right scroll arrow, then click and hold down the mouse button to scroll continuously in the particular direction. Drag the scroll box inside the scroll bar to the area of the worksheet you want to view. Excel moves the worksheet quickly to a new location in the direction you drag the scroll box. Click once inside the scroll bar, on either side of the scroll box. Excel moves the worksheet one screen display at a time.
9. Click cell C2. C2 is the active cell. A box appears around the border of the cell.
10. Click cell B6 and drag over to cell E6. This selects the range B6:E6.
11. Press and hold down Ctrl, then drag across cells A7 through A11. This selects another range, A7:A11.
12. Click any cell. This deselects the selected ranges.

13. Click the Save tool on the Standard toolbar to save the workbook.
14. Click the Close (X) button in the upper-right corner of the workbook window. This closes the workbook.

When you finish the practice exercise, your worksheet should look like the one in Figure 2.17.

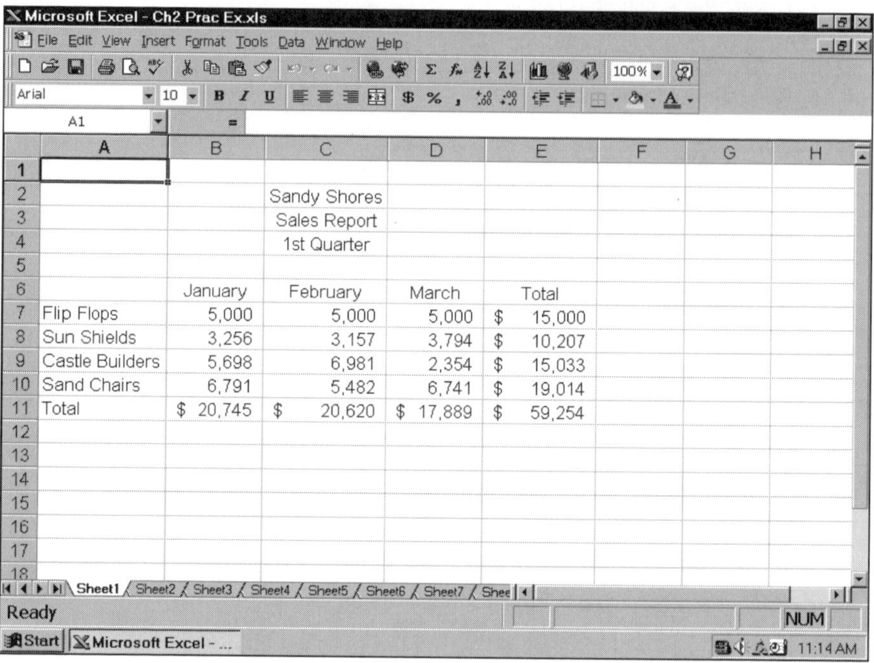

Figure 2.17 The Practice Exercise completed.

Need To Know More?

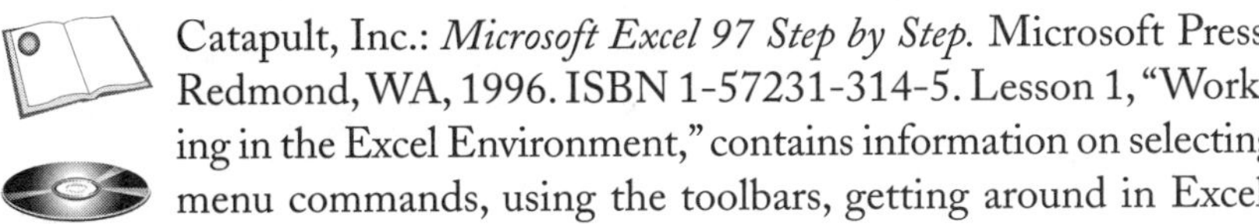

Catapult, Inc.: *Microsoft Excel 97 Step by Step.* Microsoft Press, Redmond, WA, 1996. ISBN 1-57231-314-5. Lesson 1, "Working in the Excel Environment," contains information on selecting menu commands, using the toolbars, getting around in Excel, and selecting cells.

Craig, Deborah: *How to Use Microsoft Excel 97 for Windows.* Que, Indianapolis, IN, 1996. ISBN 1-56276-469-1. Chapter 1, "Introducing Excel," tells you what Excel can do, and what is on your screen. Chapter 3, "Managing Your Workbooks," shows you how to work with a worksheet. Chapter 4, "Working with Worksheets," provides step-by-step instructions for navigating a worksheet.

Harvey, Greg: *Excel 97 for Windows for Dummies.* IDG Books Worldwide, Inc., Foster City, CA, 1996. ISBN 0-7645-0049-X. Chapter 1, "What Is All This Stuff?," introduces you to Excel basics. Chapter 7, "Maintaining Multiple Worksheets," has information on getting around worksheets in a workbook.

Neibauer, Alan: *Excel One Step at a Time.* IDG Books Worldwide, Inc., Foster City, CA, 1997. ISBN 0-7645-3139-5. Lesson 1, "Getting Started," focuses on getting started with Excel. Lesson 2, "Working with Worksheets," shows you how to work with a worksheet.

Nicholson, John R. and Sean R.Nicholson: *Discover Excel 97.* IDG Books Worldwide, Inc., Foster City, CA, 1997. ISBN 1-7645-3047-X. Chapter 1, "Diving In," discusses Excel basics.

Nossiter, Josh: *Using Microsoft Excel 97.* Que, Indianapolis, IN, 1996. ISBN 0-7897-0955-4. Chapter 1, "First Things First: Worksheet Basics," has a nice discussion of the basic worksheet skills you need to know to get around in Excel.

Reisner, Trudi: *Easy Microsoft Office.* Que, Indianapolis, IN, 1997. ISBN 0-7897-1078-1. Part I, "The Basics," instructs you how to select a menu command and use the toolbars. Part VI, "Entering and Editing Data in Excel," steps you through moving around a worksheet, moving between worksheets, and selecting cells.

Proficiency Level

If you can do the following Excel tasks, then you should take the Proficiency Excel exam:

- √ Identify elements in the Excel application window
- √ Create workbooks
- √ Enter text, numbers, and formulas
- √ Save and close workbooks
- √ Modify workbooks
- √ Use formulas and functions
- √ Format worksheets
- √ Work with ranges
- √ Use the drawing tools
- √ Preview and print workbooks
- √ Create charts
- √ Create Internet and Intranet documents

Creating Workbooks

Terms you'll need to understand:

- √ Data types
- √ Text
- √ Numbers
- √ Formulas
- √ Cell reference
- √ Folder
- √ File

Skills you'll need to master:

- √ Opening electronic workbooks
- √ Entering text and numbers
- √ Entering formulas
- √ Saving workbooks
- √ Closing workbooks

Excel Workbooks

Do you have spreadsheets that contain lots of numbers and require calculation? If so, Excel is the program for you. Excel makes it easier to create a workbook, enter data, and run formulas to calculate data quickly. Whenever you change any numbers on an Excel worksheet, your formulas are automatically recalculated and immediately give you the correct statistics.

Getting Started

As noted in Chapter 2, Excel presents a new, blank workbook when you first start the program. To create a worksheet from scratch, you can either enter data in a blank worksheet or create a new workbook using Excel's File|New command. Also, you can open an existing workbook with the File|Open command and then modify the contents of the workbook.

To create a useful worksheet, you must enter data into the cells that make up the worksheet. There are several types of data that you can enter, including text, numbers, formulas, dates, and times. Figure 3.1 shows a sample budget worksheet with text, numbers, and formulas.

Worksheets use formulas to perform calculations on the data you enter. With formulas, you can perform addition, subtraction, multiplication, and division

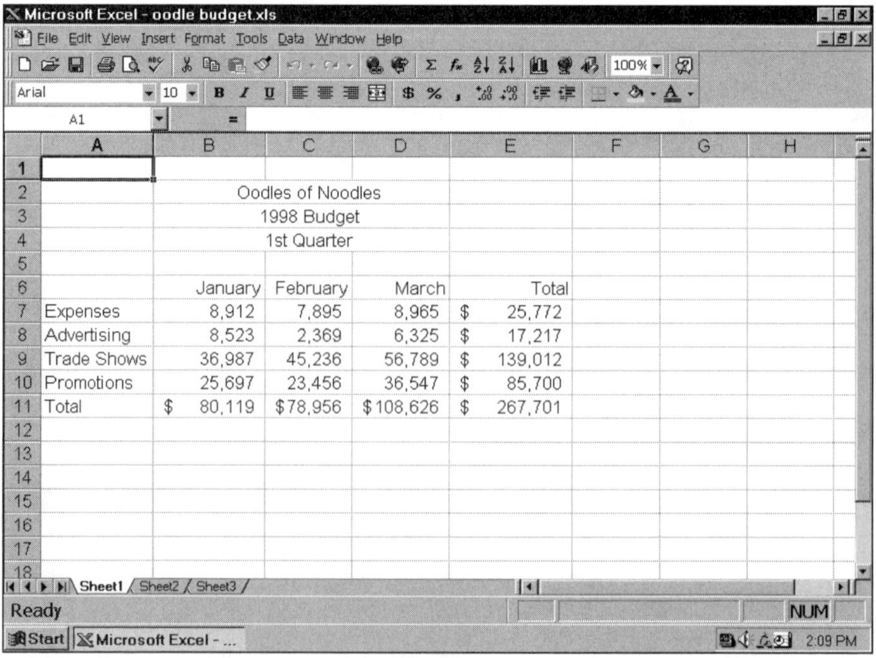

Figure 3.1 A sample budget worksheet.

using the values contained in various cells. Formulas typically consist of one or more cell addresses and/or values and a mathematical operator, such as + (addition), - (subtraction), * (multiplication), or / (division). For example, if you wanted to determine the average of the three values contained in cells A1, B1, and C1, you would enter =(A1+B1+C1)/3 in the cell where you want the result to appear.

Once you enter a formula, you can change the values in the referenced cells. Excel will automatically recalculate values based on cell changes.

In Task 1, you'll be using the File|Open command to open a workbook that is located on your companion disk. This chapter's workbook is set up for you to use when you go through the rest of the tasks in this chapter.

Task 1 Opening electronic workbooks.

1. Click the Start button on the Windows taskbar; choose Programs| Microsoft Excel. This starts the Excel program.
2. Click the Open button on the Standard toolbar. The Open dialog box should appear, as shown in Figure 3.2.
3. Click the Look In drop-down arrow, and select your hard drive, usually Drive C.
4. Select the correct folder from the files and folders list, if necessary.
5. Double-click the Ch3 Task.xls file. This is the file you want to open.

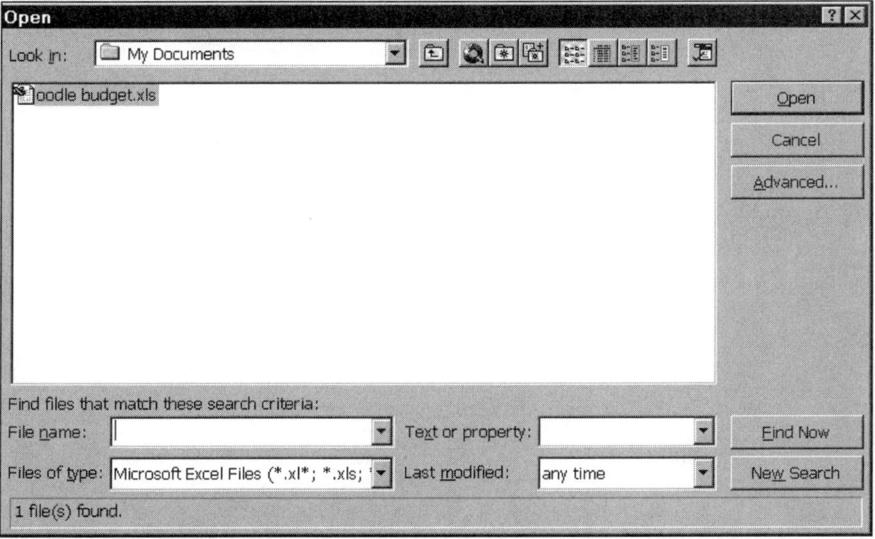

Figure 3.2 The Open dialog box.

Opening a workbook retrieves and displays an existing workbook in a workbook window. From here, you can enter data and perform Excel functions in the workbook called Ch 3 Task.

When you take the Excel exam, be prepared to open a workbook. Using the Open button on the Standard toolbar will save you a lot of time. The correct folder is already selected for you and appears in the Look In box in the Open dialog box. You just select the correct file from a list of workbook files. The files are listed in alphabetical order by default.

Task 2 Entering text and numbers.

1. Click in cell B3.
2. Type "January", then continue to enter the column headings and row headings that appear in Figure 3.3. Be sure to press Enter, Tab, or an arrow key after you type an entry. As you type, your text should appear in the cell and in the formula bar.
3. Type the numbers for January, February, and March that appear in Figure 3.3. Be sure to press Enter, Tab, or an arrow key after you type an entry. As you type, your numbers should appear in the cell and in the formula bar.

Microsoft Excel - Ch3 Task.xls

File Edit View Insert Format Tools Data Window Help

Arial 10 100% A1 =

	A	B	C	D	E	F	G	H
1			Oodles of Noodles					
2			1998 Budget					
3		January	February	March	Total			
4	Expenses	8912	7895	8965				
5	Advertising	8523	2369	6325				
6	Trade Shows	36987	45236	56789				
7	Promotions	25697	23456	36547				
8	Total							
9								
10								
11								
12								
13								
14								
15								
16								
17								
18								

1st Qtr / 2nd Qtr / Sheet3 /

Ready NUM

Figure 3.3 Budget worksheet.

If you make a mistake when typing an entry, you can use the Backspace key to make corrections. Excel does not place an entry in a cell until you press Enter, press an arrow key, press the Tab key, or click the checkmark in the Formula bar. When you type data and press Enter, Excel always moves down one cell. However, you can use the Tab key to move across to the next cell or press an arrow key to move to the next cell in the direction of your choice.

Notice that text is automatically left-aligned and numbers are automatically right-aligned in a cell. Text entries can contain letters, symbols, numbers, or any combination of these characters. The first text you might type in your worksheet is the title and perhaps a subtitle at the top center of the worksheet. Some other examples of text you would type into a worksheet are column and row headings. Column headings appear across the top of the worksheet beneath the title. Row headings appear along the left side of the worksheet, usually in column A. Column headings describe what the data represents in a column. For example, you can enter column headings to specify time periods such as years, months, days, dates, and so on. Row headings describe what the data represents in a row. For example, you can enter row headings to identify income and expense items in a budget, subject titles, and other categories.

Numeric entries contain numbers, dates, times, currency, percentages, text, and other symbols. Valid numbers must begin with a numeral (0 through 9) or one of the following symbols: + (plus sign), - (minus sign), ( ) (parentheses), , (comma), . (decimal point), $ (dollar sign), or % (percentage sign). Numbers are automatically right-aligned. You can include commas, decimal points, dollar signs, percentage signs, and parentheses in the values that you enter.

When you use formulas in your worksheet, Excel calculates your operations from left to right in the following order, giving some operators precedence over others:

1. Equations with parentheses and exponents.
2. Multiplication and division.
3. Addition and subtraction.

Returning to the earlier example, let's say that you want to determine the average of the values in cells A1, B1, and C1. If you enter =A1+B1+C1/3, you'll get the wrong answer. The value in C1 will be divided by 3, and that result will be added to A1+B1. To determine the total of A1 through C1 before dividing by three, you must enclose that group of values in parentheses, like this: =(A1+B1+C1)/3.

You'll need to know how to enter text and numbers in a worksheet. The text you type will be for a row heading at the beginning of a new row. The number you enter is at the top of a column in the new row.

It's very important to know that when a task asks you to "confirm" after you enter data in a worksheet, it means to press the Enter key.

Task 3 Entering formulas.

1. Select the cell where you want the resulting value of the formula to appear. In this case, click cell B8.

   This indicates the cell in which the formula will appear.
2. Type "=" (equal sign).
3. Type "B4".

   This identifies the first cell reference.
4. Type "+" (plus sign).

   This enters the math operator for addition.
5. Type "B5".

   This identifies the next cell reference.
6. Type "+" (plus sign).

   This enters the addition math operator.
7. Type "B6".

   This identifies the next cell reference.
8. Type "+" (plus sign).

   This enters the addition math operator.
9. Type "B7".

   This identifies the final cell reference.
10. Press Enter, and the result is calculated.

Now, you've entered your first formula. The formula should appear in the formula bar as =B4+B5+B6+B7. The correct answer is 80119.

You can also enter a formula by selecting cell references. To do so, select the cell in which the formula will appear. Type the equal sign (=). Click the first cell reference, type the operator, and click the next cell reference. Continue clicking on cells and typing operators until the formula is complete. Then, press Enter.

HOLD That Skill!

Here are some helpful hints to remember when entering text, numbers, and formulas in a worksheet:

- In some cases, you might want to enter a number as text (for example, a ZIP code). Precede your entry with a single quotation mark ('), such as '02110. The single quotation mark is an alignment prefix that tells Excel to treat the following characters as text and left-align them in the cell.
- To enter a negative number, precede it with a minus sign or surround it with parentheses.
- If you enter a number and it appears in the cell as all pound signs (#######) or scientific notation (for example, 5.28E+04), don't worry, the number is okay. This notation simply indicates that the cell is not wide enough to display the number. For a quick fix, select the cell, and choose Format|Column|AutoFit Selection. If the pound signs or scientific notation still display in the cell, choose Format Cells, and choose the Number category.
- To cancel an entry before you are done, click the Cancel button (the button with the X on it) in the Formula bar, or press Esc.
- Every formula must begin with an equal sign (=).
- When you create a formula, be sure that you do not divide by zero, use a blank cell as a divisor in a formula, or refer to a blank cell.

Saving And Closing Workbooks

You can store a copy of your workbook on a disk, making it possible to open and edit the workbook at a later time. Saving a workbook consists of naming the workbook, and then updating it as necessary.

Saving a workbook does not remove it from the screen. This requires closing the workbook. Whether you've saved a workbook or not, you can close it using the File|Close command. If you have made changes to the workbook since you last saved it, Excel gives you a chance to save the workbook.

Task 4 Saving workbooks.

1. Choose File|Save As.

   The Save As dialog box should appear as shown in Figure 3.4.

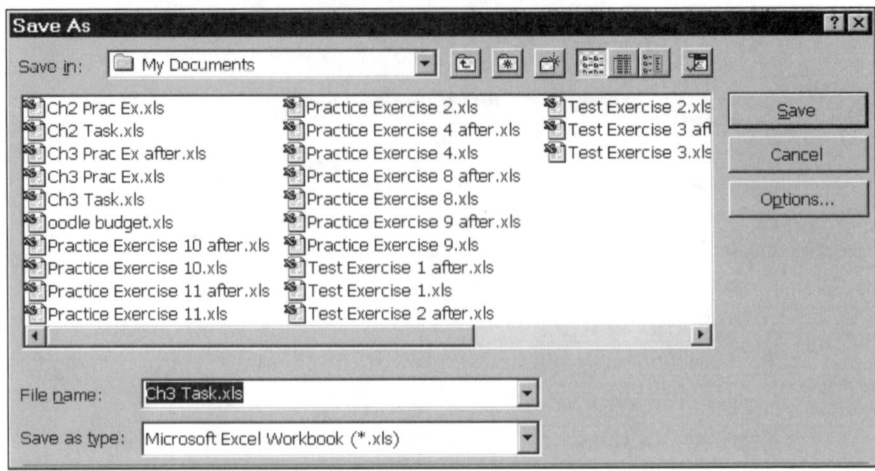

Figure 3.4 The Save As dialog box.

Note: When you save a workbook for the first time, you should click the Save button on the Standard toolbar.

HOLD That Skill!

Here are some important guidelines to keep in mind when you save a workbook:

- When naming a workbook, you can use any combination of letters or numbers up to 255 characters, including spaces, for example, 1998 BUDGET. An example of the complete path (drive letter, server name, and folder path) for a filename is C:\MY DOCUMENTS\1998 BUDGET.
- To move up a folder level in the Save As dialog box, click the Up One Level button on the Save toolbar. To move down a folder level, select a drive in the Save In box, and navigate using the files and folder list.
- To save a file you have already saved (and named), simply click the Save button on the Standard toolbar. Excel automatically saves the workbook (including any changes you entered) without displaying the Save As dialog box.
- If you want to save two versions of a worksheet—the on-screen version and the original—you can use the File|Save As command to save the on-screen version with a different name. Saving a file with a new name gives you two versions of the same workbook with differences in their data. When you save a file with a new name, you also can save the file in a different directory or drive.

2. Click the Save In drop-down arrow to change to the drive where you want to save the workbook, if necessary.
3. Double-click the folder in the files and folders list to save the file to a different folder, if necessary.
4. In the File Name text box, type a name for the workbook. For example, type "my budget".
5. Click the Save button.

The workbook is now saved on the drive and in the folder you specified. Excel 97 automatically adds .XLS to the file name as an extension. We're finished working on this workbook, so it's time to close it. Closing a workbook is explained in the next exercise.

Be sure you know how to save a workbook retaining the original name because this occurs on the test. The quick way to do this is to click the Save button on the Standard toolbar.

Task 5 Closing workbooks.

Click the Close (X) button located in the upper-right corner of the workbook.

> *Note: If you have not yet saved the workbook, you will be prompted to do so. Choose Yes to save your work, or choose No to close your workbook without saving changes.*

Closing a workbook removes the workbook window from the screen. Now, you should see just the menu bar, toolbars, Formula bar, and a blank window.

You will need to know how to close a workbook. Clicking the Workbook Window Close (X) button in the upper-right corner of the Workbook window is the fastest way to close a workbook.

Practice Exercise

The national sales manager at Sandy Shores Company is tracking the sales team and their salaries. Two salespeople have been added to the team and need to be included in the sales report. Your mission is to complete the worksheet with the information provided in the practice exercise.

Figure 3.5 shows what the worksheet contains before you go through the instructions in this exercise.

1. Open the workbook named Ch3 Prac Ex located on the companion disk.
2. In cell A9, enter the row heading Hunt, Neil.
3. Enter a $50,000 salary for Neil Hunt.
4. Give Neil Hunt a 5 percent salary increase.
5. Calculate the current salary for Neil Hunt and be sure to include the 5 percent salary increase.
6. In cell A11, enter the row heading Zola, Lars.
7. Enter a $53,000 salary for Lars Zola.
8. Give Lars Zola a 10 percent salary increase.

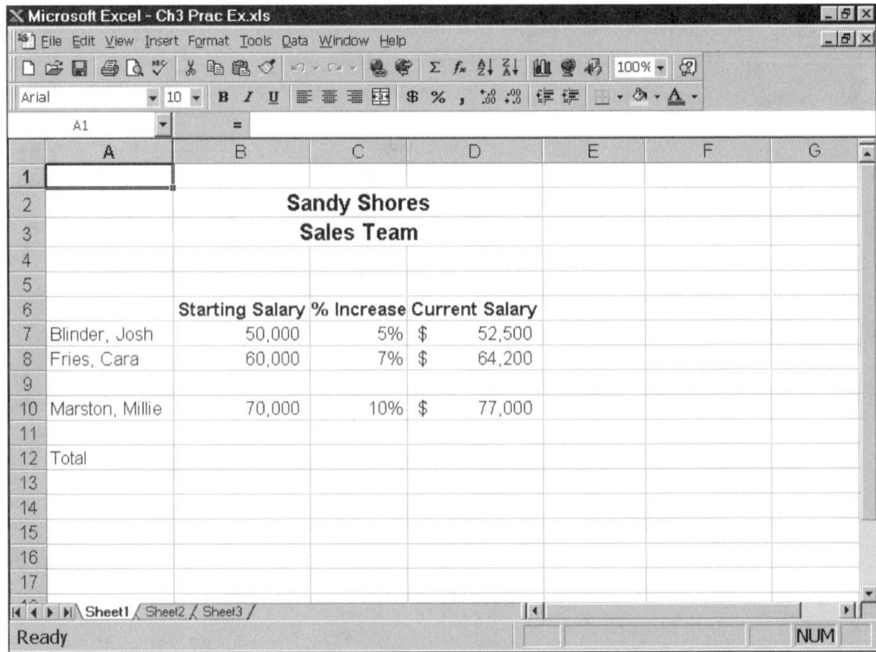

Figure 3.5 The Practice Exercise before you begin.

9. Calculate the current salary for Lars Zola with the 10 percent salary increase.
10. Calculate a total for the starting salaries.
11. Calculate a total for the current salaries.
12. Save the workbook with the same name.
13. Close the workbook.

Answers To Practice Exercise

1. Click the Open tool on the Standard toolbar, and double-click on the file name Ch3 Prac Ex.xls.
2. Click cell A9. Type the row heading "Hunt, Neil". Then, press Tab. This enters the salesperson's name.
3. In cell B9, type "50,000" for the salary, and press Tab. This enters the $50,000 salary.
4. In cell C9, type "5", and press Tab. This enters the 5 percent salary increase.
5. In cell D9, type "=". Click cell B9. Type "*" (multiplication operator), type "1.05", and press Enter. The formula B9*1.05 in cell D9 calculates a 5 percent salary increase for the $50,000 salary. The correct answer is $52,500.
6. Click cell A11. Type the row heading "Zola, Lars". Then, press Tab. This enters the salesperson's name.
7. In cell B11, type "53,000" for the salary, and press Tab. This enters the $53,000 salary.
8. In cell C11, type "10", and press Tab. This enters the 10 percent salary increase.
9. In cell D11, type "=". Click cell B11. Type "*" (multiplication operator), type "1.10", and press Enter. The formula B11*1.10 in cell D11 calculates a 10 percent salary increase for the $53,000 salary. The correct answer is $58,300.
10. Click cell B12. Type "=". Click cell B7. Type "+" (addition operator), click cell B8, type "+", click cell B9, type "+", click cell B10, type "+", and click cell B11. Press Enter. The formula adds the starting salaries in column B. The correct answer is $283,000.
11. Click cell D12. Type "=". Click cell D7. Type "+" (addition operator), click cell D8, type "+", click cell D9, type "+", click cell D10, type "+", and click cell D11. Press Enter. The formula adds the current salaries in column D. The correct answer is $304,500.

12. Click the Save tool on the Standard toolbar to save the workbook.
13. Click the Close (X) button in the upper-right corner of the workbook window. This closes the workbook.

When you finish the practice exercise, your worksheet should look like the one in Figure 3.6.

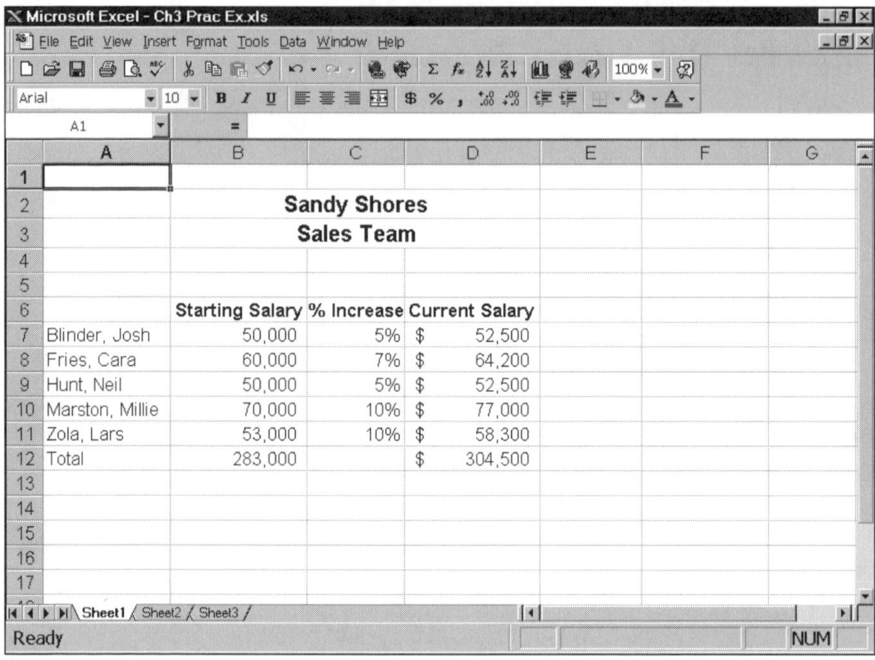

	A	B	C	D
1				
2		Sandy Shores		
3		Sales Team		
4				
5				
6		Starting Salary	% Increase	Current Salary
7	Blinder, Josh	50,000	5%	$ 52,500
8	Fries, Cara	60,000	7%	$ 64,200
9	Hunt, Neil	50,000	5%	$ 52,500
10	Marston, Millie	70,000	10%	$ 77,000
11	Zola, Lars	53,000	10%	$ 58,300
12	Total	283,000		$ 304,500

Figure 3.6 The Practice Exercise completed.

Need To Know More?

Catapult, Inc.: *Microsoft Excel 97 Step by Step.* Microsoft Press, Redmond, WA, 1996. ISBN 1-57231-314-5. Lesson 1, "Working in the Excel Environment," gives you information on entering and editing data, using simple formulas, and managing workbook files. Lesson 3, "Writing Formulas," gives a detailed explanation on adding formulas and how to open files.

Craig, Deborah: *How to Use Microsoft Excel 97 for Windows.* Que, Indianapolis, IN, 1996. ISBN 1-56276-469-1. Chapter 2, "Setting Up a Worksheet," covers how to enter data and sum numbers. Chapter 3, "Managing Your Workbooks," shows you how to save, close, and open workbooks.

Harvey, Greg: *Excel 97 for Windows for Dummies.* IDG Books Worldwide, Inc., Foster City, CA, 1996. ISBN 0-7645-0049-X. Chapter 2, "Creating a Spreadsheet from Scratch?," introduces you to entering text and numbers in worksheets and managing workbooks.

Neibauer, Alan: *Excel One Step at a Time.* IDG Books Worldwide, Inc., Foster City, CA, 1997. ISBN 0-7645-3139-5. Lesson 2, "Working with Worksheets," explores entering data and managing workbook files. Lesson 8, "Working with Formulas and Functions," has a discussion on entering formulas.

Nicholson, John R. and Sean R. Nicholson: *Discover Excel 97.* IDG Books Worldwide, Inc., Foster City, CA, 1997. ISBN 1-7645-3047-X. Chapter 3, "Managing Files and Avoiding Disasters," has information on saving, closing, and opening work books. Chapter 5, "Faster and Easier Shortcuts for Entering Data into Your Worksheets," gives you ways to enter data efficiently. Chapter 6, "New Math: Using Labels, Values, Formulas, and Functions," provides information on entering text, numbers, and formulas.

Nossiter, Josh: *Using Microsoft Excel 97.* Que, Indianapolis, IN, 1996. ISBN 0-7897-0955-4. Chapter 2, "Building a Worksheet," gives you the facts on entering data. Chapter 8, "Formulas: Excel's Recipe for Calculations," tells you everything you need to know about formulas.

Reisner, Trudi: *Easy Microsoft Office.* Que, Indianapolis, IN, 1997. ISBN 0-7897-1078-1. Part II, "Managing Files," Task 6 discusses saving and closing a file, and Task 8 covers opening a file. Part VI, "Entering and Editing Data in Excel," Task 36 teaches you how to enter text and numbers. Part VII, "Working with Formulas," Task 45 shows you how to create a formula.

Modifying Workbooks

Terms you'll need to understand:

- √ Edit mode
- √ Text orientation
- √ Copy
- √ Move
- √ Relative
- √ Absolute
- √ Sort
- √ Ascending order
- √ Descending order

Skills you'll need to master:

- √ Deleting cell contents
- √ Deleting sheets
- √ Inserting sheets
- √ Naming sheets
- √ Revising text and numbers
- √ Revising formulas
- √ Indenting text
- √ Rotating text
- √ Copying data
- √ Moving data
- √ Inserting rows and columns
- √ Deleting rows and columns
- √ Using a relative cell reference in a formula
- √ Using an absolute cell reference in a formula
- √ Sorting text and numbers

Excel Data

This chapter deals with making changes to the data you enter in your worksheet. You'll learn how to delete data and worksheets; revise text, numbers, and formulas; center text horizontally and vertically; copy and move data; insert and delete rows and columns; and create absolute formulas.

The data you enter in your worksheet is not carved in stone. Excel's editing functions enable you to make changes to your data at any time. It's a snap! You can do all kinds of things to the data in your worksheet so that it contains exactly what you want. Editing data involves basically two steps: selecting the data to tell Excel what you want to change, and then performing an Excel command to make the change. In this chapter, you'll see how easy it is to use Excel's editing commands by using the Standard toolbar to make minor and major modifications to your worksheets.

Deleting Data And Sheets

After you press Enter to place data in a cell, you can change your mind about the contents. Sometimes, you might find that a piece of data you initially typed into a cell is incorrect and needs to be changed. Excel makes it easy to erase the contents of a cell.

In addition to removing data within a cell, you can also delete an entire worksheet. If you no longer want a sheet in a workbook, you can delete it. Or, if you want to keep only one worksheet in a workbook, you can delete all the other worksheets to free up memory. Excel enables you to delete an entire worksheet in one fell swoop.

Task 1 Deleting cell contents.

1. Open the workbook Ch4 Task found on the companion disk.
2. Select cell A1 if necessary. This cell contains the data you want to delete.
3. Press Delete.
4. Select cell B4, and drag to cell D8.

   This selects the range B4:D8.
5. Press Delete.
6. Click the Undo button on the Standard toolbar. The data is restored.
7. Click any cell to deselect the cell range.

When you delete cell contents, Excel removes the data from the cell and you see an empty cell. If the empty cell is the active cell, Excel shows an empty formula bar. Deleting cell content does not remove the formatting associated with the data in the cell. If you want to clear the contents of a cell and the formatting, you can use the Edit|Clear command. This command gives you four choices for clearing cells: All (deletes cells content and formatting), Formats (deletes formatting only), Contents (deletes cell contents only), and Comments (deletes comments only). Deleting cell content does not remove the cells themselves. If you would like to delete the cells themselves, select the cell(s) you want to delete, and select Edit|Delete. Then, choose either the Shift cells left or Shift cells up option. Excel will delete the cell(s) and move the surrounding cells left or up.

You'll be asked to clear the contents of a cell. The quickest way to do this is to use the Delete key.

Task 2 Deleting sheets.

1. Click the Sheet4 worksheet tab.
2. Select Edit|Delete Sheet.

   The Delete Sheet dialog box should appear, asking you to confirm the deletion.
3. Click OK.

Excel removes the sheet from the workbook. The remaining sheets appear in the workbook.

You should know how to delete a sheet. Be sure to first click on the sheet you want to delete, and then select Edit|Delete Sheet.

Inserting And Naming Sheets

You can insert new worksheets in your workbook at any time. An advantage to having multiple worksheets is that you can copy and move worksheets within a workbook or from one workbook to another. Another advantage is that you can keep separate pages of data more organized. For example, you might want to keep each sales territory on a separate worksheet within a sales report workbook. After you insert a sheet, you can give it a name to clarify and organize your worksheet.

Task 3 Inserting sheets.

1. Click the Sheet3 worksheet tab if necessary.
2. Select Insert|Worksheet.

Excel inserts the new sheet in the workbook. The new sheet Sheet1 appears between 2nd Qtr and Sheet3.

Task 4 Naming sheets.

1. Double-click the Sheet1 worksheet tab.
2. Type “3rd Qtr”.

   This names the new worksheet.
3. Press Enter.

The worksheet name appears on the tab, as shown in Figure 4.1. If you want to change an existing worksheet name, double-click the worksheet tab, and type the new name.

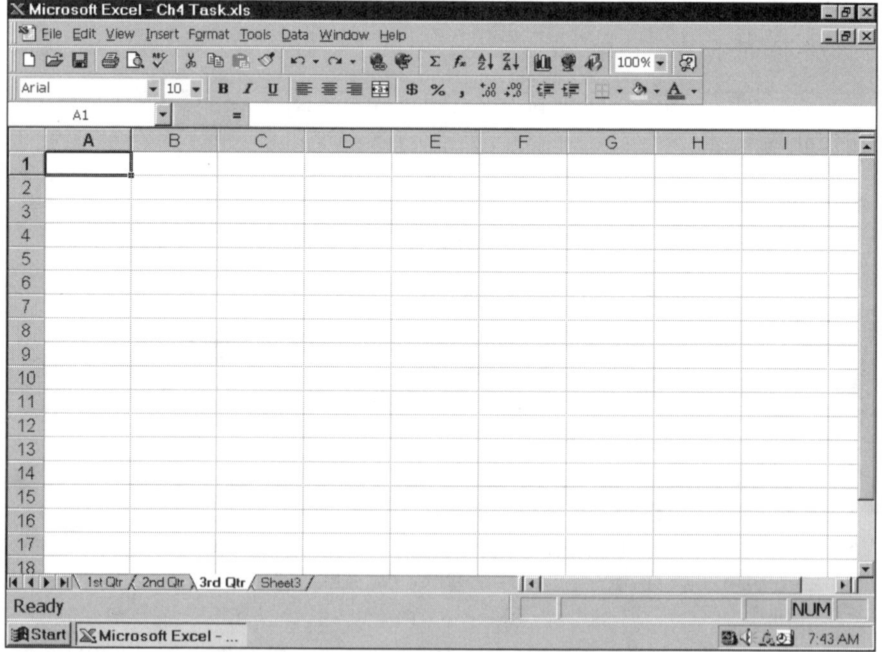

Figure 4.1 New sheet with a name in the workbook.

Revising Data

You can correct data after it is placed in a cell by editing the cell using Excel's Edit functions. You can make changes to any part (or all) of the information in a cell. When you edit data, you don't have to retype an entry. You can just make a few quick changes to correct the contents of a cell. If the changes are an entirely new entry, then you can overwrite the original information.

When you change the numbers in a worksheet, Excel automatically recalculates the formulas that refer to the number and quickly displays the new answers. This is a major advantage to working with an Excel electronic spreadsheet.

You may want to indent data to make it stand out in a column of text or numbers. For example, if you enter a date for a row heading such as June 5, you can indent the row headings, such as the days of the week (Monday, Tuesday, etc.), that appear beneath June 5. That way, the days of the week stand out and are easier to read.

To make your text look fancier, you can rotate the text so that it appears vertically instead of horizontally. Flipping the text sideways lets you print it from top to bottom rather than left to right. If you don't want to flip the text horizontally or vertically, you can angle the text by specifying the number of degrees of an angle you want to rotate the text. The text will appear slanted. You can also center the text horizontally and vertically so that it looks perfectly centered from top to bottom and left to right within a cell.

The exercises in this section describe how to revise text and numbers, revise formulas, indent text, and rotate text.

Task 5 Revising text and numbers.

1. Click the 1st Qtr sheet. Then, click cell A6. This selects the cell that contains the text you want to replace.
2. Type "Conferences", and press Enter.

   This is the new text.
3. Click cell B4.

   This selects the cell that contains the number you want to change.
4. Type "9500", and press Enter.

   This is the new number. The revised entry should appear in the cell and in the Formula bar. Notice that Excel recalculated the formula in cell B8. The new answer is 159663.

You can use the arrow keys to move the insertion point to the characters you want to change or delete. Or, you can click anywhere in the entry in the Formula bar to move the insertion point to where you want it.

Task 6 Revising formulas.

1. Double-click cell B8.

   This cell contains the formula you want to edit.

2. Click before the cell reference C7 in the Formula bar, and drag over to the end of the cell reference.

   This selects the cell reference you want to change.

3. Type "B7".

   This is the new cell reference.

4. Press Enter.

The revised formula should appear in the formula bar. The new answer 80707 should appear in the cell.

Note: Be careful not to unintentionally overwrite formulas with text or numbers. If you overwrite a formula with a number, Excel will no longer update the formula.

It's important to know how to revise a formula, especially changing a formula from one function to another.

Task 7 Indenting text.

1. Select the range A4:A7.

   This highlights the cells that contain the text you want to indent.

2. Click the Increase Indent button on the Formatting toolbar.

   The text in cells A4:A7 should appear indented.

You should be prepared to indent data in a range of cells on the exam.

Task 8 Rotating text.

1. Select the range B3:E3.

   This highlights the cells that contain the text you want to rotate.

2. Select Format|Cells.

   The Format Cells dialog box should appear.

3. Click the Alignment tab (see Figure 4.2).

4. In the Orientation section, type "60" in the Degrees box. This specifies the number of degrees you want the text rotated.

5. Click OK.

   The text in cells B3:E3 should appear slanted.

6. Select your column headings, if necessary.

7. Select Format|Cells.

   The Format Cells dialog box should appear.

8. Click the Alignment tab if necessary.

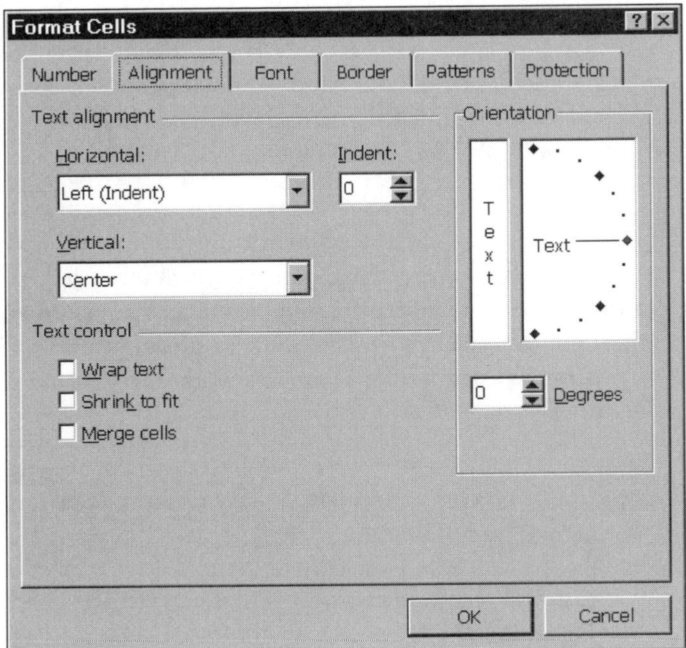

Figure 4.2 The Format Cells dialog box.

9. In the Horizontal section, choose Center.
10. In the Vertical section, choose Center if necessary.
11. Click OK.

The column headings should appear centered horizontally and vertically.

Be ready to center column headings horizontally and vertically using the Format|Cells command. Also, be sure you know how to rotate text.

Copying And Moving Data

You can save time by copying data in one or more cells in a worksheet instead of typing the same data in each cell. For example, you might want to copy text from one cell to another cell. Excel lets you copy text, numbers, and formulas, enabling you to save time and keystrokes. Excel's Edit Copy command lets you copy data to the Clipboard (a temporary storage area) and then paste it wherever you want. Then, you can paste that data again and again because it's stored on the Clipboard for your use until you copy or move different data to the Clipboard.

The drag-and-drop method also lets you copy data in a worksheet. When you drag and drop data, the data is not copied to the Clipboard. Another way to copy data is to use the Edit|Fill command. Again, data is not copied to the Clipboard when you use the Edit|Fill method. With this method, you can just drag the fill handle to copy data. The fill handle is a small box located in the lower-right corner of an active cell's border.

In addition, you can use Excel's Move command or the drag-and-drop method to remove information from one cell and place it into another cell. You do not have to go to the new cell and enter the same data and then erase the data in the old location. For example, you might want to move a title that is in the wrong cell, or you might want to move data in a worksheet because the layout of the worksheet has changed.

In the next task, you'll copy data in three ways. First, you'll copy data to the Clipboard using the Edit|Copy command. Next, you'll copy data using the drag-and-drop method by holding down the Ctrl key and using the mouse. And finally, you'll copy data using the fill handle.

Task 9 Copying data.

1. Click cell B4. This selects the first cell in the range you want to copy. Click in cell B4 and drag to cell B7. This is the last cell in the range.

Note: Be sure to position the mouse pointer inside the border of the cell you drag to highlight the range. Avoid pointing to the fill handle because you will copy the cell's content. Also, don't point to the cell's border because you'll move the cell content.

This selects the range that you want to copy.

2. Click the Copy button on the Standard toolbar.

   A marquee surrounds the range you selected.

3. Click cell B10.

   This indicates where you want the copied data to appear.

4. Click the Paste button on the Standard toolbar.
5. Press Esc to remove the marquee.

   The data should appear in the original location as well as in the new location.

6. Click cell B8.

   This selects the cell that contains the formula you want to copy.

7. Hold down the Ctrl key, and move the mouse pointer to any border of the active cell.

   The mouse pointer has a plus sign next to it, indicating that you are going to copy data using the mouse.

8. Click and drag the mouse to cell B14.

   The formula should appear in the original location as well as in the new location.

9. Click cell B8.

   This selects the cell that contains the formula you want to copy.

10. Move the mouse pointer to the small box in the lower-right corner of the active cell.

    The mouse pointer changes to a plus sign.

11. Click and drag the mouse over cells C8:D8.

The formula should appear in the original location as well as in the new locations.

Be sure you know how to copy a formula down through a column. You should also know how to copy data to fill a range of cells. You can use the Copy button on the Standard toolbar or use the fill handle technique, using the mouse to drag the formula or the text and copy it into the cells you want.

Task 10 Moving data.

1. Click cell C1.

   This action selects the data that you want to move.

2. Click the Cut button on the Standard toolbar.
3. Click cell A2.

   This indicates where you want the data to appear.

4. Click the Paste button on the Standard toolbar.

The data should be cleared in the original location and appear only in the new location.

Be sure you know how to move data to a new location in the worksheet. It's best to use the drag-and-drop method by pointing to the cell's border and dragging the contents to the new location in the worksheet.

Inserting And Deleting Rows And Columns

Inserting extra rows and columns allows you to make room for additional data. Adding more space between rows and columns makes the worksheet easier to read. You might want to delete rows or columns from a worksheet to close up some empty space. In this section, we'll insert and delete rows and columns.

Task 11 Inserting rows and columns.

1. Click row header 3. This selects the entire row.
2. Select Insert|Rows.
3. Click column header A to select the entire column.
4. Select Insert|Columns.

A new row should appear where you selected a row. All subsequent rows should shift downward. A new column should appear to the left of the column you selected. All adjacent columns should shift to the right, as shown in Figure 4.3.

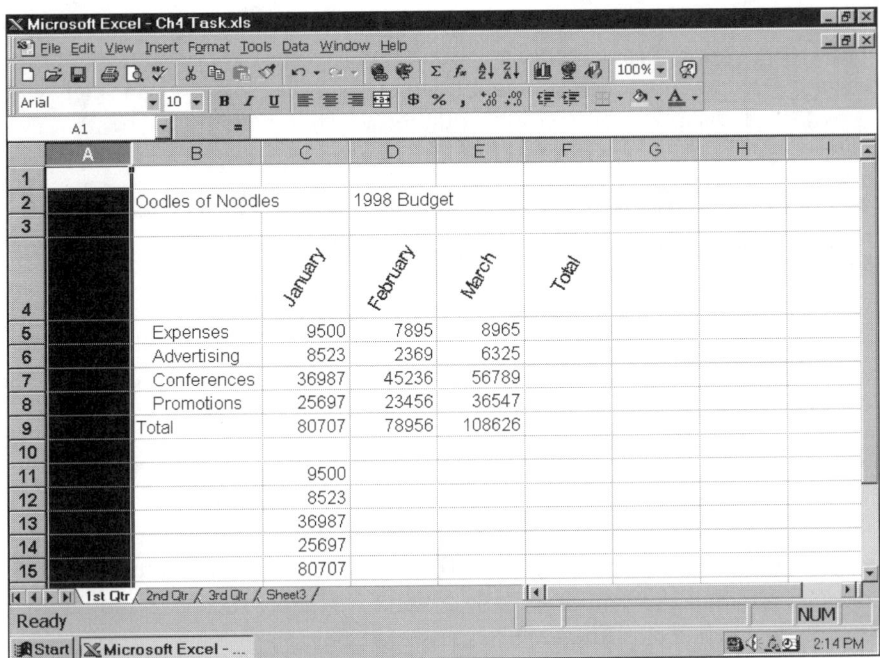

Figure 4.3 A new row and new column in the worksheet.

Be ready to insert a new row in one of the exercises on the exam. Be sure to select the correct row header by clicking on the row header number where you want the new row to appear. Remember that the new row will appear above the row you selected.

Task 12 Deleting rows and columns.

1. Click row header 1 to select the entire row.
2. Select Edit|Delete.

   The row should disappear, and all subsequent rows should shift upward.
3. Click column header A to select the entire column.
4. Select Edit|Delete.

   The column should disappear, and all adjacent columns should shift to the left.

If you see the Delete dialog box after you select Edit|Delete, you did not select the entire column. Click the Entire Column button, and then click OK.

Be sure you know how to delete a row, and be sure to select the correct row header by clicking on the row header number of the row you want to delete. Keep in mind that the row you select will disappear and all subsequent rows should shift upward.

Using Relative And Absolute Cell References In Formulas

When you copy a formula from one place in a worksheet to another, Excel adjusts the cell references in the formulas relative to the new positions in the worksheet. The formulas adjust to reflect the respective rows or columns. This is called a *relative cell reference* in a formula.

Sometimes, you might not want the cell references to be adjusted when formulas are copied—that's when *absolute cell references* become important. An absolute cell reference is a cell reference in a formula that does not change when the formula is copied to a new location. To make a relative cell reference into an absolute reference, you must add a $ (dollar sign) before the letter and number that make up the cell address. For example, $E$3.

Some formulas use mixed references. For example, the column letter might be an absolute reference, and the row number might be a relative reference. An example of a mixed relative and absolute reference in a formula is $B2/2. If you copied this formula, the row reference (row number) would be adjusted, but not the column.

The next two tasks show you the difference between using relative and absolute cell references in a formula.

Task 13 Using a relative cell reference in a formula.

1. Click cell E8, and type "=B8+C8+D8". Press Enter.

   This enters a relative formula in cell E8 and calculates the totals in row 8.

2. Click cell A9, and type "% of Total". Press Enter.

   This enters a row heading for the % of Total formulas you are going to enter in row 9.

3. Click cell B9.

   This selects a cell to indicate where you will enter the relative formula.

4. Type "=" (equal sign).
5. Click cell B8.

   This selects a cell to enter the first cell reference in the formula.

6. Type "/" (slash).

   This inserts the math operator for division.

7. Click cell E8.

   This selects a cell to enter the second cell reference in the formula.

8. Press Enter.

9. Click cell B9.

10. Click the Copy button on the Standard toolbar.

11. Click cell C9 and drag over to cell D9.

    This selects the cells where you want the relative formulas to appear.

12. Click the Paste button on the Standard toolbar.

    You should see the error #DIV/0! in cells C9 and D9, which indicates there is an error in the formulas. That's because the second cell reference needs to remain the same when copied. You need to enter absolute formulas to calculate a % of Total. Notice that the second cell reference in each relative formula changes when copied to other cells. Let's undo the erroneous results.

13. Click the Undo button on the Standard toolbar.

14. Press Esc to turn off the marquee.

Task 14 Using an absolute cell reference in a formula.

1. Click cell B9.

   This selects a cell to indicate where you will enter the absolute formula.

2. Type "=" (equal sign).

3. Click cell B8.

   This selects a cell to enter the first cell reference in the formula.

4. Type "/" (slash).

   This inserts the math operator for division.

5. Click cell E8.

   This selects a cell to enter the second cell reference in the formula.

6. Press F4 (Absolute).

7. Press Enter.
8. Click cell B9.
9. Click the Copy button on the Standard toolbar.
10. Click and drag to cells C9 and D9.

    This selects the cells where you want the absolute formulas to appear.
11. Click the Paste button on the Standard toolbar.
12. Press Esc to remove the marquee.

Notice that the second cell reference in each absolute formula remains the same when copied to other cells.

Make sure you understand absolute cell referencing. You will be required to enter an absolute formula on the exam. The test question on absolute formulas will give you some tips and hints about entering an absolute formula. Remember that when you are asked to confirm the formula, it means that you should press the Enter key after you enter the formula.

Sorting Data

The Sort feature enables you to sort text in alphabetical order and numbers in numeric order. The text and numbers can be sorted in ascending order (lowest to highest), such as from A through Z and 0 through 9, or descending order (highest to lowest), such as from Z through A and 9 through 0. Perhaps you want to sort a column of row headings so that you can easily look down the sorted column to find the information you want. Keep in mind that you can sort by any column and sort more than one column at a time.

Task 15 Sorting text and numbers.

1. Select the cells A4:D7. This is the range you want to sort.
2. Click the Sort Ascending button on the Standard toolbar.
3. Click any cell to deselect the range.

   Excel sorts the data in alphabetical order according to the item names in Column A.
4. Close the Ch4 Task workbook and save the changes.

Don't select the column headings as part of a sort range. If you accidentally do, Excel will include the headings with the data that you're sorting. You probably won't get the results you planned on.

You will be asked to sort data on the exam. The exam task on sorting data will give you the column and sort order for sorting the data. Before you sort the data, be sure to select the range of cells you want to sort and don't include the column headings in your selection.

Practice Exercise

The Sandy Shores Company budget for the first quarter needs some modification. In this practice exercise, you edit data; insert, delete, and name sheets; change the orientation of text; copy and move data; create relative and absolute formulas; and sort text and numbers.

Figure 4.4 shows what the worksheet contains before you go through the instructions in this exercise.

1. Open the workbook named Ch4 Prac Ex.
2. Delete the text Draft Version in cell B1.
3. Insert a new sheet between Sheet2 and Sheet3.
4. Change the Sheet1 name to 1st Qtr.
5. Delete Sheet4.
6. Make the 1st Qtr sheet active.
7. The February advertising expenses have changed from 50,000 to 57,000. Replace the cell entry with the new number.
8. Change 1st to First in the subtitle 1st Quarter Budget.
9. Indent the text in the range A5:A9.

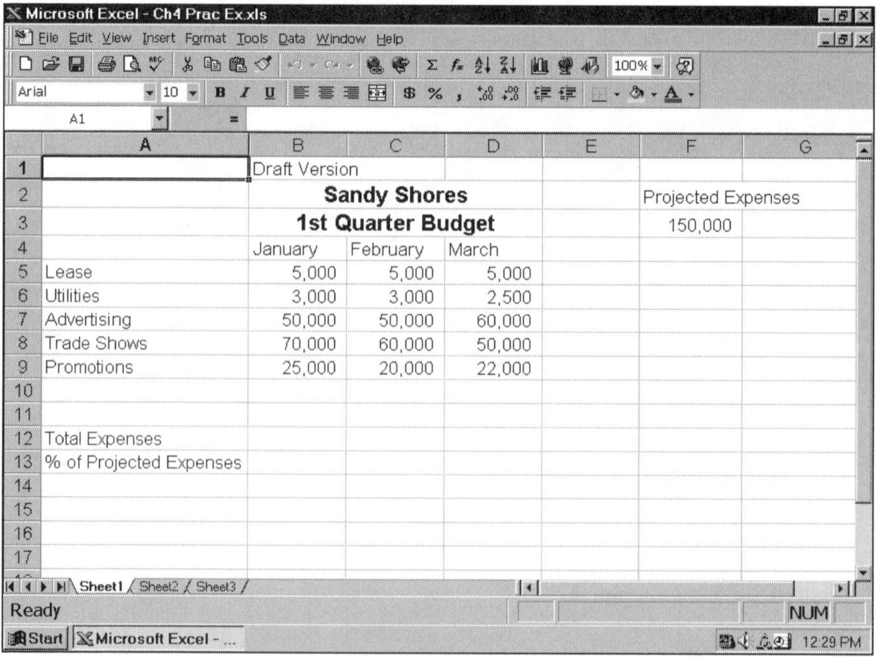

Figure 4.4 The Practice Exercise before you begin.

10. Center the column headings text horizontally and vertically.
11. Rotate the column headings text to 60 degrees.
12. Insert a new row between rows 3 and 4.
13. Delete row 12, which is an empty row.
14. Insert a new column between columns E and F.
15. Delete column E.
16. Create a relative formula to calculate the total January expenses.
17. Copy the formula for total January expenses into the total expenses for February and March.
18. Move the title Sandy Shores up to cell C1.
19. Create an absolute formula to calculate the percent of Projected Expenses for January. *Hint:* In cell B13, enter a formula that includes the Total Expenses for January in cell B12 (relative) divided by the Projected Expenses in cell F3 (absolute).
20. Using the fastest copy method, copy the absolute formula into the % of Projected Expenses for February and March.
21. Sort the budget items alphabetically (ascending order). *Hint:* Be sure to include the numbers for each budget item.
22. Save the workbook with the same name.
23. Close the workbook.

Answers To Practice Exercise

1. Click the Open tool on the Standard toolbar, and double-click on the file name Ch4 Prac Ex.xls.
2. Click cell B1. Press Delete. The text Draft Version should disappear from cell B1.
3. Click the Sheet3 tab to make Sheet3 active. This tells Excel that you want to insert a new sheet between Sheet2 and Sheet3. Choose Insert|Worksheet. Excel inserts Sheet4 between Sheet2 and Sheet3.
4. Double-click on the Sheet1 tab. Type "1st Qtr", and press Enter to name the Sheet1 tab.
5. Click on the Sheet4 tab. Choose Edit|Delete Sheet. Excel displays a message to inform you that the sheet will be deleted permanently. Choose OK to confirm the deletion.
6. Click on the 1st Qtr sheet to make it active.
7. Click cell C7. Type "57,000". This replaces 50,000 with 57,000 for the February advertising expenses.

8. Click cell C3. Press F2 (Edit). Press Home. This moves the insertion point to the beginning of the cell entry. Press Delete. This removes the number 1 in the subtitle. Type “Fir”, and press Enter. You have edited text, and the subtitle should now read *First Quarter Budget*.
9. Click in cell A5, and drag down to cells A6:A9. You have selected the row headings in the range A5:A9. Click the Increase Indent button on the Formatting toolbar. The row headings should appear indented.
10. Click in cell B4, and drag across to cells C4 and D4. You have selected the column headings in the range B4:D4. Choose Format|Cells. In the Format Cells dialog box, in the Text Alignment area, choose Center for the Horizontal option, and choose Center for the Vertical option. Click OK. The column headings should appear centered both horizontally and vertically.
11. If the column headings are not selected from Step 9, click in cell B4 and drag across to cells C4 and D4. You have selected the column headings in the range B4:D4. Choose Format|Cells. In the Format Cells dialog box, in the Orientation area, type “60” in the Degrees box. Click OK. The column headings should appear angled at 60 degrees.
12. Click the row header 4 to select the entire row 4. Choose Insert|Rows. Excel inserts a new row above row 4. All subsequent rows shift down accordingly.
13. Click the row header 12 to select the entire column. Choose Edit|Delete. Excel removes the entire row 12, which was an empty row.
14. Click the column header F to select the entire column. Choose Insert|Columns. Excel inserts a new column before column F. All subsequent columns shift to the right accordingly.
15. Click the column header E to select the entire column. Choose Edit|Delete. Excel deletes the entire column E.
16. Click cell B12. This is where you enter the formula. Type “=”. Click cell B6. Type “+” (addition operator), click cell B7, type “+”, click cell B8, type “+”, click cell B9, type “+”, and click cell B10. Press Enter. This addition formula calculates the total January expenses in column B. The correct answer is 153,000.
17. Click cell B12. Click the Copy tool on the Standard toolbar. The data is copied to the Clipboard. Click cell C12 and drag over to D12. This tells Excel where you want the formula to appear. Click the Paste tool on the Standard toolbar. Excel copies the formula

for total January expenses into the total expenses for February and March. Notice all the cell references in the relative formula adjust relative to their new positions in the worksheet. For example, B6, B7, B8, B9, and B10 change to C6, C7, C8, C9, and C10 for the February expenses. Press Esc to remove the marquee.

18. Click cell C2. Click the Cut tool on the Standard toolbar. The data is moved to the Clipboard. Click cell C1. This tells Excel where you want to move the data. Click the Paste tool on the Standard toolbar. The title Sandy Shores should appear in cell C1. Press Esc to remove the marquee. A fast way to move the title is to click on cell C2, point to any border of cell C2 until the mouse pointer changes to a diagonal arrow, and drag the cell entry into cell C1.

19. Click cell B13. This is where you enter the formula. Type "=". Click cell B12, which contains the total expenses for January. Type "/" (division operator), and then click cell F3, which contains the projected expenses. Press F4 (Absolute). Excel inserts a $ (dollar sign) before the column letter F and row number 3, making the cell reference F3 absolute. Press Enter. The formula in cell B13 should be B12/$F$3, which calculates the percent of Projected Expenses for January. The correct answer is 102%.

20. The fastest copy method is the AutoFill command. Click cell B13 if necessary, and move the mouse pointer to the fill handle (small square) in the lower-right corner of the active cell. The mouse pointer changes to a small cross. Drag the fill handle across to cell C13 and C14. Excel copies the absolute formula into the % of Projected Expenses for February and March. Click each formula in row 13 and observe what has happened. In the February absolute formula, the first cell reference is relative and so it adjusted to C12. The second cell reference E3 is absolute and did not adjust. The correct answer is 97%. When you copy a formula, the absolute cell reference does not change in the new location. The correct answer in cell D13 is 93%.

21. Select cells A6:D10. The selected range includes the budget items and the numbers for each budget item. Click the Sort Ascending tool on the Standard toolbar. The budget items should appear alphabetically.

22. Click the Save button on the Standard toolbar to save the workbook.

23. Click the Close (X) button in the upper-right corner of the workbook window. This closes the workbook.

When you finish the practice exercise, your worksheet should look like the one in Figurc 4.5.

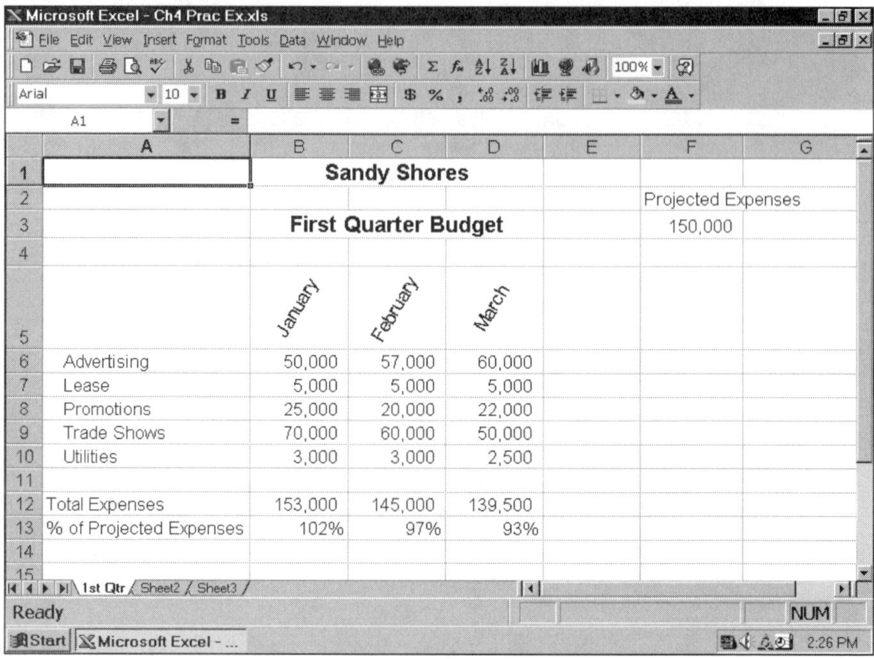

Figure 4.5 The completed Practice Exercise.

Need To Know More?

Catapult, Inc.: *Microsoft Excel 97 Step by Step*. Microsoft Press, Redmond, WA, 1996. ISBN 1-57231-314-5. Lesson 1, "Working in the Excel Environment," contains information about editing data and rearranging a worksheet using move and copy. Lesson 3, "Writing Formulas," discusses absolute formulas. Lesson 7, "Sorting and Subtotaling to Organize Your Data," talks about sorting text and numbers in a worksheet.

Craig, Deborah: *How to Use Microsoft Excel 97 for Windows*. Que, Indianapolis, IN, 1996. ISBN 1-56276-469-1. Chapter 7, "Changing Worksheet Structure," tells you how to insert columns and rows, delete cells, and move and copy data. Chapter 9, "More About Formulas and Functions," shows you how to create absolute formulas and fix formulas. Chapter 14, "Working with Lists of Data," provides step-by-step instructions for sorting text and numbers.

Harvey, Greg: *Excel 97 for Windows for Dummies*. IDG Books Worldwide, Inc., Foster City, CA, 1996. ISBN 0-7645-0049-X. Chapter 3, "Making It All Look Pretty," explains how to enhance text. Chapter 4, "Going Through Changes," talks about editing your worksheet. Chapter 7, "Maintaining Multiple Worksheets," covers inserting, deleting, and naming sheets.

Neibauer, Alan: *Excel One Step at a Time*. IDG Books Worldwide, Inc., Foster City, CA, 1997. ISBN 0-7645-3139-5. Lesson 4, "Rearranging and Previewing Worksheets," explains how to edit data. Lesson 6, "Using Worksheets and Windows," focuses on inserting, deleting, and naming worksheets. Lesson 7, "Preventing and Correcting Worksheet Errors," shows you how to create absolute formulas. Lesson 8, "Working with Formulas and Functions," tells you more about relative formulas.

Nicholson, John R. and Sean R. Nicholson: *Discover Excel 97*. IDG Books Worldwide, Inc., Foster City, CA, 1997. ISBN 1-7645-3047-X. Chapter 4, "Sprucing Up Your Worksheet," explains how to edit your data. Chapter 6, "New Math: Using Labels, Values, Formulas, and Functions," covers relative and absolute formulas. Chapter 12, "Multiplicity: Working with More Than One Worksheet," discusses inserting, deleting, and naming sheets.

Nossiter, Josh: *Using Microsoft Excel 97*. Que, Indianapolis, IN, 1996. ISBN 0-7897-0955-4. Chapter 4, "Let's Make Some Changes Around Here," has a nice discussion of editing data. Chapter 6, "Working with Worksheets and Workbooks," explains inserting, deleting, and naming sheets. Chapter 8, "Formulas: Excel's Recipe for Calculations," goes over relative and absolute formulas.

Reisner, Trudi: *Easy Microsoft Office.* Que, Indianapolis, IN, 1997. ISBN 0-7897-1078-1. The tasks in Part VI, "Entering and Editing Data in Excel," step you through editing Excel data: Task 37, "Overwriting a Cell and Erasing a Cell," Task 38, "Editing a Cell," Task 39, "Copying a Cell," Task 40, "Moving a Cell," Task 42, "Inserting and Deleting Rows and Columns." The tasks in Part VII, "Working with Formulas," show you how to create and copy formulas.

5

Using Functions

Terms you'll need to understand:

- √ Function
- √ Argument
- √ **SUM**
- √ **MIN**
- √ **MAX**
- √ **AVERAGE**
- √ Paste Function

Skills you'll need to master:

- √ Totaling numbers using the **SUM** function
- √ Finding the minimum number using the **MIN** function
- √ Finding the maximum number using the **MAX** function
- √ Averaging numbers using the **AVERAGE** function

Working With Excel Functions

In Chapter 4, you learned how to create formulas and make changes to them. Let's take that one step further by talking about a special Excel formula called a *function*. What is a function? In a nutshell, it's an abbreviated formula that performs a specific operation on a group of numbers. Excel provides more than 320 functions to help you with tasks ranging from determining loan payments to calculating investment returns. You provide the variable parts of the formula, and Excel calculates the result. If you later insert or delete rows (or columns), Excel can automatically update the results of the function. In this chapter, we'll show you how to build the most commonly used functions, such as **SUM**, **MIN**, **MAX**, and **AVERAGE**. The **SUM** function adds a group of numbers. The **MIN** function finds the minimum number in a group of numbers. The **MAX** function finds the maximum number in a group of numbers. The **AVERAGE** function calculates the average for a group of numbers.

Using The SUM, MIN, MAX, And AVERAGE Functions

A function consists of three elements: an equal sign (=), a function name, and arguments. For example, the function **=SUM(B4:B8)** adds the quantities in cells B4 through B8. The **SUM** function is the most commonly used function. **SUM** is a shortcut for entering an addition formula. You can replace a lengthy column or row total formula with a simple **SUM** function. **SUM** is the name of the function that automatically sums entries in a range. You enter the range within parentheses. For instance, first you enter **=SUM(**. You can type the function in lowercase or uppercase letters. Then, you select the range. A dashed border called a *marquee* surrounds the selected range. Finally, you enclose the function with a closing parenthesis. Entering) tells Excel that you are finished selecting the range. Excel inserts the range coordinates in the parentheses. The quickest way to enter a **SUM** function is to use the AutoSum button on the Standard toolbar.

Other commonly used functions are the **MIN**, **MAX**, and **AVERAGE** functions. The **MIN** function is a predefined formula that returns the minimum number in a range of cells. The **MAX** function is a ready-made formula that returns the maximum number in a range of cells. The **AVERAGE** function is a formula that adds the values you specify in a range and then divides the sum by the number of values in the range.

You can use Excel's Paste Function to enter any function. The Paste Function will step you through the process of inserting a function using a series of dialog

HOLD That Skill!

You need to keep some basic concepts in mind when you're using Excel's functions. Namely, every function consists of the following three elements:

- **Equal Sign (=)** Indicates that what follows is a function or formula.
- **Function Name (for example, SUM)** Indicates the operation that will be performed.
- **Argument (for example, B4:B9)** Indicates the cell addresses of the numbers that the function will act on. The argument is often a range of cells, but it can be much more complex.

boxes. In the next four tasks, we'll use the AutoSum button and the Paste Function to create basic functions in Excel.

> *Note: If the results of a formula are fractional, such as 5534.25, you can round the fractional number by using the Decrease Decimal button on the Formatting toolbar. You can click the Decrease Decimal button until Excel displays a whole number. In the example 5534.25, you would need to click the Decrease Decimal button twice to round the number two decimal places and display the whole number 5534.*

Task 1 Totaling numbers using the SUM function.

1. Open the Ch5 Task workbook located on your companion disk.
2. Click cell E5.

   This selects the cell in which you want to place the **SUM** function.
3. Double-click the AutoSum button on the Standard toolbar.

   You should see **=SUM(B5:D5)** in the formula bar and the result of the formula, 25772, in cell E5.
4. Use the AutoFill handle to copy the **SUM** formula in cell E5 down through column E (E6:E9).
5. Click cell E6.

In cell E6, you should see **=SUM(B6:D6)** in the formula bar and the result of the formula, 17217. In cell E7, the formula is **=SUM(B7:D7)**, and the correct answer is 139012. Cell E8 should contain the formula **=SUM(B8:D8)**, and the result is 85700. In cell E9, the **SUM** formula is **=SUM(B9:D9)**, and the answer is 267701.

You can click on the AutoSum tool once to instruct Excel to insert **=SUM** and the range of cells to the left of or above the selected cell. Then, you can adjust the range of cells by clicking inside the selected cell or the formula bar, and edit the range. Or, you can click on the first correct cell in the range to deselect the incorrect range, drag the mouse pointer over the rest of the correct range of cells, and press Enter.

It's important to know how to use the AutoSum tool on the Standard toolbar, because you create a **SUM** function to add numbers in a column. You should also know how to round the **SUM** function results to a whole number, so be sure to use the Decrease Decimal button on the Formatting toolbar to accomplish this.

In the next task, we'll add a MIN function, using the Paste Function to find the minimum number in a specified range.

Task 2 Finding the minimum number using the MIN function.

1. Click cell B11.

   This indicates where you want to place the MIN function.

2. Click the Paste Function button on the Standard toolbar.

   The Paste Function dialog box should appear (see Figure 5.1).

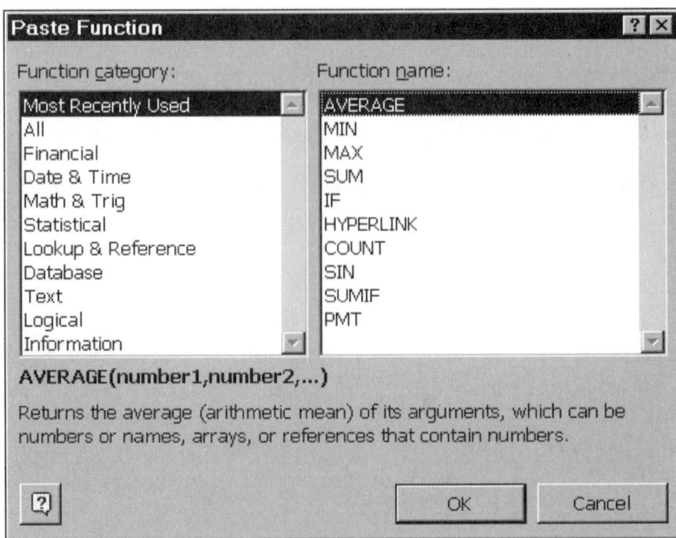

Figure 5.1 The Paste Function dialog box.

3. In the Function Category list, choose Statistical.
4. In the Function Name list, choose MIN.
5. Click OK.
6. In the Number1 box, enter "E5:E8".

   This defines the argument (in this case, the argument is a range of cells).
7. Click OK.

=MIN(E5:E8) should appear in the formula bar, and the result of the formula, 17217, should appear in cell B11. This result is the lowest number in the specified range. Advertising is the minimum value in the range.

To enter the values or cell ranges for the argument, you can type a number in the text box or drag the dialog box title bar out of the way and click on the desired cells with the mouse pointer.

In Task 3, we'll find the maximum number in a range of cells by using Excel's MAX function.

Task 3 Finding the maximum number using the MAX function.

1. Select cell B12.

   This specifies where you want the **MAX** function to appear.
2. Click the Paste Function button on the Standard toolbar.

   The Paste Function dialog box should appear.
3. In the Function Name list, choose MAX.
4. Click OK.
5. In the Number1 box, type "E5:E8" (see Figure 5.2).

   This defines the argument (in this case, the argument is a range of cells).
6. Click OK.

=MAX(E5:E8) should appear in the formula bar, and the result of the formula, 139012, should appear in cell B12. The result shown is the highest number in the specified range. Conferences are the maximum expense in the budget.

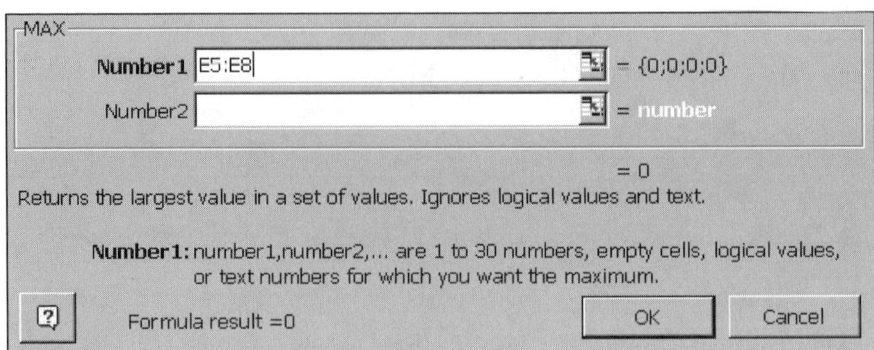

Figure 5.2 The arguments in the Number1 box in the MAX dialog box.

Be ready to use the **MAX** function to find the maximum number in a range of cells.

In the task coming up, we'll calculate the average for a group of numbers by creating an AVERAGE function with the Paste Function dialog box.

Task 4 Averaging numbers using the AVERAGE function.

1. Select cell B13.

   The **AVERAGE** function will be placed in this cell.

2. Click the Paste Function button on the Standard toolbar.

   The Paste Function dialog box should appear.

3. In the Function Name list, choose AVERAGE.
4. Click OK.
5. In the Number1 box, enter "E5:E8".

   This defines the argument (in this case, the argument is a range of cells).

6. Click OK.

   =AVERAGE(E5:E8) should appear in the formula bar, and the result of the formula, 66925.25 should appear in cell B13. The result shown is the average of the numbers in the specified range.

7. Click the Decrease Decimal button on the Formatting toolbar.

The result of the formula, 66925.3, should appear in cell B13. Excel has rounded up the fractional number one decimal place, still displaying a fractional number.

8. Click the Decrease Decimal button on the Formatting toolbar again.

   The result of the formula, 66925, should appear in cell B13. Excel has rounded up the fractional number two decimal places, resulting in a whole number.

9. Close the Ch5 Task workbook without saving the changes.

Take a look at the list of function names for the Most Recently Used option in the Function Category list in the Paste Function dialog box. The Function Name list contains the most recently used function names for the current Excel session. You can just click a function name to use it. This eliminates the step of having to choose a function category.

Remember how to use the **AVERAGE** function to calculate the average for several numbers in a range.

Practice Exercise

The Human Resources Department at the Sandy Shores Company tracks salaries and benefits for the employees. The Human Resources director needs to gather information on employee salaries and benefits for corporate headquarters. In this exercise, you'll need to calculate the total salaries, find the minimum salary, find the maximum salary, and take an average of the salaries.

Figure 5.3 shows what the worksheet contains before you go through the instructions in this exercise.

1. Open the Ch5 Prac Ex workbook located on the companion disk.
2. Total the salaries.
3. Find the minimum salary.
4. Find the maximum salary.
5. Calculate an average to find the average salary and round the results of the formula to a whole number.
6. Save the workbook with the same name.
7. Close the workbook.

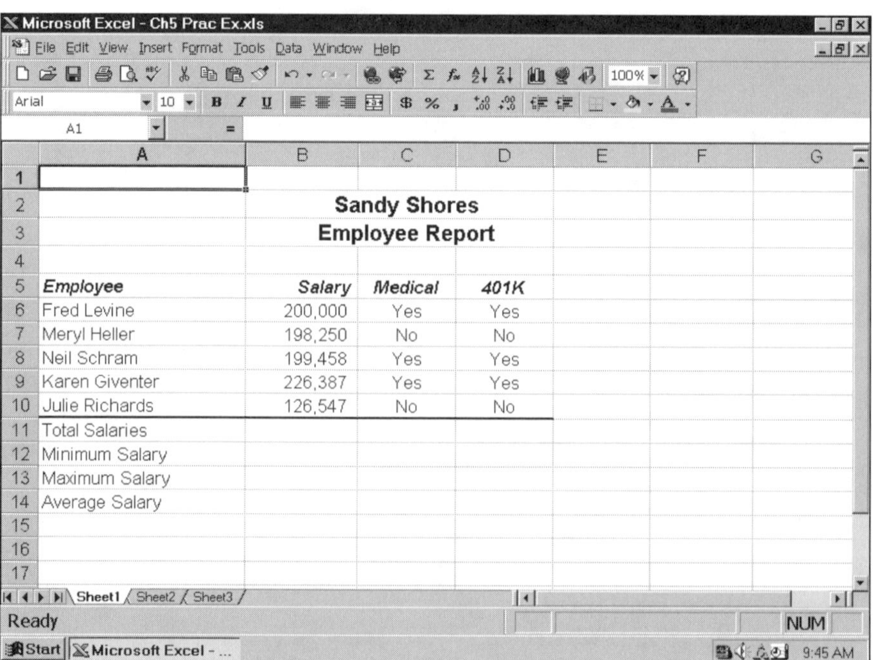

Figure 5.3 The Practice Exercise before you begin.

Answers To Practice Exercise

1. Click the Open tool on the Standard toolbar, and double-click on the file name Ch5 Prac Ex.
2. Click cell B11. Double-click the AutoSum button on the Standard toolbar. The formula **=SUM(B6:B10)** should appear in cell B11. The correct answer is 950,642. This **SUM** formula calculates a total for the salaries.
3. Click cell B12. Click the Paste Function button on the Standard toolbar. In the Function Category list, choose Statistical. In the Function Name list, choose MIN. Click OK.

   In the Number1 box, enter "B6:B10". This defines the argument (in this case, the argument is a range of cells). Click OK. **=MIN(B6:B10)** should appear in the formula bar, and the result of the formula, 126,547, should appear in cell B12. The result shown is the lowest salary in the specified range.
4. Click cell B13. Click the Paste Function button on the Standard toolbar. In the Function Category list, verify that Statistical is selected. In the Function Name list, choose MAX. Click OK. In the Number1 box, enter "B6:B10". This defines the argument (in this case, the argument is a range of cells). Click OK. **=MAX(B6:B10)** should appear in the formula bar, and the result of the formula, 226,387, should appear in cell B13. The result shown is the highest salary in the specified range.
5. Click cell B14. Click the Paste Function button on the Standard toolbar. In the Function Category list, verify that Statistical is selected. In the Function Name list, choose AVERAGE. Click OK. In the Number1 box, enter "B6:B10". This defines the argument (in this case, the argument is a range of cells). Click OK. **=AVERAGE(B6:B10)** should appear in the formula bar, and the result of the formula, 190,128.40, should appear in cell B14. The result shown is the average salary in the specified range. Click twice on the Decrease Decimal button on the Formatting toolbar. The result shown is a whole number, 190,128. Your worksheet should look like the one in Figure 5.4.
6. Click the Save button on the Standard toolbar to save the workbook.
7. Click the Close (X) button in the upper-right corner of the workbook window. This closes the workbook.

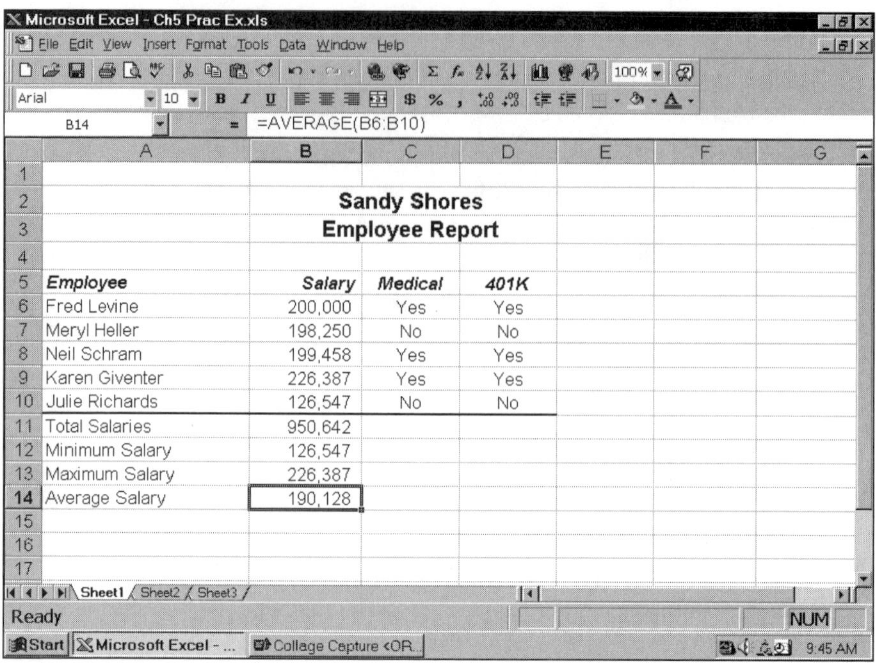

Figure 5.4 The completed Practice Exercise.

Need To Know More?

Catapult, Inc.: *Microsoft Excel 97 Step by Step*. Microsoft Press, Redmond, WA, 1996. ISBN 1-57231-314-5. Lesson 3, "Writing Formulas," tells you how to build functions.

Craig, Deborah: *How to Use Microsoft Excel 97 for Windows*. Que, Indianapolis, IN, 1996. ISBN 1-56276-469-1. Chapter 9, "More About Formulas and Functions," discusses Excel's functions.

Harvey, Greg: *Excel 97 for Windows for Dummies*. IDG Books Worldwide, Inc., Foster City, CA, 1996. ISBN 0-7645-0049-X. Chapter 2, "Creating a Spreadsheet from Scratch," explains how to create functions.

Neibauer, Alan: *Excel One Step at a Time*. IDG Books Worldwide, Inc., Foster City, CA, 1997. ISBN 0-7645-3139-5. Lesson 3, "Automating Your Work," explains how to use the AutoSum button. Lesson 8, "Working with Formulas and Functions," has a nice discussion on building functions.

Nicholson, John R. and Sean R. Nicholson: *Discover Excel 97*. IDG Books Worldwide, Inc., Foster City, CA, 1997. ISBN 1-7645-3047-X. Chapter 6, "New Math: Using Labels, Values, Formulas, and Functions," explains how to create functions.

Nossiter, Josh: *Using Microsoft Excel 97*. Que, Indianapolis, IN, 1996. ISBN 0-7897-0955-4. Chapter 9, "What are Functions?," has a good explanation of functions. Chapter 10, "Functions You'll Use Often," covers the most commonly used Excel functions.

Reisner, Trudi: *Easy Microsoft Office*. Que, Indianapolis, IN, 1997. ISBN 0-7897-1078-1. In Part VII, "Working with Formulas," refer to Task 46, "Totaling Cells with the SUM Function."

6

Formatting Worksheets

Terms you'll need to understand:

- Alignment
- Font
- Font size
- Font style
- Number format
- Column width
- Row height
- Border

Skills you'll need to master:

- Aligning data
- Changing text font, size, style, and color
- Changing number formats and modifying decimal places
- Changing column width and row height
- Adding borders and shading

Changing The Look Of Your Data

When you format a worksheet, you can change the appearance of your data. With Excel's formatting tools, you can make your worksheet more attractive and readable. You'll find it's easy to center, left-align, and right-align data in cells; change the font, font style, and font size for text; display dollar signs, commas, and percent signs; and assign the number of decimal places. You can even adjust column width to accommodate long entries, alter row height to fit small or large fonts, and apply a variety of borders to your worksheet. We'll take a look at all of these formatting options in this chapter. You'll learn how to right-align column headings, change the font and font size, and add bold to emphasize text. This chapter will also teach you how to add dollar signs and commas to numbers, change the number of decimal places, adjust column width and row height, and add borders to bring attention to a certain portion of the worksheet.

Formatting Your Data

When you enter data into a cell, numbers automatically align to the right side of the cell, and text automatically aligns to the left side of the cell. The Alignment command enables you to align data in a cell, left, center, or right. You can use the Merge And Center button on the Formatting toolbar to quickly center text in the leftmost cell across the entire range of cells you select. The Merge And Center feature is good for centering a title and subtitle at the top of a worksheet.

The default alignment is General. General alignment means that numbers are right-aligned and text is left-aligned. Aligning data is good for fine-tuning the appearance of column headings across the columns to line up the headings with the numbers that are right-aligned.

A *font* is a particular typeface and size. You can access a number of font faces, sizes, colors, and styles using Excel's Formatting toolbar. You can use the font faces provided by Windows as well as fonts designed for your printer. If Windows does not have a screen version of the printer font you select, it substitutes a font (in this case, the printout looks different than the screen). Font styles available in Excel include bold, italic, and underline. Font styles are often used to emphasize significant words and numbers. You can apply font settings to a single cell or range of cells.

Excel's Number Format command lets you display numeric values in many ways. Formatting a number means changing the way it is displayed. For example, you can format the number 100 to look like currency: $100.00. It is important that the numbers in your worksheet appear in the correct format—$100.00 is certainly different than 100%. You can also use Excel's Number Format commands to specify the number of decimal places you want. By default, the currency, comma, and percent styles display two decimal places. But if you don't want any decimal places or you just want one decimal place, you can change the display at any time.

Often, applying number and font formatting options makes an entry longer than the default column width. For example, $1,000 is only 6 characters. If you format the number as currency with two decimal places, the number will appear as $1,000.00, and it will require 9 spaces. Pound signs (#) in a cell indicate that the column is not wide enough to display the result of a formula. With Excel's Column Width and AutoFit Selection commands, you can change the width of any column at any time. The Row Height command allows you to adjust the height of any row. Small or large fonts is the determining factor for row height.

Finally, the Border command gives you many choices regarding the display of boxes around cells and ranges. For instance, you can have a single thick outline border that creates a box to emphasize the title of a worksheet. Or, you can put a double underline on the bottom of cells to draw attention to totals. For a simple but dramatic effect, you could add shading to your worksheets and specify the percentage of shading you want. You can even add a color and pattern to the shaded area, if you wish. The Color options let you choose a color for the overall shading. The Patterns options let you select a black-and-white or colored pattern that lies on top of the overall shading. You can get some beautiful and professional-looking results from adding borders and shading to your worksheets.

In the upcoming tasks, you will right-align data in a worksheet, and change the font, size, style, and color for text. You will also change number formats, modify decimal places, adjust column width and row height, as well as add borders and shading to your worksheet.

Task 1 Aligning data.

1. Open the Ch6 Task workbook located on the companion disk.
2. Select cells B4:E4.

   This selects the range you want to right-align.
3. Click the Align Right button on the Formatting toolbar.
4. Click any cell to deselect the range.

HOLD That Skill!

Here are some important concepts to remember when you're formatting a worksheet:

- By default, Excel right-aligns text and left-aligns numbers. If the data contains both text and numbers, Excel left-aligns the data. You can change the alignment of data by using the Align Left, Align Right, and Center buttons on the Formatting toolbar.
- A *font* is a set of characters that have the same typeface. You can change the font's size; add bold, italic, or underline; change its color; or add special effects, such as strikethrough, superscript, subscript, and small caps.
- The font and font sizes in the list can vary, depending on the fonts installed on the system, the type of printer you have, and the selected font.
- You can preview how a font will look in your worksheet and when printed out by using the Format Cells dialog box. In this dialog box, the Preview area shows you the effects of your font choices. The way your font and font sizes look can vary, depending on the fonts installed on the system, the type of printer you have, and the selected font.
- You can format cells before you type your text and numbers. For example, if you want a title in Bold, 12-Point Arial, click in the cell that will contain the title, then set these formats before you start typing.
- To repeat the alignment format command in another cell, choose the Edit|Repeat Format Cells command, or press the F4 (Repeat) key.
- The default width of a column is 8.11 digits. The number of digits that fit in a column depend on the font you use. The default height of a row is 13.2 points. The height of the digits that fit in a row depends on the font you use.

As you can see in Figure 6.1, Excel right-aligns the contents of each cell in the range.

Be sure you know how to center data in a range.

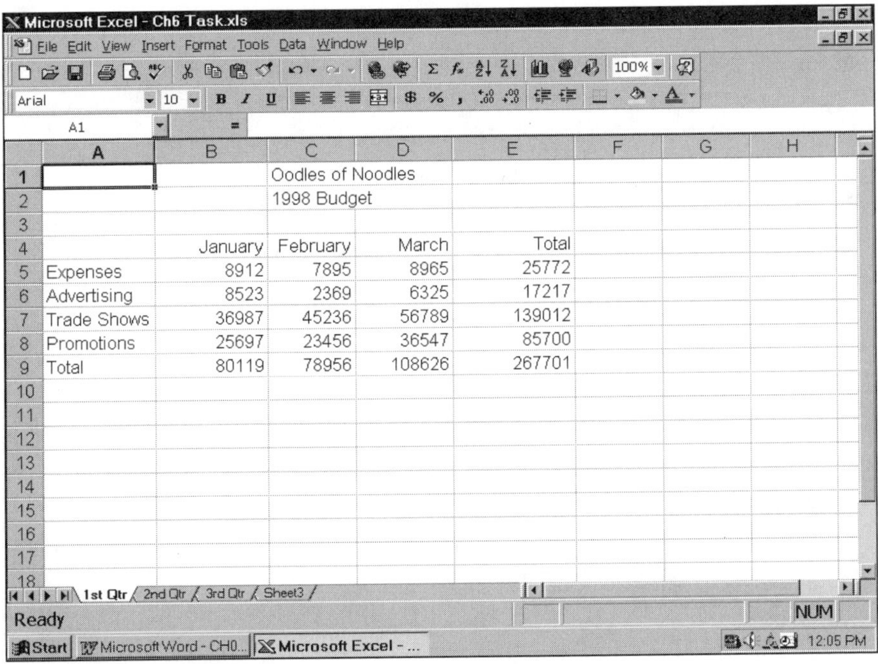

Figure 6.1 Right-aligned column headings.

Task 2 Changing text font, size, style, and color.

1. Select cell C1.

   This selects the title of the worksheet.

2. Click the drop-down arrow next to the Font box on the Formatting toolbar.

3. From the font list, choose Impact.

4. Click the drop-down arrow next to the Font Size box on the Formatting toolbar.

5. From the font size list, choose 14.

6. Click the Bold button on the Formatting toolbar.

7. Click the drop-down arrow on the Font Color button on the Formatting toolbar.

8. Choose the color Teal in the Font Color palette.

9. Click any cell to deselect the range.

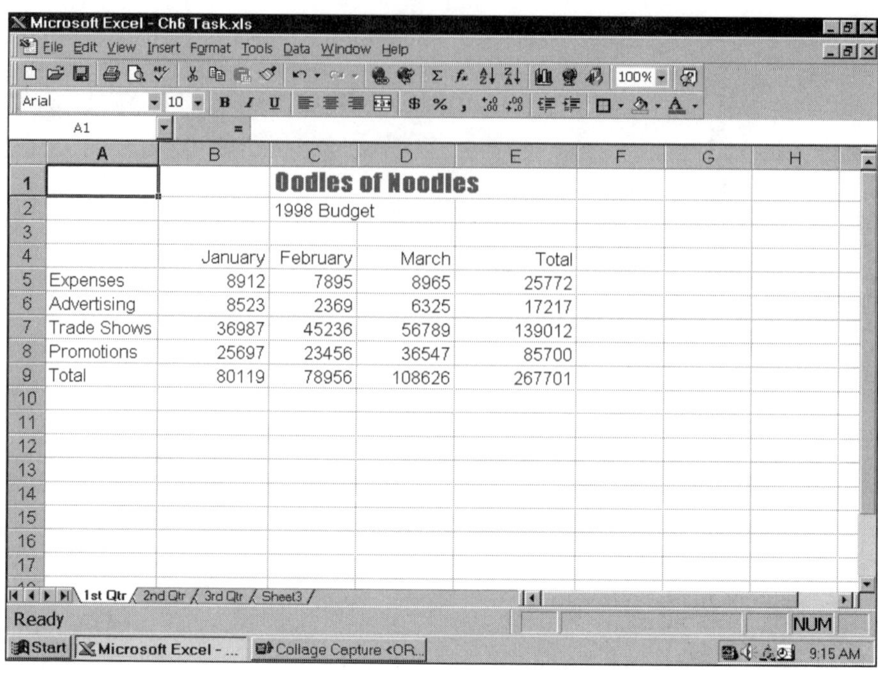

Figure 6.2 Font, size, style, and color changes.

Excel should change the font and font size of the worksheet title. As you can see in Figure 6.2, the font size is larger, the boldface style brings more attention to the title, and the font color should be teal (because this is a black-and-white book, the color won't show).

You can use keyboard shortcuts to change text attributes faster. First, select the cell(s), then press Ctrl+B for Bold, Ctrl+I for Italic, Ctrl+U for Underline, and Ctrl+5 for Strikethrough.

It's important to know how to change the font, font size, and font color for text in worksheets. You'll also need to know how to format a range with bold and italic.

Task 3 Changing number formats and modifying decimal places.

1. Select cells B9:E9.

   This selects the range in which you want to display dollar signs.

2. Click the Currency Style button on the Formatting toolbar.

   Pound signs (#) indicate that the entries are too long to fit in the column. If pound signs display on your screen, you need to widen the column (which is what you'll learn how to do in the next section). When you use the Decrease Decimal command, Excel removes as many decimal places as you specify. The comma style displays commas and two decimal places.

3. Click the Decrease Decimal button twice on the Formatting toolbar.
4. Select cells B5:E8.

   This selects the range in which you want to display commas.

5. Click the Comma Style button on the Formatting toolbar.
6. Click the Decrease Decimal button twice on the Formatting toolbar.
7. Click any cell to deselect the range.

Your worksheet should now look similar to the worksheet shown in Figure 6.3. Notice in Figure 6.3, the currency style displays dollar signs, commas, and zero decimal places.

	A	B	C	D	E
1			Oodles of Noodles		
2			1998 Budget		
3					
4		January	February	March	Total
5	Expenses	8,912	7,895	8,965	25,772
6	Advertising	8,523	2,369	6,325	17,217
7	Trade Shows	36,987	45,236	56,789	139,012
8	Promotions	25,697	23,456	36,547	85,700
9	Total	$ 80,119	$ 78,956	$ 108,626	$ 267,701

Figure 6.3 Numbers with Currency Style and Comma Style with zero decimal places.

The percent style works the same way as the comma and currency style. Be sure you know how to format a number to a percentage. To do so, click the Percent Style button on the Formatting toolbar. Don't change the number of decimal places. Just continue with the next task. In a different task, you'll need to know how to modify decimal places by rounding numbers. Be sure to use the Decrease Decimal button on the Formatting toolbar to quickly round a number.

Task 4 Changing column width and row height.

When you enter text that exceeds the width of a column, Excel spills over the text in the adjacent column (provided that the adjacent cell contains no data). If the adjacent column contains data, your entry will be truncated at the edge of the cell. The entire entry is still intact, but does not appear. When you enter numbers (or format numbers) that exceed the width of the column, Excel displays ### signs in the cell to indicate that you should expand the width of the column.

1. Move the mouse pointer to the line to the right of column letter A of column A. The mouse pointer changes to a double arrow.
2. Hold down the mouse button, and drag the mouse to make the column a width of approximately 14.00. As you're dragging the mouse, Excel displays a ScreenTip with the column width.

Excel should widen the column. If there were any pound signs (#), they should disappear and be replaced by the data. If some entries still spill over into the next column or if some cells still display pound signs, you'll need to widen the columns further.

You can use the AutoFit feature to change a column's width automatically. To use AutoFit, double-click on the line to the right of the column you want to adjust. This will adjust the width of the column based on the longest entry in the column. To make a row as tall as its tallest entry, double-click on the bottom border of the row heading. To change more than one column or row at a time, click and drag over the desired row or column headings and then double-click on the bottommost or rightmost heading border.

Task 5 Adding borders and shading.

1. Select cells B9:E9.

   This specifies the range of cells that you want to surround with a border.
2. Click the drop-down arrow next to the Borders button on the Formatting toolbar.

3. From the Borders palette, choose the last border sample.
4. Click the drop-down arrow next to the Fill Color button on the Formatting toolbar.
5. Pick the Rose color from the Color palette.
6. Click any cell to deselect the range.

   You should see a thick single line outlining the edges of the range and rose color shading. Your worksheet should resemble the one in Figure 6.4 (because this book is in black and white, you won't see the rose shading in the sample figure).

7. Close the Ch6 Task workbook without saving changes.

The outline still can be hard to see because the gridlines are displayed on screen. If you want to turn off the gridlines, choose Tools|Options, and click the View tab. In the Window Options section, choose Gridlines, and click OK.

You'll need to know how to work with borders in a worksheet. On the exam, an outline border is referred to as an automatic underline.

Microsoft Excel - Ch6 Task.xls

	A	B	C	D	E
1			Oodles of Noodles		
2			1998 Budget		
3					
4		January	February	March	Total
5	Expenses	8,912	7,895	8,965	25,772
6	Advertising	8,523	2,369	6,325	17,217
7	Trade Shows	36,987	45,236	56,789	139,012
8	Promotions	25,697	23,456	36,547	85,700
9	Total	$ 80,119	$ 78,956	$ 108,626	$ 267,701

Figure 6.4 Single outline border and shading.

Practice Exercise

The Sandy Shores Company employee report needs some sprucing up. Your job is to format the worksheet by aligning data, applying font and number formats, modifying decimal places, adjusting column width and row height, and applying borders.

Figure 6.5 shows what the worksheet contains before you go through the instructions in this exercise.

1. Open the Ch6 Prac Ex workbook located on your companion disk.
2. Right-align the Salary column heading.
3. Center the column headings and text in columns C and D.
4. Change the font for the title (not the subtitle) to 14 pt. Arial.
5. Bold the title.
6. Change the font color to blue.
7. Format the salaries in cells B6:B10 with commas and zero decimal places.
8. Format the formula results for the salaries in cells B11:B14 with dollar signs and zero decimal places.

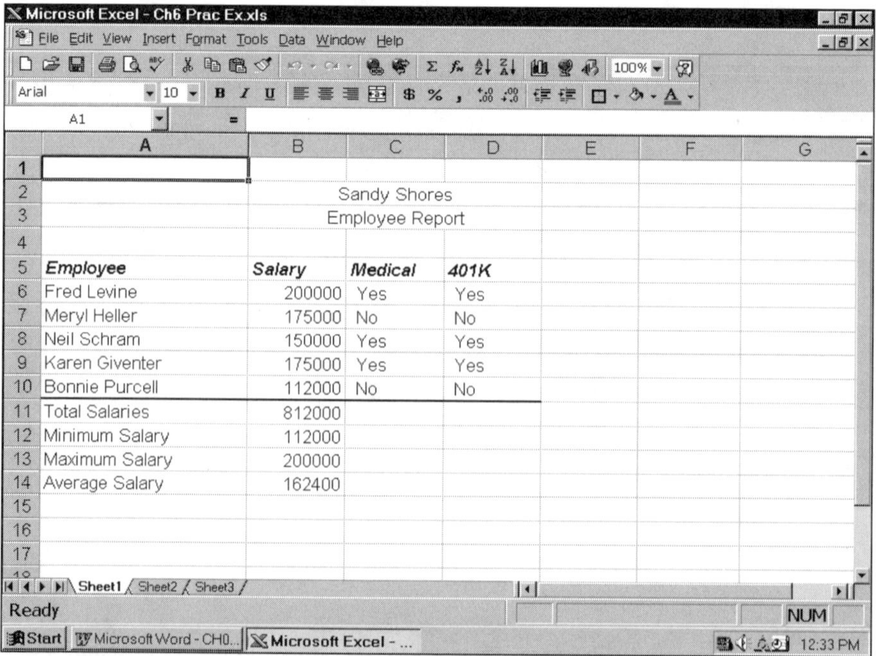

Figure 6.5 The Practice Exercise before you begin.

9. Adjust the width of column A by making the column narrower.
10. Apply a top and bottom border to the title and subtitle.
11. Add turquoise shading to the range within the top and bottom borders.
12. Save the workbook with the same name.
13. Close the workbook.

Answers To Practice Exercise

1. Click the Open tool on the Standard toolbar, and double-click on the file name Ch6 Prac Ex.
2. Click cell B5. Click the Align Right button on the Formatting toolbar. This right-aligns the Salary column heading.
3. Select the range C5:D10. Click the Center button on the Formatting toolbar. This centers the column headings and text in the selected range.
4. Click cell C2. Click the Font Size drop-down arrow on the Formatting toolbar. Choose 14. This changes the font for the title to 14 pt. Arial.
5. Click the Bold button on the Formatting toolbar. This adds bold to the text for the title.
6. Click the drop-down arrow on the Font Color button on the Formatting toolbar. Choose Blue from the color palette. This changes the font color to blue in the title.
7. Select the range B6:B10. Click the Comma Style button on the Formatting toolbar. Then, click the Decrease Decimal button twice on the Formatting toolbar. This formats the salaries with commas and zero decimal places.
8. Select the range B11:B14. Click the Currency Style button on the Formatting toolbar. Then, click the Decrease Decimal button twice on the Formatting toolbar. This formats the formula results for the salaries with dollar signs and zero decimal places.
9. Point to the column border between Columns A and B. Drag the mouse pointer to the left to reduce the white space following the entries. This adjusts the width of column A by making the column narrower.
10. Select the range B2:D3. Click the drop-down arrow next to the Borders button on the Formatting toolbar. Choose the border style in the second row, third column. This applies a top and bottom border to the title and subtitle.

11. Click the drop-down arrow on the Fill Color button on the Formatting toolbar. Choose Turquoise from the color palette. This adds turquoise shading to the range within the top and bottom borders. Your worksheet should look like the one in Figure 6.6 (because this book is in black and white, you will not see the color changes).
12. Click the Save tool on the Standard toolbar to save the workbook.
13. Click the Close (X) button in the upper-right corner of the document window. This closes the workbook.

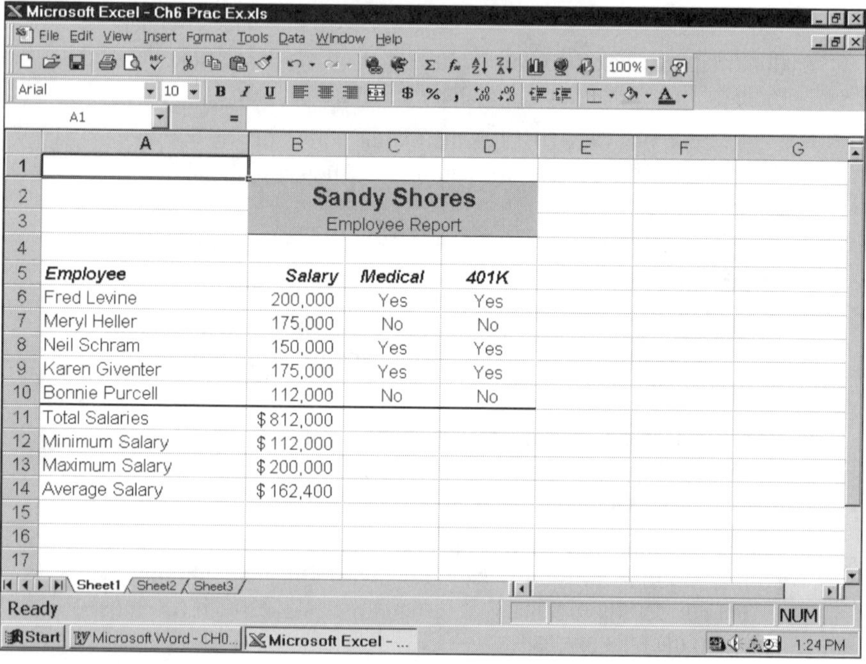

Figure 6.6 The completed Practice Exercise.

Need To Know More?

Catapult, Inc.: *Microsoft Excel 97 Step by Step*. Microsoft Press, Redmond, WA, 1996. ISBN 1-57231-314-5. Lesson 4, "Formatting Your Worksheet for a Professional Look," tells you how to format cells and format numbers.

Craig, Deborah: *How to Use Microsoft Excel 97 for Windows*. Que, Indianapolis, IN, 1996. ISBN 1-56276-469-1. Chapter 7, "Changing Worksheet Structure," explains changing column width. Chapter 8, "Improving Worksheet Appearance," shows you how to use fonts, format numbers, add borders and shading, align data, and remove formatting.

Harvey, Greg: *Excel 97 for Windows for Dummies*. IDG Books Worldwide, Inc., Foster City, CA, 1996. ISBN 0-7645-0049-X. Chapter 3, "Making It All Look Pretty," gives you instructions on formatting your worksheets.

Neibauer, Alan: *Excel One Step at a Time*. IDG Books Worldwide, Inc., Foster City, CA, 1997. ISBN 0-7645-3139-5. Lesson 5, "Formatting Worksheets," provides step-by-step instructions for formatting text and numbers in worksheets.

Nicholson, John R. and Sean R. Nicholson: *Discover Excel 97*. IDG Books Worldwide, Inc., Foster City, CA, 1997. ISBN 1-7645-3047-X. Chapter 4, "Sprucing Up Your Worksheet," covers how to format worksheets.

Nossiter, Josh: *Using Microsoft Excel 97*. Que, Indianapolis, IN, 1996. ISBN 0-7897-0955-4. Chapter 4, "Let's Make Some Changes Around Here," has a good explanation of the formatting features you need to know about in order to format your worksheets.

Reisner, Trudi: *Easy Microsoft Office*. Que, Indianapolis, IN, 1997. ISBN 0-7897-1078-1. In Part VII, "Working with Formulas," refer to Task 46, "Totaling Cells with the SUM Function."

Working With Ranges

Terms you'll need to understand:

- √ Cell name
- √ Range name
- √ Name Box
- √ Go to
- √ Define name
- √ Clear range

Skills you'll need to master:

- √ Creating and naming ranges
- √ Going to ranges
- √ Clearing ranges
- √ Formatting ranges
- √ Copying ranges
- √ Moving ranges
- √ Printing ranges

Naming, Creating, And Using Ranges

You can assign an English name to a value or a formula in a single cell or a range of cells by using the Name command. After you've assigned a name to a range, you can use the name rather than the cell addresses when specifying a cell or range of cells for use in copying, moving, erasing, formatting, or printing information on your worksheet. The cell addresses in a range are simply locations and do not describe the range itself. Defining range names provides you with a more meaningful way to reference ranges of data.

Creating and naming ranges offers several benefits. Possibly one of the biggest benefits of naming ranges is that names are easier to remember than cell addresses. In addition, formulas are often easier to define when you use range names. For instance, suppose you use the **SUM** function to add a column of numbers, and the formula reads **=SUM(C4:C9)**. If you assigned the name JULY to the range C4:C9, you could add that column using the function =SUM(JULY).

You have some flexibility when you use range names. For instance, you can redefine the cell addresses referenced by a range name by clearing a range of cell addresses from a range name or assigning new cell addresses to the range name. You can even delete a range name altogether, if you no longer need it.

HOLD That Skill!

Here are some do's and don'ts for creating and naming ranges:

- Range names can have a maximum of 255 characters.
- Range names must start with a letter.
- Range names can include letters, numbers, periods, and underlines.
- Range names cannot include spaces.
- Range names can contain lowercase and uppercase letters.
- Range names should not look like cell addresses, such as C20.
- After you type a range name in the Name Box in the formula bar, be sure to press Enter.
- Only one unique range name is allowed per workbook. For example, you can't have a range named Salary on both Sheet1 and Sheet2. You need to name the ranges Salary1 and Salary2.

Not only can you use a range name in formulas, but you can format a range of cells using a range name. For example, perhaps you want to add dollar signs to a total column. You could label the total column with the range name TOTAL, select the TOTAL range, and then apply the Currency style to TOTAL.

Naming cells and ranges also makes it easier to cut, copy, and move blocks of cells. When you need to specify a range during the copy or move operation, you can simply choose the range name instead of selecting cells on the worksheet.

Figure 7.1 shows a selected range (the column headings) and range name (ColHeadings) in the Name Box in the formula bar. In the upcoming tasks, we'll show you how to create, name, go to, and use ranges. Then, you'll clear a range and format, copy, move, and print named ranges.

Task 1 Creating and naming ranges.

1. Open the Ch7 Task workbook located on the companion disk.
2. Select cells A5:A8.

   This selects the range you want to name.

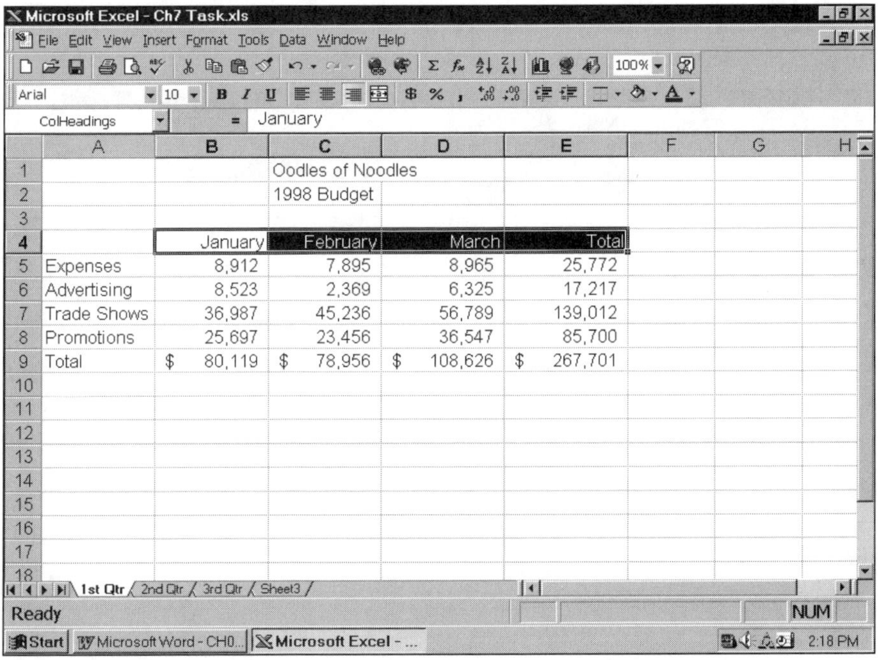

Figure 7.1 A selected range and range name in the Formula bar's Name Box.

3. Click the drop-down arrow beside the Name Box in the formula bar (see Figurc 7.2).

   You should see a list of previously created range names.

4. Click in the name box, and enter "RowHeadings".
5. Press Enter.

   Note: Be sure to press Enter after you type a range name in the Name Box in the formula bar. Otherwise, the range name will not be accepted.

   The range name should be added to the list of names in the Name Box in the Formula bar. Excel saves the name with the workbook when you save the workbook. When the range is selected, you should see the range name in the Formula bar's Name Box.

6. Click any cell to deselect the range.

Be ready to create and name a range on a worksheet.

Microsoft Excel - Ch7 Task.xls

File Edit View Insert Format Tools Data Window Help

A5 = Expenses

Name Box list: ColHeadings, namenumber, Print_Area

	A	B	C	D	E
1			Oodles of Noodles		
2			1998 Budget		
3					
4		January	February	March	Total
5	Expenses	8,912	7,895	8,965	25,772
6	Advertising	8,523	2,369	6,325	17,217
7	Trade Shows	36,987	45,236	56,789	139,012
8	Promotions	25,697	23,456	36,547	85,700
9	Total	$ 80,119	$ 78,956	$ 108,626	$ 267,701

1st Qtr / 2nd Qtr / 3rd Qtr / Sheet3

Ready NUM

Start | Microsoft Word - CH0... | Microsoft Excel - ... 2:22 PM

Figure 7.2 A list of range names in the Formula bar's Name Box.

Task 2 Going to ranges.

1. Press F5 (Go To).

   The Go To dialog box appears, as shown in Figure 7.3.

2. In the Names list, choose the range name RowHeadings.
3. Click OK.

   Excel highlights the cells that were defined for the range name.

4. Click any cell to deselect the range.

Be familiar with how to go to ranges. You'll be going to a range that is already defined for you.

Task 3 Clearing ranges.

1. Select Insert|Name, and choose Define.
2. In the Names In Workbook list, choose the range name ColHeadings.
3. Click Delete.
4. Click OK.

   Excel deletes the range name, including its cell addresses.

5. Click the Undo button on the Standard toolbar to restore the range name.

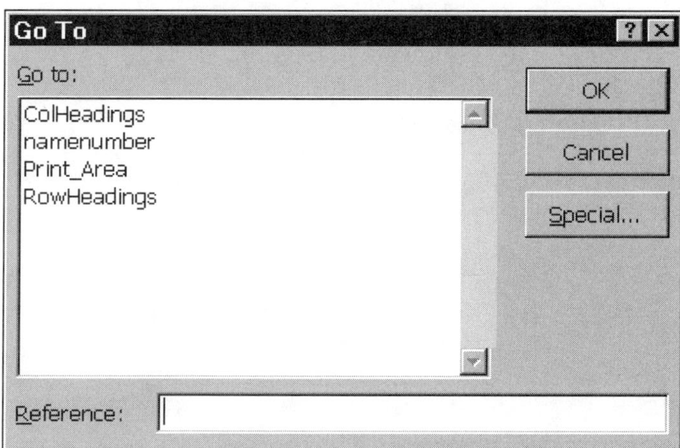

Figure 7.3 The Go To dialog box with a list of range names.

Task 4 Formatting ranges.

1. Click the drop-down arrow beside the Name Box in the formula bar.
2. Click RowHeadings.

   This selects the range you want to format.
3. Click the Italics button on the Formatting toolbar.
4. Click any cell to deselect the range.

After you select a range name, Excel should highlight the cell addresses defined for the range name. The contents of the range should appear in italics, as shown in Figure 7.4.

Task 5 Copying ranges.

1. Click the drop-down arrow beside the Name Box in the formula bar.
2. Click namenumber.

   This selects the range you want to copy.
3. Click the Copy button on the Standard toolbar.

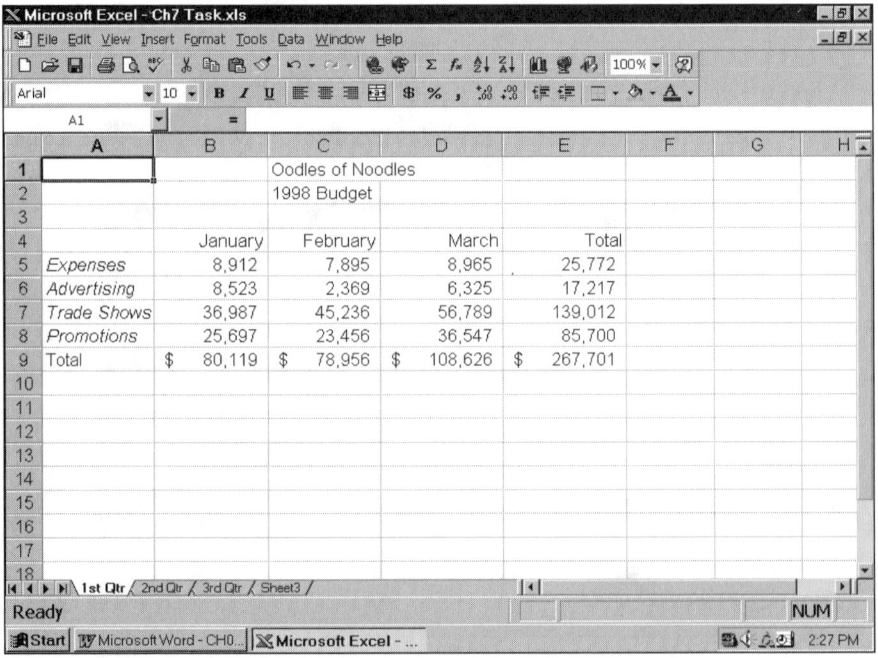

	A	B	C	D	E
1			Oodles of Noodles		
2			1998 Budget		
3					
4		January	February	March	Total
5	*Expenses*	8,912	7,895	8,965	25,772
6	*Advertising*	8,523	2,369	6,325	17,217
7	*Trade Shows*	36,987	45,236	56,789	139,012
8	*Promotions*	25,697	23,456	36,547	85,700
9	Total	$ 80,119	$ 78,956	$ 108,626	$ 267,701

Figure 7.4 A named range formatted with italics.

4. Select cell B14.
5. Click the Paste button on the Standard toolbar.
6. Press Esc to remove the copy marquee.
7. Click any cell to deselect the range.

When you select a range name, Excel should automatically highlight the cell addresses associated with the range name. The range of cells you copied should appear in the new location.

> *Note: The copied range has no range name. The range name is not part of what is copied when you copy a named range.*

Task 6 Moving ranges.

1. Click the drop-down arrow beside the Name Box in the formula bar.
2. Click ColHeadings.

   This selects the range you want to move.
3. Click the Cut button on the Standard toolbar.
4. Select cell B13.
5. Click the Paste button on the Standard toolbar.

When you specify a range name, Excel selects the cells you assigned to the range name. The range of cells you moved should appear in the new location.

> *Note: When a range is cut (rather than copied), the range name with its new location is pasted in the target cells, along with any data contained in the range.*

Task 7 Printing ranges.

1. Click the drop-down arrow beside the Name Box in the formula bar.
2. Click namenumber.

   This selects the range you want to print.
3. Press Ctrl+P. The Print dialog box opens.
4. In the Print What area, choose Selection.
5. Click OK.

When you specify a range name, Excel selects the cells you assigned to the range name. When you print a range, you are printing only the selected portion of a worksheet.

6. Close the Ch7 Task workbook without saving changes.

Practice Exercise

In the Sandy Shores Company employee report, you'll need to create and use ranges to make it easier and more efficient for others to work with the worksheet. In this practice exercise, you are going to create and name a range, go to the named range, and clear a named range. Then, you'll format a range, copy and move a named range, and finally, print a named range.

Figure 7.5 shows what the worksheet contains before you go through the instructions in this exercise.

1. Open the Ch7 Prac Ex workbook located on your companion disk.
2. Create a range name called RowHead for the employee name row headings.
3. Create a range name called ColHead for the column headings.
4. Go to the range named RowHead.
5. Clear the range name called ColHead. Then, restore the range name.
6. Format the range name called RowHead with bold text.
7. Copy the range name called ColHead to start in cell A16.

Figure 7.5 The Practice Exercise before you begin.

8. Move the range name called RowHead to start in cell A17.
9. Print the range name called RowHead.
10. Save the workbook with the same name.
11. Close the workbook.

Answers To Practice Exercise

1. Click the Open tool on the Standard toolbar, and double-click on the file name Ch7 Prac Ex.
2. Select the range A6:A10. Click in the Name Box, and enter "RowHead". Press Enter. This creates a range name called RowHead for the employee name row headings.
3. Select the range A5:D5. Click in the Name Box, and enter "ColHead". Press Enter. This creates a range name called ColHead for the column headings.
4. Press F5 (Go To), choose RowHead, and click OK. This selects the cell addresses for the range named RowHead.
5. Select Insert|Name, and then select Define. Choose ColHead, and click the Delete button. Then, click OK. This clears the range name called ColHead with its cell addresses. Next, click the Undo button on the Standard toolbar. This restores the ColHead range name.
6. If necessary, click the Name Box drop-down arrow, and choose RowHead. Click the Bold button on the Formatting toolbar. This formats the range name called RowHead with bold text.
7. Click the Name Box drop-down arrow. Choose ColHead. Click the Copy button on the Standard toolbar. Click cell A16. Then, click the Paste button on the Standard toolbar. Press Esc to remove the copy marquee. Click any cell to deselect the range. This copies the range name called ColHead to start in cell A16.
8. Click the Name Box drop-down arrow. Choose RowHead. Click the Cut button on the Standard toolbar. Click cell A17. Then, click the Paste button on the Standard toolbar. Click any cell to deselect the range. This moves the range name called RowHead to start in cell A17.
9. Click the Name Box drop-down arrow. Choose RowHead. Press Ctrl+P. In the Print dialog box, in the Print What area, choose Selection, and click OK. This prints the range name called RowHead.
10. Click the Save tool on the Standard toolbar to save the workbook.

Your worksheet should look like the one in Figure 7.6.

11. Click the Close (X) button in the upper-right corner of the document window. This closes the workbook.

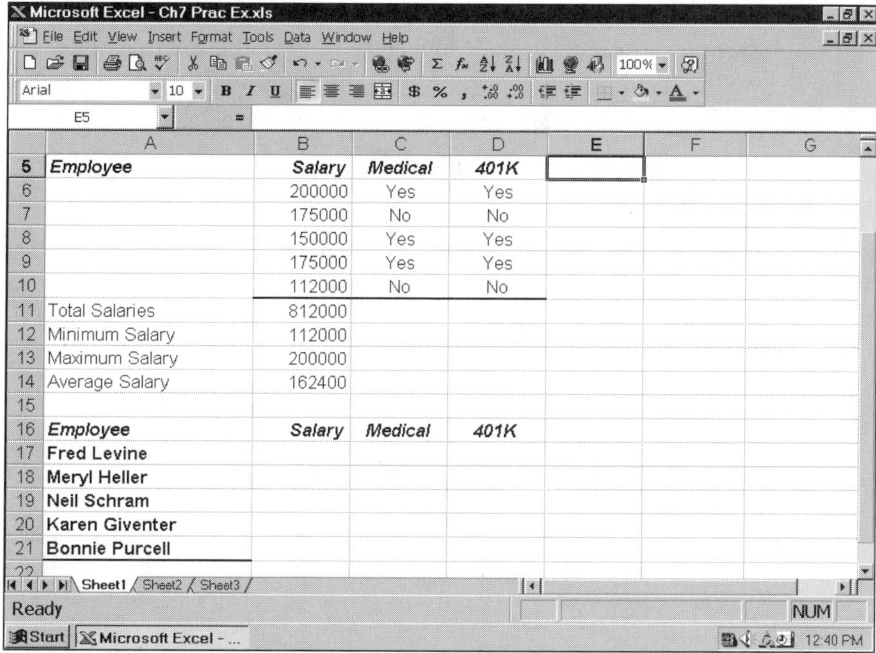

Figure 7.6 The completed Practice Exercise.

Need To Know More?

Catapult, Inc.: *Microsoft Excel 97 Step by Step*. Microsoft Press, Redmond, WA, 1996. ISBN 1-57231-314-5. Lesson 1, "Working in the Excel Environment," shows you how to rearrange worksheets by moving and copying data and working with ranges.

Craig, Deborah: *How to Use Microsoft Excel 97 for Windows*. Que, Indianapolis, IN, 1996. ISBN 1-56276-469-1. Chapter 9, "More About Formulas and Functions," tells you how to name cells and cell ranges.

Harvey, Greg: *Excel 97 for Windows for Dummies*. IDG Books Worldwide, Inc., Foster City, CA, 1996. ISBN 0-7645-0049-X. Chapter 6, "Oh, What a Tangled Worksheet We Weave," gives you instructions on naming cells.

Neibauer, Alan: *Excel One Step at a Time*. IDG Books Worldwide, Inc., Foster City, CA, 1997. ISBN 0-7645-3139-5. Lesson 3, "Automating Your Work," provides information on naming cells and ranges.

Using Drawing Tools

Terms you'll need to understand:

- √ Object
- √ Selection handles
- √ Color
- √ Border
- √ Shading
- √ Fill
- √ Pattern
- √ 3D shape
- √ WordArt

Skills you'll need to master:

- √ Creating lines
- √ Drawing objects
- √ Moving and resizing objects
- √ Modifying objects
- √ Creating 3D shapes
- √ Modifying 3D shapes
- √ Inserting pictures
- √ Inserting WordArt
- √ Modifying WordArt

Drawing Objects In Excel

Excel's drawing tools can bring out the artist in you. You can draw pictures in your worksheet to add emphasis and visual impact. Like drawing on paper, using the Draw feature takes patience and practice. This chapter introduces you to Excel's drawing tools, pictures in worksheets, and the WordArt feature that enables you to create logos and fancy-looking words in your worksheets.

Creating A Drawing

The Drawing toolbar (see Figure 8.1) offers a myriad of drawing tools for drawing and modifying lines and shapes, including 3D shapes. You can also use the drawing tools to annotate your worksheet data and charts. Any shape you draw is called an *object*.

After you draw an object, you'll see small squares, called *selection handles*, surrounding the object's border. Selection handles indicate the object is selected. The selection handles let you modify the object. Before you can move, resize, or edit an object, you must select it. Then, you can move and resize the object using the handles. You can change the color, border, and fill of objects you have created. Filling an object places a pattern inside the object to make the shape more interesting. You can also delete objects when you no longer need them.

In the next few tasks, you'll learn how to create lines and draw objects. Then, you'll move and resize the objects, as well as modify them. You'll also create a 3D shape and make some changes to it.

Task 1 Creating lines.

1. Open the Ch8 Task workbook located on the companion disk.
2. Click the Drawing button on the Standard toolbar.
3. Click the Line button on the Drawing toolbar.

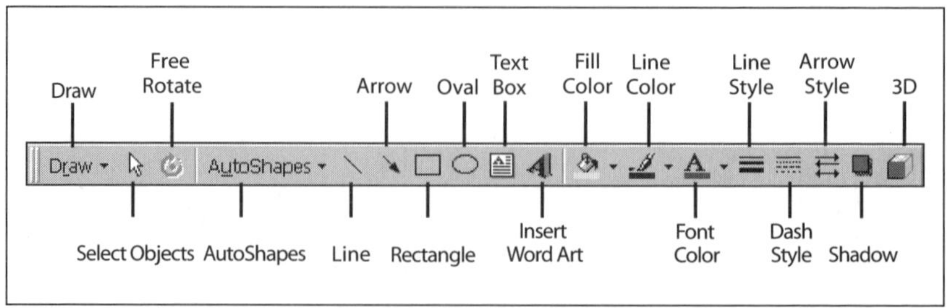

Figure 8.1 The Drawing toolbar.

HOLD That Skill!

Here are some important guidelines to remember when you work with objects:

- Click a shape tool on the Drawing toolbar, drag the crosshair pointer diagonally to draw the shape you want, and then release the mouse button.
- To draw a perfect line, square, or circle, hold down the Shift key when you drag the mouse diagonally to draw the shape.
- Before you can move, resize, or modify an object, you must select the object. Just click anywhere on the object to select it.
- A selected object displays selection handles, which are small squares surrounding the object.
- You can resize an object by pointing to a selection handle. When you see a double arrow, drag the handle until the object is the size you want.
- When you want to move an object, be sure you select it first, and then point to the object and drag it to the new location.

4. Move the cursor over cell B12. This is where you want the object to begin. The cursor changes to a cross hairs when you move it over the worksheet.
5. Click and drag your cursor from the left edge of cell B12 to the right edge of cell D12. This is where the object ends.

   Your line should look similar to the line shown in Figure 8.2. Notice the handle on each end of the line object. These handles are the selection handles that indicate the object is selected. You can drag the handles to resize the line object.
6. Click outside of the object to make the selection handles disappear.

Task 2 Drawing objects.

1. Click the Rectangle button on the Drawing toolbar.
2. Move the cursor over cell F11. This is where you want the object to begin.
3. Click and drag diagonally from the top-left corner of cell F11 to the bottom-right corner of cell G15. This is where the object ends.

   A rectangle should appear on your worksheet, as shown in Figure 8.3.
4. Click outside of the object to make the selection handles disappear.

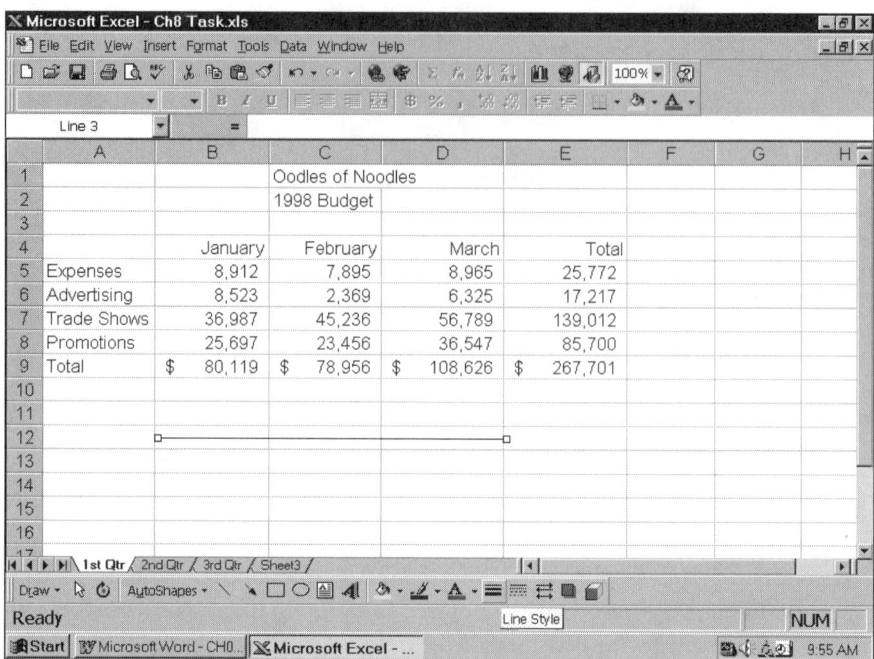

Figure 8.2 A line object.

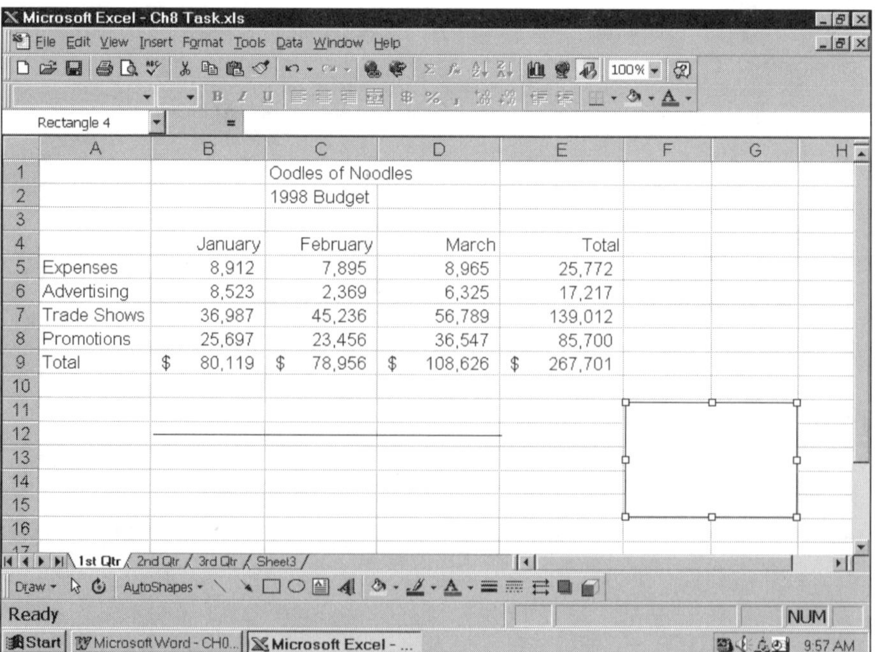

Figure 8.3 A rectangle object.

To draw a perfect square or circle, hold down the Shift key while dragging the cross-hair pointer.

Task 3 Moving and resizing objects.

1. Click the rectangle to select it.
2. Drag the object to cell B14.
3. Point to the right-middle handle until you see a double arrow.
4. Click and drag the right-middle handle one column to the right.
5. Click outside of the object to deselect it.

Your rectangle should be moved to start in cell B14 and resized as a wider rectangle.

Task 4 Modifying objects.

1. Click the rectangle to select it.
2. Click the down-pointing arrow to the right of the Fill Color button on the Drawing toolbar.
3. In the Fill palette, click a blue color patch.
4. Click outside of the object to deselect it.

Your rectangle should now be blue. The filled rectangle is shown in Figure 8.4.

Task 5 Creating 3D shapes.

1. Click the Oval tool on the Drawing toolbar.
2. Draw an oval object starting in cell E14 and ending in cell F18.
3. Click the 3D button on the Drawing toolbar.
4. Choose the 3D Style 2 from the 3D palette (place your mouse pointer over a 3D sample on the 3D palette to see the style names). See Figure 8.5.
5. Click outside of the object to make the handles disappear.

Your object should now appear as a 3D shape.

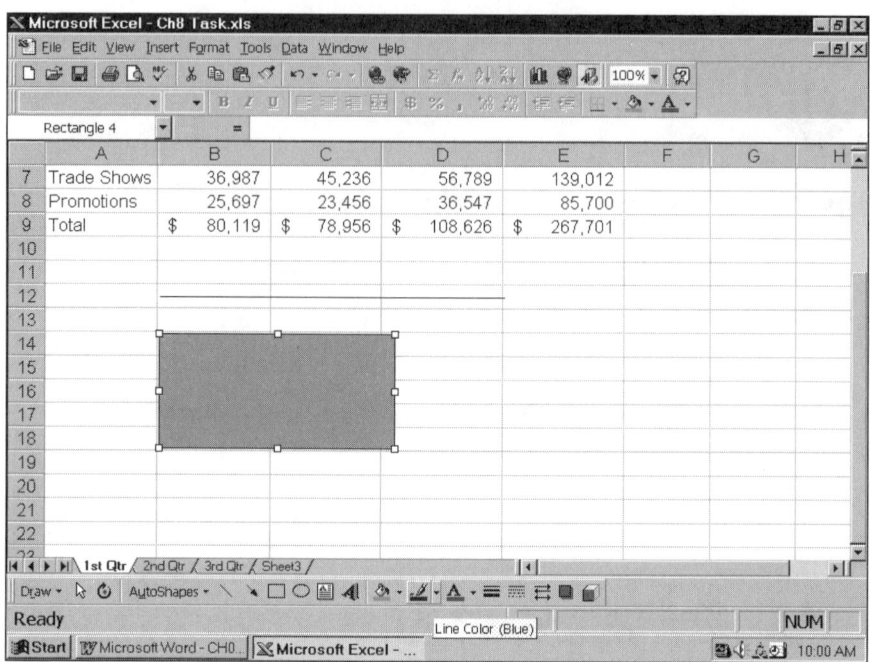

Figure 8.4 A filled rectangle.

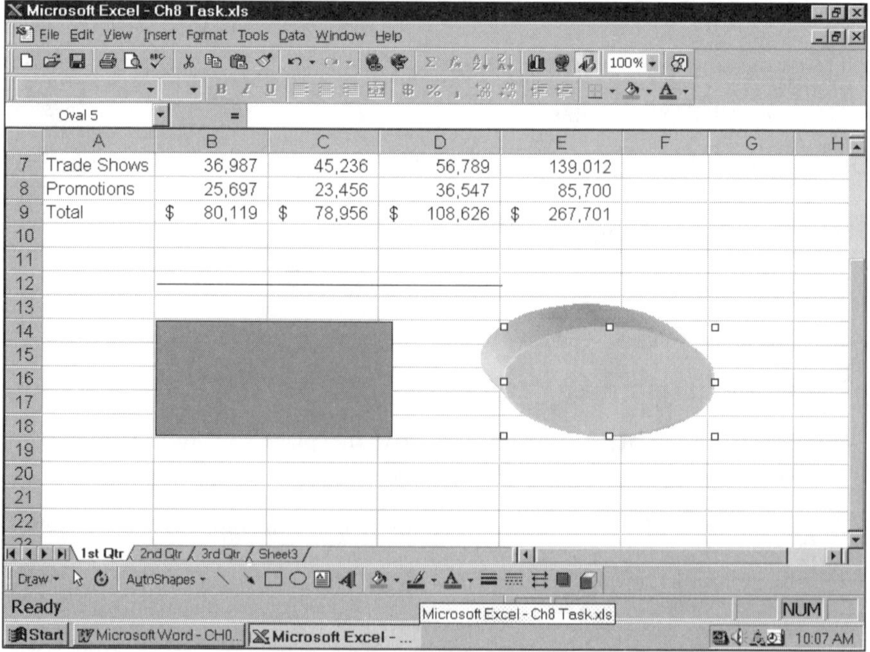

Figure 8.5 A 3D oval.

Be sure you know how to change an object to a 3D shape. Remember to select the object and then click on the 3D button on the Drawing toolbar. Once you change the object to a 3D shape, you can just continue with the next task; you don't have to deselect the object. This will save you time on the exam.

Task 6 Modifying 3D shapes.

1. Click the 3D shape to select it.
2. Click the 3D button on the Drawing toolbar.
3. Click the 3D Settings button on the 3D palette to display the 3D Settings toolbar.

   The 3D Settings toolbar gives you tools to change a 3D shape in the following ways:

   - Turn the 3D style on or off
   - Tilt the 3D shape down
   - Tilt the 3D shape up
   - Tilt the 3D shape left
   - Tilt the 3D shape right
   - Change the depth of the 3D shape
   - Change the direction of the 3D shape
   - Change the lighting on the 3D shape
   - Change the surface of the 3D shape
   - Change the 3D color
4. Click the Tilt Up button on the 3D Settings toolbar several times to change the tilt of the 3D shape.

   The 3D shape should appear with a new look, as shown in Figure 8.6.

   Note: If you want to change the depth of a 3D shape, click the Depth tool on the 3D Settings toolbar. Then, choose a point size, such as 72 pt., to make the 3D shape have more depth. Choose a lower point size to decrease the depth of the 3D shape.

5. Click the Close (X) button on the 3D Setting toolbar to close the toolbar.

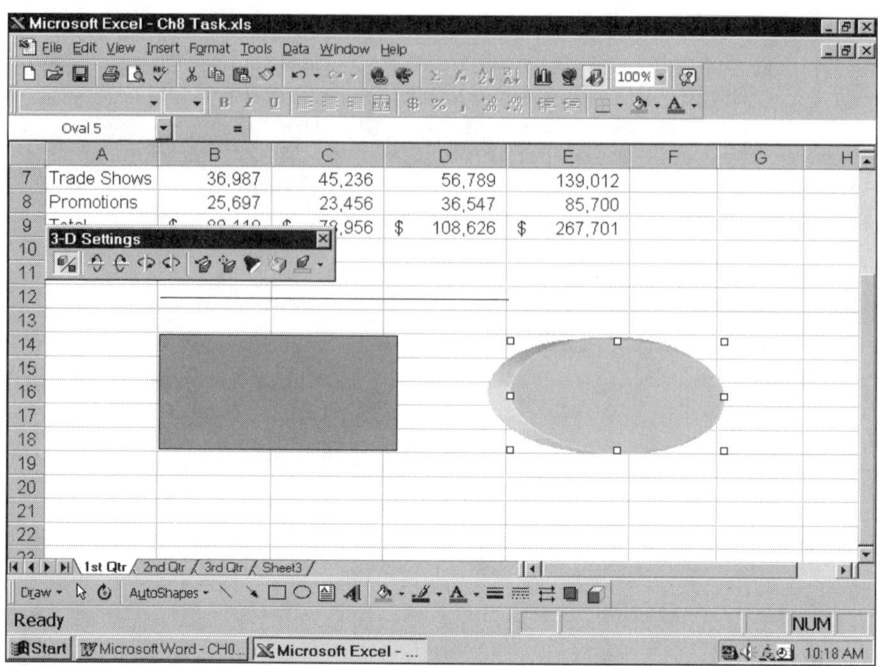

Figure 8.6 The 3D Settings toolbar and 3D circle tilted up.

6. Click outside of the object to deselect the object and make the selection handles disappear.

Inserting Pictures

Instead of drawing your own pictures in your worksheet, you can use ready-made clip art and photographs to spruce up your worksheets. There are plenty of pictures that come with Excel and so all you have to do is insert a picture wherever you want it to appear in a worksheet.

In the next task, you'll insert a picture that is stored in the Clipart folder.

Task 7 Inserting a picture.

1. Select Insert|Picture|From File.

   The Insert Picture dialog box opens.

2. Click the Up One Level button to display the C drive in the Look In box.
3. Choose the Program Files folder, the Microsoft Office folder, and then the Clipart folder.

   Note: If you have your own clip art, select the folder where it is stored.

4. Choose the 1DOLLAR.WMF picture file, and click Insert.

   The one dollar bill picture should appear in your worksheet. See Figure 8.7.

5. Click outside of the picture to deselect the object.

It's important that you know how to insert a picture in a worksheet. You don't need to resize the picture, you can just move on to the next task.

Working With WordArt

You can use WordArt to create special text effects and insert the text into your worksheet. Perhaps you want to create logos, display type, or other interesting and eye-catching text for your Excel worksheets using WordArt. You can bend, twist, turn, and angle WordArt text; change the font, font size, and font style; and add formatting features to the text using one or more colors or textures. You can even add a drop shadow to the text.

Once you insert a WordArt object into a worksheet, Excel displays the WordArt toolbar (see Figure 8.8).

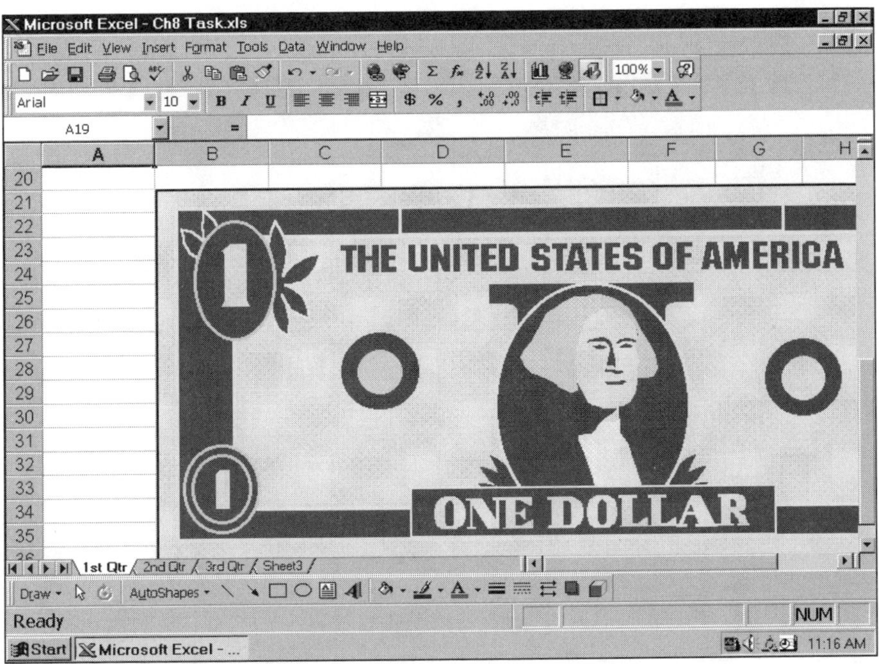

Figure 8.7 A picture in a worksheet.

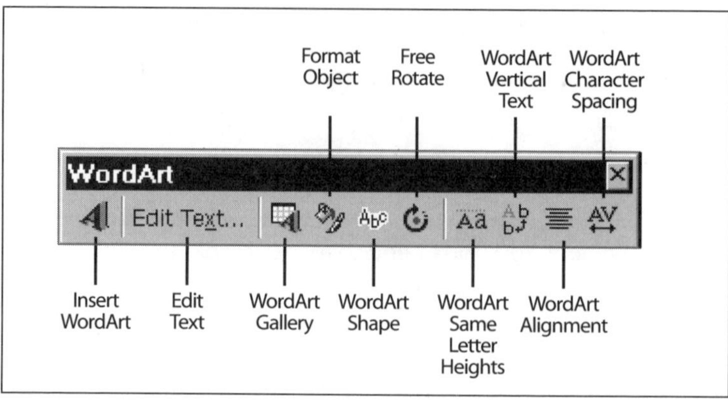

Figure 8.8 The WordArt toolbar.

In the next two tasks, you'll insert a WordArt logo, and then you'll spice it up with some formatting changes.

Task 8 Inserting WordArt.

1. Click cell A1. Then, click the Insert WordArt button on the Drawing toolbar.
2. Click a style in the WordArt Gallery (see Figure 8.9).

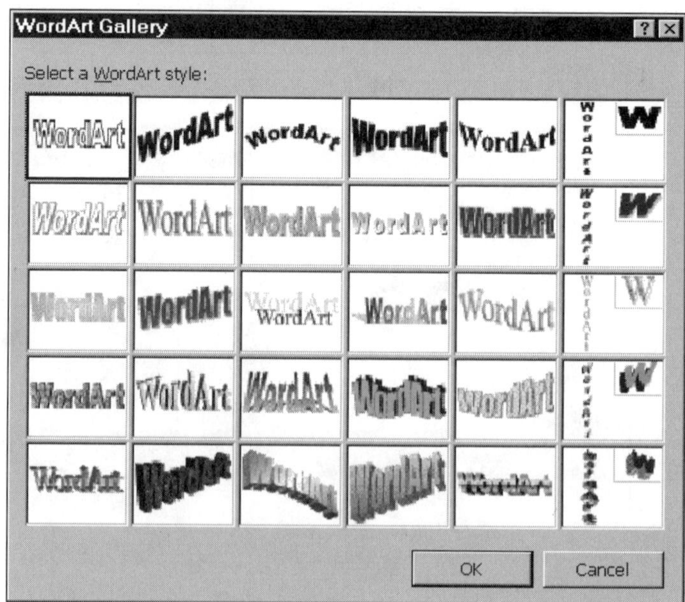

Figure 8.9 The WordArt Gallery.

3. Click OK.
4. Type "on".
5. Click OK.

   The WordArt object and WordArt toolbar should appear in your document.

6. Move the logo to the upper-left corner of the worksheet by dragging it there.
7. Click outside of the WordArt to deselect the object.

Make sure you are familiar with Excel's WordArt feature. On the test, you'll work with a WordArt logo. You need to select the WordArt logo so that you can make changes to it. When you select the logo, Excel displays the WordArt toolbar. After you're finished using the WordArt tools on the toolbar to make the necessary changes, just click any cell outside the logo, and Excel will hide the WordArt toolbar.

Task 9 Modifying WordArt.

1. Click the WordArt object to select it.
2. Click the Edit Text button on the WordArt toolbar.
3. Choose any font and font size.
4. Click OK.
5. Click the Format WordArt button on the WordArt toolbar.
6. Choose a color.
7. Click OK.
8. Click outside of the object to make the handles disappear.
9. Click the Drawing button on the Standard toolbar to close the toolbar.

   The WordArt shape should appear with its new font, font size, and color (see Figure 8.10).

10. Close the Ch8 Task workbook without saving changes.

You need to know how to change the font and font size for a WordArt title in the worksheet. You also need to know how to format the WordArt text by changing its color.

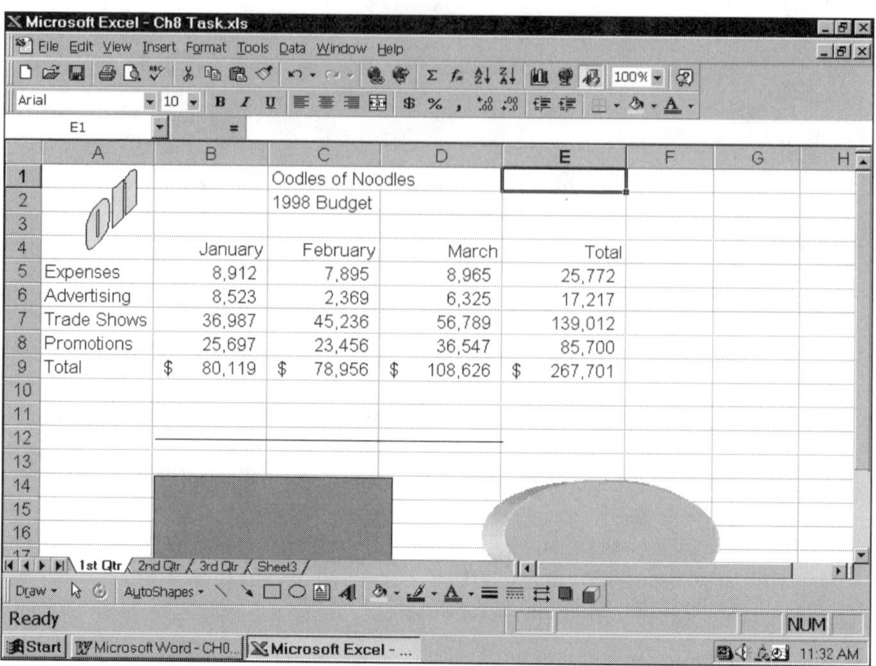

Figure 8.10 The WordArt text.

Practice Exercise

The Sandy Shores Company sales report for the first quarter needs to be spiced up. In this practice exercise, you'll draw, modify, and enhance lines as well as insert a picture and WordArt text to create a logo.

Figure 8.11 shows what the worksheet contains before you go through the instructions in this exercise.

1. Open the workbook named Ch8 Prac Ex located on the companion disk.
2. Create a horizontal line in Row 4 beneath the subtitle *1st Quarter*. *Note:* Hold down the Shift key while drawing the line.
3. Create a small circle to the right of the title.
4. Add color to the circle using the yellow fill color.
5. Create a rectangle next to the yellow circle.
6. Color the rectangle blue.
7. Make the rectangle into a 3D shape by choosing 3D Style 1.
8. Change the depth of the 3D shape to 72 pt.
9. Insert a picture of an accountant called ACCNTANT.WMF.

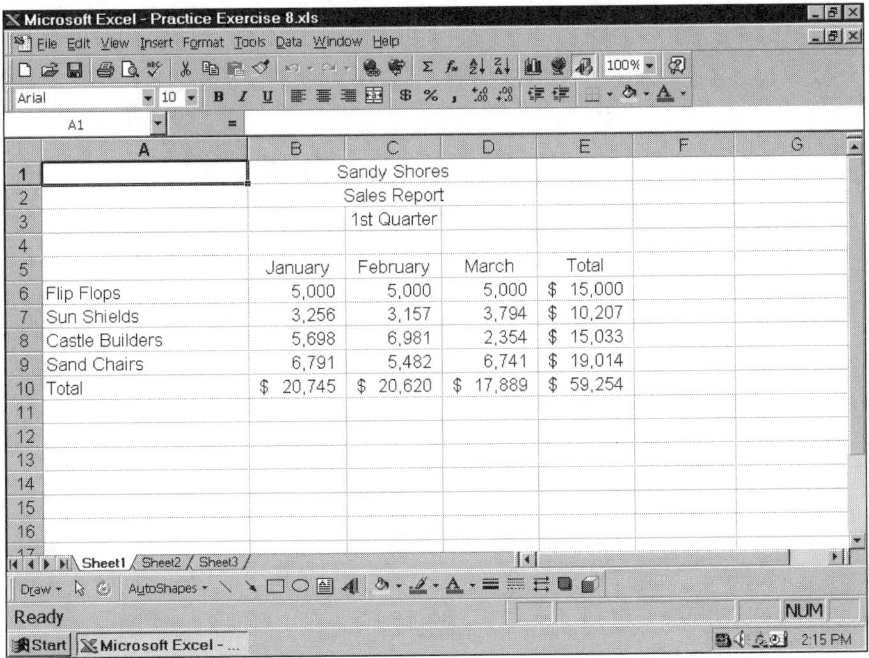

Figure 8.11 The Practice Exercise before you begin.

10. Insert WordArt by choosing the WordArt style in the second row, fifth column of the WordArt Gallery.
11. Enter "Sandy Shores" for the WordArt text.
12. Change the font size for the WordArt text to 24 pt.
13. Move the WordArt to the upper-left corner of the worksheet, near the title and subtitles, as shown in Figure 8.12.
14. Save the workbook with the same name.
15. Close the workbook.

Answers To Practice Exercise

1. Click the Open tool on the Standard toolbar, and double-click the file name Ch8 Prac Ex.
2. Click the Drawing tool button on the Standard toolbar. The Drawing toolbar appears at the bottom of the Excel window. Click the Line tool on the Drawing toolbar. Press Shift and drag the cross-hair pointer from cell B4 across to cell D4. Release the mouse button and the Shift key. This creates a horizontal line in Row 4 beneath the subtitle *1st Quarter*. The line should be selected, indicated by the selection handles at each end of the line.

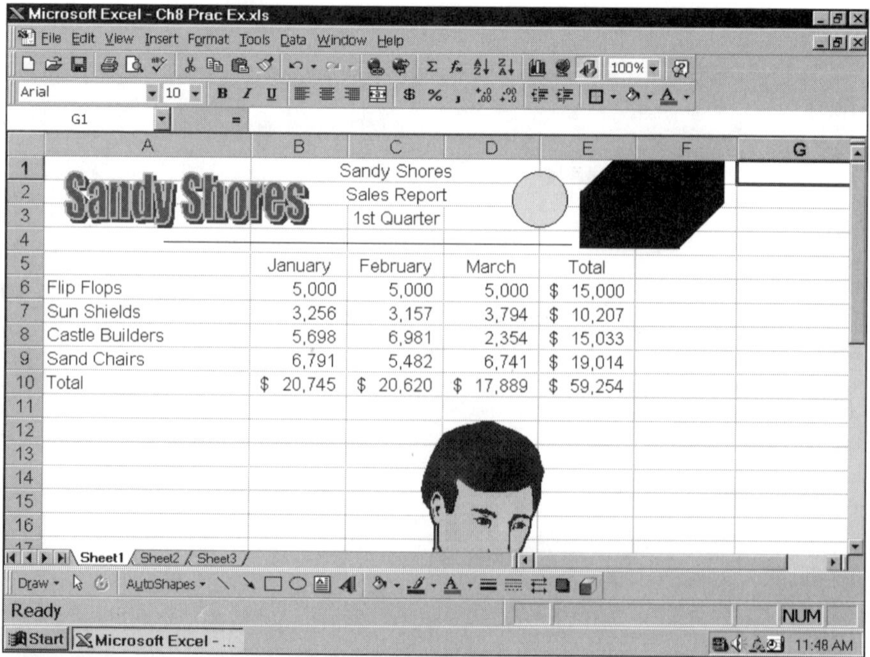

Figure 8.12 The completed Practice Exercise.

3. Click the Oval tool on the Drawing toolbar. Hold down the Shift key, and drag the cross-hair pointer diagonally from D1 to E3. Release the mouse button and Shift key. This creates a small circle next to the title. The circle should be selected, indicated by the selection handles around the circle.
4. Click the Fill Color tool on the Drawing toolbar. Choose Yellow. Excel fills the circle with the color yellow.
5. Click the Rectangle tool on the Drawing toolbar. Drag the cross-hair pointer diagonally from E1 to F3. Release the mouse button. This creates a small rectangle next to the circle. The rectangle is selected and selection handles surround it.
6. Click the Fill Color tool on the Drawing toolbar. Choose Blue. Excel fills the rectangle with the color blue.
7. Click the 3D tool on the Drawing toolbar. Choose 3D Style 1. Excel changes the blue rectangle to a 3D shape.
8. Click the 3D tool on the Drawing toolbar. Click the 3D Settings button. Click the Depth tool on the 3D Settings toolbar. Choose 72 pt. Excel displays the 3D rectangle with more depth. Click the Close (X) button on the 3D Settings toolbar to close the toolbar.
9. Select Insert|Picture|From File. Click the Up One Level button to display the C drive in the Look In box. Choose the Program Files folder, the Microsoft Office folder, and then the Clipart folder. Click on the ACCNTANT.WMF picture file. Click Insert. The accountant picture should appear below the table in your worksheet.
10. Click the Insert WordArt tool on the Drawing toolbar. In the WordArt Gallery, choose the WordArt style in the second row, fifth column. Click OK.
11. In the WordArt text box, type "Sandy Shores". Click OK. Excel adds the WordArt to the worksheet. Notice the WordArt text is in two shades of blue with a brown shadow. The WordArt toolbar appears next to the WordArt text.
12. Click the Edit Text button on the WordArt toolbar. In the Size list, choose 24 pt. Click OK. Excel reduces the size of the WordArt text from 36 pt. to 24 pt.
13. Drag the WordArt to the upper-left corner of the worksheet, near the title and subtitles. Click any cell to deselect the WordArt text.

    Your worksheet should look similar to the one shown earlier in Figure 8.12.
14. Click the Save tool on the Standard toolbar to save the workbook.
15. Click the Close (X) button in the upper-right corner of the document window. This closes the workbook.

Need To Know More?

Harvey, Greg: *Excel 97 For Windows For Dummies*. IDG Books Worldwide, Inc., Foster City, CA, 1996. ISBN 0-7645-0049-X. Chapter 8, "The Simple Art of Making Charts," gives you information on WordArt.

Neibauer, Alan: *Excel One Step At A Time*. IDG Books Worldwide, Inc., Foster City, CA, 1997. ISBN 0-7645-3139-5. Lesson 14, "Using Clip Art And WordArt," explains how to use WordArt in an Excel spreadsheet. Lesson 15, "Creating Custom Graphics," focuses on using Excel's drawing tools to create and modify your own graphics.

Printing Workbooks

Terms you'll need to understand:

- √ Preview
- √ Zoom
- √ Page break preview
- √ Print range
- √ Page setup
- √ Print area
- √ Print titles
- √ Header
- √ Footer

Skills you'll need to master:

- √ Previewing worksheets
- √ Previewing page breaks in worksheets
- √ Printing worksheets
- √ Setting the print area
- √ Setting print titles
- √ Printing the worksheet using Print Preview
- √ Printing the worksheet using Page Break Preview
- √ Printing named ranges
- √ Creating headers and footers

Printing Excel Documents

Previewing what you want to print helps you to know what the printed page will look like before you print. You can print an entire workbook or just the portion you want. Excel provides header and footer options, and you can customize your headers and footers. In this chapter, you'll preview worksheets, preview page breaks in worksheets, and print worksheets in various ways. You'll also learn how to create headers and footers that print information at the top and bottom of every page in a worksheet.

Previewing And Printing Worksheets

An Excel workbook can contain many worksheets, like pages in a loose-leaf notebook. You can print the entire workbook at once, or you can print only the pages or ranges you specify. After you set up the page with the Page Setup command and then preview your data, you can print the data. Excel provides two options to preview your worksheets before you print them out: Print Preview and Page Break Preview. Print Preview shows you how the pages in a sheet will look when printed, including headers, footers, and print titles (column and/or row headings that repeat on every page). Page Break Preview is a view that shows you where the page breaks are on a sheet, and allows you to change the page breaks to include or exclude columns and rows.

You can print selected data, selected sheets, or an entire workbook. If your workbook is already set up the way you want it to print, then you don't have to display the Print dialog box. Just click the Print button on the Standard toolbar to print your workbook. You can select a print area to tell Excel what part of the worksheet you want to print. You can also print column and row headings on the top edge and left side of your worksheet (called print titles) on every page of the printout.

In the upcoming tasks, you'll preview a worksheet and preview page breaks in a worksheet. Then, you'll print a worksheet in a variety of ways, such as select a print area, specify print titles, print the entire worksheet from the Print dialog box, print a worksheet from Print Preview, and print a worksheet from Page Break Preview. You'll also print named ranges.

Task 1 Previewing worksheets.

1. Open the Ch9 Task workbook located on the companion disk.
2. Click the Print Preview button on the Standard toolbar. Your workbook should appear in the Print Preview window (see Figure 9.1).

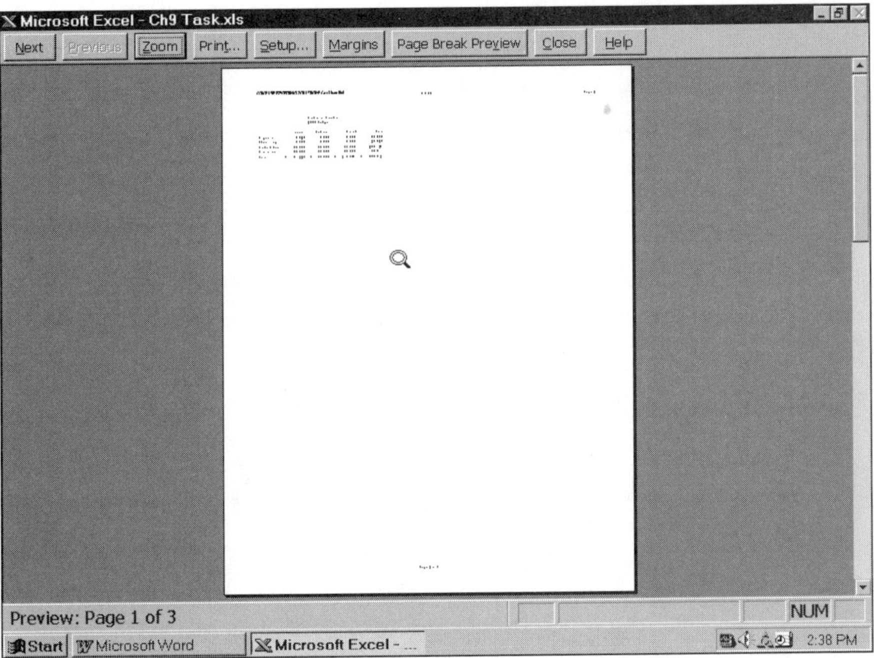

Figure 9.1 The Print Preview window.

3. Click the Zoom button on the Print Preview toolbar to zoom in.
4. Click the Zoom button again on the Print Preview toolbar to zoom out.

Note: The Next button only works if the worksheet takes up more than one page and you are not displaying the last page of the worksheet. The Previous button only works if the worksheet takes up more than one page and you're not displaying the first page of the worksheet.

5. Click the Close button on the Print Preview toolbar.

Your document window should be displayed.

Make sure that you know how to preview a worksheet before you take the exam.

Task 2 Previewing page breaks in worksheets.

1. Choose View|Page Break Preview. Excel displays your sheet in the Page Break Preview view (see Figure 9.2).

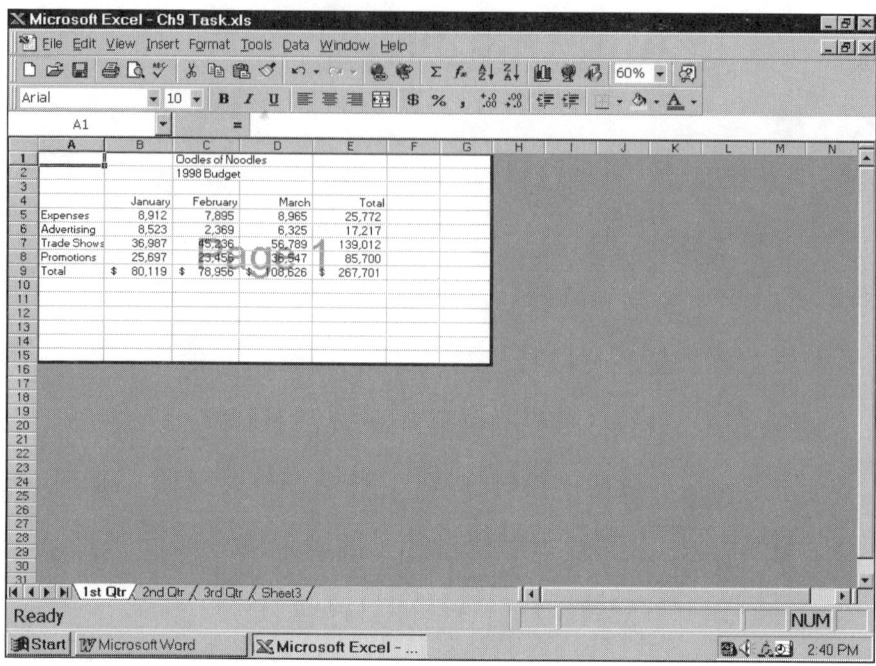

Figure 9.2 The Page Break Preview view.

Note: When you choose the Page Break Preview view, Excel will display the Welcome To Page Break Preview dialog box. This dialog box tells you that you can adjust page breaks by using the mouse. To prevent the dialog box from popping up again when going into Page Break Preview, click the Do Not Show This Dialog Again checkbox.

2. Click OK, then move the mouse pointer to the right blue border of the sheet until you see a double arrow.
3. Drag the right border to the left one column to exclude a column.
4. Move the mouse pointer to the bottom blue border of the sheet until you see a double arrow.
5. Drag the bottom border down one row to include another row.

Note: Although you can set the page breaks to columns or rows prior to the automatic page breaks, you cannot extend automatic page breaks by dragging them. You must either change the margins, orientation, or column width to give you room for additional columns or rows.

6. Choose View|Normal to return to Normal view.

Be prepared to switch to Page Break Preview and exclude a column while in that view.

Task 3 Printing worksheets.

1. Select the range B5:E9.
2. Select File|Print Area|Set Print Area.
3. Select File|Page Setup.

   The Page Setup dialog box opens.
4. Click the Sheet tab.
5. Click in the Print Titles Rows to repeat at top box.
6. Drag the Page Setup dialog box out of the way, and click cell A1 and drag down to A4.

   This selects rows 1 through 4 as the row print titles at the top edge of the worksheet that you want to repeat on every page.
7. Click in the Print Titles Columns to repeat at left box.
8. Drag the Page Setup dialog box out of the way, and click any cell in Column A.

   This selects the row headings in column A, which are the column print titles at the left edge of the worksheet that you want to repeat on every page.
9. Click OK.
10. Press Ctrl+P. The Print dialog box should appear, as shown in Figure 9.3.
11. Click OK.

Excel prints your worksheet.

It's important that you know how to print a worksheet, set a print area, and set print titles.

The next three tasks show you how to print the worksheet from Print Preview and Page Break Preview, and how to print a named range.

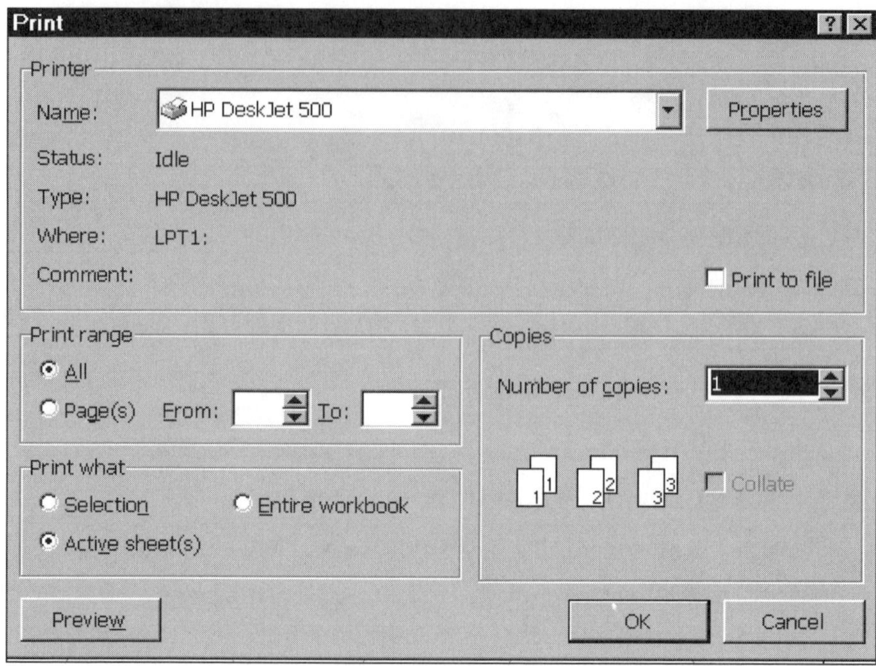

Figure 9.3 The Print dialog box.

HOLD That Skill!

Here are the Print dialog box options that you need to know about in order to print your workbooks:

- In the Printer section, you can specify the printer name, status, type, and port your printer is connected to on your computer (LPT1, LPT2, and so forth). Click the Properties button to change the printer information.
- The Print Range section lets you print one or more pages. For example, if you want to print only pages 2 through 5, select Page(s), and then type the numbers of the first and last page you want to print in the From and To boxes, respectively. You cannot print nonconsecutive pages, such as pages 5 and 10.
- In the Print What section, the Selection option lets you print the cells you selected in the worksheet, the Active Sheet(s) option prints the worksheets you selected in the workbook, and the Entire Workbook option prints the whole workbook.

- The Copies option lets you print one or more copies of the selection, worksheet, or workbook.
- The Collate option prints a complete copy of the selection, worksheet, or workbook before the first page of the next copy is printed.

Task 4 Printing the worksheet using Print Preview.

1. Click the Print Preview button on the Standard toolbar.
2. Click the Print button on the Print Preview toolbar.
3. Click OK to print the document.

Task 5 Printing the worksheet using Page Break Preview.

1. Choose View|Page Break Preview. If the Welcome To Page Break Preview dialog box is displayed, click OK.
2. Click the Print button on the Standard toolbar to print the worksheet.
3. Choose View|Normal to return to Normal view.

Before you take the exam, ensure that you know how to print directly from Page Break Preview.

Task 6 Printing named ranges.

1. Press F5 (GoTo).
2. Double-click the range name ColHeadings in the Go To list to highlight the named range on the sheet.
3. Press Ctrl+P. The Print dialog box should appear.
4. In the Print What section, choose the Selection option.
5. Click OK to print the named range called ColHeadings.

To pass the exam, you'll need to understand how to find and print a range name.

Adding Headers And Footers

If you want to print information at the top and/or bottom of every page of your printout, you can add headers and footers to your workbook. The information can include text, page numbers, the current date and time, the workbook file name, and the worksheet tab name. Excel provides predefined headers and footers that are ready to use, but you can add text and special commands to control the appearance of your headers and footers.

You can enhance your headers and footers by applying the following formatting features:

- Bold
- Italics
- Underline
- Left align
- Center
- Right align

You can also apply any font formatting, such as font, size, and effects. Left, center, and right alignment are only available by using the Left, Center, and Right sections. For example, you cannot left justify text in the Center section of the header or footer.

Be prepared to add a header and footer to a worksheet and format them with an alignment command such as right, center, or left.

Task 7 Creating Headers and Footers.

1. Select File|Page Setup. The Page Setup dialog box should appear.
2. Click the Header/Footer tab. You should see the Header and Footer dialog box, as shown in Figure 9.4.
3. Click the Header drop-down arrow, and select a header.
4. Click the Footer drop-down arrow, and select a footer.
5. Click OK.
6. Close the Ch9 Task workbook without saving changes.

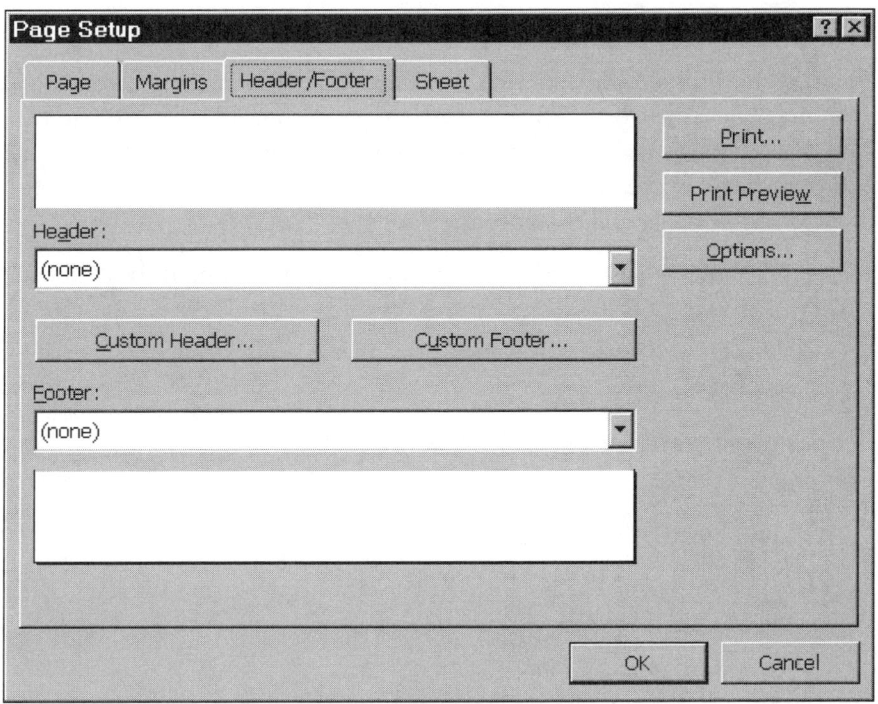

Figure 9.4 The Header/Footer tab in the Page Setup dialog box.

Use the View|Header And Footer command as a shortcut to get to the Header/Footer tab in the Page Setup dialog box.

Practice Exercise

Before you print the Sandy Shores Company budget for the first quarter, you'll need to preview the worksheet and change the page breaks in Page Break Preview. The sales manager needs to see various printouts of the budget, so you will print the worksheet, print the screen, and print a named range. You'll also need to add a header and footer to the budget.

Figure 9.5 shows what the worksheet contains before you go through the instructions in this exercise.

1. Open the Ch9 Prac Ex workbook located on the companion disk.
2. Preview the worksheet.
3. In Print Preview, zoom in on the worksheet.
4. In Print Preview, zoom out from the worksheet.
5. Close Print Preview.
6. Preview the page breaks on the worksheet.
7. In Page Break Preview, exclude column G.
8. Print the worksheet from Page Break Preview.
9. Return to Normal view.

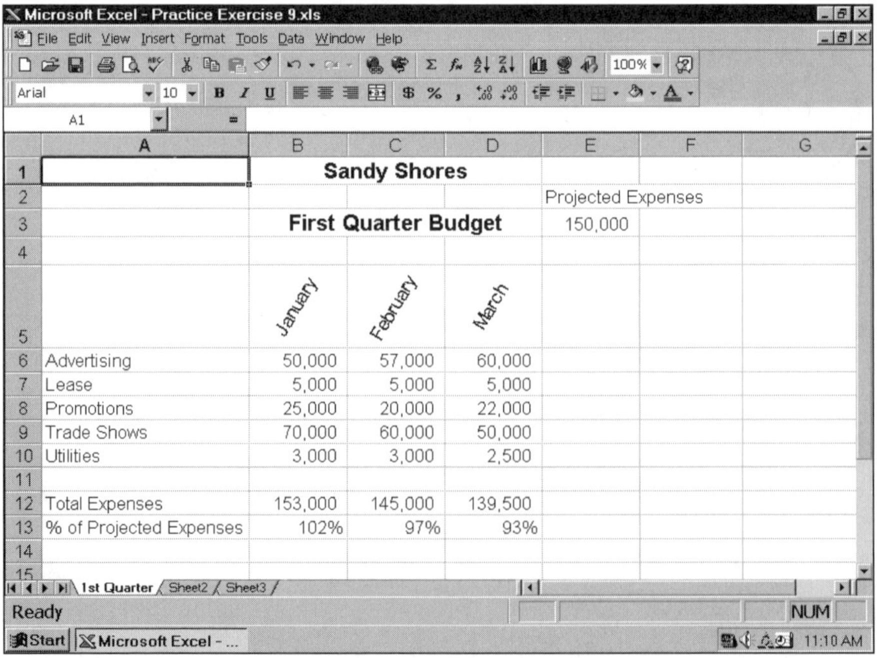

Figure 9.5 The Practice Exercise before you begin.

10. Set a print area that includes only the numbers on the worksheet, excluding the title, column, and row headings.
11. Set the row print titles to include the title and column headings. Set the column print titles to include the row headings.
12. Print the entire worksheet with the default print settings.
13. From Print Preview, print the worksheet.
14. Print the range named Total_Expenses.
15. Create a header that contains the text *1st Quarter*.
16. Create a footer that contains the text *Page 1*.
17. Preview the header and footer on the worksheet.
18. From Print Preview, print the worksheet.
19. Save the workbook with the same name.
20. Close the workbook.

Answers To Practice Exercise

1. Click the Open button on the Standard toolbar, and double-click the file name Ch9 Prac Ex.
2. Click the Print Preview button on the Standard toolbar. Excel displays the worksheet in Print Preview. The Print Preview toolbar appears at the top of the Print Preview screen.
3. Click the Zoom button on the Print Preview toolbar. Excel magnifies the worksheet so that you can see more detail on the worksheet.
4. Click the Zoom button again on the Print Preview toolbar. Excel shrinks the worksheet to show you how it will print out on a page.
5. Click the Close button on the Print Preview toolbar. This closes Print Preview.
6. Choose View|Page Break Preview. If Excel displays a dialog box informing you that you can adjust the margins by dragging them to a new location, click OK. You see the worksheet with a large Page 1 that appears in the middle of the sheet. The blue borders around the sheet represent the page breaks on the worksheet.
7. Point to the right blue border, and drag it over to column F. This excludes column G. The page break is now set at column F.
8. Click the Print button on the Standard toolbar. Excel prints the worksheet from Page Break Preview.
9. Choose View|Normal. Excel switches back to Normal view.

10. Select the range B6:D13. Select File|Print Area|Set Print Area.
11. Select File|Print Page Setup. Click the Sheet tab. Click in the Print Titles Rows to repeat at top box. Drag the Page Setup dialog box out of the way, and click cell A1 and drag down to A5. Click in the Print Titles Columns to repeat at left box. Drag the Page Setup dialog box out of the way, and click any cell in Column A. Click OK.
12. Press Ctrl+P. The Print dialog box appears. Click OK. Excel prints the entire worksheet with the default print settings.
13. Click the Print Preview button on the Standard toolbar. Click the Print button on the Print Preview toolbar. Excel prints the worksheet.
14. Press F5 (Go To). In the Go To dialog box, double-click the Total_Expenses range name. Excel highlights the range named Total_Expenses on the worksheet. Press Ctrl+P. In the Print dialog box, in the Print What section, choose the Selection option. Click OK. Excel prints the range named Total_Expenses.
15. Choose View|Header And Footer. In the Page Setup dialog box, the Header/Footer tab is selected. In the Header list, choose 1st Quarter.
16. In the Footer list, choose Page 1. Click OK. You have created a header and footer that will print on every page.
17. Click the Print Preview button on the Standard toolbar. Notice, the header appears centered at the top of the page, and the footer is centered at the bottom of the page, as shown in Figure 9.6.
18. Click the Print button on the Print Preview toolbar. Excel prints the worksheet with the header and footer from Print Preview.
19. Click the Save button on the Standard toolbar to save the workbook.
20. Click the Close (X) button in the upper-right corner of the document window. This closes the workbook.

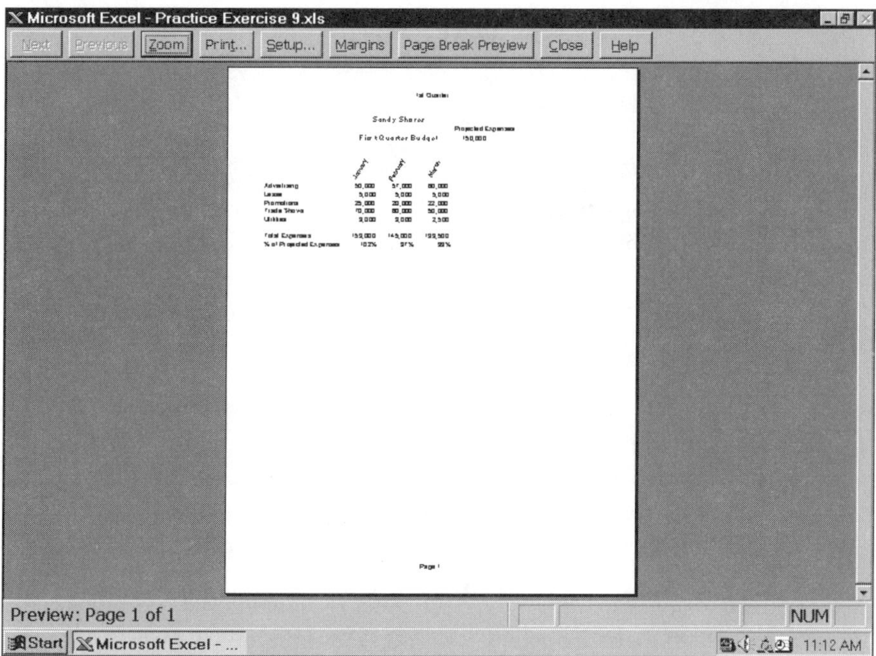

Figure 9.6 The completed Practice Exercise.

Need To Know More?

Catapult, Inc.: *Microsoft Excel 97 Step By Step*. Microsoft Press, Redmond, WA, 1996. ISBN 1-57231-314-5. Lesson 2, "Setting Up a Worksheet," tells you how to print a worksheet quickly. Lesson 3, "Writing Formulas," discusses using cell names. Lesson 4, "Formatting Your Worksheet for a Professional Look," talks about creating headers and footers. Lesson 10, "Printing Reports to Distribute Information Offline," covers the details of previewing and printing a worksheet.

Craig, Deborah: *How to Use Microsoft Excel 97 for Windows*. Que, Indianapolis, IN, 1996. ISBN 1-56276-469-1. Chapter 5, "Printing," gives you all the information you need about previewing and printing a worksheet. Chapter 9, "More About Formulas and Functions," shows you how to name cells and cell ranges.

Harvey, Greg: *Excel 97 for Windows for Dummies*. IDG Books Worldwide, Inc., Foster City, CA, 1996. ISBN 0-7645-0049-X. Chapter 5, "Printing the Masterpiece," explains how to preview and print worksheets. Chapter 6, "Oh, What a Tangled Worksheet We Weave," talks about naming cells in worksheets.

Neibauer, Alan: *Excel One Step at a Time*. IDG Books Worldwide, Inc., Foster City, CA, 1997. ISBN 0-7645-3139-5. Lesson 4, "Rearranging and Previewing Worksheets," explains how to preview worksheets. Lesson 10, "Arranging and Printing Worksheets," discusses previewing and printing worksheets.

Nicholson, John R. and Sean R. Nicholson: *Discover Excel 97*. IDG Books Worldwide, Inc., Foster City, CA, 1997. ISBN 1-7645-3047-X. Chapter 9, "Get Ready, Get Set! Go to Page Setup," explains headers and footers. Chapter 10, "Out with the New: Printing Worksheets," covers previewing and printing worksheets.

Nossiter, Josh: *Using Microsoft Excel 97*. Que, Indianapolis, IN, 1996. ISBN 0-7897-0955-4. Chapter 5, "Putting It All on Paper: Printing Worksheets and Workbooks," has a nice discussion of previewing and printing worksheets.

Reisner, Trudi: *Easy Microsoft Office*. Que, Indianapolis, IN, 1997. ISBN 0-7897-1078-1. In Part VIII, "Formatting the Worksheet," refer to Task 51, "Inserting and Removing Page Breaks for information on Page Break Preview." Task 54, "Previewing and Printing the Worksheet," shows you how to preview and print worksheets.

Creating Charts

Terms you'll need to understand:

- √ Chart types
- √ Data series
- √ Plot area
- √ Y axis
- √ X axis
- √ Categories
- √ Values
- √ Legend
- √ Gridlines

Skills you'll need to master:

- √ Creating charts
- √ Modifying charts
- √ Formatting charts
- √ Previewing charts
- √ Printing charts

Representing Data Using Excel Charts

Instead of using only a worksheet to represent data, you can create a chart to represent the same data. For example, you might want to create a chart and print the chart and worksheet together for a presentation. That way, your audience can easily see trends in a series of values. In this chapter, you'll create, modify, format, preview, and print a chart.

Creating, Modifying, And Formatting Charts

You can use Excel to create, modify, and format charts. But, before you begin to create charts, you need to be familiar with the chart elements shown in Figure 10.1.

The most common chart types include pie, bar, column (default), line, and area. Most of these basic chart types also come in 3D. A standard, flat chart is professional looking, but a 3D chart can help your audience distinguish between different sets of data. When you choose a chart type and a chart subtype,

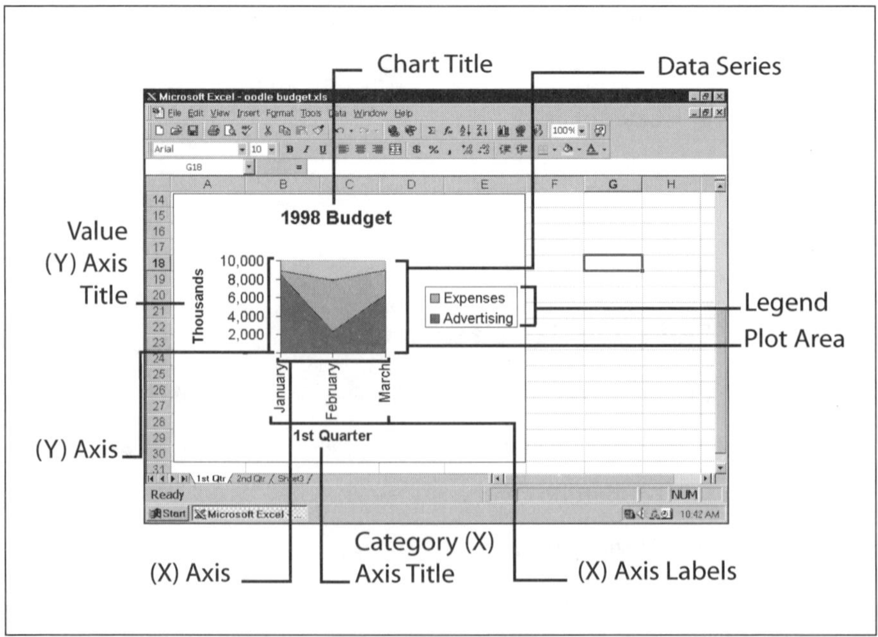

Figure 10.1 The elements of a chart.

HOLD That Skill!

Here are some terms you'll need to keep in mind when you're working with charts:

- *Data series*—The bars, pie wedges, lines, or other elements that represent plotted values in a chart. Often, the data series correspond to rows of data in your worksheet.
- *X axis*—The number of elements in a series. For most two-dimensional charts, categories are plotted along the category (X) axis, which is usually horizontal. Categories generally correspond to the columns that you have in your chart data, with the category labels coming from the column headings.
- *Y axis*—For most two-dimensional charts, data values are plotted along the value (Y) axis, which is usually vertical. The Y axis reflects the values of the bars, lines, or plot points. In a two-dimensional bar chart, the axes are reversed, with the values being plotted on the X axis and the categories on the Y axis. In a 3D chart, the Z axis represents the vertical plane, and the X axis (distance) and Y axis (width) represent the two sides on the floor of the chart.
- *Legend*—The element that designates the separate categories of a chart. For example, the legend for a column chart shows what each column of the chart represents.
- *Gridlines*—The lines that depict the X-axis and Y-axis scale of the data series. For example, major gridlines for the Y axis will help you follow a point from the X or Y axis to identify a data point's exact value.

you can display interesting and meaningful results based on your worksheet data in a professional manner. The following chart types are available:

- Column
- Bar
- Line
- Pie
- XY (Scatter)
- Area
- Doughnut

- Radar
- Surface
- Bubble
- Stock
- Cylinder
- Cone
- Pyramid

The easiest way to create a chart in Excel is to use the Chart Wizard. The Chart Wizard leads you step-by-step through the task of creating a chart. Excel plots the data and creates the chart where you specify on the worksheet.

After you create a chart, you'll have a variety of chart tools at your disposal to format and edit the chart. You can use the Chart toolbar to change legends, gridlines, X axis, Y axis, background, colors, fonts, titles, labels, and much more (see Figure 10.2). In the upcoming tasks, you'll create a default chart (clustered column chart) using the Chart Wizard. Then, you'll modify the chart by moving it to a different location, and you'll resize the chart. Finally, you'll change the appearance of the chart by changing the legend and the category axis text.

Task 1 Creating charts.

1. Open the Ch10 Task workbook stored on the companion disk (see Figure 10.3).
2. Select cells A4 through D8 to identify the range you want to chart.

   Note: When you create a chart, make sure the range you select includes the labels, but doesn't include the totals. If you are charting the totals, make sure you only select the total rows and not the data that creates them.

3. Click the Chart Wizard button on the Standard toolbar. The Chart Wizard—Step 1 Of 4—Chart Type dialog box should appear, displaying the chart types. The Clustered Column Chart is the default chart type.

Figure 10.2 The Chart toolbar.

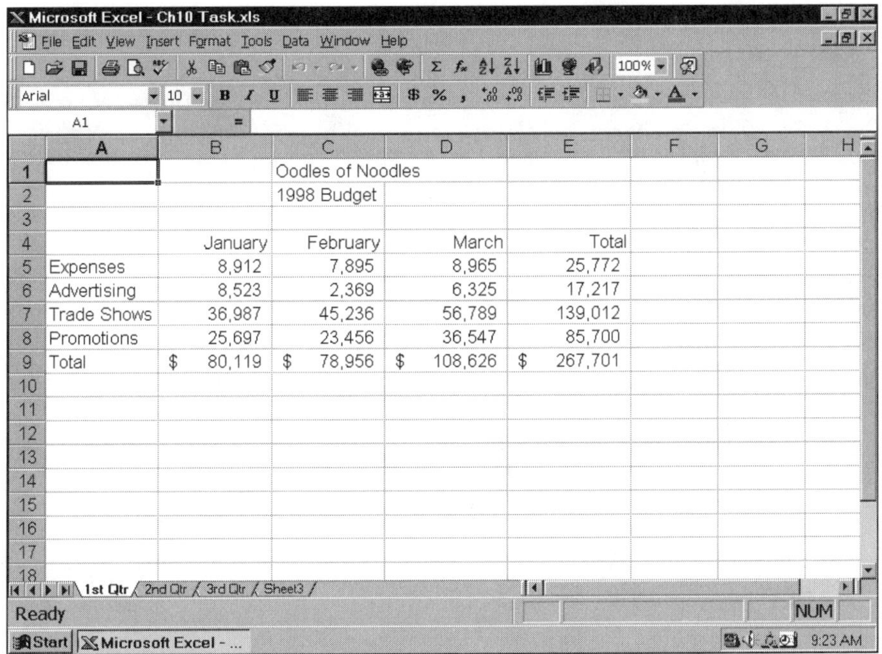

Figure 10.3 The workbook when first opened.

4. Click the Next button. This accepts the Clustered Column chart type, and the Chart Wizard—Step 2 Of 4—Chart Source Data dialog box should appear with a sample chart.

5. Choose the Rows option. Each area represents the values for each budget category by month. January, February, and March are the category (X) axis labels. The budget category names appear in the legend for the data series.

6. Click the Next button. Excel displays the Chart Wizard—Step 3 Of 4—Chart Options dialog box. The dialog box contains a sample chart and options for adding titles, changing the legend, and formatting other elements in the chart.

7. On the Titles tab, click the Chart Title text box, and type "1998 Budget".

8. Click the Next button. You should see the Chart Wizard—Step 4 Of 4—Chart Location dialog box. You can place the chart on a separate *chart sheet* or as an object in an existing worksheet. A chart sheet is a separate element from the worksheet and is stored in the current workbook. Keep the As Object In option and 1st Qtr sheet selected.

To return to a previous Chart Wizard dialog box while using the Chart Wizard, click the Back button. To go to the next Chart Wizard dialog box, click the Next button. You can stop the process of creating a chart by clicking the Cancel button in any Chart Wizard dialog box.

9. Click the Finish button.
10. Click the Save button on the Standard toolbar to save the file.

The chart appears near the top of the worksheet, and the plot area is too small to see the data series areas in the chart. Selection handles surround the border of the chart. You also should see a Chart toolbar. Figure 10.4 shows the clustered column chart and the Chart toolbar. In the next task, you will move and resize the chart, making it easier to see the elements of the chart.

> *Note: If you don't see the Chart toolbar, select View|Toolbars|Chart. If the Chart toolbar is docked next to the Standard or Formatting toolbar, point to the Chart toolbar (not on a button), and drag it into the worksheet area, so that it's near the chart.*

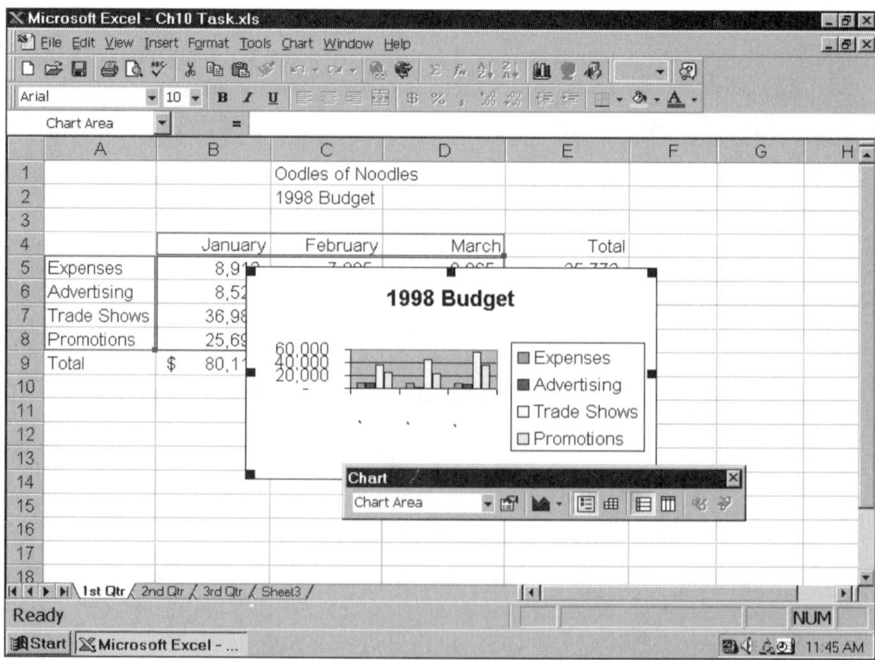

Figure 10.4 The clustered column chart and Chart toolbar.

HOLD That Skill!

You should remember some basic concepts when creating a chart in Excel:

- You must select data before you can create a chart.
- If you change any data in the specified chart range, Excel will update the chart accordingly, to reflect the new data in the worksheet.
- You can choose a chart type from the Chart Type list and then choose a chart subtype from the Chart Sub-type gallery. A description of the chart type appears in the lower-right side of the Chart Wizard dialog box when you click on a chart subtype.
- You can plot a series in rows or columns. The chart will look different depending on your choice, so make sure you choose a setup that fits your needs best.
- You can add labels to the Category (X) axis (along the bottom of the chart) and Value (Y) axis (along the left side of the chart).
- In the last Chart Wizard dialog box, you can specify where you want to place the chart. You have two choices: As New Sheet and As Object In. The As New Sheet option lets you insert the chart on a separate chart sheet. A chart sheet is a separate element from the worksheet and is stored in the current workbook. The As Object In option enables you to insert the chart as an object in the worksheet that contains the data you're charting.

Be sure you know how to create a chart using the Chart Wizard. The exam requires you to create using the default settings. You enter a title for the chart, too. You'll insert the chart as an object. The Chart toolbar will appear after you create the chart. You can close the Chart toolbar when you're taking the exam, because you won't need it.

Task 2 Modifying charts.

1. Point to the chart. When you see a four-headed arrow, drag the chart downward to move the chart below the worksheet with the upper-left corner of the chart starting in cell A11.
2. Point to the right-middle selection handle. When a double-headed arrow appears, drag it to the right to column D, to make the chart wider.
3. Drag the bottom-middle selection handle down to the bottom edge of row 25, to make the chart taller. The chart appears in the range A11:D25.

4. Click any cell in the worksheet to deselect the chart. The selection handles and the Chart toolbar disappear.

The chart appears below the worksheet, and you should be able to see all the elements in the chart (see Figure 10.5).

After you create the chart in the exam, you'll be required to move the chart beneath the worksheet. You'll have to resize the chart to fit it into the specified range.

Task 3 Formatting charts.

1. Select the chart by clicking anywhere on it. You should see the Chart toolbar. See Figure 10.2 for more information on the Chart toolbar tools.
2. Click the Legend button to remove the legend.
3. Click the Legend button again to add the legend.
4. Click the Chart Objects drop-down arrow on the Chart toolbar, and choose Category Axis.
5. Click the Format Axis button on the Chart toolbar.

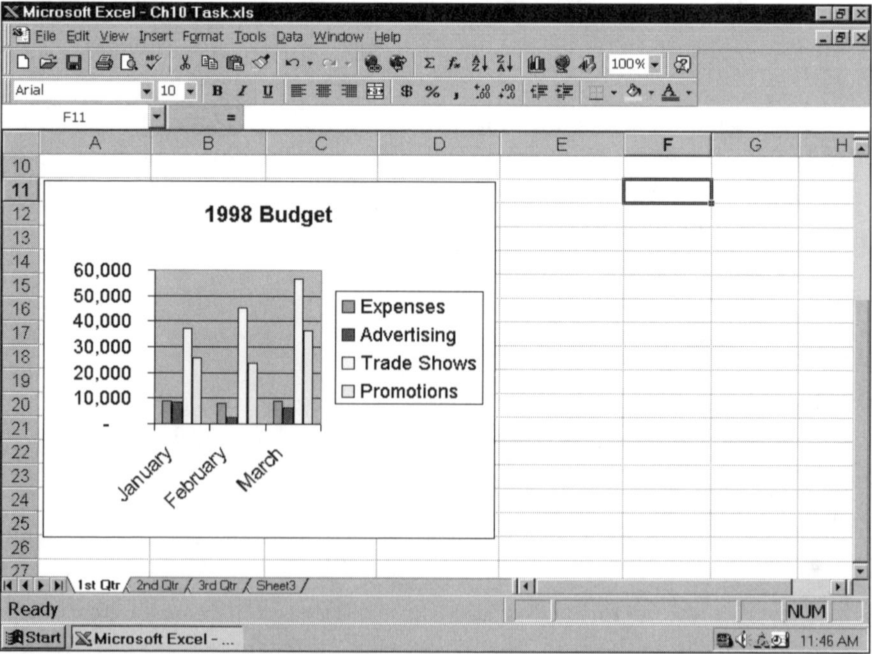

Figure 10.5 Modified column chart.

The Format Axis dialog box opens.

6. Click the Font tab.
7. Click the Courier New font and Bold style.
8. Click OK.
9. Click the Angle Text Upward button to angle the category axis text upward.
10. Change the legend text "Expenses" to "Samples" by clicking on cell A5 in the worksheet. Then, type over the data with the new text.

Figure 10.6 shows the formatted column chart. As you can see, it is easy to format your charts using the Chart toolbar. Now that you know how to create and modify your charts, you'll need to know how to preview and print your charts.

Be ready to change the category axis to a different font on a chart provided with the worksheet on the exam. You can select Category Axis from the Chart Objects drop-down list on the Chart toolbar, and change the font and font style. You will also be required to change a description in a legend. To do so, type over

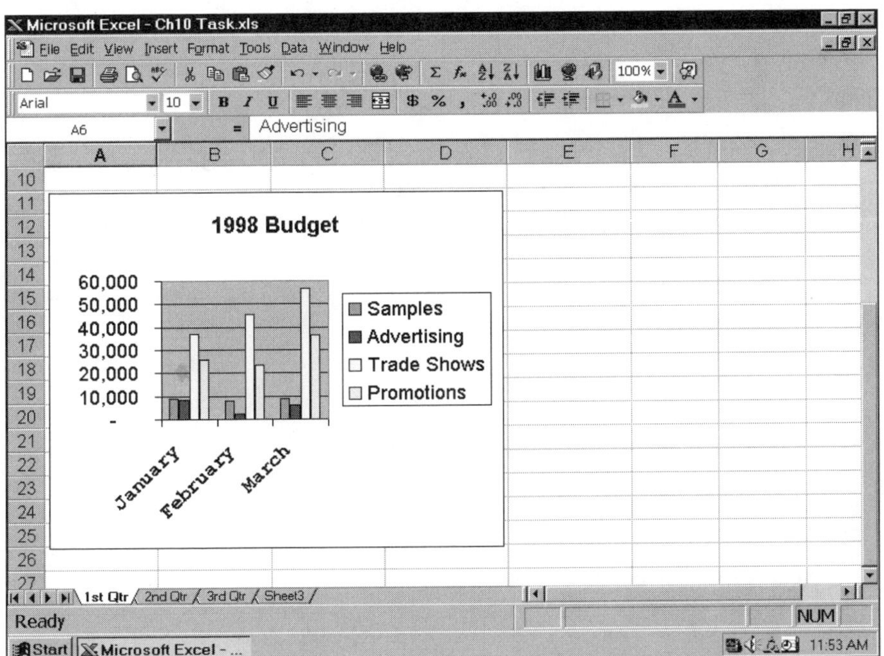

Figure 10.6 Formatted column chart.

the column heading in the worksheet, and the legend description on the chart will change to reflect the change you made in the worksheet.

Previewing And Printing Charts

You can preview and print your charts just as you can preview and print your worksheets. If a chart is an object in a worksheet, it will print when you print the worksheet that contains the chart. If you create a chart on a separate chart sheet, you can print the chart separately by printing only the chart sheet. The following tasks show you how to preview the chart to see how the worksheet and chart look before printing them. Then, you'll print the worksheet with the chart.

Task 4 Previewing charts.

1. Click the chart if it isn't already selected.
2. Click the Print Preview button on the Standard toolbar.

   Note: If the chart is selected before using Print Preview, Excel displays only the chart in the Preview window. To preview both the worksheet and chart, be sure to deselect the chart by clicking on any cell in the worksheet.

The chart appears the way it will print out.

When you take the exam, you'll be required to display and print your chart only using Page Preview. Be sure to click on the chart to ensure the chart is selected in the worksheet. Then, preview the chart and print it from the preview window. Due to the way the exam is designed, the document won't actually be printed out during the exam.

Task 5 Printing charts.

1. Click the Print button on the Print Preview toolbar, or click the Print button on the Standard toolbar.
2. If necessary, click OK.

   Excel prints the chart.
3. Close the Ch10 Task workbook without saving changes.

Practice Exercise

The sales director at the Sandy Shores Company is going to give a presentation at the annual Sandy Shores sales conference. The director says that a picture is worth a thousand words and, therefore, would like to use a column chart to present the sales data in the sales reports worksheet. In this practice exercise, you'll create a column chart and then modify and format the chart. You'll also preview the chart before printing it. Then, you'll print the chart to prepare the sales director for the presentation.

Figure 10.7 shows what the worksheet contains before you go through the instructions in this exercise.

1. Open the Ch10 Prac Ex workbook stored on the companion disk.
2. Select the range A6:D10. This is the data range you'll be charting.
3. Create a chart, and use the default chart type.
4. Plot the chart data in rows.
5. Add a chart title called *Sandy Shores Sales*.
6. Insert the chart as an object in Sheet1.
7. Save the workbook with the same name.

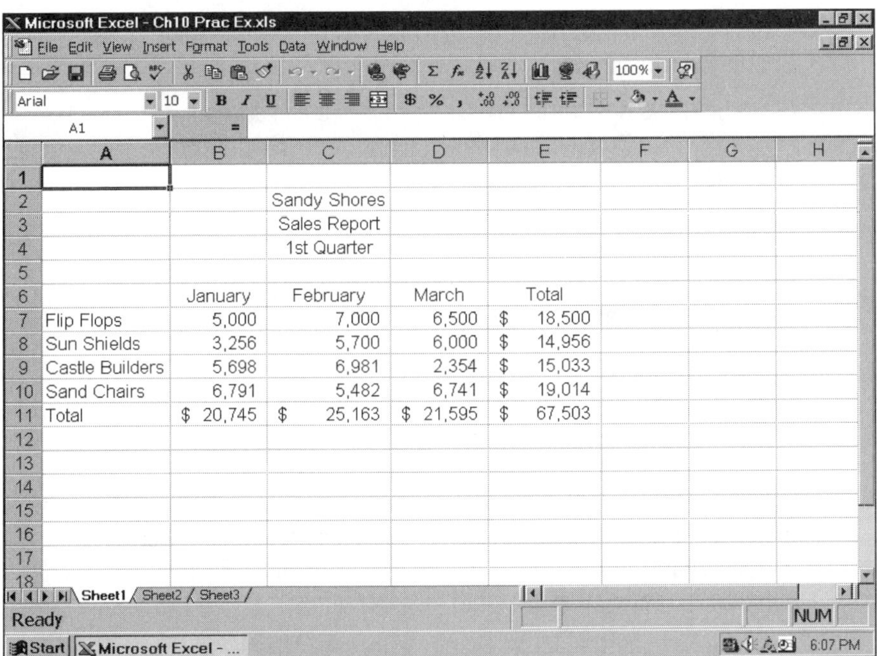

Figure 10.7 The Practice Exercise before you begin.

8. Display the clustered column chart beneath the worksheet.
9. Make the area chart wider and taller by resizing it to fit the range A13:E30.
10. Change the category axis text to Bold Times New Roman.
11. Change the legend text “Castle Builders” to “Castle Molds”.
12. Preview the clustered column chart.
13. Print the clustered column chart.
14. Save the workbook with the same name.
15. Close the workbook.

Answers To Practice Exercise

1. Click the Open button on the Standard toolbar, and double-click the file name Ch10 Prac Ex.
2. Click in cell A6, and drag diagonally to cell D8. This selects the data range A6:D10, which is the range you'll be charting.
3. Click the Chart Wizard button on the Standard toolbar. Excel opens the Chart Wizard—Step 1 Of 4—Chart Type dialog box and shows the chart types. The Clustered Column Chart is the default chart type.

   Click the Next button. The Chart Wizard—Step 2 Of 4—Chart Source Data dialog box appears with a sample chart.
4. Click the Rows option (if necessary) to plot the chart data in rows. Click the Next button. The Chart Wizard—Step 3 Of 4—Chart Options dialog box appears. You should see a sample chart and options for adding titles, changing the legend, and formatting other elements in the chart.
5. With the Titles tab selected, click in the Chart Title box, and type “Sandy Shores Sales”. This adds the chart title to the area chart.
6. Click the Next button. The Chart Wizard—Step 4 Of 4—Chart Location dialog box appears. From here, you can choose how you want to insert the chart.

   Accept the As Object In option and Sheet1 default selections. This tells Excel to insert the chart as an object on Sheet1. Click the Finish button to create the chart. Excel displays the area chart and the Chart toolbar in Sheet1. The chart contains selection handles, indicating that the chart is selected.
7. Click the Save button on the Standard toolbar. This saves the workbook with the same name, including the area chart.

8. Point to the chart, and drag it to the blank area beneath the worksheet. This moves the chart.
9. Point to the chart, and drag the upper-left corner of it to cell A13. Point to the right-middle selection handle until you see a double arrow. Drag the handle to the right-hand border of column E. This makes the chart wider. Then, use the vertical scroll box to scroll down to see the bottom of the chart. Point to the bottom-middle selection handle, and drag the border down to the bottom edge of row 30. This makes the chart taller. Now, you should see the entire plot area of the chart.
10. With the chart selected, click the Chart Objects drop-down arrow on the Chart toolbar, and choose Category Axis. Click the Format Axis button on the Chart toolbar. In the Format Axis dialog box, click the Font tab. Choose the Times New Roman font and Bold style. Click OK.
11. Click on cell A9 in the worksheet. Then, type Castle Molds and press Enter.
12. Click on the chart to select it, if necessary. Then, click the Print Preview button on the Standard toolbar. Excel shows the clustered column chart in Print Preview.
13. Click the Print button on the Print Preview toolbar. The Print dialog box appears. Click OK to print the clustered column chart.
14. Click the Save button on the Standard toolbar to save the workbook.

    Your worksheet should look like the one in Figure 10.8.
15. Click the Close (X) button in the upper-right corner of the document window. This closes the workbook.

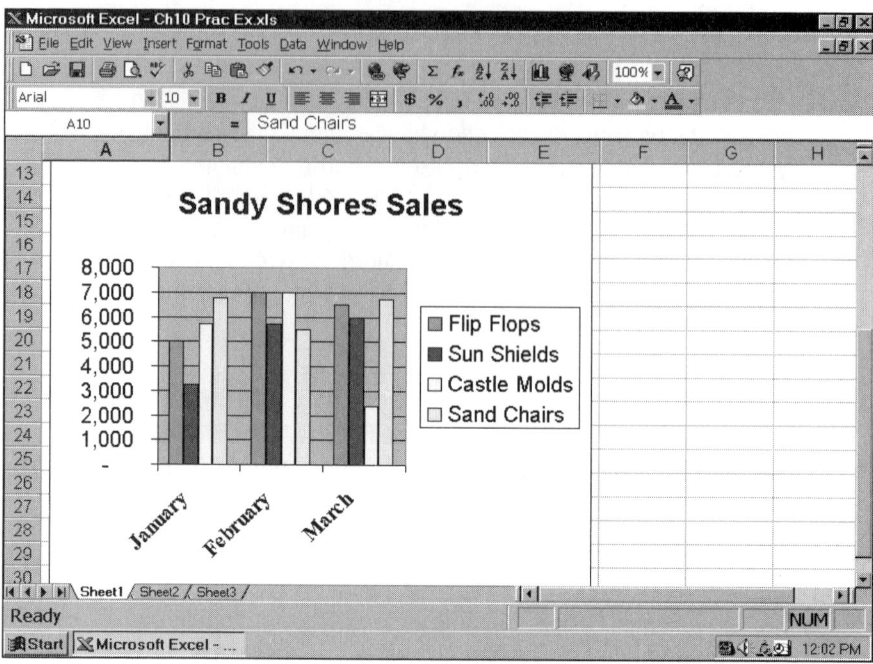

Figure 10.8 The completed Practice Exercise.

Need To Know More?

Catapult, Inc.: *Microsoft Excel 97 Step By Step*. Microsoft Press, Redmond, WA, 1996. ISBN 1-57231-314-5. Lesson 9, "Charting to Assess Trends and Relationships," tells you all about creating, modifying, and formatting charts. Lesson 10, "Printing Reports to Distribute Information Offline," shows you how to print worksheets and charts.

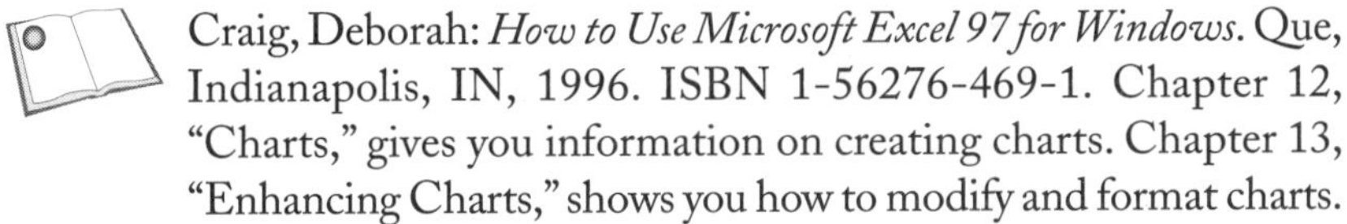

Craig, Deborah: *How to Use Microsoft Excel 97 for Windows*. Que, Indianapolis, IN, 1996. ISBN 1-56276-469-1. Chapter 12, "Charts," gives you information on creating charts. Chapter 13, "Enhancing Charts," shows you how to modify and format charts.

Harvey, Greg: *Excel 97 for Windows for Dummies*. IDG Books Worldwide, Inc., Foster City, CA, 1996. ISBN 0-7645-0049-X. Chapter 8, "The Simple Art of Making Charts," explains how to create, modify, and format charts.

Neibauer, Alan: *Excel One Step at a Time*. IDG Books Worldwide, Inc., Foster City, CA, 1997. ISBN 0-7645-3139-5. Lesson 13, "Creating Charts and Maps," shows you how to create, modify, and format all kinds of charts.

Nicholson, John R. and Sean R. Nicholson: *Discover Excel 97*. IDG Books Worldwide, Inc., Foster City, CA, 1997. ISBN 1-7645-3047-X. Chapter 7, "Pretty Pictures: Creating Cool Charts," explains how to create, modify, and format charts.

Nossiter, Josh: *Using Microsoft Excel 97*. Que, Indianapolis, IN, 1996. ISBN 0-7897-0955-4. Chapter 11, "Charts Explained (in English)," gives you a lot of information about chart types and how to create charts. Chapter 12, "Editing Charts," covers how to edit and format charts.

Reisner, Trudi: *Easy Microsoft Office*. Que, Indianapolis, IN, 1997. ISBN 0-7897-1078-1. In Part VI, "Entering and Editing Data in Excel," see Task 44, "Creating and Printing a Chart," for step-by-step instructions on creating, modifying, and printing charts.

Chapter 11

Creating Internet And Intranet Documents

Terms you'll need to understand:

- Internet
- Intranet
- HTML
- Internet Assistant Wizard
- HTML document
- Hyperlink
- Web browser

Skills you'll need to master:

- Saving Excel data as an HTML document
- Creating hyperlinks in Excel workbooks
- Browsing the Web within Excel

Networking With Excel

In Excel, you can publish a workbook as a Web page on the Internet or on your company's intranet. The Internet is a collection of computers scattered around the world that are connected together. The Web is a collection of documents that contain links (known as hyperlinks) to other Web documents. Web documents, known as *Web pages*, can be stored on a system configured with server software in order to be viewed on the Internet.

Text used to link information on different Web pages is called *hypertext*. Web pages are designed using a computer coding language called *Hypertext Markup Language*, commonly referred to as HTML. HTML documents can contain text and references to graphics and other pages. HTML documents can be browsed by any computer that has a Web browser or text editor. Hyperlinks link Web pages together and can contain both text and graphic links. You can click on hypertext or a hyperlink graphic to access a Web page. From that Web page, you can click on another hyperlink, either text or a graphic, to view another Web page, and so on.

An intranet is a smaller version of the Internet. Intranets are usually designed to meet a specific company's needs. An intranet's HTML documents are stored on one or more servers within a company and are accessible only to employees within the company.

This chapter shows you how to save worksheet data as an HTML document that you can publish as a Web page. You'll also learn how to create hyperlinks in Excel workbooks. The hyperlinks will enable you to access a Web page on the Internet and browse the Web from within Excel.

Creating A Web Page From Worksheet Data

You can convert Excel data and charts into HTML format and publish the information on the Web. As mentioned earlier, every Web page is designed using HTML. Each Web document is basically a plain text file containing formatting instructions for the text, graphics, and links that make up the Web page. The text file is called the Web page's *HTML source code*, because the formatting instructions are written in HTML. The Web recognizes files created using HTML and displays HTML documents as Web pages. You can save your Excel data and charts as HTML documents.

HOLD That Skill!

Here are some items to consider when you save worksheet data as an HTML document:

- You can save an entire worksheet or just a portion of a worksheet as an HTML document.
- The File|Save As HTML command converts worksheet data into an HTML document that is readable on the Internet or on an intranet.
- When you select File|Save As HTML, Excel steps you through four Internet Assistant Wizard dialog boxes.
- In most cases, you can keep the default options in each Internet Assistant Wizard dialog box. The only option you need to select is the type of code page in the last dialog box. Usually, the code page is US/Western European, unless you are using Excel somewhere else in the world. In this case, choose the appropriate code page.
- After you create the HTML document, you can add the document to your company FTP site or ask the Webmaster in your company how you can publish your document on the Web.

Task 1 Saving Excel data as an HTML document.

1. Open the Ch11 Task workbook stored on the companion disk.
2. Press F5 (Go To).
3. Select Annual_Report_Data, the range name you want to save as HTML, and click OK. Excel selects the range A1:E9.
4. Select File|Save As HTML. The Internet Assistant Wizard Step 1 Of 4 dialog box should open. The item in the list box is the range A1:E9, which should already be selected (see Figure 11.1).
5. Click the Next button. The Internet Assistant Wizard—Step 2 Of 4 dialog box should appear. The first option should already be selected. This is the option you want, because Excel will create a new HTML Web page from the selected data, including a header, table, and footer.
6. Click the Next button. The Internet Assistant Wizard—Step 3 Of 4 dialog box should pop up. The title and header should already be there.
7. Click the Next button. The Internet Assistant Wizard—Step 4 Of 4 dialog box should open. The US/Western European code page option should be selected.

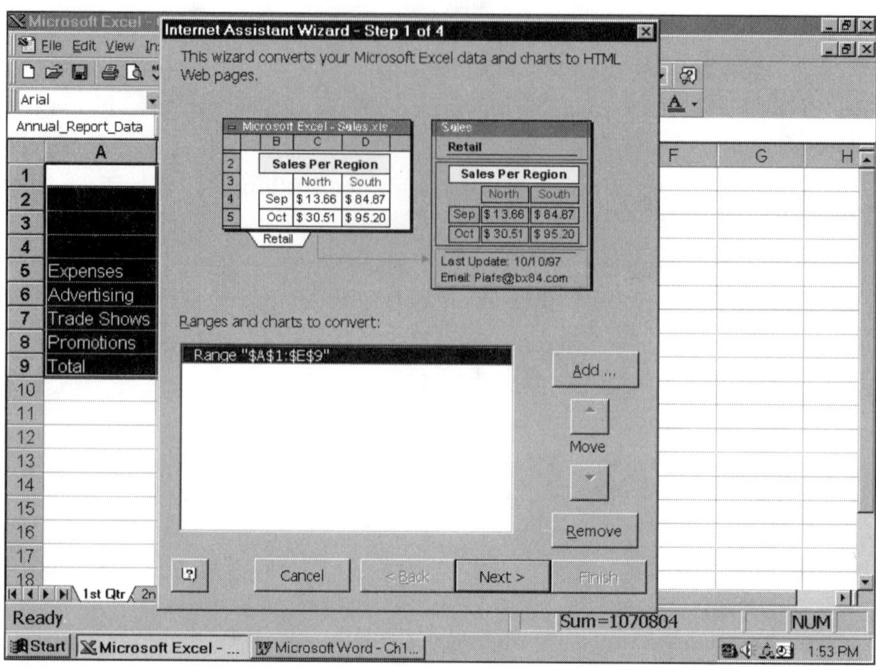

Figure 11.1 The Internet Assistant Wizard—Step 1 Of 4 dialog box.

8. In the File path box, enter the path and file name "C:\My Documents\Annual Report.htm" (see Figure 11.2).
9. Click the Finish button.

Excel converts the selected data to HTML format so that it can be published on the Web. The file extension .HTM is added to the HTML data file name. For example, Annual Report.HTM.

To return to a previous Internet Assistant Wizard dialog box, click the Back button. To go to the next Internet Assistant Wizard dialog box, click the Next button. You can stop the process of creating an HTML document by clicking the Cancel button in any Internet Assistant Wizard dialog box.

Be ready to save a named range as an HTML file. You'll want to accept all the default settings in each Internet Assistant Wizard dialog box and enter a file path and name for the HTML document in the last dialog box.

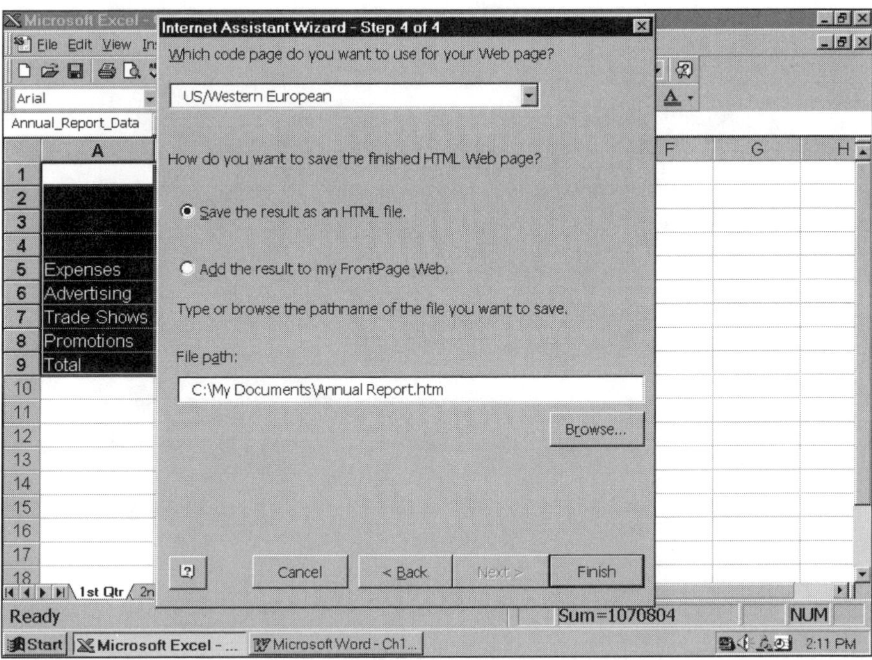

Figure 11.2 The code page and file path in the Internet Assistant Wizard—Step 4 Of 4 dialog box.

Creating A Hyperlink To A Web Page

Hyperlinks create connections among Web pages. As mentioned earlier, hyperlinks can appear as linked text or images. You can recognize hypertext, because it looks different than the regular text on a page. Generally, hypertext appears in a different color from normal text, and it changes color after you've used it. In addition, hypertext links on Web pages are usually underlined to help you identify them in the surrounding text. Excel supports hypertext, and you can use hyperlinks when designing Web pages and linking Office 97 documents. For example, you can link a memo in Microsoft Word 97 to an Excel workbook. You can also create a hyperlink in Excel that links to a Web site on the Internet, which is the process depicted in the next task.

Task 2 Creating hyperlinks in Excel workbooks.

1. Click in cell A11 to deselect the range. Then, click the Insert Hyperlink button on the Standard toolbar. The Insert Hyperlink dialog box should open (see Figure 11.3).

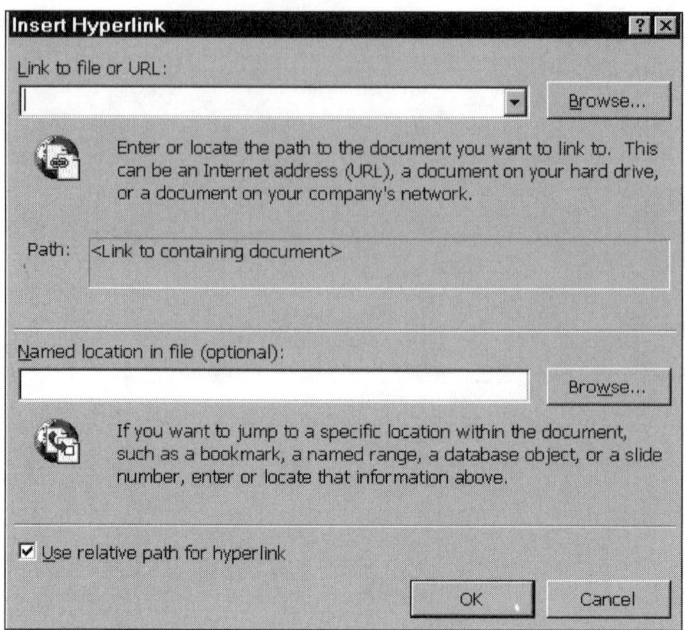

Figure 11.3 The Insert Hyperlink dialog box.

2. In the Link To File Or URL box, click the drop-down arrow, and choose http://. Then, type a URL (Uniform Resource Locator). For example, type "www.microsoft.com".
3. Click OK to insert the hyperlink. Excel should create the hyperlink in cell A11 as the link to the specified URL. The hyperlink should appear in blue text and underlined.
4. Move the mouse pointer over cell A11. Notice the mouse pointer changes to a hand with a pointing finger.
5. Establish an Internet connection.
6. Click the hyperlink.

The Web toolbar should appear. Clicking on the hyperlink should open your browser and bring you to the Web page you requested in the link.

Browsing The Web From Within Excel

You can browse the Web as much as you want directly from within Excel. You don't have to leave the program and start Microsoft Internet Explorer or any other browser you might normally use. Just be sure you have an active Internet connection before you use Excel to browse the Internet.

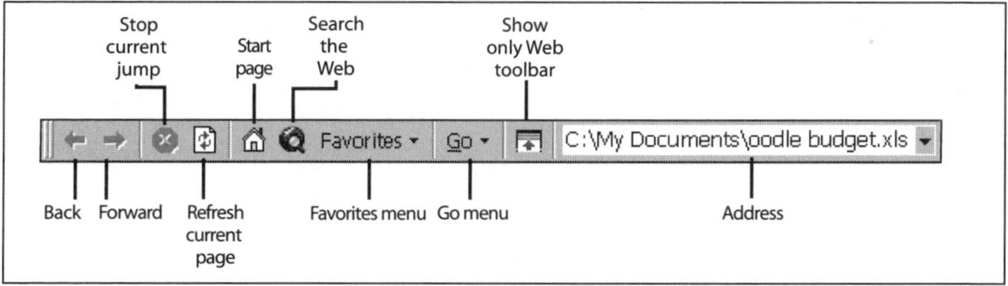

Figure 11.4 The Web toolbar.

Excel provides a Web toolbar for browsing the Web at any time (see Figure 11.4). The tools on the Web toolbar enable you to browse the Web in the following ways:

- Browse back through Web pages.
- Browse forward through Web pages.
- Stop current jump to cancel the loading of a page you selected (use this when a page is taking too long to load).
- Refresh the current Web page with the latest data.
- Jump to the Start page (your home page).
- Search the Web by opening the default browser (even if it's Netscape) and displaying a search page.
- Use the Favorites menu to store your favorite Web site addresses in the Favorites folder, and go to specific Web sites provided on the Favorites menu.
- Use the Go menu to navigate through Web pages.
- Show only the Web toolbar, to optimize the available screen space for viewing Web pages.
- Use the Address box to enter a URL, which is a Web site address for a page you want to look at.

Task 3 Browsing the Web within Excel.

1. Click the Address text box on the Web toolbar, and enter "www.coriolis.com", which is the URL for The Coriolis Group home page.
2. Press Enter. The Web page you requested should appear.
3. Click on any link on the Web page to go to another Web page.
4. Click the Back button on the Web toolbar. This moves backward one page.

5. Click the Forward button on the Web toolbar. This moves forward one page.
6. Click the Refresh Current Page button on the Web toolbar. This reloads the current Web page and updates it with the latest information.
7. Click the Favorites button.
8. Choose Add To Favorites. This stores the current Web address in your Favorites Folder.
9. Close your Web browser.
10. Click the Web Toolbar button on the Standard toolbar. The Web toolbar disappears.
11. Close the Ch11 Task workbook without saving changes.

Practice Exercise

The accounting manager at the Sandy Shores Company would like to publish a portion of the annual report worksheet at the Sandy Shores Web site on the Internet. In this practice exercise, you'll save a named range as an HTML document. You'll also create a hyperlink in an Excel workbook that will link you to a Web site, and you'll browse the Web from within Excel using the Web toolbar.

Figure 11.5 shows what the worksheet contains before you go through the instructions in this exercise.

1. Open the Ch11 Prac Ex workbook stored on the companion disk.
2. Go to the range named *Annual_Report_Data.*
3. Save the named range as an HTML document.
4. Keep all the path defaults, and then name the document MYWEBPAGE.
5. In cell A15, create a hyperlink to the Web site **www.amazon.com**.
6. Use the hyperlink to go to the Web site you requested.
7. Go to the Web site **www.ingrambook.com** by using the Address box on the Web toolbar.
8. Click links in the Web site to browse.

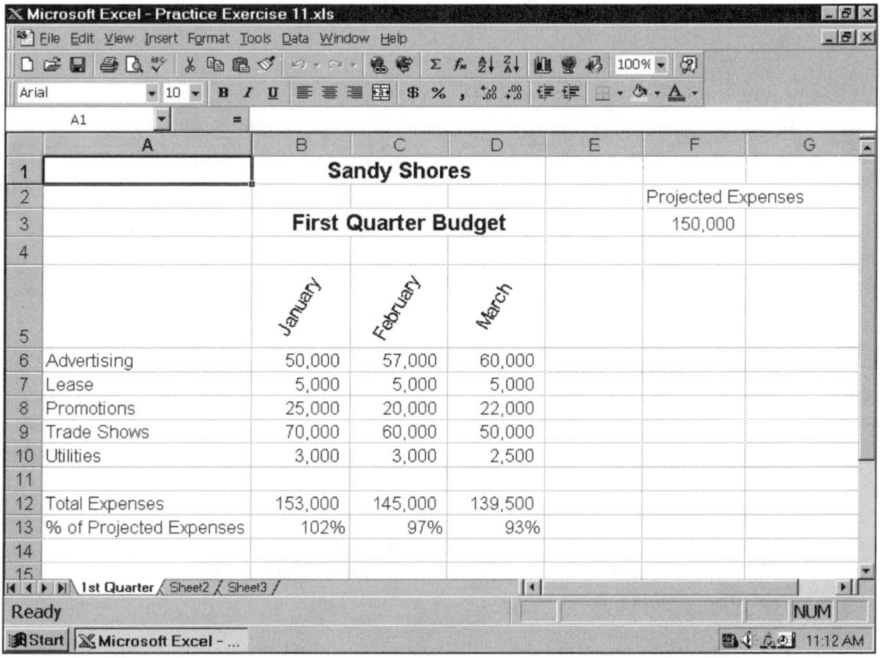

Microsoft Excel - Practice Exercise 11.xls

	A	B	C	D	E	F	G
1			Sandy Shores				
2						Projected Expenses	
3			First Quarter Budget			150,000	
4							
5		January	February	March			
6	Advertising	50,000	57,000	60,000			
7	Lease	5,000	5,000	5,000			
8	Promotions	25,000	20,000	22,000			
9	Trade Shows	70,000	60,000	50,000			
10	Utilities	3,000	3,000	2,500			
11							
12	Total Expenses	153,000	145,000	139,500			
13	% of Projected Expenses	102%	97%	93%			
14							

Figure 11.5 The Practice Exercise before you begin.

9. Browse backward one page.
10. Browse forward one page.
11. Refresh the current Web page.
12. Store the current Web address in your Favorites folder.
13. Close your Web browser and then hide the Web toolbar.
14. Save the workbook with the same name.
15. Close your Internet connection. Then, close the workbook.

Answers To Practice Exercise 11

1. Click the Open button on the Standard toolbar, and double-click the file name Ch11 Prac Ex.
2. Press F5 (Go To), and select the range named Annual_Report_Data. Click OK. Excel highlights the named range, which contains the data you are going to save as an HTML document.
3. Select File|Save As HTML. The Internet Assistant Wizard—Step 1 Of 4 dialog box opens. The first item in the list box is the range name, which is already selected. The Office Assistant might ask if you want any help with the HTML feature.
4. Click the Next button. The Internet Assistant Wizard—Step 2 Of 4 dialog box appears. The first option is already selected. This is the one you want because Excel will create a new HTML Web page from the selected data, including a header, table, and footer. Click the Next button. The Internet Assistant Wizard—Step 3 Of 4 dialog box displays. Keep the title and header that are already there. Click the Next button. The Internet Assistant Wizard—Step 4 Of 4 dialog box opens. The US/Western European code page is selected. In the File path box, type C:\MY DOCUMENTS\MYWEBPAGE.htm. Click the Finish button.
5. Click cell A15. Choose Insert|Hyperlink or click the Insert Hyperlink button on the Standard toolbar. The Insert Hyperlink dialog box opens. In the Link To File Or URL box, click the drop-down arrow, and choose http://. Then, type "**www.amazon.com**". Click OK. Excel creates the hyperlink in cell A15. The hyperlink appears in blue text and underlined.
6. Establish a connection to the Internet, if you are not already connected. Move the mouse pointer over the hyperlink. When the mouse pointer changes to a hand with a pointing finger, click the hyperlink. The hyperlink brings you to the Web page you requested in the link.
7. Type "www.ingrambook.com" in the Address text box on the Web toolbar. Press Enter. The Ingram Book Group Web page should appear.

8. Click any of the links on the Web page to go to other pages on the Web.
9. Click the Back button on the Web toolbar. This moves backward one page.
10. Click the Forward button on the Web toolbar. This moves forward one page.
11. Click the Refresh Current Page button on the Web toolbar. This reloads the current Web page and updates it with the latest information.
12. Click the Favorites button. Choose Add To Favorites. This stores the current Web address in your Favorites Folder.
13. Close your Web browser by exiting the browser program. Click the Web toolbar button on the Standard toolbar. The Web toolbar disappears.
14. Click the Save button on the Standard toolbar to save the workbook.

    When you finish the practice exercise, your worksheet should look like the one shown in Figure 11.6.

15. Close your Internet connection the way you normally would. Click the Close (X) button in the upper-right corner of the document window to close the workbook.

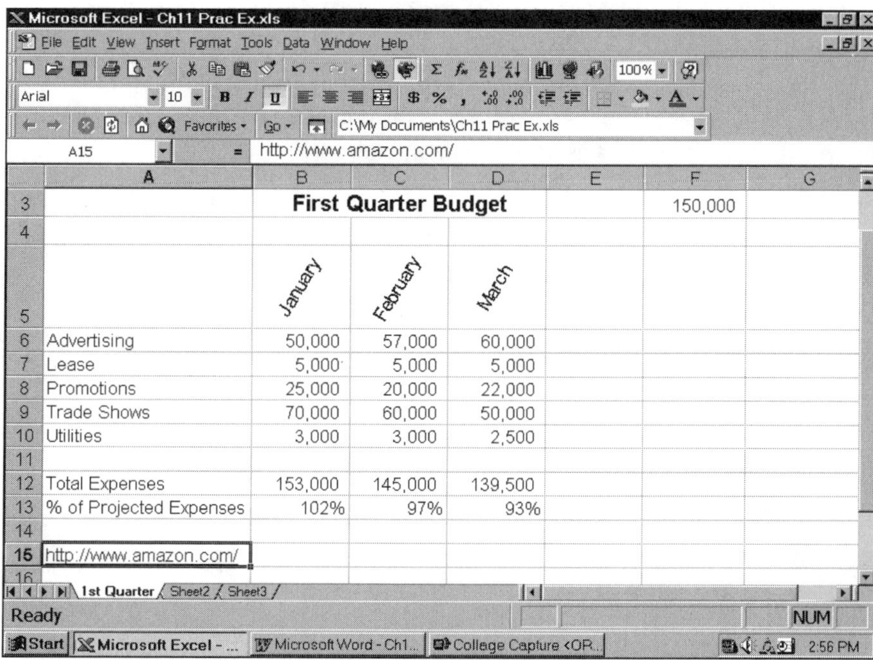

Figure 11.6 The completed Practice Exercise.

Need To Know More?

Craig, Deborah: *How to Use Microsoft Excel 97 for Windows*. Que, Indianapolis, IN, 1996. ISBN 1-56276-469-1. Chapter 18, "Excel and the Internet," gives you information on hyperlinks, creating Web pages, and viewing files on the Web.

Harvey, Greg: *Excel 97 for Windows for Dummies*. IDG Books Worldwide, Inc., Foster City, CA, 1996. ISBN 0-7645-0049-X. Chapter 10, "Of Hyperlinks and HTML," explains how to create hyperlinks and Web pages using Excel worksheet data.

Neibauer, Alan: *Excel One Step at a Time*. IDG Books Worldwide, Inc., Foster City, CA, 1997. ISBN 0-7645-3139-5. Lesson 9, "Excel on the World Wide Web," shows you how to create hyperlinks and Web pages, as well as browse the Web from within Excel.

Nicholson, John R. and Sean R. Nicholson: *Discover Excel 97*. IDG Books Worldwide, Inc., Foster City, CA, 1997. ISBN 1-7645-3047-X. Chapter 16, "Hyperlinking: There and Back Again," explains how to create and use hyperlinks in an Excel workbook.

Nossiter, Josh: *Using Microsoft Excel 97*. Que, Indianapolis, IN, 1996. ISBN 0-7897-0955-4. Chapter 22, "There's a World of Data on the World Wide Web," gives you information on how to browse the Web from Excel, create hyperlinks, and save worksheet data as an HTML document.

Reisner, Trudi: *Easy Microsoft Office*. Que, Indianapolis, IN, 1997. ISBN 0-7897-1078-1. In Part XI, "Using Microsoft Office and the World Wide Web," Task 75, "Publishing a Word Document as a Web Page," gives you an idea of how to create a Web page so that you can create your own Web page with worksheet data. Task 77, "Browsing the Web from Within Microsoft Office," shows you how to browse the Web using the Web toolbar.

Sample Proficiency Level Test

Congratulations. You've almost finished the Proficiency test chapters, and you're just about ready for the test. Now, wouldn't you like to walk into the testing center and ace the exam? Go for it—you can do it! This chapter tells you what to expect, what to memorize, how to prepare, and it even provides a sample test that you can run through. You can look up the answers for the sample test in the following chapter.

What You Need To Know About The Excel Exam

There are approximately 40 tasks on the Proficiency Excel Exam. When you start the test, Excel opens, and an instruction box appears. The time limit of the exam is 60 minutes. Answer only the questions you know in the task you are working on. When the time is up, Excel closes, the test questions window closes, and you can no longer answer questions. A progression bar appears while the exam software checks your test answers. After your test answers are checked, the exam software calculates your score. The scoring information is given to the test administrator.

Working Within The Framework

The Excel Exam is somewhat of a progressive exam in which you must complete the first step to get to the second, and so on. If you can't answer a question or complete a task, proceed to the next test question.

Deciding What To Memorize

Often, there is more than one way to accomplish the same task. You should learn to use shortcuts, such as shortcut menus, and toolbar buttons to perform tasks in the fastest way possible. The exam requires that you perform tasks in a certain way; you must complete the tasks within the allotted time.

Scoring Information

Immediately after you finish the test, the exam software will calculate your score. The scoring information process takes about an hour. After the results are in, your test administrator will notify you as to whether you passed or failed. If you pass the exam, a certificate will be mailed to you within two weeks of the test date. If you fail the exam, you can retake it.

Preparing For The Test

The first thing you should do to prepare for the Excel exam is carefully read the appropriate chapters in this book. Read Chapters 1 through 13 for the Proficiency Excel Exam and study Chapters 14 through 25 to prepare for the Expert Excel Exam. In each chapter, step through each task and read all the exam alerts, tips, and notes. Make sure you go through the practice projects, too. The next thing you should do is study and practice the information provided in the books and CDs referenced in the "Need To Know More?"

section at the end of each chapter in this book. Another way to prepare for the test is to take Excel classes or get one-on-one Excel tutoring from a certified Excel trainer. If you do some or all of these things, you will be well prepared for the test.

Taking The Test

When you take an Excel exam, the test administrator will give you two wipe-off boards (laminated paper) or plain white paper with several marker pens. You can use these boards or paper as a scratch pad. The test administrator will instruct you as to when you can begin taking the test. The test administrator will be available for any questions you might have while you are taking the test. When the test is over, the test administrator will notify you of your test results.

Test Exercises

There are three test exercises in this chapter. Each test exercise starts with a scenario and is similar to the practice projects presented in earlier chapters. Read the scenario first. A figure showing the original worksheet is provided. You'll be working on three worksheets—a different one for each exercise. You should familiarize yourself with the worksheet before you proceed to the test questions. A set of test questions is provided for each exercise. Carefully read the test questions before you start working in Excel. In order to answer the test questions, you need to perform Excel tasks. The answers to the questions are provided in Chapter 13.

Exercise 1

The Human Resources Department at the Crunchy Granola Company tracks its employees in an Excel worksheet. Your job is to work on the employee report and complete it so that the Human Resources Manager can make some management decisions based on the figures in the report.

Figure 12.1 shows what the worksheet contains before you work through the instructions in this exercise.

1. Open the workbook called Test Exercise 1.
2. Add an employee named *Meryl Heller* to the beginning of the list. Her date of hire is 9/18/91, and her salary is $50,000. *Hint:* Format the salary with a comma and zero decimal places.
3. Meryl Heller was given a raise. Calculate a 20 percent increase in pay for Meryl. *Hint:* Format the % Salary Increase with a percent sign and zero decimal places. Format the New Salary with a dollar sign and zero decimal places.
4. Change the word *Avg* to *Average* in cell A14.
5. Calculate a total for the salaries before the raises.

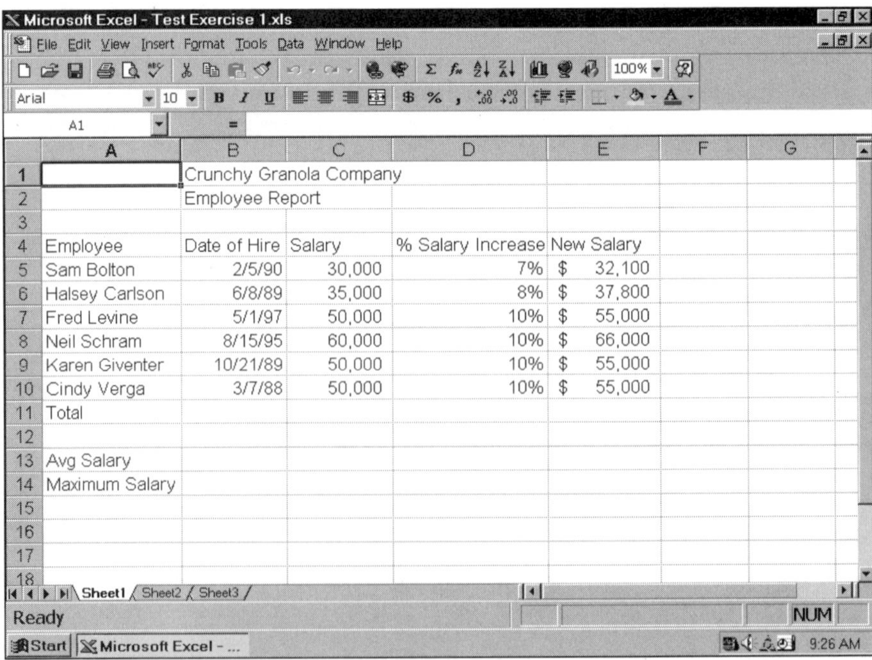

Figure 12.1 Test Exercise 1 before you begin.

6. Calculate an average of the salaries after the raises, and place the answer in cell B14.
7. Calculate the maximum salary after the raises, and place the answer in cell B15.
8. Copy the addition formula for the salaries before the raises to calculate a total for the new salaries. *Hint:* Format the total new salaries with a dollar sign and zero decimal places.
9. Change the title's font face to Impact and font size to 18 points.
10. Wrap the text in the column headings.
11. Center the column headings horizontally and vertically.
12. Go to the range named *Avg_Max.*
13. Print the range named *Avg_Max.*
14. Change the sheet name for Sheet1 to *Salary.*
15. Insert a new sheet between Sheet2 and Sheet3.
16. Name the new sheet *401K.*
17. Make the Salary sheet active.
18. Save the file with the same name.
19. Close the workbook.

Exercise 2

The track coach at the Happy Dale High School monitors the athletes' progress using an Excel worksheet. Your mission is to enhance the worksheet and create a chart to show the athletes and their progress. Then, the track coach can look at the trends in the data plotted in the chart and present the information to the athletes at their next meeting.

Figure 12.2 shows what the worksheet contains before you work through the instructions in this exercise.

1. Open the workbook called Test Exercise 2.
2. Change the WordArt font to Garamond and the font size to 20 points.
3. Change the font color for the WordArt text to Sea Green.
4. Go to the range named Weekday.
5. Format the column headings at a 60-degree angle in the range named Weekday.

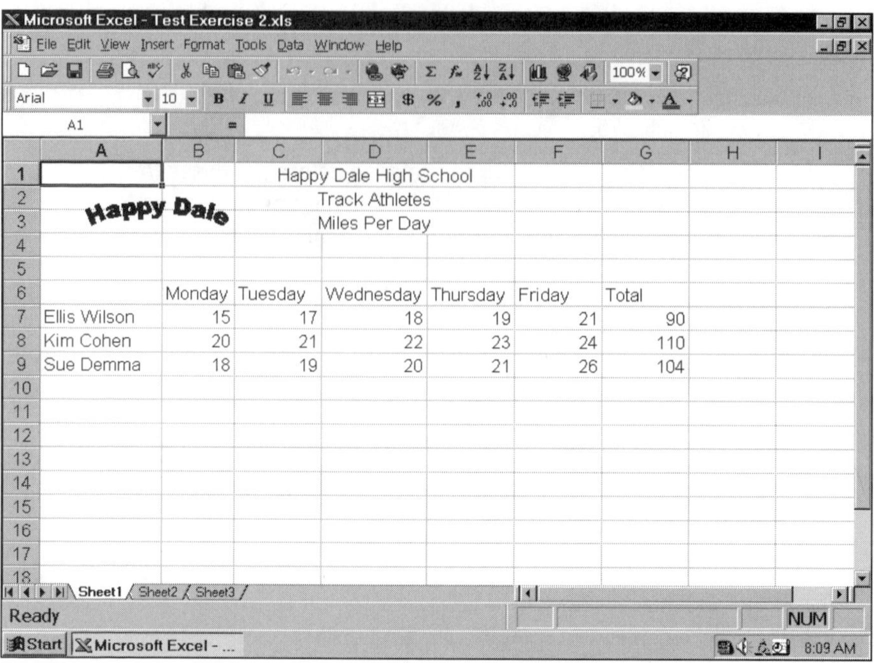

Figure 12.2 Test Exercise 2 before you begin.

6. Select the data range A6:F9, and indicate that you want to create an Area chart. *Hint:* Keep the Chart Wizard open to perform the following steps.
7. Choose the Area chart subtype.
8. Plot the data series in rows.
9. Add the chart title *Happy Dale Athletes*.
10. Add the Category X-axis title *Week 1*.
11. Add the Value Y-axis title *Miles*.
12. Show no legend.
13. Insert the chart as an object in Sheet1.
14. Save the workbook with the same name.
15. Move the chart to appear beneath the worksheet.
16. Resize the chart to fit in the range A11:F30.
17. Preview the page breaks in the worksheet.
18. Exclude column G in Page Break Preview.
19. Print the worksheet and chart from Page Break Preview, then return to normal view.

20. Save the workbook with the same name.
21. Close the workbook.

Exercise 3

The sales department at the Educational Toy Company uses an Excel worksheet to track the toy sales on a quarterly basis. The company has a Web site on the Internet and needs to add the sales information to the Web site. You'll need to create an HTML document to prepare the sales figures for the company Web site.

Figure 12.3 shows what the worksheet contains before you work through the instructions in this exercise.

1. Open the workbook called Test Exercise 3.
2. Calculate the percentage of projected sales for all toys sold in April, and place the result in cell B11. *Hint:* Create an absolute formula. Divide the total sales for April by the projected sales. The projected sales is an absolute cell reference. Format the results with a percent sign and zero decimal places.
3. Copy the absolute formula across row 11 into the % Projected Sales for May and June.

Microsoft Excel - Test Exercise 3.xls

	A	B	C	D	E
1			Educational Toy Company		
2			Sales Report		
3					
4		*April*	*May*	*June*	*Total*
5	Spin and Learn	68,000	70,000	71,000	$ 209,000
6	Etch a Picture	56,000	35,000	48,000	$ 139,000
7	Pick a Color	51,000	45,000	58,000	$ 154,000
8	Total	$ 175,000	$ 150,000	$ 177,000	$ 502,000
9					
10	Projected Sales	200,000			
11	% Projected Sales				

Figure 12.3 Test Exercise 3 before you begin.

4. Go to the range named *Second_Quarter*.
5. Save the range name Second_Quarter as an HTML document. Keep all the defaults, and name the file SECOND QTR in the file path C:\MY DOCUMENTS\.
6. Set the print area to B5:E8.
7. Set print titles to repeat the titles and headings in rows 1 through 4.
8. Print the worksheet from the Page Setup dialog box.
9. Save the workbook with the same name.
10. Close the workbook.

Answers To Sample Proficiency Level Test

This chapter contains the answers to the Chapter 12 test exercises. Each set of answers contains step-by-step instructions. A figure shows the completed worksheet for each exercise, showing you what your worksheets should look like after you perform the Excel tasks necessary to complete the exercises presented in Chapter 12.

Exercise 1

1. Click the Open button on the Standard toolbar, and double-click the file Test Exercise 1. This opens the Test Exercise 1 workbook.
2. Click row header 5. Choose Insert|Rows. Excel inserts a new row beneath row 4, and the data in all subsequent rows shifts down. Click cell A5, type "Meryl Heller". Press Tab, type "9/18/91" in cell B5, press Tab, type "50000" in cell C5, and press Enter. Click on cell C5, and click the Comma Style button on the Formatting toolbar. Then, click twice on the Decrease Decimal button on the Formatting toolbar. The employee named Meryl Heller should appear as the first item in the list, with the date of hire and salary. The salary is formatted with a comma and zero decimal places.
3. In cell D5, type ".20". Press Enter. Click cell D5, and click the Percent Style button on the Formatting toolbar. Then, press Tab. This enters the 20 percent increase in salary in cell D5 and makes cell E5 the active cell. Type "=", click cell C5, type "+(" (addition operator and left parenthesis), click cell C5, type "*" (multiplication operator), and click cell D5, type ")" (right parenthesis), and press Enter. Click cell E5, and click the Currency Style button on the Formatting toolbar. Then, click twice on the Decrease Decimal button on the Formatting toolbar. The formula calculates a 20 percent increase in pay. The correct answer is $60,000.
4. Click cell A14, press F2 (Edit), and click between the *v* and the *g* in Avg. Type "era", press the right arrow key, and type "e". This changes the word *Avg* to *Average* in cell A14.
5. Click cell C12. Double-click the AutoSum button on the Standard toolbar. This inserts the sum function =SUM(C5:C11), which calculates a total for the salaries. The correct answer is 325,000.
6. Click cell B14. Type "=AVERAGE(". Select the range E5:E11, and type ")". Press Enter. This inserts the average function =Average (E5:E11), which calculates an average of the new salaries. The average salary is $51,557.
7. In cell B15, type "=MAX(". Select the range E5:E11, and type ")". Press Enter. This inserts the maximum function =MAX(E5:E11), which calculates the maximum salary in the new salaries column. The maximum salary is $66,000.
8. Click cell C12. Click the Copy button on the Standard toolbar. Click cell E12. Click the Paste button on the Standard toolbar. Press Esc to remove the copy marquee in cell C12. This copies the addition formula for the salaries into the cell for total new salaries. The correct formula is =SUM(E5:E11), and the correct

answer is 360900. Click the Currency Style button on the Formatting toolbar. Then, click twice on the Decrease Decimal button on the Formatting toolbar. This formats the total new salaries with a dollar sign and zero decimal places.

9. Click cell B1. This selects the title. Click the Font drop-down arrow on the Formatting toolbar. Choose Impact. Click the Font Size drop-down arrow on the Formatting toolbar. Choose 18. This changes the font face to Impact and the font size to 18 points for the title.
10. Click cell A4, and drag to cell E4. This selects the column headings in the range A4:E4. Choose Format|Cells. Click the Alignment tab. In the Text Control section, choose the Wrap Text option. This indicates to wrap the column heading text after the dialog box is closed.
11. In the Format Cells dialog box, in the Alignment tab, choose Center from the Horizontal list box, and choose Center from the Vertical list box. Click OK. Excel wraps the column heading in column D, and aligns all the column headings horizontally and vertically.
12. Press F5 (Go To), and double-click Avg_Max. Excel highlights the range A14:B15, which is named *Avg_Max*.
13. Press Ctrl+P. The Print dialog box opens. In the Print What section, choose Selection, and click OK. Excel prints the Avg_Max range.
14. Double-click the Sheet1 tab, type "Salary", and press Enter. This changes the sheet name from *Sheet1* to *Salary*.
15. Click on the Sheet3 tab. Choose Insert|Worksheet. Excel inserts a new sheet, called *Sheet1*, between Sheet2 and Sheet3.
16. Double-click the Sheet1 tab, type "401K", and press Enter. This names the new sheet *401K*.
17. Click the Salary sheet tab to make the Salary sheet active.
18. Click the Save button on the Standard toolbar to save the workbook with the same name.

    When you finish the test procedures in Test Exercise 1, your worksheet should look like the one in Figure 13.1.
19. Click the Close (X) button in the upper-right corner of the document window. This closes the workbook.

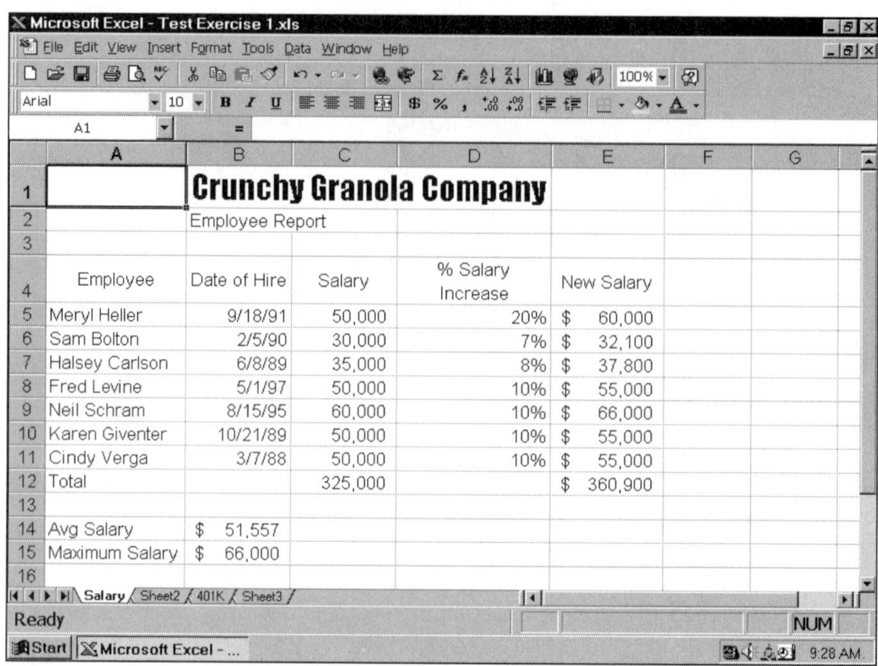

Crunchy Granola Company

Employee Report

Employee	Date of Hire	Salary	% Salary Increase	New Salary
Meryl Heller	9/18/91	50,000	20%	$ 60,000
Sam Bolton	2/5/90	30,000	7%	$ 32,100
Halsey Carlson	6/8/89	35,000	8%	$ 37,800
Fred Levine	5/1/97	50,000	10%	$ 55,000
Neil Schram	8/15/95	60,000	10%	$ 66,000
Karen Giventer	10/21/89	50,000	10%	$ 55,000
Cindy Verga	3/7/88	50,000	10%	$ 55,000
Total		325,000		$ 360,900
Avg Salary	$ 51,557			
Maximum Salary	$ 66,000			

Figure 13.1 The completed Test Exercise 1.

Exercise 2

1. Click the Open button on the Standard toolbar, and double-click the file Test Exercise 2. This opens the Test Exercise 2 workbook.
2. Click on the WordArt logo Happy Dale. The WordArt toolbar appears. Click the Edit Text button on the WordArt toolbar. Choose the Garamond font and a font size of 20 points. Click OK. Excel changes the WordArt text to the Garamond font and a font size of 20 points.
3. Click the Format WordArt button on the WordArt toolbar. Click the Colors and Lines tab (if necessary), and in the Fill section, click the Color drop-down arrow, and choose Sea Green. Click OK. Excel changes the font color for the WordArt text to Sea Green. Click any cell in the worksheet to deselect the WordArt text.
4. Press F5 (Go To), and double-click Weekday. Excel highlights the range B6:F6, which is named *Weekday*.
5. Choose Format|Cells. In the Format Cells dialog box, click the Alignment tab. In the Orientation area, type "60" in the Degrees box. Click OK. The column headings appear angled at 60 degrees.

6. Click cell A6, and drag diagonally to cell F9. This selects the data range A6:F9 that you'll be charting. Click the Chart Wizard button on the Standard toolbar. Excel opens the Chart Wizard—Step 1 Of 4—Chart Type dialog box and shows the chart types. The Clustered Column chart is the default chart type. In the Chart Type list, choose the Area chart type.
7. Choose the Area chart subtype in the Chart Sub-type gallery. Then, click the Next button. The Chart Wizard—Step 2 Of 4—Chart Source Data dialog box appears with a sample chart.
8. Click the Rows option (if necessary) to plot the chart data in rows. Click the Next button. The Chart Wizard—Step 3 Of 4—Chart Options dialog box appears. You should see a sample chart and options for adding titles, changing the legend, and formatting other elements in the chart.
9. With the Titles tab selected, click in the Chart Title box, and type "Happy Dale Athletes". This adds the chart title to the area chart.
10. Click in the Category (X) Axis box, and type "Week 1". This adds a category X-axis title called *Week 1* at the bottom of the chart along the X axis.
11. Click in the Value (Y) Axis box, and type "Miles". This adds a value Y-axis title called *Miles* to the left of the Y axis.
12. Click the Legend tab, and click the Show Legend checkbox to remove the checkmark. This removes the legend from the chart. Click the Next button. The Chart Wizard—Step 4 Of 4—Chart Location dialog box appears. From here, you can choose how you want to insert the chart.
13. Leave the As Object In option and Sheet1 selected. This tells Excel to insert the chart as an object on Sheet1. Click the Finish button to create the chart. Excel displays the area chart and the Chart toolbar in Sheet1. The chart contains selection handles, indicating that the chart is selected.
14. Click the Save button on the Standard toolbar. This saves the workbook with the same name, including the area chart.
15. Point to the chart, and drag it to the blank area beneath the worksheet. This moves the chart.
16. Point to the chart, and drag the upper-left corner to cell A11. Point to the right-middle selection handle until you see a double arrow. Drag the right-hand handle to the right border of column F. This makes the chart wider. Then, use the vertical scroll box to scroll down to see the bottom of the chart, if necessary. Point to the bottom-middle selection handle, and drag the border down to

the bottom edge of row 30. This makes the chart taller. Now, you should see the entire plot area of the chart in the range A11:F30. Click in an empty cell to deselect the chart.

17. Choose View|Page Break Preview. Excel displays a dialog box informing you that you can adjust the page breaks by dragging them to a new location. Click OK. You see the worksheet with the chart that appears at the bottom of the sheet. The zoom percentage is at 60%, so you'll need to scroll down to see the chart. The blue borders around the sheet represent the page breaks on the worksheet.
18. Point to the right blue border, and drag it over to column F. This excludes column G. The page break is now set at column F.
19. Click the Print button on the Standard toolbar. Excel prints the worksheet and chart that you see in Page Break Preview. Choose View|Normal. Excel switches back to Normal view.
20. Click the Save button on the Standard toolbar to save the workbook with the same name.

    When you finish the test procedures in Test Exercise 2, your worksheet should look like the one in Figure 13.2.

21. Click the Close (X) button in the upper-right corner of the document window. This closes the workbook.

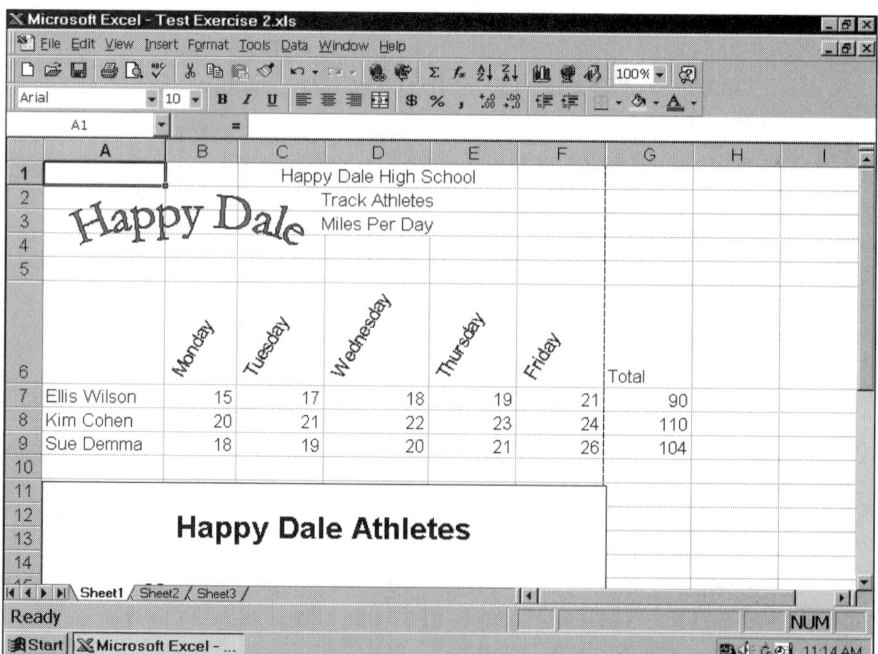

Figure 13.2 The completed Test Exercise 2.

Exercise 3

1. Click the Open button on the Standard toolbar, and double-click the file Test Exercise 3. This opens the Test Exercise 3 workbook.
2. Click cell B11. This is where you enter the absolute formula. Type "=". Click cell B8, which contains the total sales for April. Type "/" (division operator), and then click cell B10, which contains the projected sales. Press F4 (Absolute). Excel inserts a $ (dollar sign) before the column letter B and row number 10, making the cell reference B10 absolute. Press Enter. The formula in cell B11 should be =B8/$B$10, which calculates the % Projected Sales. Click cell B11, and click the Percent Style button on the Formatting toolbar. The correct answer is 88%.
3. The fastest copy method is the AutoFill command. Move the mouse pointer to the fill handle (small square) in the lower-right corner of the active cell. The mouse pointer changes to a small cross. Drag the fill handle across to cell C11 and D11. Excel copies the absolute formula into the % Projected Sales for May and June. Select each cell that contains an absolute formula in row 11, and notice what has happened. The absolute formula for May is C8/$B$10. This formula contains both relative and absolute cell references, sometimes referred to as a mixed formula. The first cell reference is relative, so it adjusted to C8. The second cell reference B10 is absolute and did not adjust. The correct answer is 75%. When you copy a formula, the absolute cell reference does not change in the new location. The absolute formula for June is =D8/$B$10. The correct answer in cell D11 is 89%.
4. Press F5 (Go To), and double-click Second_Quarter. Excel highlights the range A4:D8, which is named *Second_Quarter*.
5. Choose File|Save As HTML. The Internet Assistant Wizard—Step 1 Of 4 dialog box opens. The first item in the list box is the range name, which is already selected. Click the Next button. The Internet Assistant Wizard—Step 2 Of 4 dialog box appears. The first option is already selected. This is the one we want because Excel will create a new HTML Web page from the selected data, including a header, table, and footer. Click the Next button. The Internet Assistant Wizard—Step 3 Of 4 dialog box pops up. The title and header are already there. Click the Next button. The Internet Assistant Wizard—Step 4 Of 4 dialog box opens. The US/Western European code is already in the code page list box. In the File Path box, enter C:\MY DOCUMENTS\SECOND QTR.HTM. Click the Finish button. Excel converts the selected

data to HTML format so that it can be published on the Web. The file extension .HTM is added to the HTML data file name, such as SECOND QTR.HTM.

6. Select the range B5:D8. Select File|Print Area|Set Print Area. This sets the print area with the range B5:D8. Click any cell to deselect the range.
7. Select File|Page Setup. Click the Sheet tab. In the Print Titles section, click in the Rows to repeat at top box. Drag the Page Setup dialog box down toward the bottom of the worksheet so that it doesn't cover up the top portion of the worksheet. Click any cell in row 1 and drag down to row 4. This sets print titles to repeat the titles and headings in rows 1 through 4.
8. Click the Print button in the Page Setup dialog box. The Print dialog box opens. Click OK to print the worksheet.
9. Click the Save button on the Standard toolbar to save the workbook with the same name.

   When you finish the test procedures in Test Exercise 3, your worksheet should look like the one in Figure 13.3.

10. Click the Close (X) button in the upper-right corner of the document window. This closes the workbook.

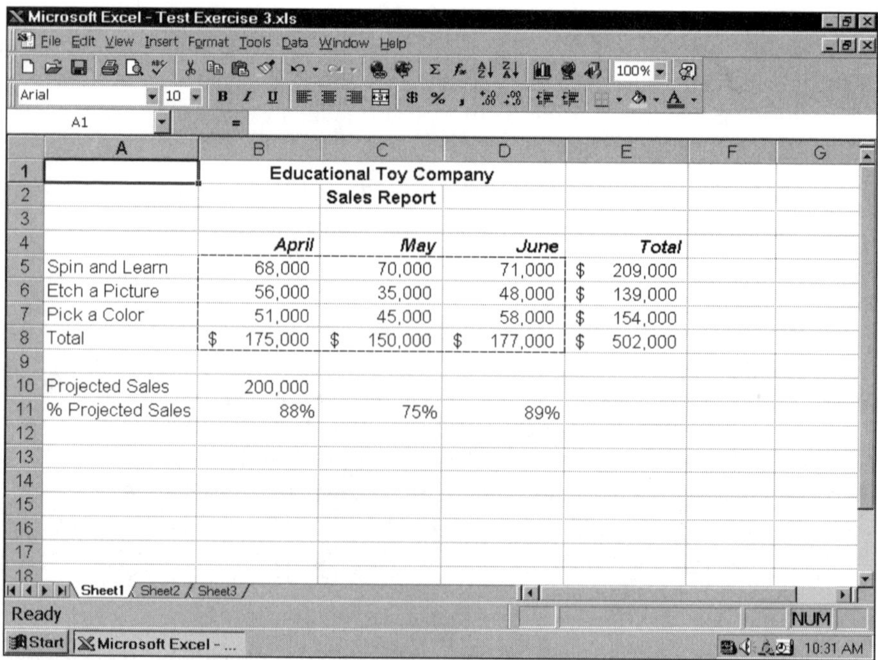

	A	B	C	D	E
1		Educational Toy Company			
2			Sales Report		
3					
4		*April*	*May*	*June*	*Total*
5	Spin and Learn	68,000	70,000	71,000	$ 209,000
6	Etch a Picture	56,000	35,000	48,000	$ 139,000
7	Pick a Color	51,000	45,000	58,000	$ 154,000
8	Total	$ 175,000	$ 150,000	$ 177,000	$ 502,000
9					
10	Projected Sales	200,000			
11	% Projected Sales	88%	75%	89%	

Figure 13.3 The completed Test Exercise 3.

Expert Level

If you can do the following Excel tasks, then you should take the Expert Excel exam:

- √ Use templates
- √ Format worksheets with custom formats, styles, and AutoFormat
- √ Audit worksheets
- √ Use the Lookup Wizard
- √ Link worksheets and workbooks
- √ Import and export data
- √ Sort and query data in an external database
- √ Manage data in an Excel list
- √ Create and run macros
- √ Share workbooks
- √ Preview and print workbooks

14

Using Templates

Terms you'll need to understand:

- √ Template
- √ Built-in template
- √ NORMAL.XLT
- √ Spreadsheet Solutions
- √ Village Software
- √ Comment
- √ Lock a sheet

Skills you'll need to master:

- √ Using built-in templates
- √ Creating templates from existing Excel workbooks
- √ Customizing templates

Using Templates In Excel

What's a *template*? A template is a collection of patterns and tools for creating a category of workbooks. You can format a template, add macros, insert text and graphics, and change the page layout so that the template includes key information.

Every workbook is based on a template. The default template is NORMAL.XLT. A template can help you create workbooks that are consistent and customize your workbooks to suit a particular need. For example, if you create a weekly budget report and you don't want to re-create the entire report each week, you can save one of your reports (or use one of Excel's built-in templates) as a customized template and then insert new numbers in the basic format each week. You can create templates using existing workbooks, or you can use or modify the general purpose templates supplied by Excel.

When you save a workbook as a template or use an Excel built-in template, you can create additional workbooks based on the template. These workbooks will include the same text, formatting, macros, and other elements included in the template.

In this chapter, you'll learn how to create a workbook using built-in Excel templates, create templates from existing workbooks, and customize your templates.

Working With Existing Templates

Excel 97 provides various built-in templates that can help you plan your finances and run your business. Some of these templates include:

- Expense Statement
- Invoice
- Purchase Order
- Village Software (allows you to order customized spreadsheets from a software company)

In the upcoming task, you'll create a new workbook using a predefined Excel template called Expense Statement.

Task 1 Using built-in templates.

1. In Excel, choose File|New. The New dialog box should appear, showing two tabs: General and Spreadsheet Solutions.
2. Click the Spreadsheet Solutions tab.

3. Click the Expense Statement.xlt template icon. This is the template you want to use. You should see a sample of the template in the Preview area, as shown in Figure 14.1.
4. Click OK.

   Excel then asks you whether to enable macros associated with the template.
5. Choose Enable Macros.

   Excel copies the template into a new workbook, ready for you to add information.
6. Choose File|Save As.
7. Name the workbook My Expenses, and click OK.
8. Close the workbook.

It's important to know how to use a built-in template to create a new workbook.

Creating Templates

You can save time by saving your favorite workbook as a template. The next task shows you how to create a template from an Excel workbook.

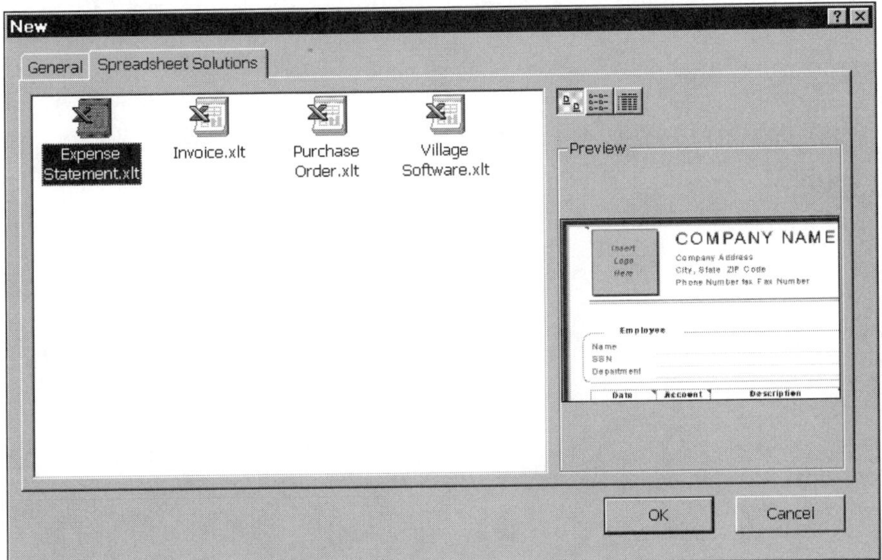

Figure 14.1 The Spreadsheet Solutions templates in the New dialog box.

Task 2 Creating templates from existing Excel workbooks.

1. Open the Ch14 Task workbook located on your companion disk. This is the workbook you want to save as a template. Your template can include text, formatting, macros, and so on.
2. Choose File|Save As to display the Save As dialog box.
3. Type a name for the template in the File Name text box.
4. Select Template from the Save As Type drop-down list box (see Figure 14.2).
5. Click Save.

   The template is created and saved. When you use this template, you will find it on the General tab in the New dialog box.
6. Click the Close (X) button to close the template.

Before you take the exam, you'll need to know how to create a template from an existing Excel workbook.

Editing Templates

You can modify a built-in template at any time. For instance, you can add a note to a cell, hide the comments, change the template options, or add your company information to the template as needed.

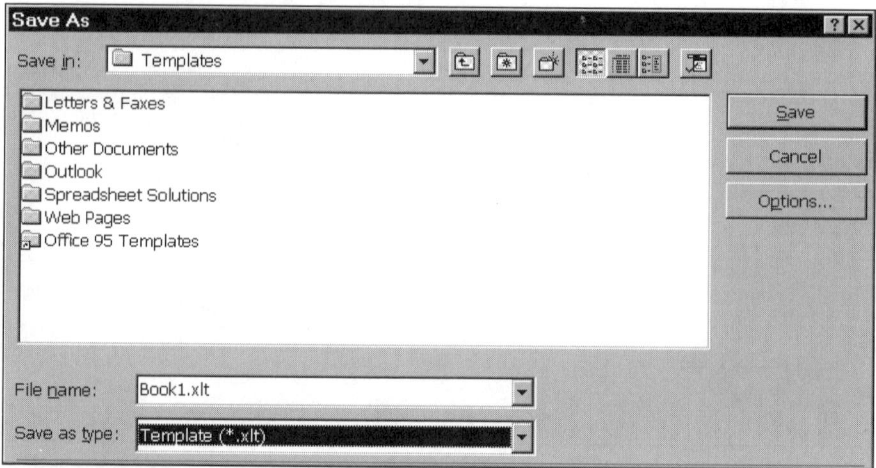

Figure 14.2 The Save As dialog box.

HOLD That Skill!

Keep the following in mind when creating templates:

- In the Save As Type drop-down list, choose Template (*.xlt) so that the Templates folder appears in the Save In box. Be sure to save all your templates in the Templates folder so that you can find your templates easily.
- When you create a new template, Excel adds the template to the General tab in the New dialog box.
- Do not click the New button on the Standard toolbar to create a template. Doing so will create a new workbook based on Normal.xlt and will not display the New dialog box.

Excel provides a floating Template toolbar that you can position anywhere on a template. This toolbar is only available when you open a template file. A Template toolbar assumes the name of the template currently open. For example, Figure 14.3 shows the toolbar with the name *Expense*. This toolbar helps you work with the template more easily and provides the following tools:

- **Size To Screen/Return To Size** Displays the Expense Statement template zoomed in at a percentage that depends on the size of your monitor and the resolution. For example, on a 14" monitor at 800×600 resolution, you will see the template at 70 percent and when you click the Size To Screen/Return to Size button, Excel displays the template at 43 percent. On a 17" monitor at 800×600 resolution, the template is at 85 percent magnification and 60 percent when you size the template to the screen.
- **Hide Comments/Display Comments** Hides and displays comments entered in cells.
- **New Comment** Lets you add a comment to a cell to further explain the data that can be entered in that cell.
- **Template Help** Provides help on working with the template.
- **Display Example/Remove Example** Displays and hides sample data in the cells.

Figure 14.3 The Expense Statement template toolbar.

- **Assign A Number** Assigns a unique number to the form.
- **Capture Data In A Database** Transfers data from the form to a database.

You can use Excel 97's Comments feature to enter information in the template. Comments are the same as cell notes. Comments help you get started and lead you through filling in the template form. To view comments, move the mouse pointer over a red triangle on the built-in template. You should then see a box containing a helpful comment.

Task 3 Customizing templates.

1. Open the My Expenses workbook that you created in Task 1. This workbook contains the template you want to customize. The template document with a Template toolbar should appear, as shown in Figure 14.4.
2. Click the Customize button at the top of the template (you might need to scroll right to see the button). Excel should insert a new worksheet before the template worksheet. For example, the Customize Your Statement worksheet appears before the Expense Statement worksheet.

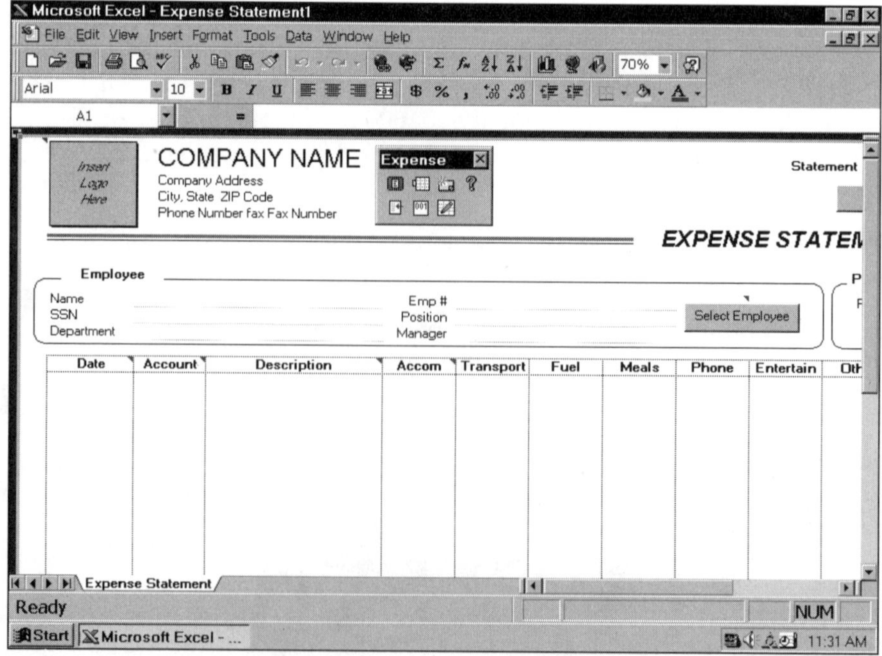

Figure 14.4 The Expense Statement template.

3. Click the Expense Statement worksheet tab. Excel displays the Expense Statement form zoomed in at 70 percent. Depending on your monitor size and resolution, your zoom percentage may be different.
4. Click the Size To Screen/Return To Size button on the Template toolbar. Excel reduces the Expense Statement form to a magnification of 43 percent. Depending on your monitor size and resolution, your zoom percentage may be different.
5. Click the Size To Screen/Return To Size button again on the Template toolbar. Excel returns the Expense Statement form to a magnification of 70 percent. Depending on your monitor size and resolution, your zoom percentage may be different.
6. Click the Display Example/Remove Example button on the Template toolbar. Excel shows sample data in the first row of the Expense Statement. This gives you an idea of what kind of data you could enter in the Expense Statement form.
7. Type any data in the second row of the form that is similar to the data in the first row.
8. Click the Hide Comments/Display Comments button on the Template toolbar. Excel hides the comment indicator (red triangle) for the comments in the Expense Statement.
9. Click the Hide Comments/Display Comments button again on the Template toolbar. Excel displays the comment indicators (red triangle).
10. Move the mouse pointer over a Comment (red triangle) to display helpful information.
11. Click on the number for Transport in the second row, type any number, and press Enter. This changes the transportation amount on the form.
12. Click the Customize Your Statement tab.
13. In the Company Name box, type your own company name. In the Phone Number box, type your own phone number.
14. Click the Lock/Save Sheet button at the top of the template. The Lock/ Save Sheet dialog box should appear, as shown in Figure 14.5. The locking options enable you to lock the changes you made to the template. Locking the template means that you cannot edit or delete the template.
15. Choose a locking option.
16. Click OK.

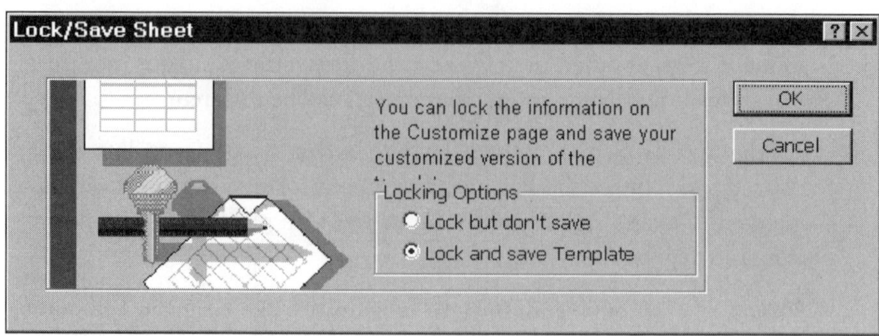

Figure 14.5 The Lock/Save Sheet dialog box.

If you choose the Lock And Don't Save option, you will be returned to the customized version of the template. You cannot make changes to the template until you click the Unlock This Sheet button at the top of the customized version of the template. In the Unlock This Sheet dialog box, click OK. Then, you can make changes to the template.

If you choose the Lock And Save Template option, you'll see the Save As dialog box. Enter a name for the template in the File Name text box, and click Save. You should be returned to the customized version of the template.

You'll need to know how to customize a template by deleting a column. You won't have to unlock the sheet, but be sure to use the shortcut menu to delete the column. Right-click on the column you want to delete, choose Delete from the shortcut menu, and then choose Entire Column. Any other method you use to delete the column will not work.

Practice Exercise

An expense form is needed to record sales expenses incurred by the salespeople at the Sandy Shores Company. The first quarter budget should be made into a template so that budgets can be quickly and easily created from a template pattern. Your job is to create a new template based on the Expense Statement template and create a template based on the existing Sandy Shores budget.

Figure 14.6 shows what the worksheet contains before you go through the instructions in this exercise.

1. Open the Ch14 Prac Ex workbook file stored on the companion disk.
2. Create a new template based on the practice exercise workbook, and name it MY TEMPLATE.
3. Close the template.
4. Create a new workbook based on the Expense Statement built-in template.
5. Customize the Expense Statement template by adding the Sandy Shores Company name to the sheet.

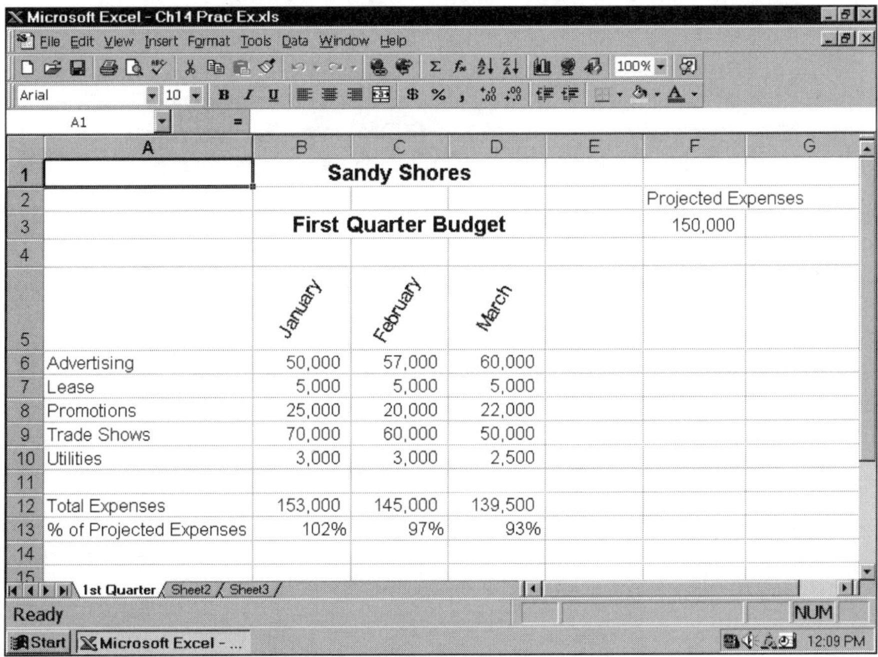

Figure 14.6 The Practice Exercise before you begin.

6. Lock and save the sheet with the name SS EXPENSE FORM.
7. Close the template.

Answers To Practice Exercise

1. Click the Open tool on the Standard toolbar, and double-click on the file name Ch14 Prac Ex.
2. Choose File|Save As. The Save As dialog box appears. Type “MY TEMPLATE” in the File Name text box. Select Template from the Save As Type drop-down list box, and click Save. This creates a new template based on the practice exercise workbook called MY TEMPLATE.XLT.
3. Click the Close (X) button in the upper-right corner of the template window. This closes the template.
4. Choose File|New. Click the Spreadsheet Solutions tab. Double-click on the Expense Statement icon. This creates a new template based on Excel’s built-in Expense Statement template. Choose Enable Macros. The Expense Statement form appears.
5. Scroll right if needed. Click the Customize button. Click the Customize Your Statement tab. Click in the Company Name text box, and type “Sandy Shores Company”. Press Enter.
6. Click the Lock/Save Sheet button at the top of the template. The Lock/Save Sheet dialog box appears. Choose the Lock And Save Template option. Click OK. You should see the Save As dialog box. Enter the name “SS EXPENSE FORM” in the File Name text box, and click Save. An information box is displayed with the path of the new template. Click OK. You are returned to the customized version of the template.

   Your completed worksheet should look like the one in Figure 14.7.
7. Click the Close (X) button in the upper-right corner of the template window. This closes the template.

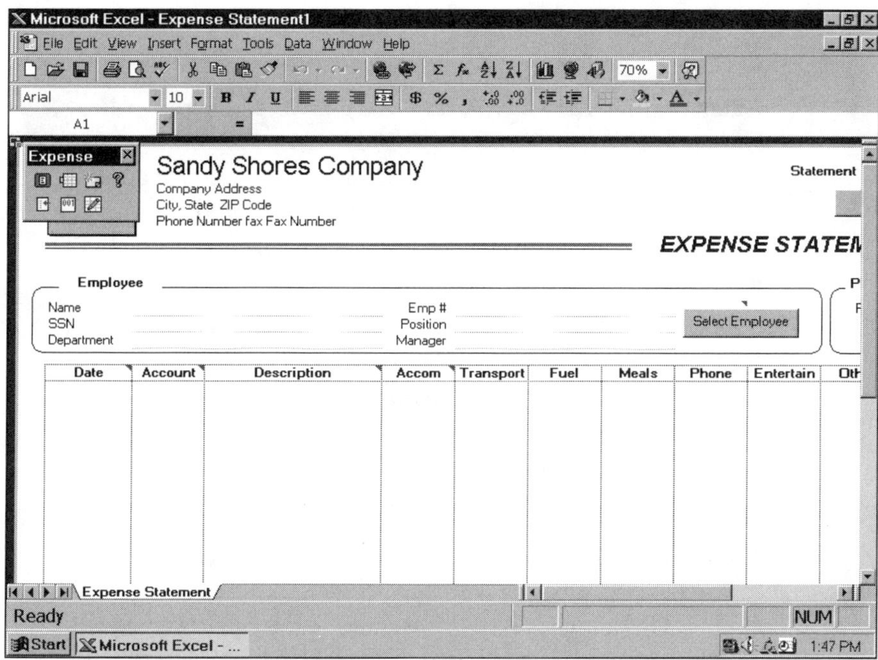

Figure 14.7 The completed Practice Exercise.

Need To Know More?

Catapult, Inc.: *Microsoft Excel 97 Step By Step*. Microsoft Press, Redmond, WA, 1996. ISBN 1-57231-314-5. Lesson 4, "Formatting Your Worksheet for a Professional Look," tells you about saving a workbook as a template and editing templates. Lesson 5, "Consolidating Multiple Lists," tells you all about using built-in templates.

Craig, Deborah: *How to Use Microsoft Excel 97 for Windows*. Que, Indianapolis, IN, 1996. ISBN 1-56276-469-1. Chapter 17, "Automating Your Work with Macros and Templates," gives you information on using built-in templates, as well as creating and customizing templates.

Nicholson, John R. and Sean R. Nicholson: *Discover Excel 97*. IDG Books Worldwide, Inc., Foster City, CA, 1997. ISBN 1-7645-3047-X. Chapter 13, "Macros and Templates and Styles (Oh, My!)," explains how to use built-in templates and create and customize templates.

Nossiter, Josh: *Using Microsoft Excel 97*. Que, Indianapolis, IN, 1996. ISBN 0-7897-0955-4. Chapter 18, "Data Maps and Templates for Data That Fits a Mold," gives you information on how to use built-in templates and create and customize templates.

Formatting Worksheets

Terms you'll need to understand:

- √ Format
- √ Custom format
- √ Format Painter
- √ Style
- √ AutoFormat
- √ Table format

Skills you'll need to master:

- √ Applying formats
- √ Creating custom formats
- √ Copying formats using Format Painter
- √ Using existing styles
- √ Defining styles
- √ Defining styles by example
- √ Copying existing styles from another workbook
- √ Applying AutoFormat

Formatting Excel Data

In this chapter, you'll learn how to apply accounting, fraction, and scientific formats to numbers; customize the appearance of numbers in your worksheets; and copy formats. In addition, you'll explore how to use and create styles, and apply AutoFormats to your worksheets.

Applying Formats

Numeric values are usually more than just numbers. Often, they represent a dollar value, date, percentage, or some other real value. You can select a value's format type in the Format Cells dialog box, or you can customize how a value displays. Excel offers a wide range of custom number formats. Table 15.1 defines Excel's numeric formats and presents the available formatting options for each category.

In Task 1, you'll apply a currency format that contains a dollar sign, commas, and two decimal places for both positive and negative numbers. Negative numbers will appear in red.

Table 15.1 Excel's numeric formats.

Format	Example	Description
General	N/A	Excel's default number format. The General format has no specific number format. In other words, a cell can contain a number with a decimal point, dollar sign, comma, or percent sign. You can also enter a date, time, or fraction in a cell. Excel will automatically display the value using the format you enter.
Number	1,500.50	Use for general display of numbers. The default Number format displays numbers with two decimal places, a comma for a thousands separator, and a minus sign preceding negative numbers. You can change the number of decimal places, remove the thousands separators, and display negative numbers in red or black, preceded by a minus sign or enclosed in parentheses.
Currency	$1,500.50	Use for general monetary values. The default Currency format displays numbers with two decimal places, a dollar sign, and a minus sign preceding negative numbers. You can change the number of decimal places, remove the dollar sign, and display negative numbers in red or black, preceded by a minus sign or enclosed in parentheses.

(continued)

Table 15.1	Excel's numeric formats *(continued)*.	
Format	**Example**	**Description**
Accounting	$1,500.00	Use for aligning dollar signs and decimal points in a column. The default Accounting format displays numbers with two decimal places and a dollar sign. You can change the number of decimal places and remove the dollar sign.
Date	7/2	Use to display date and time serial numbers. The default Date format displays month and day numbers separated by a slash. You can change the slashes to appear as hyphens and specify to show the year and time. You can perform calculations on the date values. To display only the time portion, use the Time format.
Time	11:00	Use to display time and date serial numbers. The default Time format displays the hour and minutes separated by a colon. You can also display date and time serial numbers as time values with hours, minutes, seconds, and AM or PM. You can perform calculations on the time values. To display only the date portion, use the Date format.
Percentage	98.50%	Use to display percentage values. The default Percentage format displays two decimal places. This setting multiplies the value in a cell by 100 and displays the result with a percent sign. You can assign the number of decimal places to appear.
Fraction	1/2	Use to display fractions. The default Fraction format displays one digit on either side of the slash. You can change the number of digits you want to appear on either side of the slash and the fraction type, such as halves, quarters, eighths, and so on.
Scientific	1.50E+03	Use to display numbers in scientific notation. The default Scientific format displays two decimal places.
Text	135RV90	Use to display both text and numbers in a cell as text. Excel displays the entry exactly as typed. Calculations cannot be performed on text cells.
Special	02112	Use to format numbers representing ZIP codes, phone numbers, and social security numbers.
Custom	00000	Use to create a custom number format. You can create a custom format using any of the format codes in the Type list and then make changes to those codes. In this format, # represents a number placeholder, and 0 represents a zero placeholder.

Task 1 Applying formats.

1. Open the file called Ch15 Task workbook located on your companion disk.
2. Select cell B9. This cell contains the value that you want to format.
3. Choose Format|Cells, or press Ctrl+1. The Format Cells dialog box should appear.
4. Click the Number tab, if necessary.
5. In the Category list, click Currency. The sample box should display the default format for the selected category, and the Negative Numbers list should show you the formatting options available for displaying negative numbers, as shown in Figure 15.1.
6. In the Negative Numbers list, select the second option, $1,234.10 that appears in red. This specifies how Excel should format negative numbers.
7. Click OK.

Excel should apply the format to the numbers in the cells you selected.

When you select a category, a list of format types for that category appears. The sample shows what a number will look like with the selected format type.

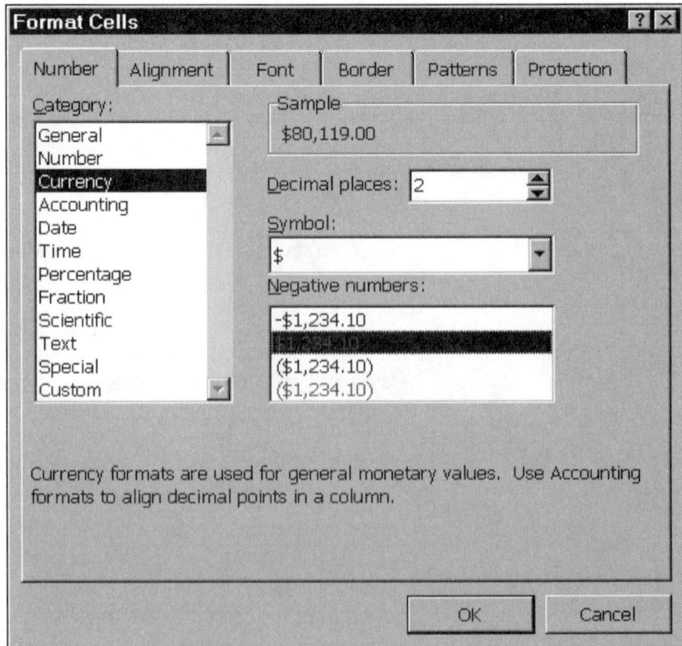

Figure 15.1 The Currency number default format and format options.

In addition to using the preformatted settings, you can type your own format to create a custom format. In the next section, we'll look at creating custom formats.

Be sure you know how to format telephone numbers. To do so, select the cell range that you want to format. Choose Format|Cells, click the Number tab, choose Special, and then choose Phone Number. Click OK to apply the special format to the cell range you selected. You should also know how to change numbers to two decimal places with the 1000 separator, which is the comma style. You can do this by selecting the cell range, and clicking the Comma Style button on the Formatting toolbar. Another formatting change you'll need to perform is to change whole numbers to two decimal places. Just select the range, and click the Increase Decimal button on the Formatting toolbar twice.

Creating Custom Formats

You can create a custom number format by choosing the Custom category on the Number tab in the Format Cells dialog box. If you select the Custom category, you will see format codes. In the next task, we'll apply a custom format to numbers on a worksheet.

Task 2 Creating custom formats.

1. Select the range B5:D8. This cell range contains the values that you want to format.
2. Choose Format|Cells, or press Ctrl+1. The Format Cells dialog box should appear.
3. Click the Number tab, if necessary.
4. In the Category list, select Custom. The Sample box should display the first number in your range, and the Type list box displays the custom formats, as shown in Figure 15.2.
5. In the Type list, select #,##0. This is a starting point for the custom format you want to use.
6. Click before the first # in the Type text box, and type "$" followed by a space. When you select a format type, Excel shows you a formatted sample number. This custom format will display a dollar sign followed by a space with commas and zero decimal places.
7. Click OK.

Excel should apply the custom format to the numbers you selected.

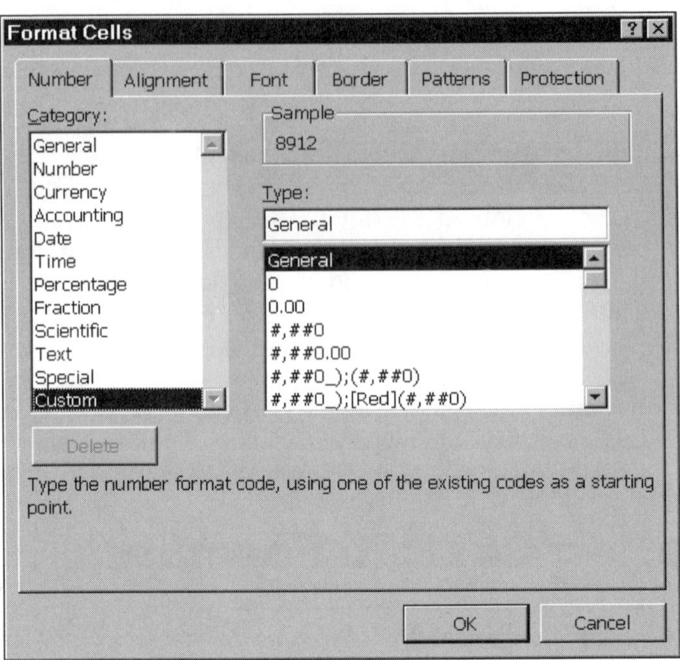

Figure 15.2 The Custom formats in the Format Cells dialog box.

When the label or the format of a number appears how you want it, you don't have to repeat the formatting process for the remaining labels or numbers that you want to format. You can copy formats to other data.

Copying Formats

Excel provides two ways to copy and paste formats—you can use copy and paste commands or you can use the Format Painter. To use copy and paste commands, you use the Edit|Copy command and then the Edit|Paste Special command. When you use the Paste Special command, you select Formats from the Paste options in the Paste Special dialog box.

The second way to copy formats is to use the Format Painter tool in the Standard toolbar. Format Painter applies the format from one cell or group of cells to another. This feature enables you to copy and paste formats that you have already used in a workbook. The Format Painter tool is the fastest way to copy the formatting of one label or number to all the others that must match it. In Task 3, we'll copy a format using the Format Painter tool.

Task 3 Copying formats using Format Painter.

1. Click cell B9.
2. Click the Format Painter tool on the Standard toolbar. A copy marquee should surround cell B9. The mouse pointer should change to a white cross with a paintbrush. The cross and paintbrush indicate that you are copying formats, as shown in Figure 15.3.
3. Move the mouse into the active cell.
4. Click and drag the mouse pointer across cells C9 and D9.
5. Release the mouse button.
6. Click any cell to deselect the range.

The copied formatting should be applied to the selected cells.

To undo formatting that you have copied, click the Undo button on the Standard toolbar.

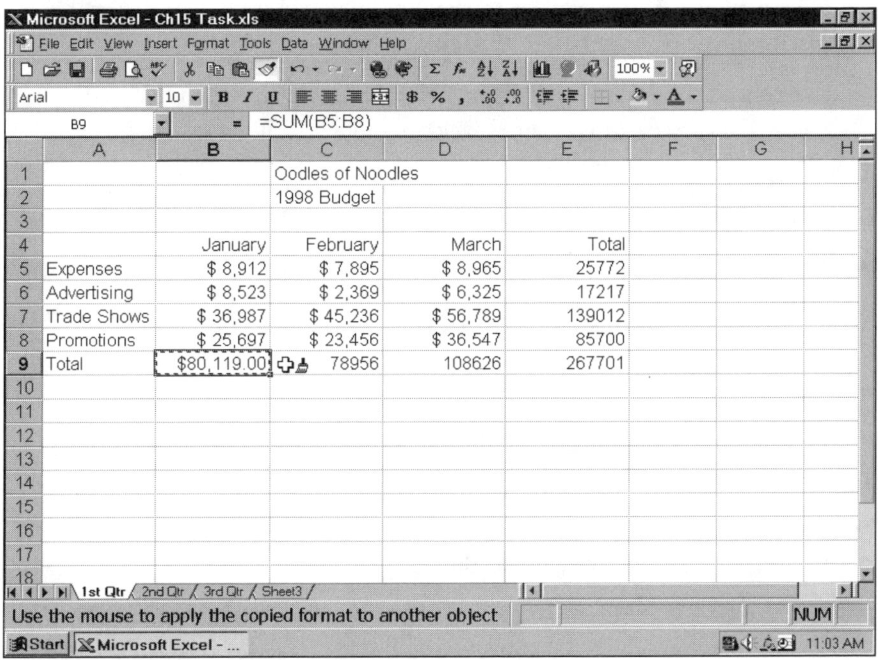

Figure 15.3 The Format Painter mouse pointer.

You've learned how to format cells, making each type of formatting change individually. By using styles, you can apply several types of formatting to a cell or cell range all at once.

Using Styles

What is a *style*? A style is a group of cell-formatting options that you apply to a cell or cell range. When you change a style's definition, the change affects the formatting of all cells formatted with that style. In Chapter 6, you enhanced a spreadsheet by applying various formats to cells. Styles allow you to apply several formats to a selected cell or cell block in one step by assigning a named style.

Excel has six predefined styles:

- **Normal** The default style. Number is set to General (lets you enter a value with a decimal point, dollar sign, comma, or percent sign, and as a date or time), font to Arial, size to 10-point, numbers are right aligned, text is left aligned, no borders or patterns, and Protection is set to locked.
- **Comma** Number is set to the Comma style with two decimal places. Negative numbers are black and enclosed in parentheses.
- **Comma (0)** Number is set to the Comma style with zero decimal places. Negative numbers are black and enclosed in parentheses.
- **Currency** Number is set to the Currency style with two decimal places. Negative numbers are black and enclosed in parentheses.
- **Currency (0)** Number is set to the Currency style with zero decimal places. Negative numbers are black and enclosed in parentheses.
- **Percent** Number is set to the Percent style with zero decimal places. Negative numbers are black and preceded by a minus sign.

To save time, save your favorite formatting combinations as styles. You can create your own styles in various ways:

- **Define the style** Create a style, and assign one or more formatting attributes to it.
- **Define by example** Select a cell that contains the formatting you want to use, and create a style based on that cell.
- **Copy a format** Select a cell in another workbook that contains the formatting you want to use, and copy the list of styles into the new workbook.

In the next four tasks, you'll look at various ways to work with styles. You'll use an existing style to change the format of column headings and define a new style from scratch. Then, you'll define a style by example, using a format that a cell contains, and finally, you'll copy styles from one workbook to another.

Task 4 Using existing styles.

1. Select B4:E4. This selects the cell range you want to format.
2. Select Format|Style. The Style dialog box should appear, as shown in Figure 15.4.
3. Click the down arrow to the right of the Style Name list box. The ColumnHeads style is already selected. This is the style you want to use. A checkmark next to a style attribute means that the style includes the attribute.
4. Click OK.
5. Click any cell to deselect the range.

The style should be applied to the selected cell range. Anything you type in the cell or cell range should be formatted according to the style you selected.

Task 5 Defining styles.

1. Choose Format|Style. The Style dialog box should appear.
2. In the Style Name list box, type "RowHeads". This names the new style.

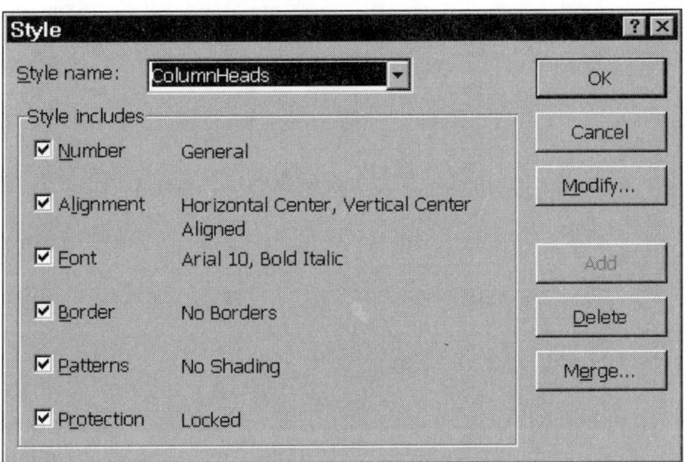

Figure 15.4 The Style dialog box.

3. Click the Add button. The style should be added to the Style Name list, and you should be able to modify it.
4. You can remove the checkmark from any attribute checkbox that you do not want to include in the style. Click the Number checkbox to exclude the Number format in the style.
5. Click on the Modify button. Excel displays the Format Cells dialog box, as shown in Figure 15.5.
6. You can use the tabs in the Format Cells dialog box to change format attributes and enter your preferences. Click the Font tab, and choose Italic, in the Font Style list box.
7. Click OK to save the settings and return to the Style dialog box.
8. Click OK to create and save the style.
9. Select A5:A9. This selects the cell range you want to format.
10. Select Format|Style. The Style dialog box should appear.
11. Click the down arrow to the right of the Style Name list box, and select RowHeads.
12. Click OK to apply the style.

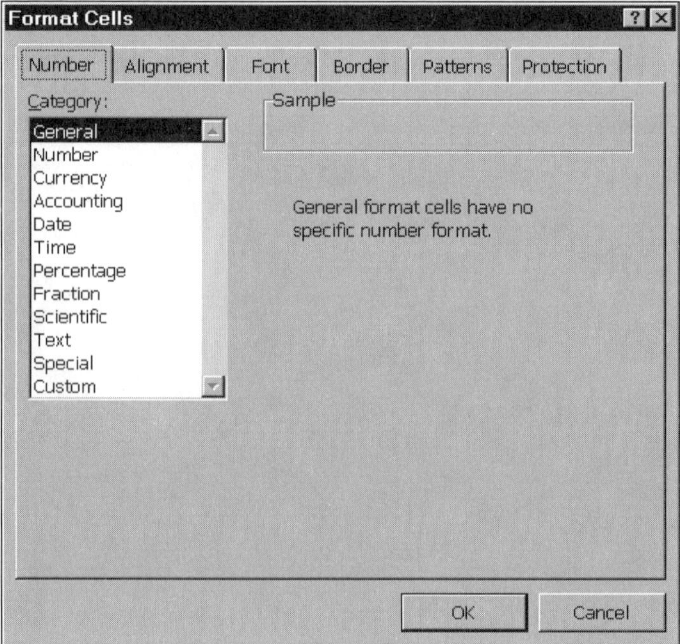

Figure 15.5 The Format Cells dialog box.

The style should be applied to the selected cell range. Anything you type in the cell or cell range should be formatted according to the style you applied.

Note: If you apply a style to one or more cells and then modify the style later, any changes you enter will immediately be applied to all cells you formatted with that style.

Be sure you know how to apply a style to a cell range.

Task 6 Defining styles by example.

1. Select cell B5. This cell contains the formatting that you want to copy.
2. Choose Format|Style.
3. In the Style Name list box, type CustomCurrency. This is a name for the style.
4. Click the Add button. The named style with the formatting from the selected cell should be added to the Style Name list box.
5. Click OK.

When you enter the same type of data into a large worksheet, it is sometimes convenient to change the default format in the style called Normal. Then, you can change the format for only those cells that are exceptions. Note that when you change the default Normal style, it affects all the cells in the worksheet and every sheet in the workbook. When you create a new workbook, Excel uses the default format settings, not the modified version of the Normal style. You can change the default settings for number format, alignment, and other settings. To do so, modify any of the format settings for the Normal style.

Task 7 Copying existing styles from another workbook.

1. Click the New button on the Standard toolbar. This creates a new workbook. This is the workbook you want to copy styles to.
2. Select Format|Style.
3. Click the Merge button. The Merge Styles dialog box should open, as shown in Figure 15.6.
4. Select Ch15 Task.xls. This is the name of the worksheet to copy from.

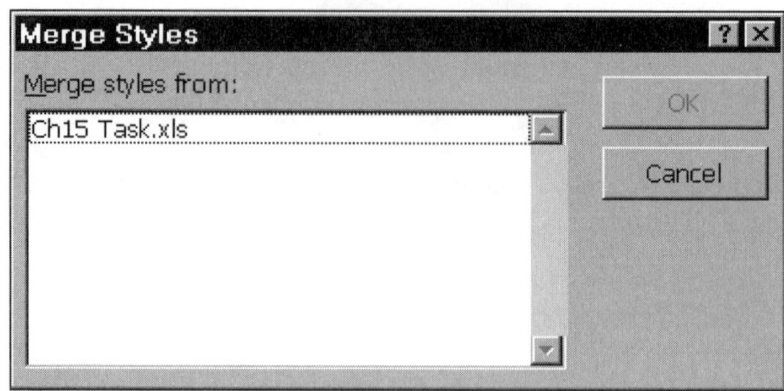

Figure 15.6 The Merge Styles dialog box.

5. Click OK to close the Merge Styles dialog box.
6. Click OK.
7. Save the new workbook with the name My Merge Styles.

   All the existing styles from the workbook should be copied to the current workbook.
8. Close the workbook.

Note: To modify a style, select Format|Style, display the style in the Style Name drop-down list box, and click the Modify button. Then, you can make any changes to the formats for the style. To delete a style, display the style name in the Style Name drop-down list box, and click the Delete button. Excel removes the style from the workbook.

Instead of using individual cell formatting or styles, you can simply use any of Excel's predefined AutoFormats to format all the data in your worksheet at once.

HOLD That Skill!

Remember, each style contains specifications for one or more of the following options:

- **Number** Controls the appearance of values, such as dollar values and dates.
- **Font** Specifies the type style, type size, and any attributes for text contained in the cell, such as bold, italic, or underline.
- **Alignment** Specifies general, left, right, or center alignment.

- **Border** Specifies the border placement and line style options for the cell.
- **Patterns** Adds specified shading to the cell.
- **Protection** Allows you to protect or unprotect a cell. By protecting cells in your worksheet, you lock the cells so that they cannot be edited or deleted. However, if you protect a cell or cell range, the cells are not locked until you protect a worksheet by selecting Tools|Protection|Protect Sheet.

Using AutoFormats

Excel offers the AutoFormat feature to take some of the pain out of formatting. AutoFormat provides you with 16 pre-designed table formats that you can apply to a worksheet. In the next task, you'll use the AutoFormat feature to format a table.

Task 8 Applying AutoFormat.

1. In the Ch15 Task workbook, select the cell range A4:E9. This range contains the data you want to format.
2. Choose Format|AutoFormat. The AutoFormat dialog box should appear, as shown in Figure 15.7.
3. In the Table Format list, choose Colorful 2. This is the pre-designed format you want to apply. When you select a format, Excel should show you what it will look like in the Sample area. If you want to exclude certain elements from the AutoFormat, click the Options button, and choose the elements that you want to turn off.

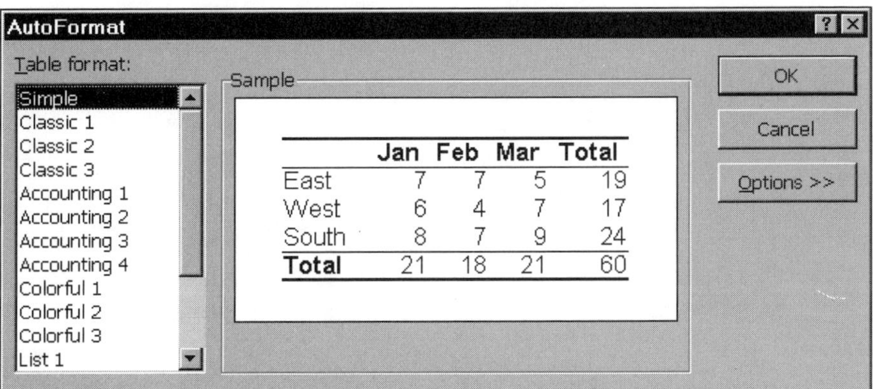

Figure 15.7 The AutoFormat dialog box.

4. Click OK, and click on any cell to deselect the table.

   Excel should format your table to appear like the one in the preview area.

5. Close the Ch 15 Task workbook without saving changes.

Note: If you don't want to keep the changes implemented by AutoFormat, click the Undo button on the Standard toolbar.

Be prepared to use AutoFormat to format a worksheet. Before you apply the AutoFormat style, make sure you select the cell range in the table that you want to format.

Practice Exercise

The Sandy Shores company is going through an annual audit, and, therefore, the spreadsheets need to look professional. In this exercise, you'll format the data in the worksheet with number formats, custom formats, styles, and AutoFormats. Figure 15.8 shows what the worksheet contains before you work through the instructions in this exercise.

1. Open the Ch15 Prac Ex workbook file located on the companion disk.
2. Select cell B11, and apply the Accounting format with zero decimal places.
3. Select the range B6:D10.
4. Create a custom format as #,##0, and apply it to the selected range.
5. Copy the format in cell B11 to the range C11:D11.
6. Select the range B1:B2.
7. Apply the Title style to title and subtitle.
8. Select the column headings in the worksheet.

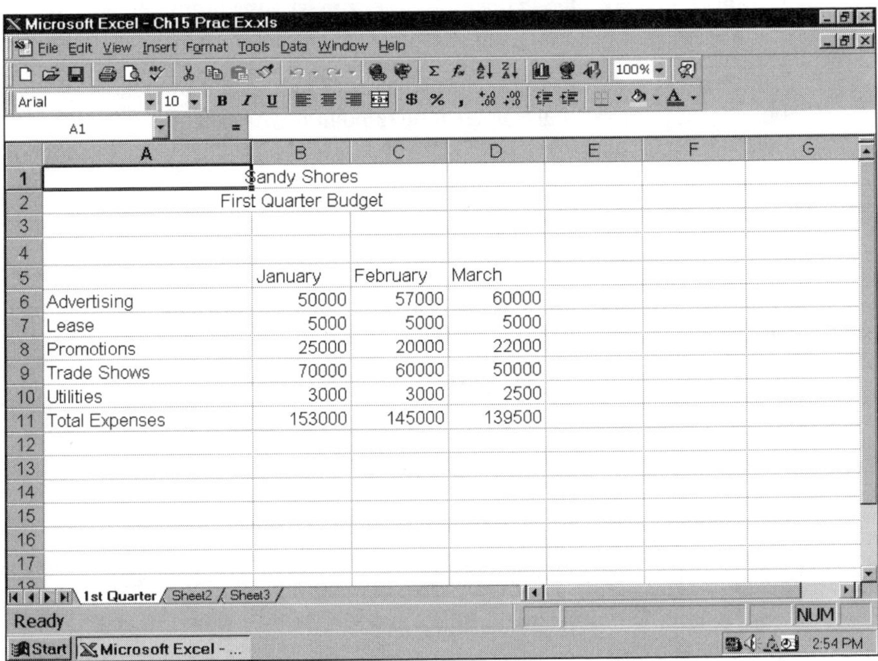

Figure 15.8 The Practice Exercise before you begin.

9. Create a style named Headings, based on Normal, with 12 point Century Gothic, Bold Italic. *Note:* If you don't have Century Gothic, choose any font. If Excel doesn't display the entire text for the column headings in each column, choose a smaller point size until you see all the text.
10. Modify the Headings style to 10 point.
11. Apply the Classic 2 AutoFormat to the range A5:D11.
12. Save the workbook with the same name.
13. Close the workbook.

Answers To Practice Exercise

1. Click the Open button on the Standard toolbar, and double-click the file name Ch15 Prac Ex.
2. Click on cell B11. Choose Format|Cells, and click the Number tab. Choose the Accounting category, and change the number of decimal places to 0. Click OK. This applies the Accounting format with zero decimal places.
3. Click cell B6 and drag to D10. This selects the range B6:D10.
4. Choose Format|Cells. Choose the Custom category. Select the custom format #,##0, and click OK. This applies the comma format with zero decimal places to the selected range.
5. Click cell B11. Then, click the Format Painter tool on the Standard toolbar. Drag the Format Painter mouse pointer over cells C11 and D11. This copies the format in cell B11 to the range C11:D11.
6. Click cell B1 and drag to B2. This selects the range B1:B2.
7. Choose Format|Style. The Style dialog box opens. Click the Style name drop-down arrow, and choose Title. Click OK. This applies the Title style to the title and subtitle.
8. Click cell B5 and drag to cell D5.
9. Choose Format|Style. The Style dialog box opens. Type "Headings" in the Style Name text box. Click the Add button. Click the Modify button, then click the Font tab. Choose Century Gothic from the Font list, Bold Italic from the Font style list, and 12 from the Size list. Click OK to close the Format Styles dialog box. This creates a style named Headings, based on Normal and formatted with 12 point Century Gothic, Bold Italic. Click OK to close the Style dialog box.

10. Choose Format|Style. The Style dialog box opens. Click the Style name drop-down arrow, and choose Headings, if necessary. Click the Modify button. Click the Font tab. Choose 10 from the Size list. Click OK to close the Format Cells dialog box. Click OK again, to close the Style dialog box. This modifies the Headings style to 10 point. You should see the column headings font decrease in size.
11. Click in cell A5 and drag to cell D11. Choose Format|AutoFormat. Select the Classic 2 style in the Table Format list. Click OK, then click on any cell to deselect the table. This applies the Classic 2 AutoFormat to the range A5:D11. Notice that the AutoFormat feature overrides any previously applied styles.

    Your worksheet should look like the one in Figure 15.9.
12. Click the Save button on the Standard toolbar to save the workbook.
13. Click the Close (X) button in the upper-right corner of the workbook window. This closes the workbook.

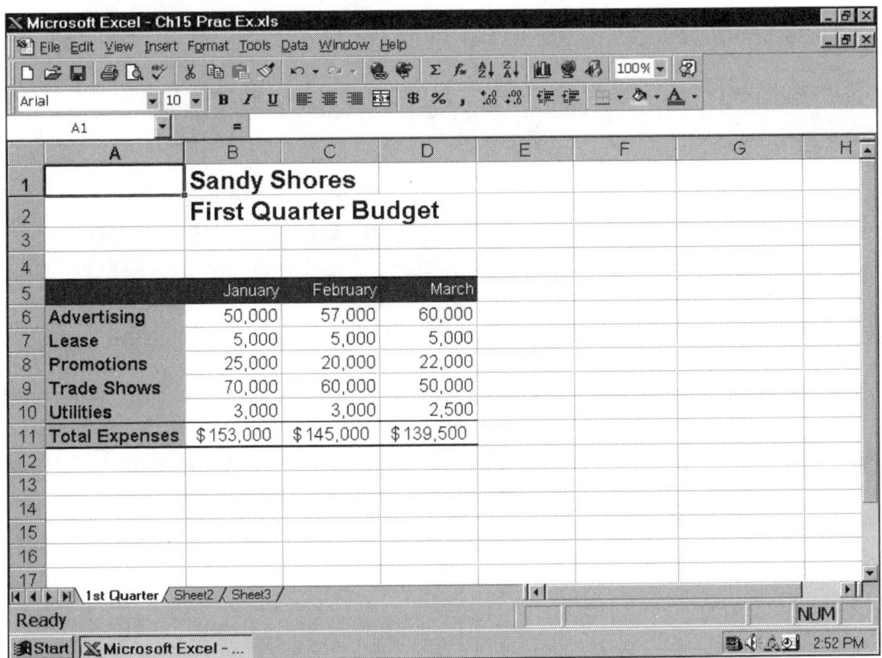

Figure 15.9 The completed Practice Exercise.

Need To Know More?

Catapult, Inc.: *Microsoft Excel 97 Step By Step*. Microsoft Press, Redmond, WA, 1996. ISBN 1-57231-315-5. Lesson 4, "Formatting Your Worksheet for a Professional Look," tells you how to format cells and numbers.

Craig, Deborah: *How to Use Microsoft Excel 97 for Windows*. Que, Indianapolis, IN, 1996. ISBN 1-56276-469-1. Chapter 8, "Improving Worksheet Appearance," gives you all the information you need on formatting numbers and removing formatting. Chapter 10, "Formatting Shortcuts," shows you how to copy formats, use AutoFormats, and apply styles.

Harvey, Greg: *Excel 97 for Windows for Dummies*. IDG Books Worldwide, Inc., Foster City, CA, 1996. ISBN 0-7645-0049-X. Chapter 3, "Making It All Look Pretty," explains how to format numbers in your worksheet.

Neibauer, Alan: *Excel One Step at a Time*. IDG Books Worldwide, Inc., Foster City, CA, 1997. ISBN 0-7645-3139-5. Lesson 5, "Formatting Worksheets," explains how to format numbers in worksheets.

Nicholson, John R. and Sean R. Nicholson: *Discover Excel 97*. IDG Books Worldwide, Inc., Foster City, CA, 1997. ISBN 1-7645-3047-X. Chapter 4, "Sprucing Up Your Worksheet," explains formatting numbers in worksheets. Chapter 13, "Macros and Templates and Styles (Oh, My!)," covers using and creating styles in worksheets.

Nossiter, Josh: *Using Microsoft Excel 97*. Que, Indianapolis, IN, 1996. ISBN 0-7897-0955-4. Chapter 7, "Not Just a Pretty Face: Formatting Makes Data Easier to Read," has a nice discussion of formatting worksheets.

16

Auditing Worksheets

Terms you'll need to understand:

- √ Audit
- √ Tracer
- √ Precedent
- √ Dependent
- √ Trace error
- √ Comment
- √ Constants

Skills you'll need to master:

- √ Checking and reviewing data
- √ Tracing cell precedents
- √ Tracing cell dependents
- √ Tracing cell errors
- √ Adding and viewing comments

Using Excel's Audit Features

Excel's audit features are useful tools to help you detect problems in your worksheet formulas. Excel provides an Auditing toolbar to help you find errors on your worksheets, attach comments to cells, and track problems in your worksheet formulas.

This chapter defines the auditing terms you'll need to know before you audit a worksheet. In addition, you'll explore the Auditing toolbar, use Auditing tools to check and review worksheet data, learn how values are determined, and track problems in formulas.

Checking And Reviewing Data

Using auditing tools can help you understand, visualize, and troubleshoot the relationships among cell references, formulas, and data. Before you audit a worksheet, you'll need to be familiar with the following auditing terms:

- **Constant** Cells with contents that are not to be included in a formula. Cells containing values that do not begin with an equal sign are considered to be constants, whether they are numbers or text.
- **Dependent** Cells that contain formulas that refer to other cells.
- **Error** Values that result from an incorrect cell reference or formula.
- **Precedent** Cells that are referred to directly by a formula.
- **Tracer** A visual tool that enables you to find precedents, dependents, and errors in any cell in a worksheet. Tracers are graphic displays, such as arrows, that visually show where formulas get their values. Tracers show a relationship between cells and illustrate precedent and dependent relationships.

When you're auditing worksheets, you might want to use the Go To Special command to quickly search for comments, precedents, dependents, or any other auditing information.

Using The Go To Special Command

The Go To Special command helps you find the following information while auditing worksheets:

- Comments
- Constants
- Formulas that meet a particular criteria

- Blank cells
- Cells in the current region or array
- Cells that do not fit a pattern in a row or column
- Precedents
- Dependents
- Last active cell in your sheet
- Visible cells
- Objects

To use the Go To Special command, press F5 (Go To), and click the Special button in the Go To dialog box. In the Go To Special dialog, select the item you want to go to, and click OK.

In the upcoming task, you'll prepare for auditing data in a worksheet by displaying the Auditing toolbar. Notice that before using tracers, the task involves verifying that the Hide All option is not selected in the Options dialog box.

Task 1 Checking and reviewing data.

1. Open the Ch16 Task workbook located on your companion disk.
2. To verify that the Hide All option is turned off, choose Tools|Options. The Options dialog box should appear.
3. Click the View tab, if necessary.

   In the Objects section, verify that the Hide All option button is not selected and that the Show All option button is selected (displays with a black circle in the radio button).
4. Click OK.
5. Choose Tools|Auditing|Show Auditing Toolbar. The Auditing toolbar should open, as shown in Figure 16.1.

The Auditing toolbar provides the following tools to audit worksheets:

- **Trace Precedents** Draws arrows from all cells that supply values directly to the formula in the active cell (precedents).

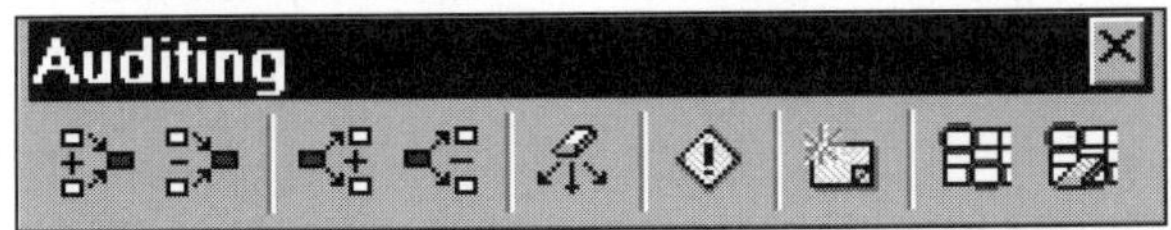

Figure 16.1 The Auditing toolbar.

- **Remove Precedent Arrows** Deletes a level of precedent tracer arrows from the active worksheet.
- **Trace Dependents** Draws arrows from the active cell to cells with formulas that use the values in the active cell (dependents).
- **Remove Dependent Arrows** Deletes a level of dependent tracer arrows from the active worksheet.
- **Remove All Arrows** Deletes all tracer arrows from the active worksheet.
- **Trace Error** Draws an arrow to an error value in the active cell from cells that might have caused the error.
- **New Comment** Displays a comment text box next to a cell you selected that will contain text or audio comments.
- **Circle Invalid Data** Identifies incorrect entries with circles. Incorrect entries are values outside the limits you set by using the Data Validation feature (discussed in Chapter 20).
- **Clear Validation Circles** Hides circles around incorrect values in cells.

With the Auditing toolbar displayed, you are ready to trace precedents, that is, find the cells that are referenced in a formula.

When you audit a worksheet, it's a good idea to display the Auditing toolbar and have it handy instead of choosing the Auditing commands from the Tools menu. When you finish using the toolbar, click the Close (X) button to close the toolbar.

Finding Cells Referenced In A Formula

You can trace the precedents of a cell to figure out the relationship between a formula and its cell references. In Task 2, you'll trace the precedent of a cell.

Task 2 Tracing cell precedents.

1. Select cell E5. This is the cell that contains the formula you want to trace.
2. Click the Trace Precedents tool on the Auditing toolbar. Excel should display a tracer arrow on the worksheet, as shown in Figure 16.2.
3. Double-click the point of the tracer arrow (blue or solid arrow) to select the cells leading up to the cell at the point end of the arrow.

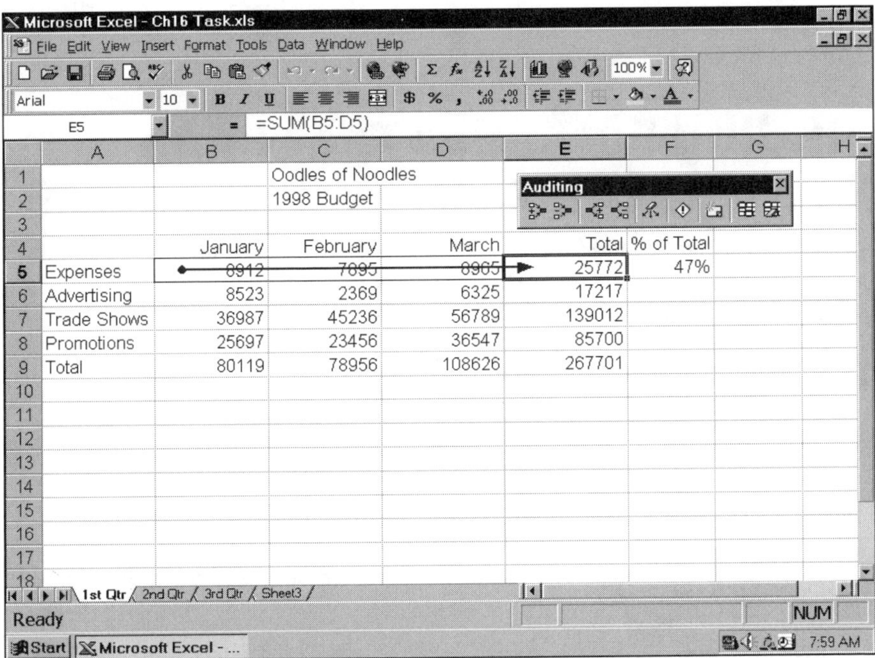

Figure 16.2 Precedent tracer arrow on the active worksheet.

4. Double-click the tracer arrow again to select the cell at the point end of the arrow.
5. Select cell F5. This cell contains the formula you want to trace.
6. Click the Trace Precedents tool on the Auditing toolbar. Excel should display a tracer arrow on the worksheet.
7. Double-click the point of the external worksheet arrow (dashed arrow with spreadsheet icon). The Go To dialog box should open.
8. Select the item in the Go To list, and click OK. Excel should display the selected sheet (2nd Qtr sheet tab).
9. Click the 1st Qtr sheet tab. This returns you to the original worksheet.
10. Click the Remove Precedent Arrows tool on the Auditing toolbar to remove one level of tracer arrows.

Be ready to trace the precedents of a cell. It's advisable to use the Auditing toolbar to do this. When you are asked to select them, double-click the point of the tracer arrows. When you finish using the toolbar, be sure to close it.

You've traced precedents. Now, you'll learn how to trace dependents. Dependents are formulas that contain cell references.

Finding Formulas That Refer To A Specific Cell

You can trace the dependents of a cell to determine the relationship between a cell reference and the formula that contains the cell reference. The next task depicts how to trace the dependents of a cell.

Task 3 Tracing cell dependents.

1. Select cell B5. This is the cell dependent that you're going to trace.
2. Click the Trace Dependents tool on the Auditing toolbar. Excel should display tracer arrows on the worksheet, as shown in Figure 16.3.
3. Double-click the point of the tracer arrow (blue or solid arrow) to select the cell at the point end of the arrow.
4. Double-click the point of the tracer arrow again to select the cell at the opposite end of the arrow.

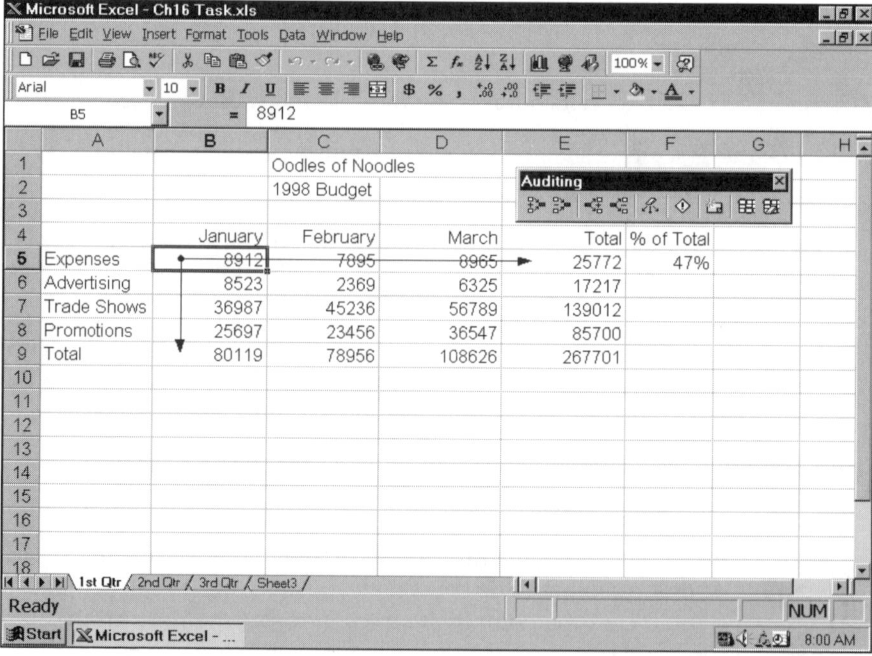

	A	B	C	D	E	F
1			Oodles of Noodles			
2			1998 Budget			
3						
4		January	February	March	Total	% of Total
5	Expenses	8912	7895	8965	25772	47%
6	Advertising	8523	2369	6325	17217	
7	Trade Shows	36987	45236	56789	139012	
8	Promotions	25697	23456	36547	85700	
9	Total	80119	78956	108626	267701	

Figure 16.3 Dependent tracer arrows on the active worksheet.

5. Click the Remove Dependent Arrows tool on the Auditing toolbar to remove the tracer arrows.

After tracing precedents and dependents, you can also trace any errors in your worksheet. If you have formulas that produce errors, Excel's Trace Errors feature can help you find and correct the errors.

Be ready to trace the dependents of a cell. The fastest and most efficient way to do this is to use the Auditing toolbar. When you are asked to select them, double-click the point of the tracer arrows.

HOLD That Skill!

When you audit a worksheet to trace the precedents or dependents of a cell, Excel displays any combination of the following symbols:

- **Blue or solid arrow** Indicates direct precedents or dependents of the selected formula.
- **Red or dotted arrow** Indicates formulas that refer to error values.
- **Dashed arrow attached to a spreadsheet icon** Refers to external worksheets.

Finding Errors

You can trace errors in a cell to find out where the error is on the worksheet and then correct the error. Some of the error values that can appear in a cell include:

- **#DIV/0!** Occurs when you create a formula that divides by 0 (zero) or divides by a cell that is empty.
- **#N/A** Occurs when you have a value that is not available to a function or a formula.
- **#NAME?** Occurs when Excel doesn't recognize text in a formula.
- **#NULL!** Occurs when you specify an intersection of two areas that do not intersect. For example, you might have an incorrect range operator (not using a comma to separate two ranges, such as =SUM(B1:B8,F4:F8) or incorrect cell reference.
- **#NUM!** Occurs when you use an unacceptable argument in a function that should be a numeric argument, or a formula's result is a number that is too large or too small for Excel to display. Excel displays values between $-1*10^{307}$ and $1*10^{307}$.

- **#REF!** Occurs when a cell reference is not valid, such as when you delete cells that refer to formulas or paste cells onto cells that are referred to by other formulas.
- **#VALUE!** Occurs when you use the wrong type of argument in a function or wrong operand in a formula.

In the next task, you'll see how you can trace an error that appears in a cell.

Task 4 Tracing cell errors.

1. Select cell E6, press F2, press the End key, type "=/0", and press Enter. You should see the #DIV/0! in cell E6. This is an error value that is traceable.
2. Select cell E6, click the Trace Error tool on the Auditing toolbar. Excel should display an error tracer arrow on the worksheet, as shown in Figure 16.4.
3. Double-click the point of error tracer arrow (red, dotted, blue, or solid arrow) to select the cell at the base of the arrow.
4. Double-click the point of the tracer arrow again to select the cell at the point end of the arrow.

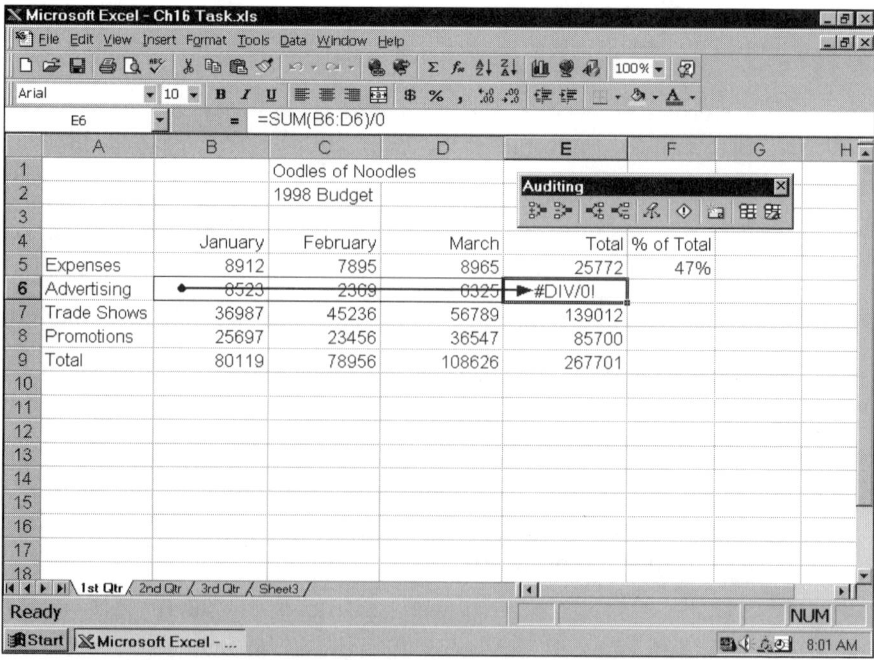

Figure 16.4 An error tracer arrow on the active worksheet.

HOLD That Skill!

When you trace errors in a worksheet, Excel displays any combination of the following symbols:

- **Red or dotted arrow** Indicates the first precedent formula that contains an error.
- **Blue or solid arrow** Indicates the precedents of the first formula producing an error.
- **Dashed arrow attached to a spreadsheet icon** Refers to external worksheets.

5. In cell E6, type =SUM(B6:D6). This corrects the error. The error tracer arrow should disappear.
6. Click the Close (X) button on the Auditing toolbar to close the toolbar.

After you audit a worksheet, you might want to further clarify the data by entering a comment next to the cell that needs an explanation. That way, others who use the worksheet can understand what is happening with the data in the worksheet.

Adding Comments To Your Worksheet

You can add comments to your worksheets using Excel's auditing features or the Insert Comment command. Adding comments is useful if you are going to share your work with others. Some explanation might be necessary to clarify certain portions of a worksheet or workbook. Adding comments is also helpful to track your work or trace your footsteps if you are using complex formulas and references. Comments enable you to remind yourself of how a portion of a worksheet operates and insert questions or comments for others to read.

In the next task, you'll add a comment to explain the data in a cell, and then you'll view the comment.

Task 5 Adding and viewing comments.

1. Select cell E5. This is the cell for which you want to enter a comment.
2. Choose Insert|Comment. You should see a box with an insertion point in it appear next to cell C5.

3. In the Comment box, type “Get March advt figures and chg formula”. Notice your name appears in the comment, followed by the text you entered. Click on another cell to close the comment. Notice a red triangle displays in the upper-right corner of the cell that contains the comment.

   Note: Comments cannot be closed by pressing Enter—that just adds a blank line. To close a comment, click another cell.

4. To view a comment, point to the cell that contains the comment. The comment should pop up, as shown in Figure 16.5.
5. Close the Ch16 Task workbook without saving changes.

   Note: If you select multiple cells, Excel will place the comment in the first cell you select in the range.

You need to know how to insert a comment. You'll enter one comment in a cell.

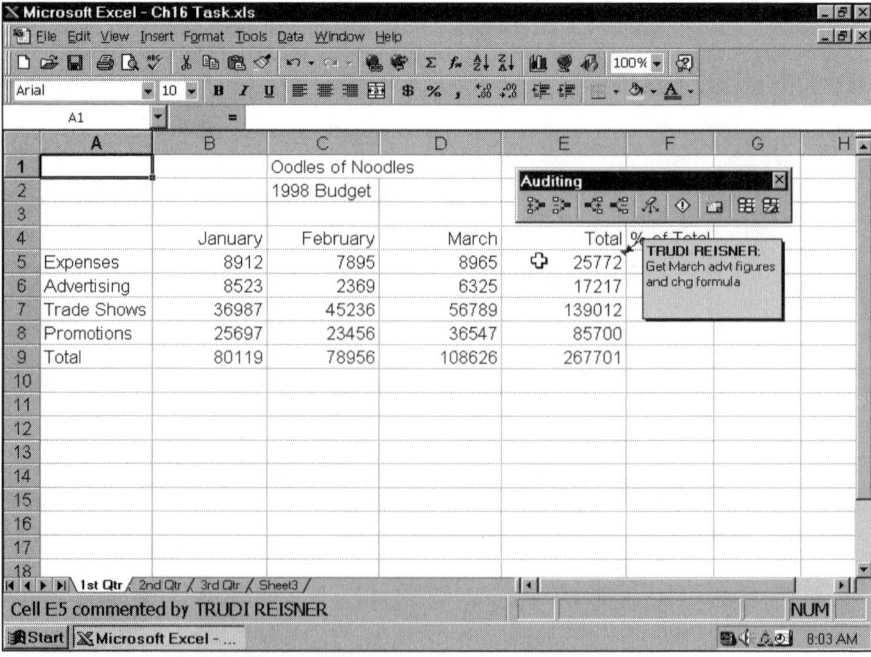

Figure 16.5 Viewing a comment.

Practice Exercise

The accounting supervisor at Sandy Shores Company needs to audit the worksheets before tax time. Your job is to use Excel's auditing tools to trace precedents, dependents, and errors. Figure 16.6 shows what the worksheet contains before you go through the instructions in this exercise.

1. Open the Ch16 Prac Ex workbook stored on the companion disk.
2. Display the Auditing toolbar.
3. Trace the precedents for the formula in cell B11.
4. Remove the precedent arrow.
5. Trace the dependents for the cell C6.
6. Remove the dependent arrow.
7. Select cell E6, which contains an error value.
8. Trace the error in cell E6.
9. Remove all the tracer arrows on the active worksheet.
10. In cell E6, enter the comment "Get projected expenses and calculate %" for the cell.

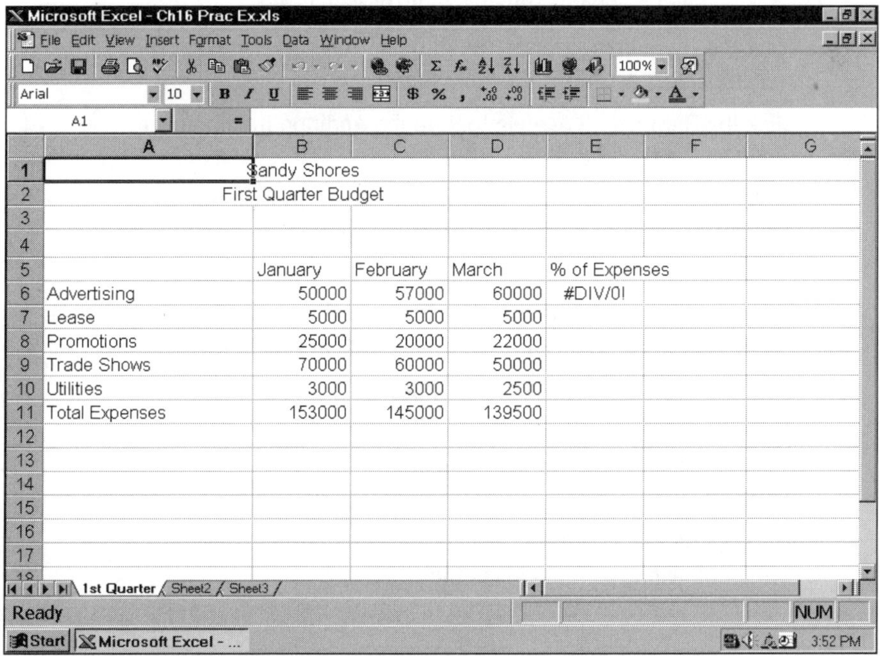

	A	B	C	D	E
1		Sandy Shores			
2		First Quarter Budget			
3					
4					
5		January	February	March	% of Expenses
6	Advertising	50000	57000	60000	#DIV/0!
7	Lease	5000	5000	5000	
8	Promotions	25000	20000	22000	
9	Trade Shows	70000	60000	50000	
10	Utilities	3000	3000	2500	
11	Total Expenses	153000	145000	139500	

Figure 16.6 The Practice Exercise before you begin.

11. Read the comment you just entered.
12. Hide the Auditing toolbar.
13. Save the workbook with the same name.
14. Close the workbook.

Answers To Practice Exercise

1. Click the Open button on the Standard toolbar, and double-click on the file name Ch16 Prac Ex.
2. Choose Tools|Auditing|Show Auditing Toolbar. The Auditing toolbar opens.
3. Click cell B11. Click the Trace Precedents tool on the Auditing toolbar. Excel displays a tracer arrow on the worksheet.
4. Click the Remove Precedent Arrows tool on the Auditing toolbar to remove the tracer arrow.
5. Click cell C6. Click the Trace Dependents tool on the Auditing toolbar. Excel displays a tracer arrow on the worksheet.
6. Click the Remove Dependent Arrows tool on the Auditing toolbar to remove the dependent tracer arrow.
7. Click on cell E6, which contains an error value.
8. Click the Trace Error tool on the Auditing toolbar. Excel displays an error tracer arrow on the worksheet.
9. Click the Remove All Arrows tool on the Auditing toolbar. Excel removes the tracer arrow.
10. With cell E6 selected, click the New Comment tool on the Auditing toolbar, and type "Get projected expenses and calculate %." for the comment. Click another cell to close the comment.
11. Point to cell E6 that contains the comment. Excel displays the comment so that you can read it, as shown in Figure 16.7.
12. Click the Close (X) button in the upper-right corner of the Auditing toolbar. The Auditing toolbar disappears.
13. Click the Save button on the Standard toolbar to save the workbook.
14. Click the Close (X) button in the upper-right corner of the workbook window. This closes the workbook.

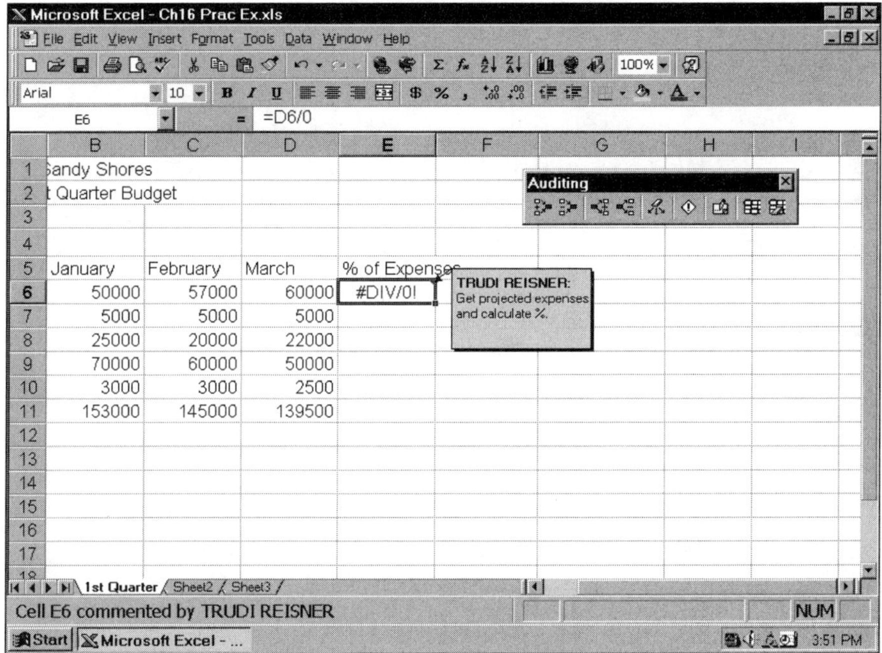

Figure 16.7 The completed Practice Exercise.

Need To Know More?

Catapult, Inc.: *Microsoft Excel 97 Step By Step*. Microsoft Press, Redmond, WA, 1996. ISBN 1-57231-316-5. Lesson 12, "Sharing a Workbook with Others," tells you how to review changes in a workbook.

Neibauer, Alan: *Excel One Step at a Time*. IDG Books Worldwide, Inc., Foster City, CA, 1997. ISBN 0-7645-3139-5. Lesson 7, "Preventing and Correcting Worksheet Errors," explains how to validate cell entries and audit your worksheets.

Nicholson, John R. and Sean R. Nicholson: *Discover Excel 97*. IDG Books Worldwide, Inc., Foster City, CA, 1997. ISBN 1-7645-3047-X. Chapter 11, "Numbers Do Lie: Checking Your Work," explains how to perform data validation to audit your worksheets. Chapter 16, "Sharing the Workload: Group Projects," covers tracking changes in worksheets.

Nossiter, Josh: *Using Microsoft Excel 97*. Que, Indianapolis, IN, 1996. ISBN 0-7897-0955-4. Chapter 14, "More Analyzing and Auditing, Too," talks about auditing worksheets.

17

Working With Workbooks

Terms you'll need to understand:

- √ External references
- √ Sheet references
- √ 3D references
- √ Linking formula
- √ Sheet range
- √ Cell range

Skills you'll need to master:

- √ Referencing another worksheet in a formula
- √ Building a formula to link several worksheets
- √ Building a formula to link workbooks
- √ Updating links manually
- √ Arranging open workbooks
- √ Moving among open workbooks

Linking Data In Excel Workbooks

Linking is the process of dynamically updating data in a worksheet from data in another source worksheet. When data is linked, any changes you make to the original data are reflected in the linked data.

Linking is accomplished through special formulas that contain references known as *external references*. An external reference can refer to a cell in a different worksheet in the same workbook, or any other worksheet in any other workbook. This chapter introduces you to creating formulas that link data from other worksheets and workbooks. You'll also learn how to arrange multiple workbooks on screen.

Linking Workbooks

Excel lets you link data from other worksheets and workbooks in several ways. You can:

- Reference another worksheet in a linking formula using sheet references.
- Reference several worksheets in a linking formula using 3D references.
- Reference another workbook in a linking formula.

If you have a lot of data and you create many worksheets to store this data, you might have a formula in one worksheet that needs to use data from another sheet. These formulas are called *sheet references*. Sheet references are useful because you don't have to create redundant data in numerous sheets.

Suppose you have a formula that needs to reference a cell range that has two or more sheets in a workbook. This might happen if you have identical worksheets for different sales territories. You also might have several worksheets that have totals calculated and entered in identical cell addresses. You can add all these totals to get a grand total by referencing the sheet and cell addresses in one formula. These cell addresses are called *3D references*. You set up a 3D reference by including a sheet range, which names the beginning and ending sheets, and a cell range, which names the cells to which you are referring. For example, a formula that contains 3D references might look like this:

```
=SUM(SHEET1:SHEET5!B6:B11)
```

This formula references Sheet1 through Sheet5 and adds the data appearing in cells B6 through B11.

When you are linking workbooks, there are some special names for the workbooks that you need to know about. The workbook that contains a linking

HOLD That Skill!

Here are some important concepts to remember when you build linking formulas:

- You can type a linking formula in the cell where you want the results to appear.
- If you're referencing a cell in another sheet, the syntax is **Sheet!Cell**. When you enter a linking formula to reference a cell in another sheet, include the sheet name followed by an ! (exclamation mark) and the cell reference.
- If you're referencing a cell in more than one sheet, the syntax is **SheetX:SheetY!Cell**. When you enter a linking formula to reference a cell in more than one sheet, include the first sheet name, a : (colon), the last sheet name, an ! (exclamation mark), and the cell reference(s).
- If you're referencing a cell in another workbook, the syntax is **[Book]Sheet!Cell**. When you enter a linking formula to reference a cell in another workbook, include the workbook name enclosed in brackets, the sheet name followed by an ! (exclamation mark), and the cell reference.

formula is called the *dependent workbook*, and the workbook that contains the linked data is called the *source workbook*.

The next three tasks show you how to build linking formulas to reference a cell in another worksheet, reference a range of cells in three worksheets, and reference a cell on a sheet in another workbook.

Task 1 Referencing another worksheet in a formula.

1. Open the Ch17 Task workbook located on your companion disk. This workbook will contain the linking formula.
2. Click the 2nd Qtr sheet tab.
3. Click cell A12. This cell will contain the linking formula.
4. Type "=".
5. Click the 1st Qtr sheet tab.
6. Click cell E9.

7. Press Enter.

8. Click cell A12. In cell A12, you should see the linking formula ='1st Qtr'!E9, which links the data in cell E9 on the 2nd Qtr sheet to cell A12 on the 1st Qtr sheet. The correct result is 267701.

9. Click the Currency Style button on the Formatting toolbar.

10. Click twice on the Decrease Decimal button on the Formatting toolbar.

You should now see $267,701 in cell A12 on the 2nd Qtr sheet as shown in Figure 17.1.

> *Note: If you know which cells you want to reference, you can type the entire linking formula in a cell. If you're not sure of the cell address that you want to reference on another sheet, you can start typing your formula and then switch to the sheet that you want to reference when you get to that part of the formula. Then, use your mouse, and click the cell or range of cells that you want to include in your formula. The cell or range reference will appear automatically in your formula. To complete the process, press Enter to calculate.*

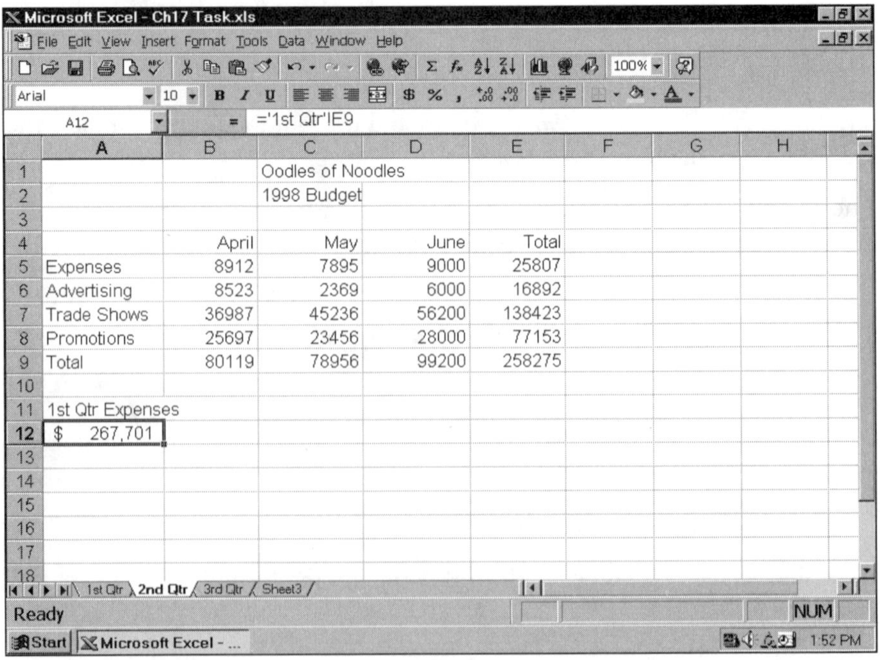

	A	B	C	D	E
1			Oodles of Noodles		
2			1998 Budget		
3					
4		April	May	June	Total
5	Expenses	8912	7895	9000	25807
6	Advertising	8523	2369	6000	16892
7	Trade Shows	36987	45236	56200	138423
8	Promotions	25697	23456	28000	77153
9	Total	80119	78956	99200	258275
10					
11	1st Qtr Expenses				
12	$ 267,701				

Figure 17.1 A linking formula that references another sheet.

When the sheet name contains spaces, such as Sales Report 98, you need to insert single quotation marks around the name when you are making sheet references.

Make sure you know how to link two sheets using a linking formula that references a cell on another worksheet.

In the upcoming task, you'll create a linking formula that references a range of cells on three sheets and totals the expenses for January, April, and July.

Task 2 Building a formula to link several worksheets.

1. Click the 3rd Qtr sheet tab.
2. Click cell A12. This cell will contain the linking formula.
3. Type "=SUM('1st Qtr:3rd Qtr'!B5:B8)".
4. Press Enter.
5. Click cell A12. In cell A12, you should see the linking formula **=SUM(**'1st Qtr:3rd Qtr'!B5:B8), which links the data in the range of cells B5 through B8 on the 1st Qtr sheet through the 3rd Qtr sheet. The correct result is 240357.
6. Click the Currency Style button on the Formatting toolbar.
7. Click twice on the Decrease Decimal button on the Formatting toolbar.

You should now see $240,357 in cell A12 on the 3rd Qtr sheet as shown in Figure 17.2.

> ***Note:** Another way to include 3D references in your formulas is to use the mouse and click the worksheets that you want to include in your formula. To do so, start typing your formula in the cell where you want the answer to appear. When you get to the point where you need to use the 3D reference, click the first worksheet tab that you want to include in your reference, press and hold the Shift key if the worksheets are consecutive, click the last worksheet that you want to include, and select the cells you want to reference. If the worksheets are nonconsecutive, press and hold the Ctrl key, click the worksheets you want to include, and select the cells you want to reference. When you finish entering your formula, press Enter.*

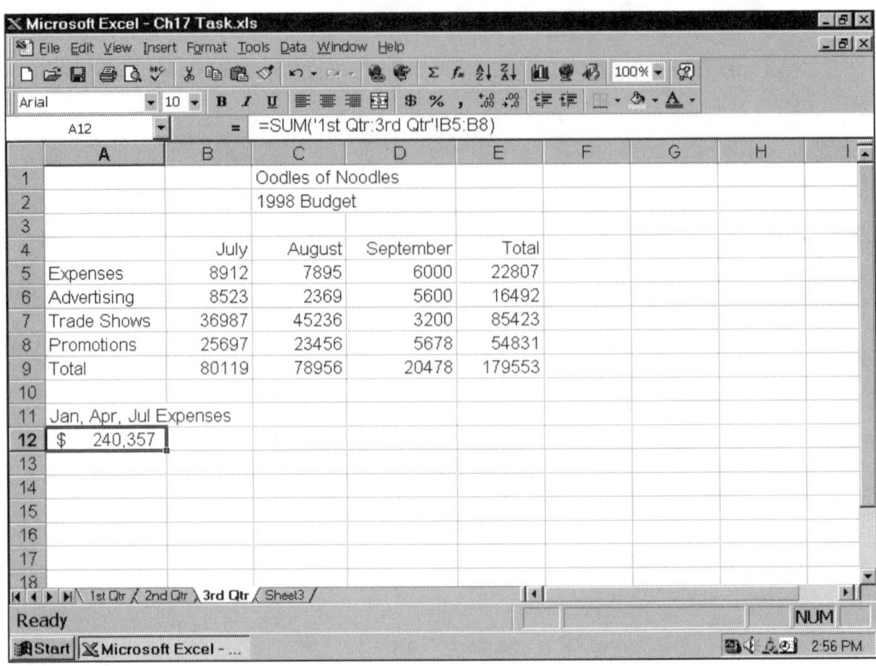

Figure 17.2 A linking formula that references several sheets.

Task 3 Building a formula to link workbooks.

1. Open the Ch17 Task3 located on your companion disk. This is the workbook that you want to link to the first workbook.
2. Choose Window, and select the Ch17 Task workbook. This is the workbook that will contain the linking formula.
3. Click the 1st Qtr sheet tab.
4. Click cell A12. This cell will contain the linking formula.
5. Type "=", click cell E9, and type "+".
6. Choose Window, and select the Ch17 Task 3 workbook.
7. In the 1st Qtr sheet, click cell E9. This is the cell that contains the data you want to link to the first workbook.
8. Press Enter.
9. Click cell A12. In cell A12, you should see the linking formula =E9+'[Ch17 Task 3.xls]1st Qtr'!$E$9, which links the data in cell E9 on the 1st Qtr sheet of the Ch17 Task 3 workbook. The correct result is 535487.

10. Click the Currency Style button on the Formatting toolbar.
11. Click twice on the Decrease Decimal button on the Formatting toolbar.
12. Close the Ch 17 Task3 workbook.

You should now see $535,487 in cell A12 on the 1st Qtr sheet as shown in Figure 17.3.

It's important that you know how to create a linking formula to link two workbooks. You can use the Window menu command to switch between workbooks. Remember that the syntax for a linking formula that links workbooks is **[Book]Sheet!Cell**.

Using Multiple Workbooks

When working with multiple workbooks and linking formulas, you need to know how the links get updated. If you change data in cells that are referenced in linking formulas, will the formula results be updated automatically? Yes, as long as both workbooks are open. If the data in the source workbook is changed while the dependent workbook—the one which contains a linking formula—is closed, then the linked data will not be immediately updated. The next time you open the dependent workbook, Excel will inquire whether you want to

Microsoft Excel - Ch17 Task.xls

A12 = =E9+'[Ch17 Task3.xls]1st Qtr'!$E$9

	A	B	C	D	E	F	G
1			Oodles of Noodles				
2			1998 Budget				
3							
4		January	February	March	Total		
5	Expenses	8912	7895	8965	25772		
6	Advertising	8523	2369	6325	17217		
7	Trade Shows	36987	45236	56789	139012		
8	Promotions	25697	23456	36547	85700		
9	Total	80119	78956	108626	267701		
10							
11	1st Qtr 97 & 98 Expenses						
12	$ 535,487						

1st Qtr / 2nd Qtr / 3rd Qtr / Sheet3

Figure 17.3 A linking formula that references another workbook.

update the data. To update all the linked data in the workbook, choose Yes. If you choose No, or if you have links that are manually updated, you can update the links yourself.

With Excel's Copy command, you can copy data from one workbook to another. For example, you open two workbooks: one that contains a quarterly sales report and another with the annual sales report. To make things easier, you might want to copy the first quarter projected sales figures in the first workbook to the second workbook. The original data in the first workbook remains intact. A copy of the data appears in the second workbook. To switch from one workbook to another, you can use any of the methods mentioned later in this section.

There are times when you may have more than one workbook open at a time. You can open as many workbooks as will fit in your computer's memory. When you open multiple workbooks, you will need to know how to manage them.

Suppose you want to see all the open workbooks at a glance. You can do just that by arranging them on the screen for easy viewing. Excel makes it easy to have multiple workbooks open and to avoid getting lost in a maze of multiple workbooks. With the help of Excel's Window Arrange command, you can arrange your workbooks in windows in four ways:

- **Tiled** Arranges the open workbooks in small windows displayed in a tiled fashion on the screen.
- **Horizontal** Displays the open workbooks in windows as horizontal bands across your workspace.
- **Vertical** Organizes the open workbooks in windows as vertical bands in your Excel window.
- **Cascade** Layers the open workbooks in windows on the screen.

Whether you arrange the open workbooks using one of the arrange options or you leave them on top of each other in the order in which you opened them, you can move among open workbooks very easily. Excel provides several easy ways to get to the workbook you want. You can use the mouse, shortcut keys, or the Window menu to move to the workbook of your choice. To move among open workbooks, you can:

- Click a visible part of a workbook window.
- Press Ctrl+F6 to move from one workbook window to another.
- Open the Window menu. At the bottom of the Window menu, you should see a list of workbook names, allowing you to switch to any open workbook. Simply select the name of the workbook you want to display.

In the next task, you'll first make a change to the data that a linking formula references. Then, you'll update the links manually to refresh the data in the worksheets you linked. In Task 5, you'll copy data from one open workbook to another. In Task 6, you'll arrange the open workbooks on the screen in various ways using the four Arrange Windows options: Tiled, Horizontal, Vertical, and Cascade. Finally, in Task 7, you'll move among open workbooks using the mouse, shortcut keys, and the Window menu.

Task 4 Updating links manually.

1. In the Ch 17 Task workbook, click cell D5.
2. Type "9050", then press Enter.
3. Choose Edit|Links. The Links dialog box should open, as shown in Figure 17.4. The Source File list box contains a list of all linking resources used in the active workbook. The link reference you want to update, in this case, Ch 17 Task3.xls, is already selected.
4. Click Update Now.

   Note: The Update Now button in the Links dialog box is available only if the source workbook is not already open, and if any linked formulas have been changed since the last update. In the Links dialog box, you can click the Change Source button to change the link reference. Or, you can open the source worksheet by clicking the Open Source button in the Links dialog box.

5. Click OK. The linked formula in cell A12 is updated from 535,487 to the new value of 535,572.

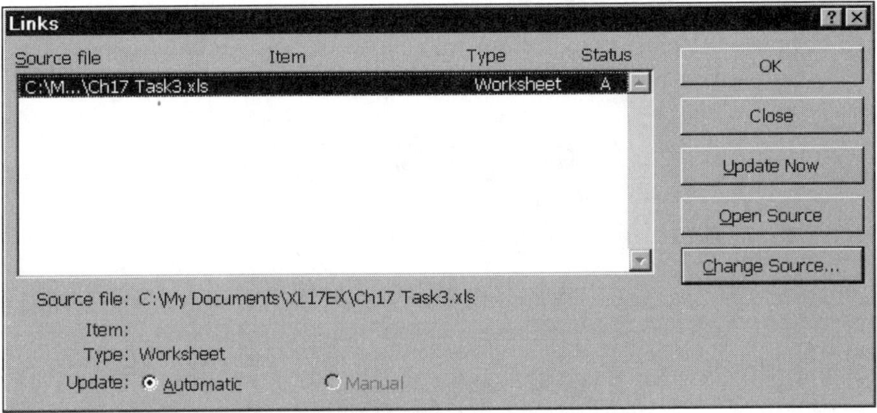

Figure 17.4 The Links dialog box.

Task 5 Copying data between workbooks.

1. Open the Ch 17 Task3 workbook.
2. Press Ctrl+F6 to switch to the Ch 17 Task workbook.
3. In the 1st Qtr sheet, select B5:C8.
4. Click the Copy button on the Standard toolbar.
5. Press Ctrl+F6 to switch to the Ch 17 Task3 workbook.
6. In the 1st Qtr sheet, click cell B20.
7. Click the Paste button on the Standard toolbar.

The data you copied and pasted into the second workbook should appear starting in row 20.

Be prepared to copy and paste a range of cells from one workbook to another. It's best to use the Window menu command to switch between workbooks.

Task 6 Arranging open workbooks.

1. Open the following three workbooks: Ch17 Task3.xls, Ch17 Prac Ex.xls, and Ch17 Prac Ex2.xls. Now, you should have four workbooks open.
2. Choose Window|Arrange. The Arrange Windows dialog box should open, as shown in Figure 17.5.
3. Choose the Tiled option if necessary, and click OK. You should see the workbooks arranged in a tiled format.
4. Choose Window|Arrange.
5. Choose the Horizontal option, and click OK. You should see the workbooks arranged in horizontal bands.

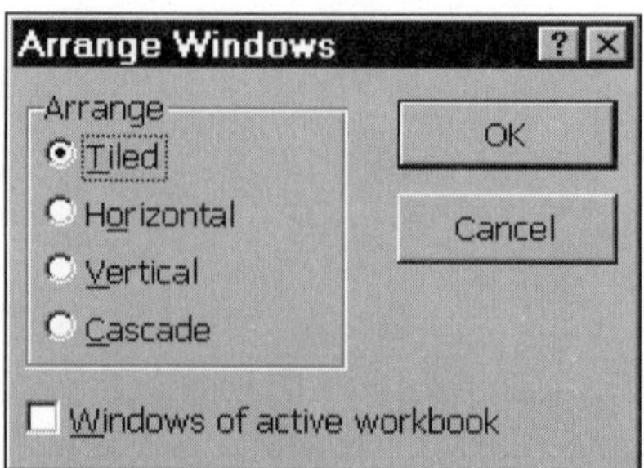

Figure 17.5 The Arrange Windows dialog box.

6. Choose Window|Arrange.
7. Choose the Vertical option, and click OK. You should see the workbooks arranged in vertical bands.
8. Choose Window|Arrange.
9. Choose the Cascade option, and click OK. You should see the workbooks arranged in a layered effect.

Task 7 Moving among open workbooks.

1. Double-click the Ch17 Task workbook title bar. The workbook should appear in a full-size window on the screen.
2. Press Ctrl+F6 to move to the next open workbook (Ch17Prac Ex2).
3. Press Ctrl+F6 to move to the other workbook (Ch17 Prac Ex).
4. Choose Window. The Window menu should open, and you should see a list of workbook names at the bottom of the menu (see Figure 17.6).
5. Choose the Ch17 Task3.xls workbook from the Window menu.

   The workbook you selected should appear in a full-size window on the screen.
6. Close the Ch17 Task3 workbook.
7. Close all the rest of the open workbooks.

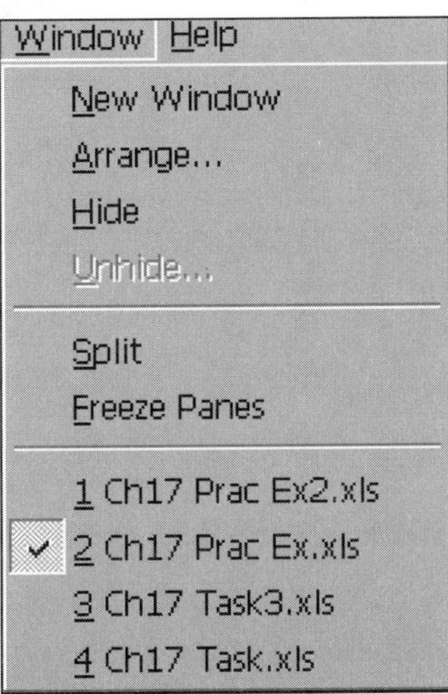

Figure 17.6 Workbook names on the Window menu.

Practice Exercise

It's the end of the first quarter and the National Sales Manager at Sandy Shores Company is comparing two sales reports: One workbook contains the sales figures for the Eastern territory and another workbook contains the sales figures for the Western territory. Your mission is to create linking formulas to calculate data on two sheets, then several sheets, and, finally, to link the two workbooks. Next, you will update the links and arrange the workbooks on the screen for easy viewing. Finally, you'll practice moving among the open workbooks in several ways.

Figure 17.7 shows what the Ch17 Prac Ex workbook contains before you go through the instructions in this exercise.

1. Open the Ch17 Prac Ex workbook file located on the companion disk.
2. Create a linking formula in cell A14 in the 1st Quarter sheet to link cell E11 in the 2nd Quarter.
3. Create a linking formula in cell A17 in the 1st Quarter sheet to total the expenses in the 1st Quarter, 2nd Quarter, and 3rd Quarter sheets.

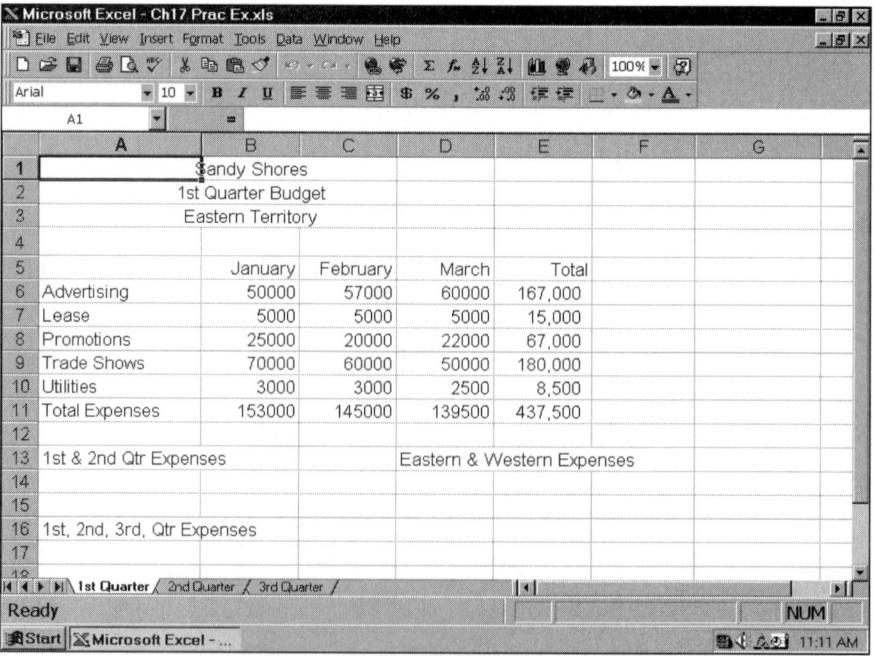

Figure 17.7 The Practice Exercise before you begin.

4. Open the Ch17 Prac Ex2 workbook file located on the companion disk.
5. Switch back to the Ch17 Prac Ex workbook.
6. In the Ch17 Prac Ex workbook, create a linking formula in cell D14 in the 1st Quarter sheet to link to cell E11 in the 1st Quarter sheet in the Ch17 Prac Ex2 workbook.
7. Switch to the Ch17 Prac Ex2 workbook. In the 1st Quarter sheet, in cell B6, change the number to 55000. Switch back to the Ch17 Prac Ex workbook. *Note:* The links update automatically.
8. In the Ch17 Prac Ex workbook, on the 1st Quarter sheet, copy and paste the range B6:C10 to the cell B25 on the 1st Quarter sheet in the Ch17 Prac Ex2 workbook.
9. Arrange both workbooks on the screen in a tiled fashion.
10. Use the Horizontal Arrange Windows option to arrange both workbooks.
11. Display both workbooks in a vertical arrangement.
12. Arrange the workbooks in a cascade fashion.
13. Move from one workbook to another using the mouse.
14. Navigate among the workbooks using the shortcuts keys.
15. Move to the Ch17 Prac Ex2 workbook with the Window menu.
16. Save the Ch17 Prac Ex2 workbook with the same name.
17. Close the Ch17 Prac Ex2 workbook.
18. Save the Ch17 Prac Ex workbook with the same name.
19. Close the Ch17 Prac Ex workbook.

Answers To Practice Exercise

1. Click the Open button on the Standard toolbar, and double-click the file name Ch17 Prac Ex.
2. Click cell A14 in the 1st Quarter sheet, and type "=". Click cell E11. Type "+" (plus sign). Then, click the 2nd Quarter sheet tab, and click cell E11. Press Enter. This creates a linking formula to link cell E11 on the 1st Quarter worksheet with cell E11 on the 2nd Quarter worksheet. The correct formula is =E11+'2nd Quarter'!E11. The correct answer is 875,000.
3. Click cell A17 in the 1st Quarter sheet, and type "=SUM('1st Quarter:3rd Quarter'!E11)". Press Enter. The correct result is 1,312,500. This linking formula links the data on the 1st Quarter, 2nd Quarter, and 3rd Quarter sheets.

4. Click the Open button on the Standard toolbar, and double-click the file name Ch17 Prac Ex2. This opens a second workbook.
5. Select Window, and choose Ch17 Prac Ex. This switches back to the first workbook.
6. In the Ch17 Prac Ex workbook, in the 1st Quarter sheet, click cell D14. Then, type "=". Select Window, and choose Ch17 Prac Ex2. Click cell E11 in the 1st Quarter sheet. Press Enter. The correct formula is ='[Ch17 Prac Ex2.xls]1st Quarter'!$E$11. The correct result is 437500. This links both workbooks.
7. Choose Window, and click Ch 17 Prac Ex2 at the bottom of the menu. This switches to the Ch 17 Prac Ex2 workbook. In cell B6, type "55000", then press Enter. This changes the number in the workbook. Choose Window, and click Ch 17 Prac Ex at the bottom of the menu. Notice the links update automatically because all associated workbooks are currently open. The correct answer is 442500.
8. In the Ch17 Prac Ex workbook, on the 1st Quarter sheet, select the range B6:C10. Click the Copy button on the Standard toolbar. Press Ctrl+F6. In the Ch17 Prac Ex2 workbook, on the 1st Quarter sheet, click cell B25. Click the Paste button on the Standard toolbar. This copies the data from the Ch17 Prac Ex workbook to the Ch17 Prac Ex2 workbook.
9. Choose Window, Arrange. Select the Tiled option, and click OK. This arranges both workbooks on the screen in a tiled fashion.
10. Choose Window, Arrange. Select the Horizontal option, and click OK. This arranges both workbooks in horizontal bands across the screen.
11. Choose Window, Arrange. Select the Vertical option, and click OK. This arranges both workbooks in vertical bands on the screen.

    When you get to this point in the Practice Exercise, your Ch17 Prac Ex workbook should look like the one in Figure 17.8.
12. Choose Window, Arrange. Select the Cascade option, and click OK. This arranges the workbooks in a cascade fashion.
13. Click the visible part of a workbook. This displays an entire workbook.
14. Press Ctrl+F6 to navigate the workbooks using the shortcuts keys.
15. Select Window, and choose Ch17 Prac Ex2. This should move you to the Ch17 Prac Ex2 workbook using the Window menu.

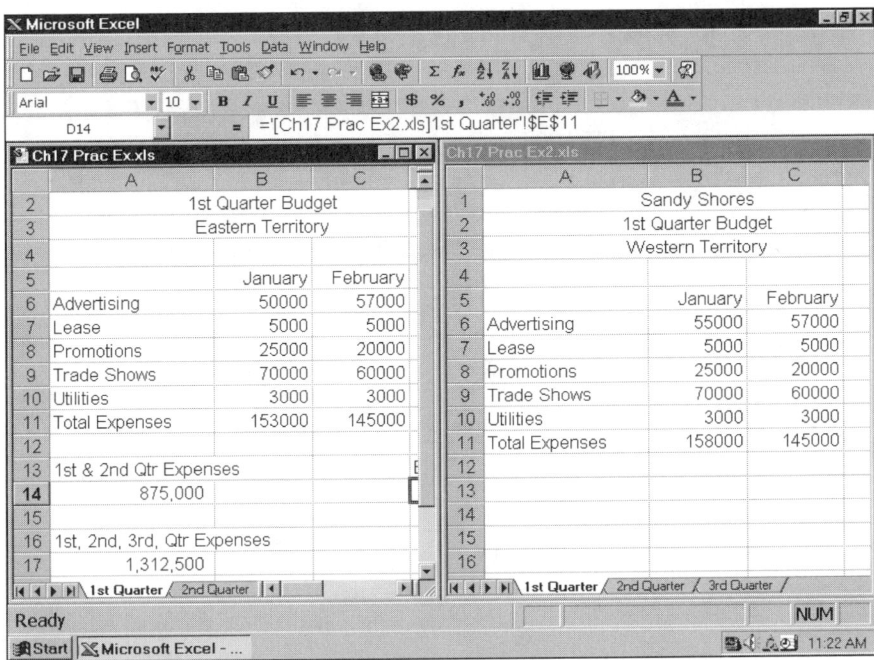

Figure 17.8 The completed Practice Exercise.

16. Click the Save button on the Standard toolbar to save the Ch17 Prac Ex2 workbook with the same name.
17. Click the Close (X) button in the upper-right corner of the Ch17 Prac Ex2 workbook window. This closes the workbook.
18. Click the Save button on the Standard toolbar to save the Ch17 Prac Ex workbook with the same name.
19. Click the Close (X) button in the upper-right corner of the workbook window. This closes the workbook.

Need To Know More?

Catapult, Inc.: *Microsoft Excel 97 Step By Step*. Microsoft Press, Redmond, WA, 1996. ISBN 1-57231-314-5. Lesson 1, "Working in the Excel Environment," tells you how to move and copy sheets. Lesson 5, "Consolidating Multiple Lists," discusses consolidating data from several worksheets. Lesson 13, "Integrating Microsoft Excel with Other Programs," covers linking worksheets and workbooks.

Craig, Deborah: *How to Use Microsoft Excel 97 for Windows*. Que, Indianapolis, IN, 1996. ISBN 1-56276-4617-1. Chapter 15, "Working with Multiple Worksheets," gives you information on copying and moving data between sheets and building formulas to link data.

Nicholson, John R. and Sean R. Nicholson: *Discover Excel 97*. IDG Books Worldwide, Inc., Foster City, CA, 1997. ISBN 1-7645-3047-X. Chapter 12, "Multiplicity: Working with More Than One Worksheet," explains how to work with multiple worksheets.

Nossiter, Josh: *Using Microsoft Excel 97*. Que, Indianapolis, IN, 1996. ISBN 0-78177-01755-4. Chapter 17, "Linking Workbooks, Sharing Workbooks," covers how to create formulas to link the data in workbooks.

18

Importing And Exporting Data

Terms you'll need to understand:

- √ Import
- √ Export
- √ External data
- √ Data source
- √ Query Wizard
- √ ASCII data
- √ Table
- √ Field
- √ Record

Skills you'll need to master:

- √ Choosing an external data source
- √ Importing ASCII data
- √ Exporting data to other applications

Using Excel To Transfer Data

Excel's list management features enable you to transfer data in two ways. You can *import* and *export* data using Excel. Unless you are going to type your data into Excel, you can import data into a worksheet. Importing data means that you automatically bring data in from whatever source currently holds it. This chapter shows you how to select a data source and import data from a database. You'll also learn how to import text files from other programs. Once your data is in Excel, you might want to export your data so that you can use it in another program. (Of course, you'll want to manage your data while it is in Excel. Chapters 19 and 20 explain how to manage data in an Excel database.) Exporting Excel data lets you save your Excel data as a different file type so that you can use it in another program. In this chapter, we'll focus on importing and exporting Excel data.

Before we go any further, let's review a few database terms that you need to understand when working with Excel lists and databases:

- **Field** One category of a record. A field can be thought of as a column in an Excel database. For example, Name, Address, and Zip Code are fields.
- **Record** A row of related fields. For example, a customer record can be a set of 10 fields of data, all relating to one customer.
- **Table** A collection of information arranged in rows and columns. For example, an Excel worksheet is a table. Tables are organized by topic or by related item, such as customers, serial numbers, and so forth. From a database perspective, the rows and columns equate to records and fields.

You can use Excel's Microsoft Query to perform several data import and export tasks. You can use Microsoft Query to perform complex query operations, but you can also do a lot with the Query Wizard, which uses Microsoft Query to obtain results. The Query Wizard is much easier to use, and you'll learn how to import data using the Query Wizard in this chapter.

Importing Data From Other Applications

Excel, Microsoft Query, and Query Wizard give you an opportunity to take advantage of the power of importing data. Microsoft Query helps you import data from a wide range of sources, including the following:

- Microsoft Excel
- Microsoft Access

- Microsoft FoxPro
- Microsoft SQL Server
- ASCII Text
- dBASE
- Paradox

The first time you use Query Wizard, you will need to define a new *data source* using the Create New Data Source feature. A data source tells the Query Wizard where to go to get data. After you use Query Wizard to access a data source, you can use the wizard to sort, filter, display, and send information to the application of your choice, such as Excel. You'll learn how to sort data in Chapter 19 and how to filter and display data in Chapter 20.

In some cases, you might want to import data that exists in ASCII or plain text format. This usually happens when you have another program that exports its data in this format, such as an accounting system. Excel uses its Text Import Wizard to help you bring in data that isn't formatted for Excel. When you import ASCII data, the Text Import Wizard steps you through a series of dialog boxes, asking you to choose options to define the ASCII data you're importing. You should always see what your ASCII data file actually contains in the Data Preview box in each Text Import Wizard dialog box. That way, you can easily choose the definition options you want. The definition options include the following:

- Original data type
- Delimiters
- Treat consecutive delimiters as one
- Text qualifier
- Column data format

HOLD That Skill!

When you define your ASCII data, you need to select from the available Text Import Wizard options. It's important to know what these options are:

- There are two original data type options: delimited and fixed width. A delimited file contains a character such as a comma, space, or tab that separates each field. A fixed-width file contains fields that are aligned in columns with spaces between each field. All fields are in exactly the same position on each line. Sometimes, the fields are all together, and it might be hard to see where each field begins and ends.

- Use the Data Preview area in the Text Import Wizard dialog boxes to see what the ASCII file actually contains. If the file contains heading information, set the Start Import At Row field to the number of lines that Excel should skip. For example, if you're importing an accounting report, the first few lines might contain report heading information that you really don't want in your Excel worksheet.
- In the Delimiters area, choose the appropriate character that will separate each field. The most common delimiter character is the comma. Other popular delimiters are tabs and spaces. If your files use more than one kind of delimiter, the Text Import Wizard allows you to choose multiple delimiters.
- The Treat Consecutive Delimiters As One option eliminates any empty fields from your data input. Often, a null field (empty field) will simply show up with, for example, two commas next to each other. Selecting this option causes Excel to skip empty fields. However, be careful about choosing this option, because it might leave you with data that isn't aligned in the correct column in the final worksheet.
- Many ASCII files distinguish text fields by enclosing the text within quotation marks or some other character. This lets Excel know which fields are text and which are numbers. If your files use a special extra delimiter for text fields, you can choose that character in the Text Qualifier drop-down list.
- The Column Data Format option lets you change the format for the data in each column. The default format is General; however, it's not a good idea to keep this choice for some types of fields. Sometimes, numeric data should be treated as text. For example, a product list might contain model numbers that lead with zeroes. If you import that column as General, the values will be entered into Excel as numbers, and any leading zeroes will be lost. You can prevent this from happening by choosing the Text option in the Column Data Format area. That way, Excel will treat the column as text and display the leading zeroes.

The following task steps you through the process of choosing an external data source by using the Create New Data Source feature.

Task 1 Choosing an external data source.

1. Open the Ch18 Task workbook located on your companion disk.
2. Choose Data|Get External Data.
3. Choose Create New Query. The Choose Data Source dialog box should open (see Figure 18.1). You should see <New Data Source> selected in the Databases tab.

   Note: If you are working on a network, your Choose Data Source dialog box may contain a list of different data sources than you see in Figure 18.1.

   Note: Be sure that the Use The Query Wizard To Create/Edit Queries checkbox is selected.

4. Click OK. The Create New Data Source dialog box should appear (see Figure 18.2). There are four steps in this dialog box. Notice that steps two through four are grayed out (unavailable). As you complete each step, the next becomes available. You need to complete only three of them. The fourth step is optional.
5. Next to step 1, type "My Data". This is the data file name that you're going to use for the data source.
6. In step 2, choose Microsoft Access Driver (*.mdb). This is the driver that will be used to access the data.

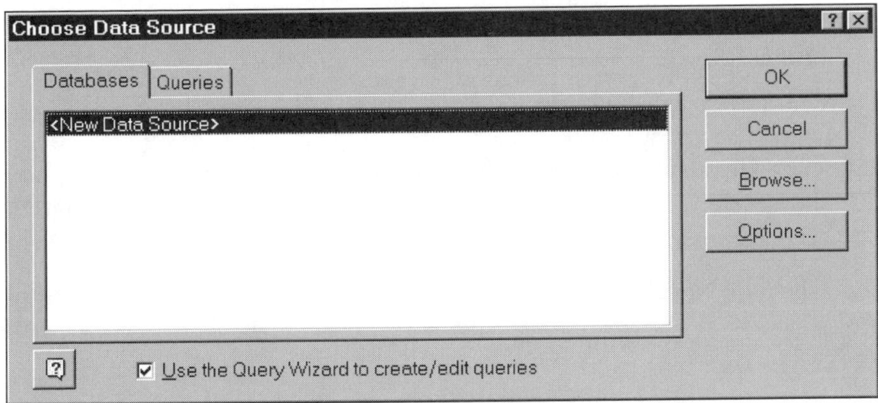

Figure 18.1 The Choose Data Source dialog box.

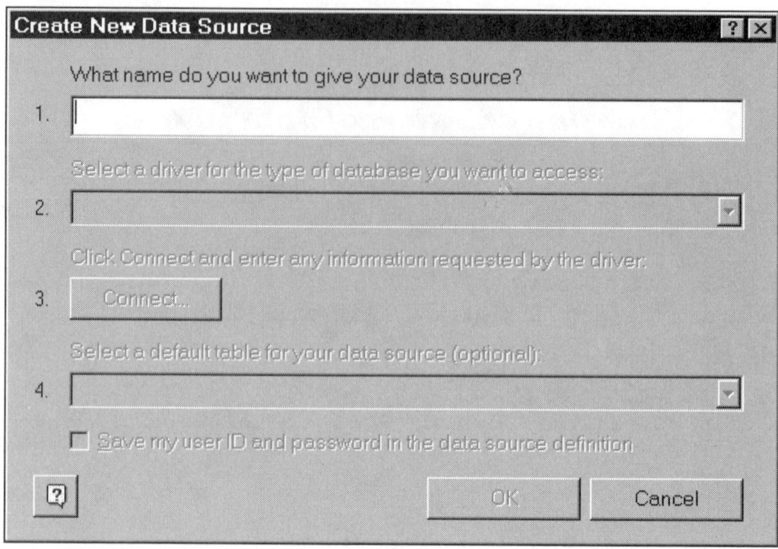

Figure 18.2 The Create New Data Source dialog box.

7. For step 3, click the Connect button. You should see a dialog box that lets you further define the data source.

8. Click the Select button, and double-click on the SALES94.mdb file name. Click OK.

9. Click OK again to close the Create New Data Source dialog box and return to the Choose Data Source dialog box. The My Data file should be selected.

10. Click OK. The Query Wizard should appear.

Note: If Microsoft Query is unavailable, it means that you chose the Typical installation option during Setup, and Microsoft Query is not installed on your computer. You'll need to install Microsoft Query by running the Microsoft Office 97 Setup program.

11. With Customers selected in the Available Tables And Columns box on the left side of the dialog box, click the right arrow button. This copies the Customer fields into the Columns In Your Query box on the right.

12. Click the Next button.

13. Click the Next button again.

14. Click the Next button one more time.

15. Click the Finish button.

16. Choose New Worksheet, and click OK.

The Query Wizard should place the imported data in a new worksheet called Sheet1. You should see the customer information from the SALES94 Microsoft Access database, as shown in Figure 18.3. The External Data toolbar should appear on screen.

Be sure you know how to create a new data source and create a new query that imports data from a Microsoft Access 97 database. You'll need to select fields in the Access database. Skip the Query Wizard dialog boxes that ask you to filter and sort the data, and Excel will bring you to the last dialog box. This is where you'll tell Excel to place the imported information in a specific cell on an Excel worksheet.

In the upcoming task, you'll import ASCII data into an Excel worksheet.

Task 2 Importing ASCII data.

1. Click the Open button on the Standard toolbar.
2. In the Files Of Type drop-down list, choose Text Files (*.prn; *.txt; *.csv).

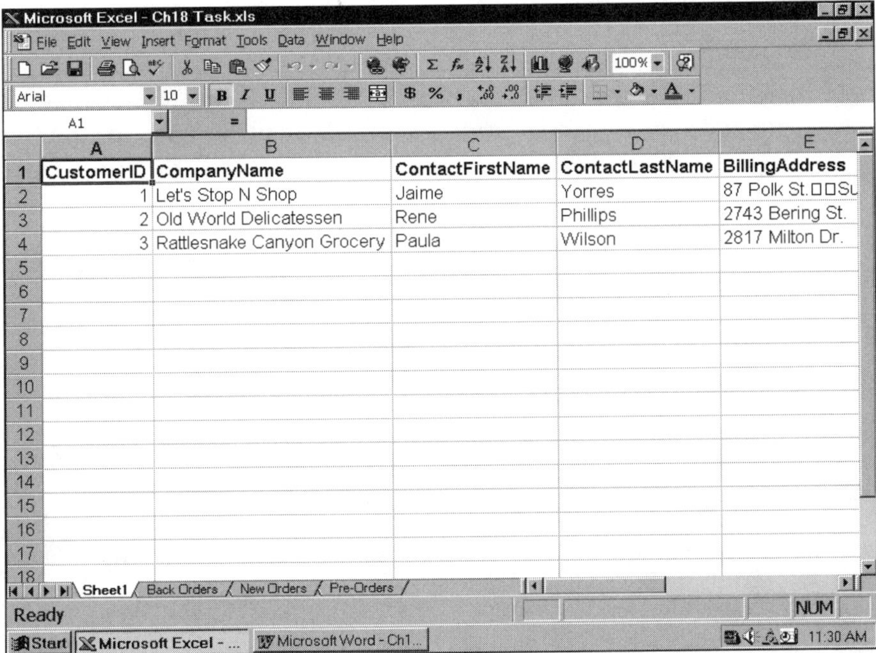

Figure 18.3 The customer information from the Access database.

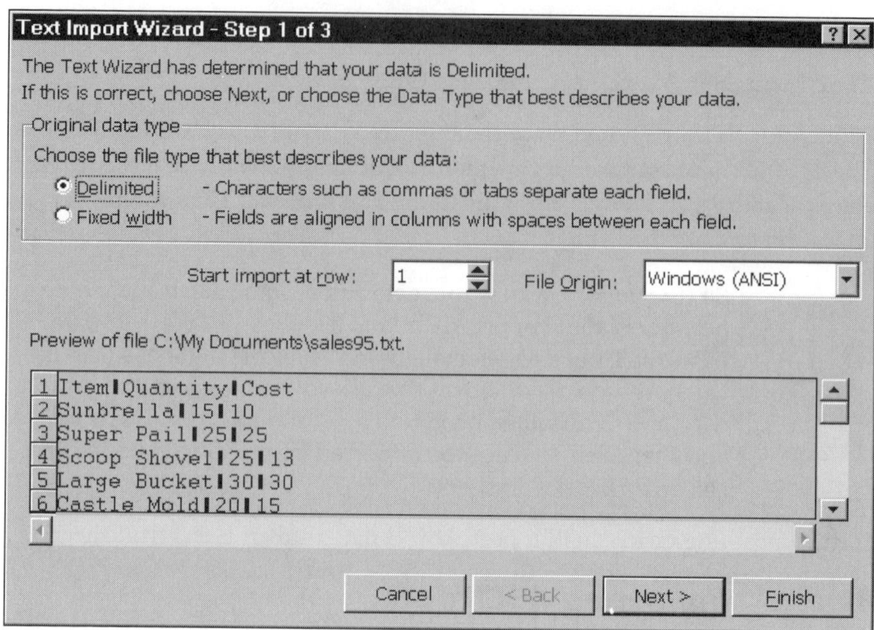

Figure 18.4 The Text Import Wizard—Step 1 Of 3 dialog box.

3. Choose the ASCII text file named sales95.txt, and click Open. The Text Import Wizard—Step 1 Of 3 dialog box should appear (see Figure 18.4). Notice the ASCII file in the Preview window at the bottom of the dialog box.

4. Click the Next button. The Text Import Wizard—Step 2 Of 3 dialog box should open. In the Delimiters area, Tab should be selected. You know this is correct because the data lines up in the preview box at the bottom of the dialog box.

5. Click the Next button. You should see the Text Import Wizard—Step 3 Of 3 dialog box.

6. Click the Finish button.

   The Import Text Wizard should place the imported data in a workbook called SALES95.txt and on a worksheet called sales95, as shown in Figure 18.5.

7. Close the SALES95 workbook. The workbook closes without prompting you to save it.

It's essential to know how to import a text file in Excel.

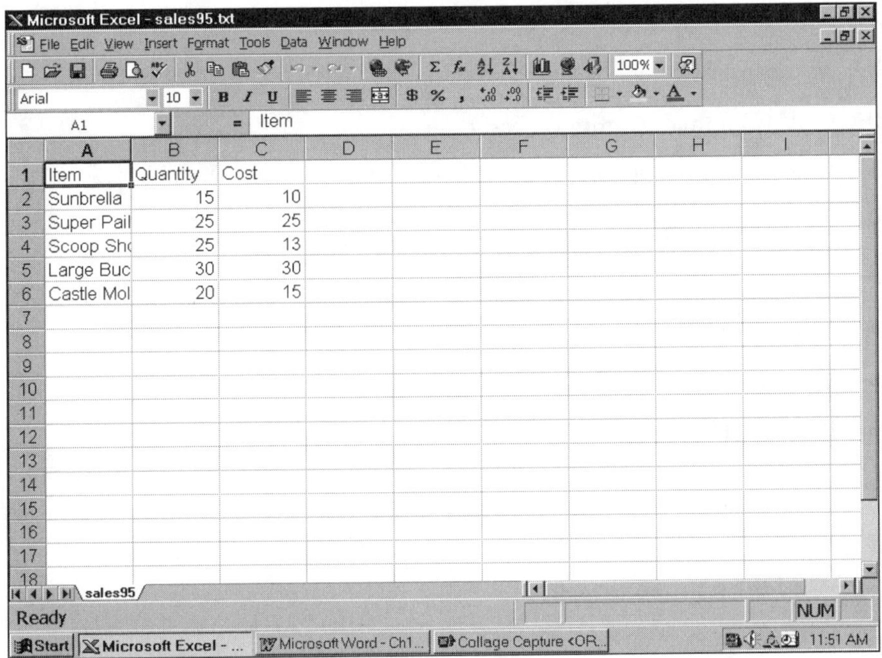

Figure 18.5 The imported data in the sales 95 worksheet in the SALES95.TXT workbook.

Exporting Data To Other Applications

What if you want to share information between Excel and another Office program. You can make use of the information you create in Excel in other Office programs, and vice versa. Depending on how you want the information to appear, you can share the information in various ways. For example, you can update the information if the original file changes and choose with whom you want to share the information. When you want to use an Excel workbook in another program, you simply save the workbook in a format the other program can use. The formats appear in the Save As Type drop-down list in the Save As dialog box.

You can save your Excel workbook in the following formats:

- Microsoft Excel Workbook (*.xls)
- Template (*.xlt)
- Formatted Text (Space delimited) (*.prn)
- Text (Tab delimited) (*.txt)

- Microsoft Excel 5.0/95 Workbook (*.xls)
- Microsoft Excel 97 & 5.0/95 Workbook (*.xls)
- CSV (Comma delimited) (*.csv)
- Microsoft Excel 4.0 Worksheet (*.xls)
- Microsoft Excel 3.0 Worksheet (*.xls)
- Microsoft Excel 2.1 Worksheet (*.xls)
- Microsoft Excel 4.0 Workbook (*.xlw)
- WK4 (1-2-3) (*.wk4)
- WK3,FM3 (1-2-3) (*.wk3)
- WK3 (1-2-3) (*.wk3)
- WK3,FMT (1-2-3) (*.wk1)
- WK1,ALL (1-2-3) (*.wk1)
- WK1 (1-2-3) (*.wk1)
- WKS (1-2-3) (*.wks)
- WQ1 (Quattro Pro/DOS) (*.wq1)
- DBF 4 (dBASE IV) (*.dbf)
- DBF 3 (dBASE III) (*.dbf)
- DBF 2 (dBASE II) (*.dbf)
- Text (Macintosh) (*.txt)
- Text (OS/2 or MS-DOS) (*.txt)
- CSV (Macintosh) (*.csv)
- CSV (OS/2 or MS-DOS) (*.csv)
- DIF (Data Interchange Format) (*.dif)
- SYLK (Symbolic Link) (*.slk)
- Microsoft Excel Add-In (*.xla)

Unless a complete Excel 97 installation was done, all of the above mentioned filters may not be available. To make them available, run the Microsoft Office 97 Setup program.

The following task demonstrates how to export data in an Excel worksheet to another application. You'll save the file in a tab-delimited text format and store it in the specified directory.

Task 3 Exporting data to other applications.

1. With the Ch18 Task workbook on the screen, choose File|Save As. You should see the Save As dialog box.
2. Click the Save As Type drop-down arrow. You should see a list of file formats.
3. Choose Text (Tab delimited) (*.txt). (See Figure 18.6.)
4. In the File Name box, type "My Export".
5. In the Save In box, choose the My Documents directory.
6. Click Save.

   Excel displays a dialog box informing you that only the current worksheet is saved.
7. Click OK to continue.

   Excel should save your file in the tab-delimited text format in the My Documents directory. You should see a message informing you that the selected file type doesn't support workbooks that contain multiple sheets and asking if you want to save the active sheet or all the sheets.
8. Click OK to save the active sheet.

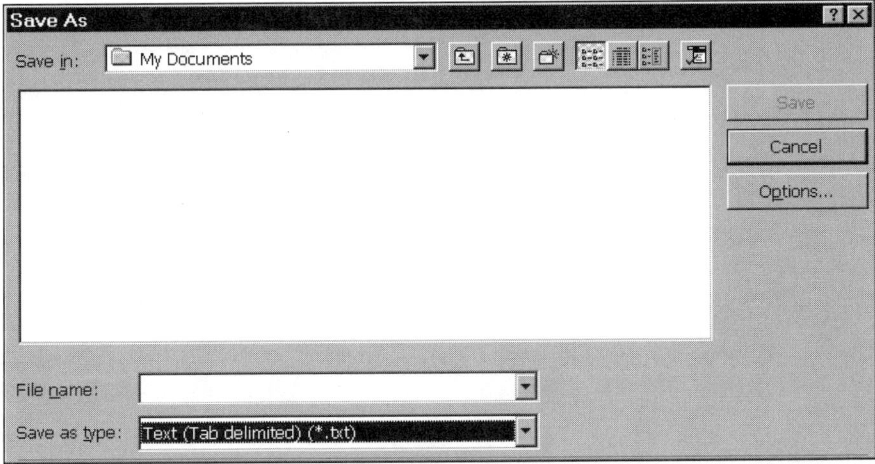

Figure 18.6 The Text (Tab delimited) format selected in the Save As dialog box.

9. Close the My Export workbook. You should see a message stating that the file isn't saved in an Excel 97 format and asking if you want to save the changes.
10. Click No. This saves the file in the TXT format and closes the workbook.

You'll need to know how to export a worksheet as a tab-delimited text file. You'll be instructed to save the file with a particular file name and in a specific directory.

Practice Exercise

The Sandy Shores Company has been using Microsoft Access to manage its databases. One particular Access database named sales94 needs to be imported into Excel. Also, an Excel worksheet needs to be exported to another application in a different format. You'll need to perform these tasks, because you're the resident Excel expert. You're going to create a new query for an external data source, import ASCII data, and export data.

Figure 18.7 shows what the worksheet contains before you go through the instructions in this exercise.

1. Open the Ch18 Prac Ex workbook located on your companion disk.
2. Create a new query that imports data from the Microsoft Access 97 database sales94.mdb file. (*Note:* Create a new data source.) Name the new data source My Data 2. Select the Orders columns. Place the imported information in a new worksheet.
3. Import the ASCII data file named sales95.txt.
4. Export the Sales Records worksheet in the Ch18 Prac Ex workbook as a tab-delimited text file with the name My Export 2.TXT

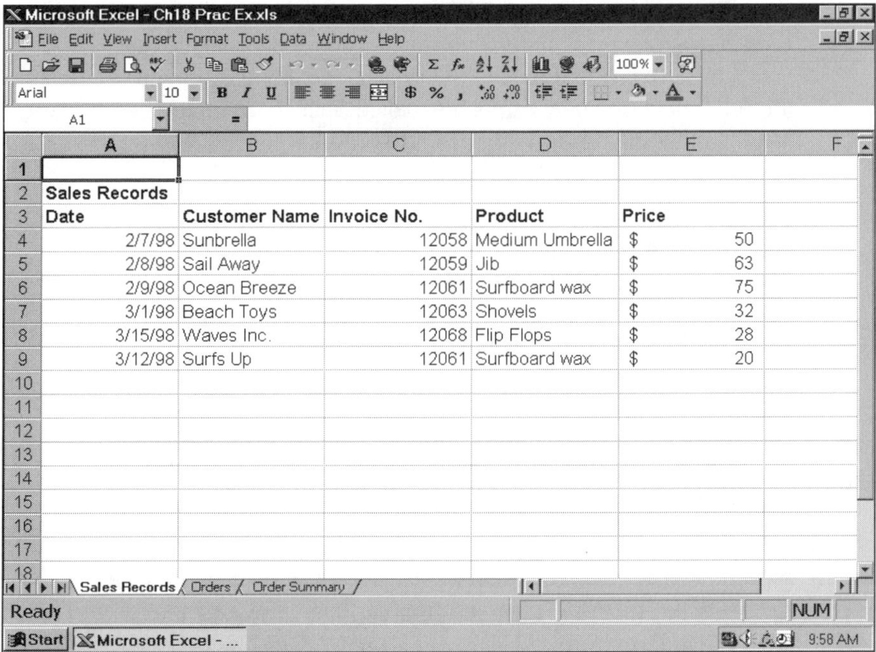

	A	B	C	D	E
1					
2	Sales Records				
3	Date	Customer Name	Invoice No.	Product	Price
4	2/7/98	Sunbrella	12058	Medium Umbrella	$ 50
5	2/8/98	Sail Away	12059	Jib	$ 63
6	2/9/98	Ocean Breeze	12061	Surfboard wax	$ 75
7	3/1/98	Beach Toys	12063	Shovels	$ 32
8	3/15/98	Waves Inc.	12068	Flip Flops	$ 28
9	3/12/98	Surfs Up	12061	Surfboard wax	$ 20

Figure 18.7 The Practice Exercise before you begin.

into the My Documents directory. Save only the active sheet and close the workbook without saving any changes.

Answers To Practice Exercise

1. Click the Open button on the Standard toolbar, and double-click the file name Ch18 Prac Ex.
2. Choose Data|Get External Data. Choose Create New Query. The Choose Data Source dialog box opens. You should see <New Data Source> selected in the Databases tab. Click OK. The Create New Data Source dialog box appears. Next to step 1, type "My Data 2". This is the data file name that you're going to use for the data source. In step 2, choose Microsoft Access Driver (*.mdb). This is the driver that will be used to access the data. For step 3, click the Connect button. A dialog box displays that lets you further define the data source. Click the Select button, and double-click on the SALES94.mdb file name. Click OK. Click OK again to close the Create New Data Source dialog box and return to the Choose Data Source dialog box. The My Data 2 file should be selected. Click OK. The Query Wizard should appear. Select Orders in the Available Tables And Columns box on the left side of the dialog box. Then, click the right arrow button. This copies the Orders fields into the Columns In Your Query box on the right. Click the Next button. Click the Next button again. Click the Next button one more time. Click the Finish button. Choose New Worksheet, and click OK. The Query Wizard should place the imported data in a new worksheet called Sheet1. You should see the customer information from the SALES94 Microsoft Access database.
3. Click the Open button on the Standard toolbar. In the Files of Type drop-down list, choose Text Files (*.prn; *.txt; *.csv). Choose the ASCII text file named sales95.txt, and click Open. The Text Import Wizard—Step 1 Of 3 dialog box appears. Notice the ASCII file in the Preview window at the bottom of the dialog box. Click the Next button. The Text Import Wizard—Step 2 Of 3 dialog box opens. In the Delimiters area, make sure Tab is selected. Click the Next button. You see the Text Import Wizard—Step 3 Of 3 dialog box. Click the Finish button. Excel places the imported data in a workbook called SALES95.TXT. Close the workbook.
4. Click the Sales Records sheet tab. Choose File|Save As. The Save As dialog box displays. Click the Save As Type drop-down arrow. A list of file formats displays. Choose Text (Tab delimited) (*.txt), if necessary. In the File Name box, type "My Export 2". In the

Save In box, choose the My Documents directory. Click Save. This exports the data as a tab-delimited text file with the name My Export 2.TXT into the MY DOCUMENTS directory. Click OK to save the active sheet. Click the Close Window (X) button in the upper-right corner of the document window. Click No. This saves the workbook in its existing format and then closes it.

When you finish the practice exercise, your worksheet should look like the one in Figure 18.8.

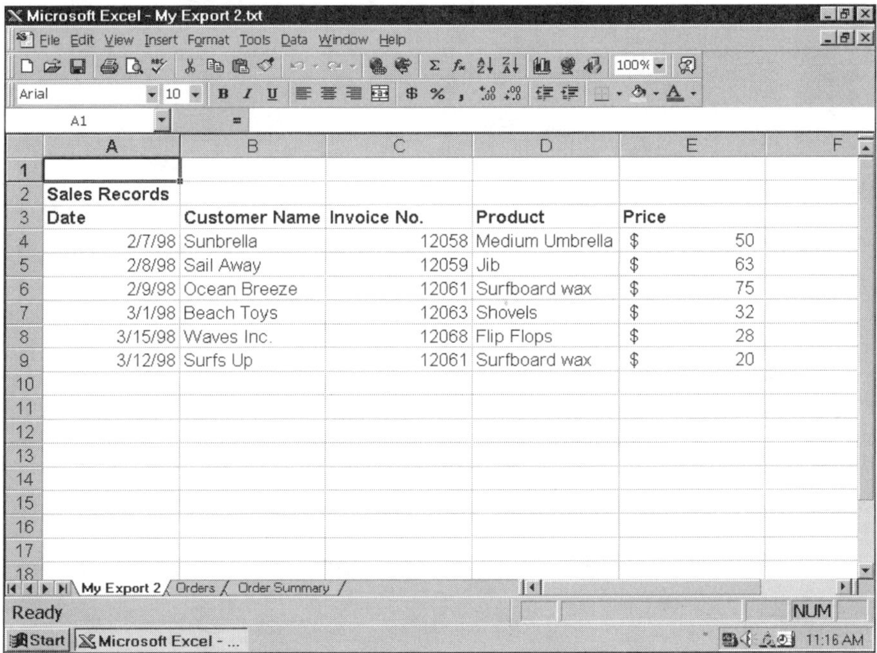

Figure 18.8 The completed Practice Exercise.

Need To Know More?

Catapult, Inc.: *Microsoft Excel 97 Step By Step*. Microsoft Press, Redmond, WA, 1996. ISBN 1-57231-314-5. Lesson 8, "Creating Pivot Tables to Summarize Data," covers how to get external data into a worksheet.

Nossiter, Josh: *Using Microsoft Excel 97*. Que, Indianapolis, IN, 1996. ISBN 0-7897-0955-4. Chapter 20, "Exchanging Data with Other Programs," has a good discussion on importing data from other programs and exporting data to other programs.

19

Managing Data With An External Database

Terms you'll need to understand:

- √ Sort
- √ Field
- √ Sort key
- √ Ascending order
- √ Descending order
- √ Query Wizard

Skills you'll need to master:

- √ Sorting a list with Data Sort
- √ Sorting data using a custom sort order
- √ Sorting data with Query Wizard
- √ Querying data using the Query Wizard

Using Excel Lists

In an Excel list, you can sort the data and arrange the rows of a database list in a particular order, based on the contents of the fields or columns. The Sort feature allows you to sort your data in ascending or descending order. You can use the Data Sort command or the Query Wizard to sort your data. The Data Sort command sorts data in an Excel list or database. The Query Wizard sorts data in an external database. Querying data is the process of retrieving specific information from a database to create a list in an Excel worksheet. Excel's Query Wizard lets you create a simple query to retrieve data in an external database and place that data in an Excel worksheet. You can also filter and sort data in an external database and place the imported data in an Excel worksheet. In this chapter, you'll learn how to sort data in an Excel list using the Data Sort command, and you'll learn how to query data using the Query Wizard.

Sorting Data

There are a couple of ways to sort your data in Excel:

- Use Excel's Data Sort command to sort data in an Excel list.
- Use the Query Wizard to sort data in an external database.

Either way you sort your data, you can specify how Excel should reorder the data rows. If you specify an *ascending* sort order, the lowest number, the beginning of the alphabet, or the earliest date appears first in the list. Excel uses the following order for an ascending sort:

- Numbers
- Text and text that includes numbers
- Logical values
- Error values
- Blanks

Descending order starts with the highest number, the end of the alphabet, or the latest date. Sorting in descending order reverses the order mentioned in the preceding list, except for blanks, which are always sorted last.

The Data Sort command enables you to perform simple sort operations as well as complex sorts. You can do a simple sort operation by sorting one or more columns of data in ascending and descending order. The first field (column), called a *key*, that you choose to sort by is called the *primary sort*. The second field, or second key, you specify is called the *secondary sort*. The second sort field is only used if there is duplicate data in the first sort field. If you select a third field (key) for the sort operation, that is a called a *tertiary sort*. The third sort field is only used if there is duplicate data in the first and second sort fields. If your rows have row headings, you can use the Sort dialog box to choose an option in the My List Has area to specify that your rows contain labels. If your rows do not have row headings, the My List Has area in the Sort dialog box is unavailable.

With a more complex sort operation, the Data Sort command lets you specify certain information about your data to refine the sort results. When you select Data|Sort and click the Options button in the Data Sort dialog box, you should see the following sort options:

- First Key Sort Order
- Case Sensitive
- Orientation

The First Key Sort Order option lets you sort your data based on the names of the week, days, and months. For instance, if your primary sort is by names of the month, you can specify the first key sort order by selecting January, February, March, and so on, in the First Key Sort Order list. If you want a sort dependent on upper- and lowercase, you can choose the Case Sensitive option when you sort data in a list. By default, Excel sorts data from top to bottom; however, you can ask Excel to sort a list from left to right instead. The Sort Left To Right option in the Orientation area lets you do this.

HOLD That Skill!

The following guidelines should be considered when sorting data in Excel:

- Use the Data Sort command to sort data in an Excel list.
- Use the Query Wizard to sort data in an external database, and then place the sorted data in an Excel worksheet.
- Before you perform any sort operation, be sure to select the range you want to sort. If you select the column headings in the list, Excel will automatically identify that the column headings are present. However, you might want to check the Header Row option in the My List Has area in the Sort dialog box to ensure that the header rows are activated. Then, Excel will not sort the column heading with the other data in the list. If your list does not have field names, choose the No Header Row option in the My List Has area.

- Specify ascending order to sort data from 0 through 9 and A through Z.
- Specify descending order to sort data from Z through A and 9 through 0.
- Specify any special sort options to refine your data sort results. For example, you can specify the first key sort order, determine whether you want the sort to be dependent on uppercase and lowercase letters, choose the sort orientation (top to bottom or left to right), and tell Excel what your list contains, such as row headings.

In Chapter 4, you learned how to sort data using the Sort Ascending button on the Standard toolbar to do a simple sort. You sorted by one column of data in a worksheet. In the next two tasks, you'll see how to use the Data Sort command to sort data in a list. In Task 1, you'll perform a simple sort based on two columns in ascending order. In Task 2, you'll perform a more complex sort using a custom sort order that sorts data by month, depends on uppercase letters, and sorts the list from left to right.

Task 1 Sorting a list with Data Sort.

1. Open the Ch19 Task workbook located on your companion disk.
2. In the Back Orders sheet, select cells A4:G13.

   Note: Ensure that the full width of the list is selected. If you neglect to include some columns, Excel will not sort them with the other data, resulting in scrambled records. If you sort by columns, the same problem can occur if you do not select the full column height. If this happens, or for any other reason you do not like the results of the sort, you can undo the sort immediately by using the Edit|Undo command, pressing Ctrl+Z, or clicking the Undo button on the Standard toolbar.

3. Select Data|Sort. The Sort dialog box should appear, as shown in Figure 19.1. Notice that Excel has automatically detected the header row, even though it was not selected. In the My List Has area, be sure the Header Row option is selected. This ensures that the field names will not be sorted among the data.

If you want to sort by one field (column), you can use the Sort Ascending and Sort Descending buttons on the Standard toolbar to quickly sort your list. Excel will sort the entire list, except column headings. These buttons use the default sort options described earlier in this chapter.

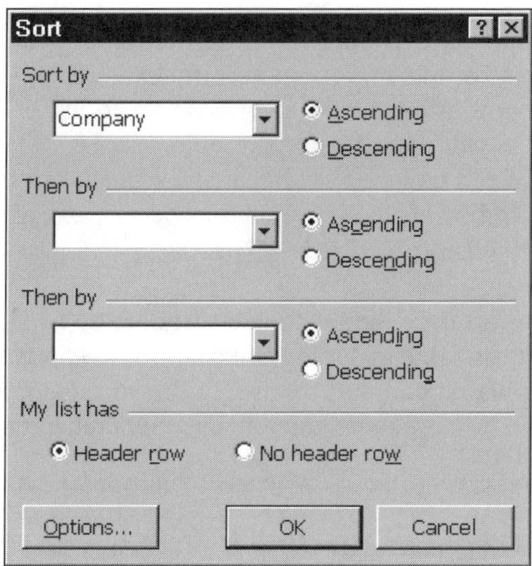

Figure 19.1 The Sort dialog box.

4. Click the Sort By drop-down arrow to see the field headings.
5. Choose Company. This is the name of the first field (primary sort field) by which you want to sort.

   Note: If your data does not have labels (column headings) in a header row (first row), then, select the first cell at the top of the column by which you want to sort.

6. Ascending is the default sort order. Make sure this option is selected.
7. Click the Then By drop-down arrow.
8. Choose Date. This is the name of the secondary sort field by which you want to sort.
9. Ascending is the default sort order. Make sure this option is selected.
10. Click OK.
11. Click any cell to deselect the range.

Excel should sort the data in alphabetical order according to the company names in Column A and the dates in Column B, from top to bottom. Where the company names are the same, the records are sorted in ascending order based on the Date field.

If you want to sort a column that contains both numbers and numbers that contain text characters (for example, 1, 1A, 2, 2A), format all the entries as text, so they will sort together. Otherwise, the numbers will sort first (for example, 1, 2, 1A, 2A). Also, the alignment would be incorrect, because Excel aligns numbers left and text right, by default. To format numbers as text, precede the number with an apostrophe (such as '1).

It's important to know how to sort data by two fields. Be sure to select the table including the column headings and exclude the last row that contains totals. Use the Sort dialog box to sort a field in descending order and another field in descending order.

In the upcoming task, you'll see how to sort columns based on row contents.

Task 2 Sorting data using a custom sort order.

1. In the Back Orders sheet, select cells A4:G13.
2. Select Data|Sort. The Sort dialog box should display.
3. In the My List Has area, be sure the Header Row option is selected. This ensures that the field names will not be sorted among the data.
4. Click the Options button. The Sort Options dialog box should appear, as shown in Figure 19.2.
5. In the Orientation area, choose the Sort Left To Right option.
6. Click OK. The Sort Options dialog box closes.
7. In the Sort By drop-down list, choose the row name Row 3.
8. Click OK.
9. Click any cell to deselect the range.

   Excel should sort the data from left to right in Row 3.

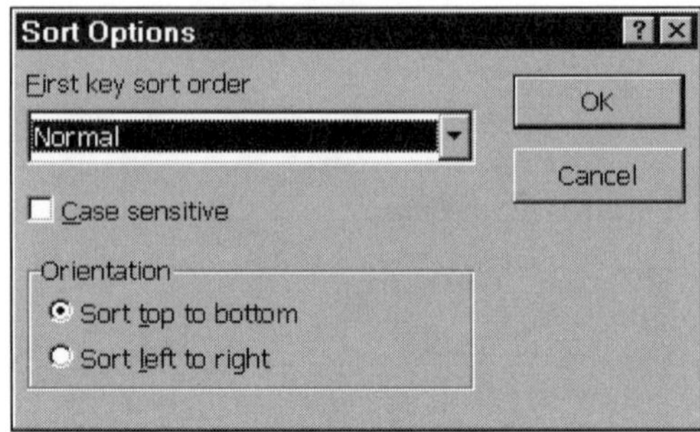

Figure 19.2 The Sort Options dialog box.

In the following task, you'll perform a simple sort using the Query Wizard to sort three fields (columns) and specify to sort the third field in descending order.

Task 3 Sorting data with Query Wizard.

1. In the Back Orders sheet, choose Data|Get External Data.
2. Choose Create New Query. The Choose Data Source dialog box should open. You should see <New Data Source> selected in the Databases tab.
3. Click OK. The Create New Data Source dialog box should appear.
4. Next to step 1 on the Create New Data Source dialog box, type "My Sort Data". This is the name of the database query you are creating.
5. In step 2, choose Microsoft Access Driver (*.mdb). This is the driver that will be used to access the data.
6. For step 3, click the Connect button. You should see a dialog box that lets you further define the data source.
7. Click the Select button, choose sales94.mdb, and click OK.
8. Click OK, then click OK again. This should close the Create New Data Source dialog box and return you to the Choose Data Source dialog box. The My Sort Data file should be selected.
9. Click OK. The Query Wizard should appear.
10. In the Available Tables And Columns list, choose Customers. Click the right arrow button to display the fields in the box on the right.
11. Click the Next button.
12. Click the Next button again, to continue. The Query Wizard—Sort Order dialog box should appear, as shown in Figure 19.3.
13. In the Sort By list, choose CustomerID. Specify ascending order.
14. Click the Next button.
15. Click the Save Query button.
16. Type "Customer ID Query from My Sort Data" for the query name, and click the Save button. Excel automatically adds the DQY file type to the query file name.
17. Click the Finish button.
18. Select the New Worksheet option, and click OK.

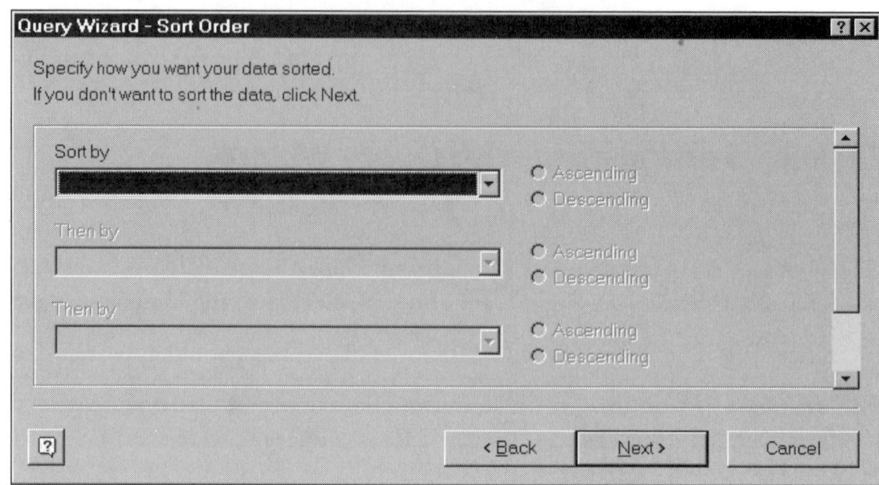

Figure 19.3 The Query Wizard—Sort Order dialog box.

The Query Wizard should place the data in a new worksheet called Sheet1.

Note: When you want to run the query again, simply choose Data|Get External Data, and select Run Database Query. Then, choose the query name by double-clicking it. The Query Wizard will run the query and ask you to specify in which cell on the worksheet you want the data to appear. Click a cell in the worksheet, and click OK. Excel will display the data starting in the cell you selected.

Querying Data

Querying data in a database can be quite complex, but Query Wizard makes it much easier to set up queries that perform exactly as intended. Query Wizard will walk you through the process of querying data, making it as quick and painless as possible. You choose the columns you want to include in your query by double-clicking the column names in the Query Wizard—Choose Columns dialog box. Then, you can save the query to use over and over.

The following task illustrates how to query data using the Query Wizard.

Task 4 Querying data using the Query Wizard.

1. Click the Back Orders sheet tab.
2. Choose Data|Get External Data.

3. Choose Create New Query. The Choose Data Source dialog box should open.
4. Click OK. The Create New Data Source dialog box should appear.
5. Next to step 1 on the Create New Data Source dialog box, type "My First Query". This is the data file name you're going to use for the data source.
6. In step 2, choose Microsoft Access Driver (*.mdb). This is the driver that will be used to access the data.
7. For step 3, click the Connect button. You should see a dialog box that lets you further define the data source.
8. Click the Select button, choose sales94.mdb, and click OK.
9. Click OK, then click OK again. This should close the Create New Data Source dialog box and return you to the Choose Data Source dialog box. The My First Query file should be selected.
10. Click OK. The Query Wizard should appear.
11. In the Available Tables And Columns list, choose Orders. Click the right arrow button to display the fields in the box on the right.
12. Click the Next button. The Query Wizard—Filter Data dialog box should open.
13. In the Column To Filter list, choose OrderDate. On the right, click the drop-down arrow for OrderDate, and choose Is Greater Than. Then, click the drop-down arrow in the next box on the right, and choose 1995-02-01 00:00:00. See Figure 19.4.

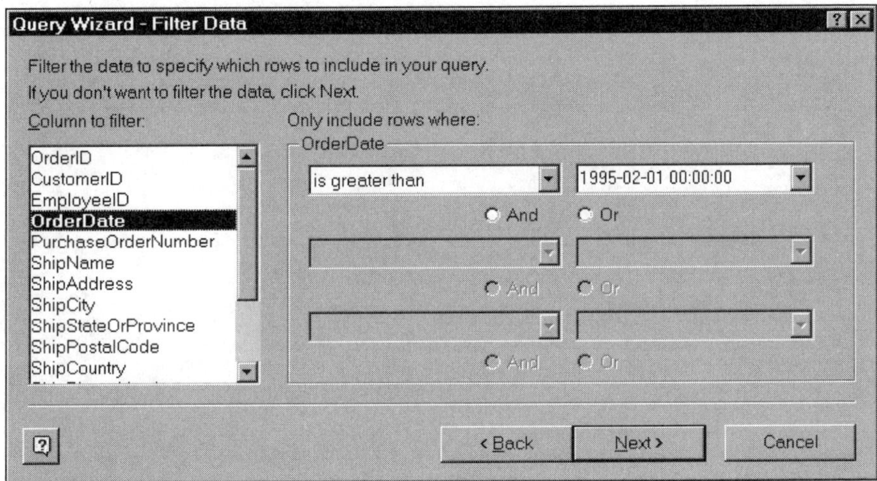

Figure 19.4 The Query Wizard—Filter Data dialog box.

14. Click the Next button to continue. The Query Wizard—Sort Order dialog box should open.
15. In the Sort By list, choose EmployeeID. Specify ascending order.
16. Click the Next button.
17. Click the Save Query button.
18. Type "Order Date Query from My First Query" for the query name, and click the Save button.
19. Click the Finish button.
20. Click cell A17 on the Back Orders sheet, and click OK.

    The Query Wizard should place the data in the Back Orders worksheet starting in cell A17.
21. Browse the records. Notice only certain records have been selected—those meeting the specified criteria. This is fewer than the original records contained in the unfiltered database file. Also, notice that the records are now sorted according to the Employee ID field.

Be sure you know how to create a new query that imports data from a Microsoft Access 97 database (you'll be given the name of the Access database). You'll need to create a new data source and select fields for the query. A field will need to be sorted in descending order. Then, you'll have to save the query with a specified query name. Finally, you'll be required to place the imported information into a specific cell on a worksheet.

Practice Exercise

In Chapter 18's Practice Exercise, the Sandy Shores Company needed to import a Microsoft Access database into Excel. You created a new data source to accomplish this. Now, the marketing manager at Sandy Shores Company has requested that you execute a query to retrieve specific data in the external database and create a list in Excel. In this Practice Exercise, you'll be using the same Microsoft Access database that you used in the Chapter 18 Practice Exercise, which is called sales94.mdb.

Figure 19.5 shows what the worksheet contains before you go through the instructions in this exercise.

1. Open the Ch19 Prac Ex workbook.
2. In the Sales Records worksheet, sort the data by Customer Name in ascending order and the Price in descending order.
3. In the Sales Records worksheet, sort the data by row 3 in ascending order from left to right. Widen column A, if necessary.
4. Create a new query called Sort Customer using the sales94.mdb file. (*Hint:* Do not close the Query Wizard.)
5. Use the Query Wizard to sort the Customer data by Customer ID in ascending order.

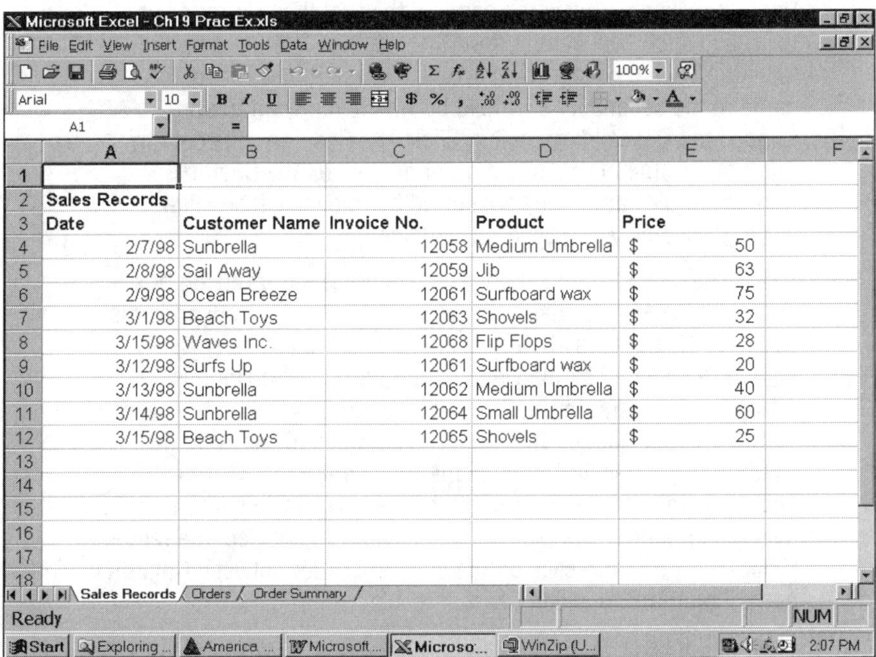

Figure 19.5 The Practice Exercise before you begin.

6. Import the sorted data into cell A15 on the Sales Records worksheet.
7. In the Sales Records worksheet, create a new query that imports data from the Microsoft Access 97 database sales94.mdb file. (*Hint:* Create a new data source, but don't close the Query Wizard.) Name the query file My Customer.
8. Display the fields for the Orders table.
9. Filter the CustomerID field using the criteria Is Less Than 3.
10. Put the field Customer ID in descending order.
11. Save the query as Customer ID Query from My Customer.
12. Place the imported information in A25 on the Sales Records worksheet.
13. Save the workbook with the same name.
14. Close the workbook.

Answers To Practice Exercise

1. Click the Open button on the Standard toolbar, and double-click the file name Ch19 Prac Ex.
2. Select cells A4:E12. Choose Data|Sort. The Sort dialog box should appear. Click the Sort By drop-down arrow. Choose Customer Name. This is the name of the first field (primary sort field) by which you want to sort. Choose the Ascending option. Click the Then By drop-down arrow. Choose Price. This is the name of the secondary sort field by which you want to sort. Choose the Descending option. Click OK. This sorts the data by Customer Name in ascending order and, when the Customer Names are the same, they are sorted by Price in descending order. Click any cell to deselect the range.
3. Select cells A4:E12, and choose Data|Sort. The Sort dialog box opens. In the My List Has area, be sure the Header Row option is selected. This ensures that the field names will not be sorted among the data. Click the Options button. The Sort Options dialog box appears. In the Orientation area, choose the Sort Left To Right option. Click OK. The Sort dialog box displays. In the Sort By drop-down list, choose the row name Row 3. Click OK. This sorts the data by Row 3 (the header row) from left to right in the Sales Records worksheet. Click any cell to deselect the range. If necessary, double-click on the column border between Column A and Column B to widen Column A.
4. Choose Data|Get External Data. Choose Create New Query. The Choose Data Source dialog box opens. You should see <New

Data Source> selected in the Databases tab. Click OK. The Create New Data Source dialog box appears. Next to step 1, type "Sort Customer". This is the data file name you're going to use for the data source. In step 2, choose Microsoft Access Driver (*.mdb). This is the driver that will be used to access the data. For step 3, click the Connect button. A dialog box that lets you further define the data source appears. Click the Select button. Choose sales94.mdb, and click OK. Click OK, then click OK again. This closes the Create New Data Source dialog box and returns you to the Choose Data Source dialog box. The Sort Customer file is selected. Click OK. The Query Wizard appears. In the Available Tables And Columns list, choose Customers. Click the right arrow button to display the fields in the box on the right.

5. Click the Next button. Click the Next button to continue. The Query Wizard—Sort Order dialog box opens. In the Sort By list, choose CustomerID. Specify ascending order. Click the Next button. Click the Finish button.

6. Click cell A15 on the Sales Records worksheet, and click OK. This sorts the data by Customer ID in ascending order and places the imported data beginning in cell A on the Sales Records worksheet (see Figure 19.6).

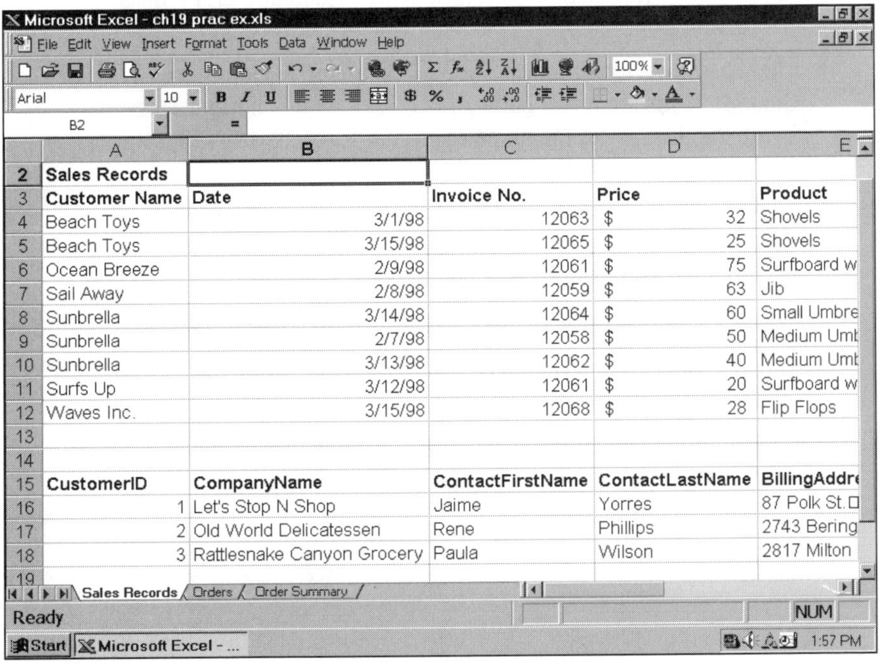

	A	B	C	D	E
2	Sales Records				
3	Customer Name	Date	Invoice No.	Price	Product
4	Beach Toys	3/1/98	12063	$ 32	Shovels
5	Beach Toys	3/15/98	12065	$ 25	Shovels
6	Ocean Breeze	2/9/98	12061	$ 75	Surfboard w
7	Sail Away	2/8/98	12059	$ 63	Jib
8	Sunbrella	3/14/98	12064	$ 60	Small Umbre
9	Sunbrella	2/7/98	12058	$ 50	Medium Umb
10	Sunbrella	3/13/98	12062	$ 40	Medium Umb
11	Surfs Up	3/12/98	12061	$ 20	Surfboard w
12	Waves Inc.	3/15/98	12068	$ 28	Flip Flops
13					
14					
15	CustomerID	CompanyName	ContactFirstName	ContactLastName	BillingAddre
16	1	Let's Stop N Shop	Jaime	Yorres	87 Polk St.
17	2	Old World Delicatessen	Rene	Phillips	2743 Bering
18	3	Rattlesnake Canyon Grocery	Paula	Wilson	2817 Milton

Figure 19.6 The completed Sort Customer query Practice Exercise.

7. Choose Data|Get External Data. Choose Create New Query. The Choose Data Source dialog box opens. You should see <New Data Source> selected in the Databases tab. Click OK. The Create New Data Source dialog box appears. Next to step 1, type "My Customer". This is the data file name you're going to use for the data source. In step 2, choose Microsoft Access Driver (*.mdb). This is the driver that will be used to access the data. For step 3, click the Connect button. You should see a dialog box that lets you further define the data source. Click the Select button. Choose sales94.mdb, and click OK. Click OK, then click OK again. This closes the Create New Data Source dialog box and returns you to the Choose Data Source dialog box. The My Customer file should be selected. Click OK. The Query Wizard appears.
8. In the Available Tables And Columns list, choose Orders. Click the right arrow button to display the fields in the box on the right. Click the Next button.
9. In the Column To filter list, choose CustomerID. On the right, click the drop-down arrow for CustomerID, and choose Is Less Than. Then, click the drop-down arrow in the next box on the right, and choose 3. Click the Next button.
10. In the Sort By list, choose CustomerID. Specify descending order. This sorts the CustomerID field in descending order. Click the Next button.
11. Click the Save Query button. Type "Customer ID Query from My Customer" for the query name, and click the Save button. This saves the query with the name Customer ID Query from My Customer.
12. Click the Finish button. Click cell A25 on the Sales Records worksheet, and click OK. This places the imported information beginning in cell A25 on the Sales Records worksheet.

    Now your worksheet should look like the one in Figure 19.7.
13. Click the Save button on the Standard toolbar to save the workbook.
14. Click the Close (X) button in the upper-right corner of the document window. This closes the workbook.

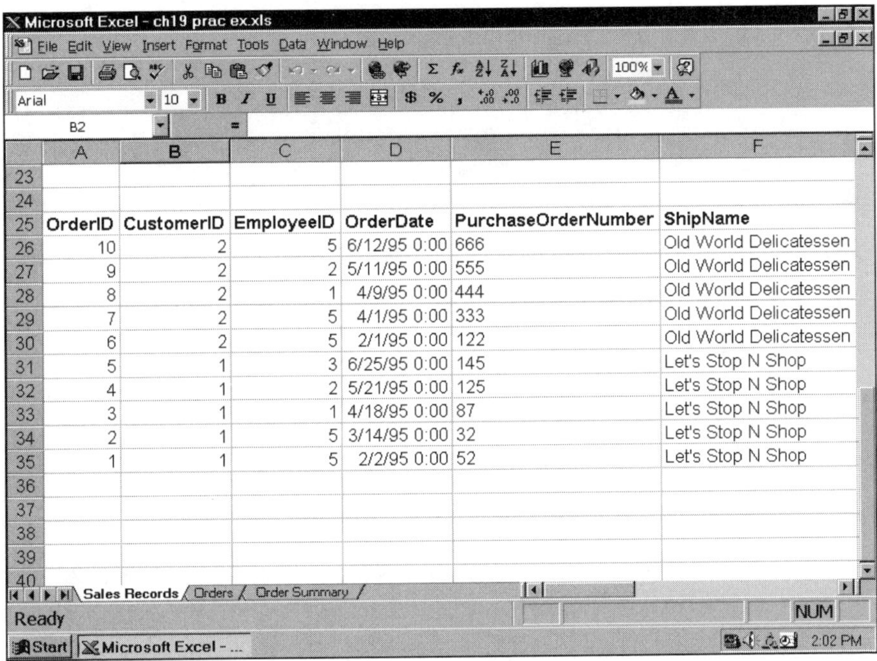

Figure 19.7 The completed Customer ID query Practice Exercise.

Need To Know More?

Catapult, Inc.: *Microsoft Excel 97 Step By Step*. Microsoft Press, Redmond, WA, 1996. ISBN 1-57231-314-5. Lesson 7, "Sorting and Subtotaling to Organize Your Data," tells you how to sort a list of information.

Craig, Deborah: *How to Use Microsoft Excel 97 for Windows*. Que, Indianapolis, IN, 1996. ISBN 1-56276-469-1. Chapter 14, "Working with Lists of Data," shows you how to sort, search, and find records in an Excel list.

Harvey, Greg: *Excel 97 for Windows for Dummies*. IDG Books Worldwide, Inc., Foster City, CA, 1996. ISBN 0-7645-0049-X. Chapter 9, "How to Face a Database," explains how to sort and query data in Excel lists.

Nicholson, John R. and Sean R. Nicholson: *Discover Excel 97*. IDG Books Worldwide, Inc., Foster City, CA, 1997. ISBN 1-7645-3047-X. Chapter 14, "Making a List: Excel's Database Features," gives you information on sorting and querying data in Excel lists.

Nossiter, Josh: *Using Microsoft Excel 97*. Que, Indianapolis, IN, 1996. ISBN 0-7897-0955-4. Chapter 15, "Databases in a Nutshell," has a nice discussion of sorting and querying Excel lists.

Working With Data In An Excel List

Terms you'll need to understand:

- √ Filter
- √ Extract
- √ Pivot table
- √ Data map
- √ Data validation
- √ Conditional formatting
- √ Logical formula (**IF**)
- √ Lookup function

Skills you'll need to master:

- √ Using filters
- √ Extracting data
- √ Creating pivot tables
- √ Creating data maps
- √ Validating data
- √ Circling invalid data
- √ Setting up conditional formatting
- √ Building logical formulas (**IF**)
- √ Looking up a value

Using Excel Lists

In the previous chapter, you were introduced to sorting and querying data in an external database. In this chapter, you'll learn about querying lists by extracting data to display a subset of data that you alter. In addition, you'll use filters to display a subset of data that you can't alter. To further your database knowledge, you'll explore data analysis and pivot tables. This chapter shows you how to use many other useful features, such as data maps, data validation, conditional formatting, logical (IF) formulas, and the Lookup Wizard.

Querying Data In Excel Lists

Chapter 19 shows how to query an external database using Query Wizard. In this chapter, you'll query a list or database, and Excel will place the data wherever you specify on the worksheet.

One way to query data in a list is to use *filters*. A filter enables you to work with a subset of your data without moving or sorting the data. The AutoFilter command inserts drop-down arrows next to column headings in an Excel list or database. Selecting an item from a drop-down list hides all rows except rows that contain the selected value. You can edit and format the cells that are visible.

There might be times when you want to work with a subset of your data. For instance, you might want to extract a partial list of data to give to someone who doesn't need the entire database list. Or, maybe you want to create a report using a filtered view of the data, uncluttered by extraneous information. You can filter your data and move it somewhere else, such as to another worksheet, workbook, or application. At some point, you might want to delete unwanted records from the data. You can accomplish this by filtering or extracting data from your list.

HOLD That Skill!

Consider these helpful hints when filtering data in Excel:

- You can filter only one list at a time on a worksheet.
- Choose Data|Filter. If there is a checkmark next to the AutoFilter command, select the AutoFilter command to turn it off before selecting another Excel list.
- Data stored to the left or right of the Excel list can be hidden when you filter the list. If other data shares the worksheet with the list, store it in rows above or below the list area or on another sheet in the workbook.

- You can display five types of criteria:
  - **All** Displays all records in the field.
  - **Custom** Displays the Custom AutoFilter dialog box that enables you to create **AND** or **OR** criteria.
  - **Exact Values** Displays only records with this exact value in the field.
  - **Blanks** Displays all records with blanks in the field.
  - **Nonblanks** Displays all records with values that are not blanks in the field.

You can extract data to copy to another worksheet by using the AutoFilter method. With this method, you copy and paste data wherever you want to put it.

Task 1 shows you how to use filters to display specific data in a list. Task 2 shows you how to extract data from a database.

Task 1 Using filters.

1. Open the Ch20 Task workbook file located on the companion disk.
2. Select cell A4. This selects a cell within the list you want to filter.
3. Select Data|Filter, and choose AutoFilter. You should see drop-down arrows next to each column heading in the list, as shown in Figure 20.1.
4. Click the drop-down list for the Store column. The drop-down list shows the unique values for the column.

You can click the column heading and press Alt+Down Arrow to see a drop-down list of data you want to display.

5. Select Top 10. Change the number 10 to 4, and click OK to show the top 4 items. You should see four records, and the rest of the records should be hidden. The blue arrow on the filter button indicates the filtered data is based on criteria you selected in the Store column.
6. Click the drop-down list for the Quantity column. Choose Custom. In the dialog box, choose is greater than, and choose 3. Click OK. You should see two records, and the rest of the records should be hidden, as illustrated in Figure 20.2.

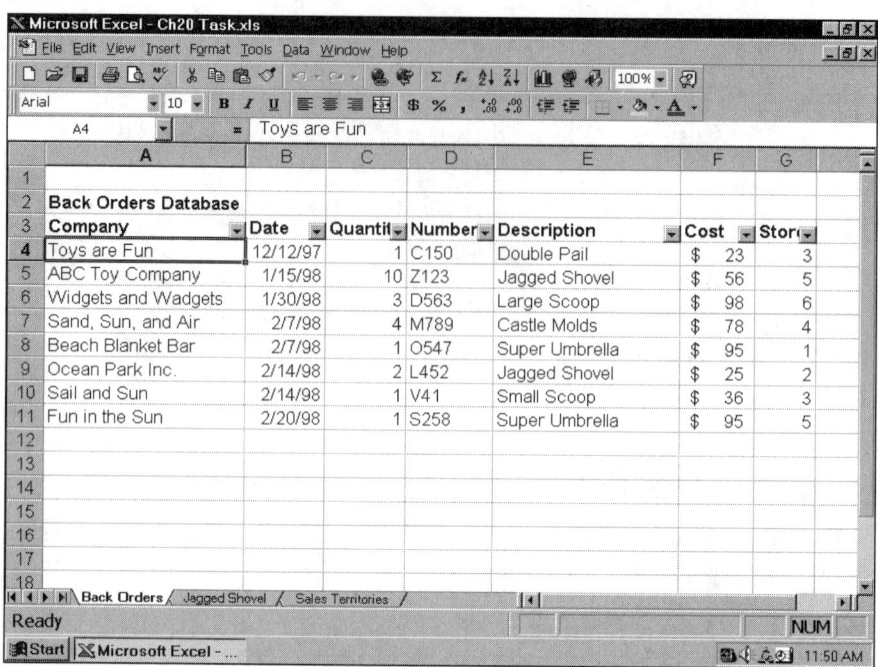

Back Orders Database

Company	Date	Quantity	Number	Description	Cost	Store
Toys are Fun	12/12/97	1	C150	Double Pail	$ 23	3
ABC Toy Company	1/15/98	10	Z123	Jagged Shovel	$ 56	5
Widgets and Wadgets	1/30/98	3	D563	Large Scoop	$ 98	6
Sand, Sun, and Air	2/7/98	4	M789	Castle Molds	$ 78	4
Beach Blanket Bar	2/7/98	1	O547	Super Umbrella	$ 95	1
Ocean Park Inc.	2/14/98	2	L452	Jagged Shovel	$ 25	2
Sail and Sun	2/14/98	1	V41	Small Scoop	$ 36	3
Fun in the Sun	2/20/98	1	S258	Super Umbrella	$ 95	5

Figure 20.1 Filter drop-down arrows next to column headings.

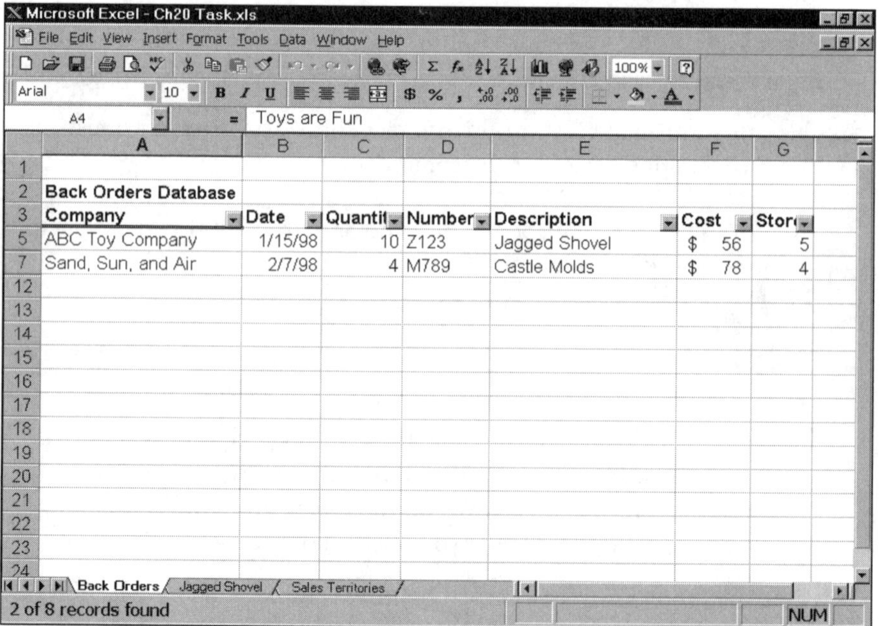

Back Orders Database

Company	Date	Quantity	Number	Description	Cost	Store
ABC Toy Company	1/15/98	10	Z123	Jagged Shovel	$ 56	5
Sand, Sun, and Air	2/7/98	4	M789	Castle Molds	$ 78	4

Figure 20.2 Filtered list showing two records.

7. Select Data|Filter, and choose AutoFilter. This removes the drop-down arrows from the column headings in the list, redisplays the hidden rows, and turns off the AutoFilter feature for this list.

You'll need to know how to use filters in order to pass the exam. You'll be asked to filter out records that meet two criteria, using Top 10 and Custom.

Task 2 Extracting data.

1. Cell A4 should already be selected. Select Data|Filter|AutoFilter to display the column drop-down arrows. Click the drop-down list for the Description column. The drop-down list shows an alphabetical list of unique values for the column.
2. Select Jagged Shovel. This is the criterion you want to display. You should see two records, and the rest of the records should be hidden, as illustrated in Figure 20.3.
3. Select all the filtered data in the range A3:G9.
4. Click the Copy tool on the Standard toolbar.

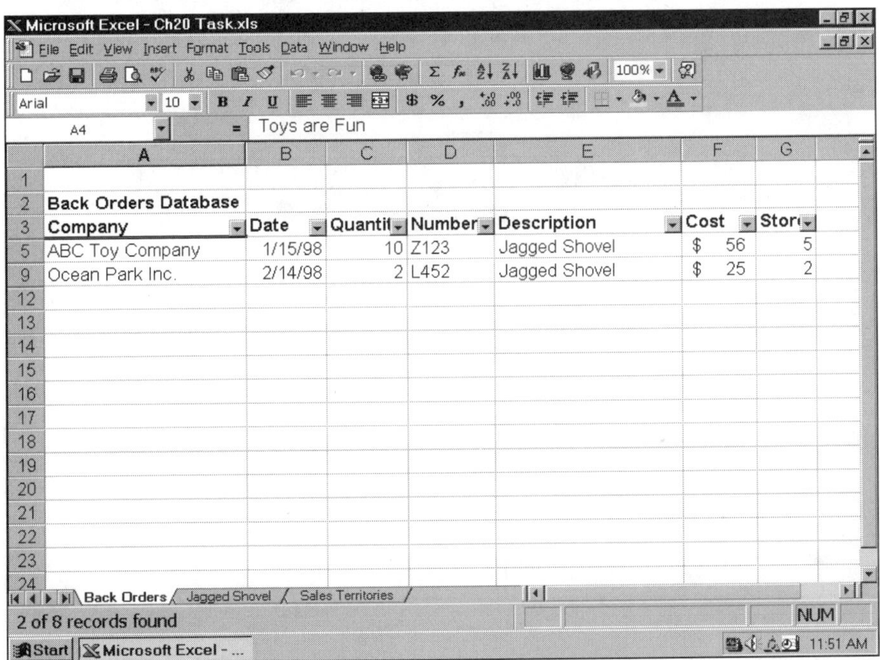

Figure 20.3 Filtered data showing two records.

5. Click the Jagged Shovel sheet tab.
6. Click cell B2. This is the cell that will be the top-left corner of the new list.
7. Click the Paste tool on the Standard toolbar.

   Excel copies the data to the new location, as shown in Figure 20.4.
8. Click any cell to deselect the range.
9. Click the Back Orders sheet tab.
10. Click any cell to deselect the range.
11. Press Esc to remove the copy marquee.
12. Select Data|Filter|AutoFilter. This removes the drop-down arrows from the column headings in the list, turns off the AutoFilter feature for this list, and displays all the list data.

This section shows you how to filter and extract data. In the next section, you'll learn another way to work with data in an Excel list—you'll learn how to use a pivot table.

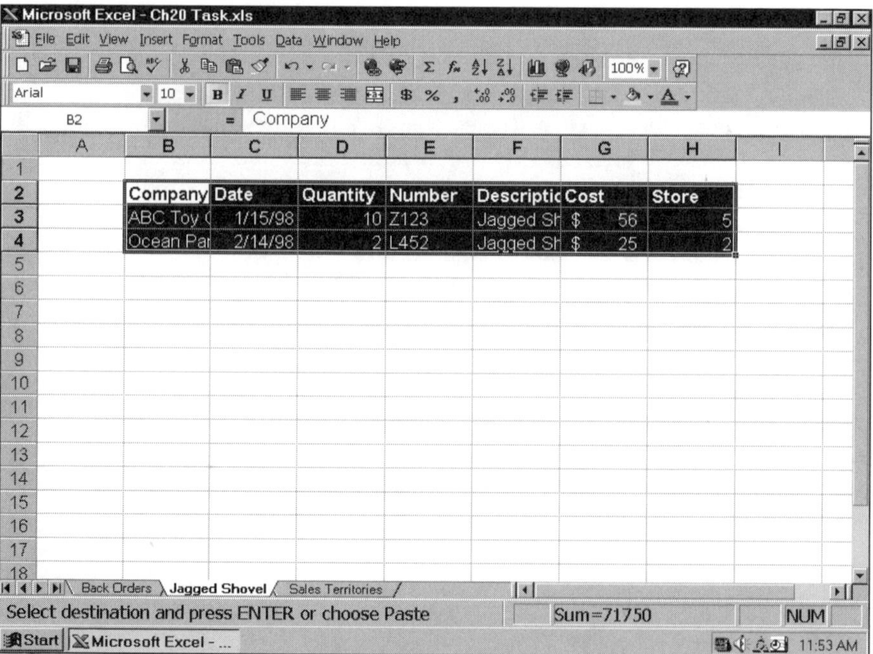

Figure 20.4 Extracted data in a new list.

Working With Pivot Tables

A pivot table lets you analyze, summarize, and manipulate data in lists and tables. Pivot tables offer flexible and intuitive analysis of data. Although the data that appears in pivot tables looks like any other worksheet data, you cannot directly enter or change the data in the data area of a pivot table. The pivot table itself is linked to the source data, and what you see in the cells of the table are read-only amounts. However, you can change the formatting (Number, Alignment, Font, Border, Patterns) and choose from a variety of computation options such as SUM, AVERAGE, MIN, and MAX.

You can create a pivot table from several sources. The default, and most common choice, is to create a pivot table from an Excel list or database. You can also create a pivot table from data in an external data source, multiple consolidation ranges, or another pivot table.

The following task illustrates how to create a pivot table from an Excel list or database.

Task 3 Creating pivot tables.

1. Click any cell in the Back Orders sheet, which contains the data in the Excel database that you want to use to create a pivot table.
2. Choose Data|PivotTable Report. The PivotTable Wizard—Step 1 Of 4 dialog box should open. The Office Assistant should ask you if you want help with pivot tables.

   Note: From this point, until the pivot table appears in the worksheet, you are working in the PivotTable Wizard.

3. In the Where Is The Data That You Want To Analyze? area, choose Microsoft Excel List Or Database, if it's not already selected. This tells Excel the source of the tabular data.
4. Click the Next button to continue. The PivotTable Wizard—Step 2 Of 4 dialog box should appear. In the Range box, the range should be $A$3:$G$11.

   Note: If the range is incorrect, click in the Range box, and type the correct range. This defines the data range you want to change. A quick way to specify the range in the Range box is to highlight the range in the worksheet.

5. Click the Next button. The PivotTable Wizard—Step 3 Of 4 dialog box should appear, as shown in Figure 20.5. The fields appear on buttons to the right in the dialog box. These currently are the column fields. There are four areas you can define to create your PivotTable: ROW, COLUMN, DATA, and PAGE.

   You drag the field buttons to the areas to define the layout of your PivotTable. For example, to summarize the values in a field in the body of the table, place the field button in the DATA area. To arrange items in a field in columns with the labels across the top, place the field button in the COLUMN area. To arrange items in a field of rows with labels along the side, place the field button in the ROW area. To show data for one item at a time, that is, one item per page, place the field button in the PAGE area.
6. Drag the Cost button to the DATA area.
7. Drag the Date button to the ROW area.
8. Drag the Company button to the COLUMN area. Let's average the numbers instead of summing them.
9. Double-click on the Sum of Cost button in the DATA area. The PivotTable Field dialog box should open.

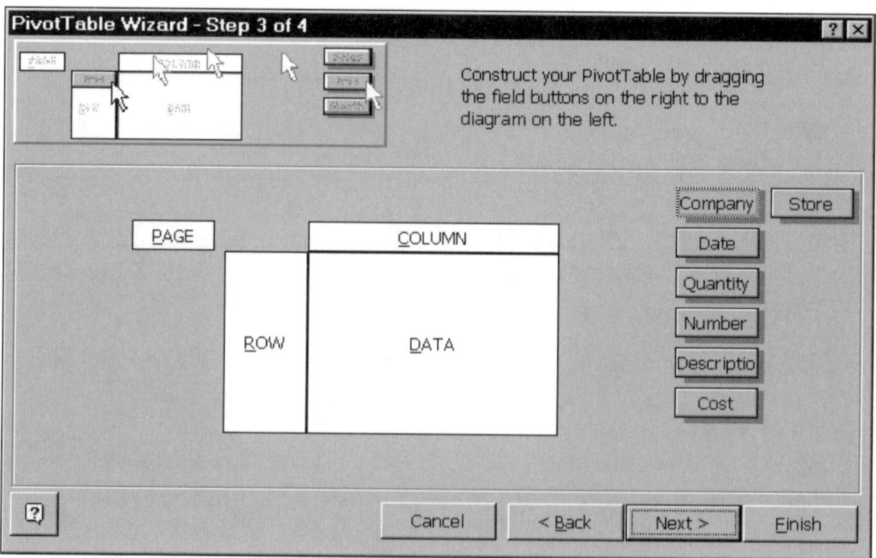

Figure 20.5 The PivotTable Wizard—Step 3 Of 4 dialog box.

10. Choose Average. Then, click the Number button. Choose Currency, and click OK. Click OK again.
11. Click the Next button. The PivotTable Wizard—Step 4 Of 4 dialog box should appear.
12. Choose New Worksheet, if necessary.
13. Click the Finish button.

    The PivotTable Wizard places the table in the new worksheet called Sheet1, as you can see in Figure 20.6. The PivotTable toolbar should appear.

Be sure you know how to create a pivot table based on an Excel database in a worksheet. You'll have to drag a field button into the DATA area. Then, you'll need to change the Sum button in the DATA area to an Average button to average the data and change the formatting to currency. You'll be required to place the pivot table on a new worksheet.

You've seen how to analyze, summarize, and manipulate data in an Excel list using a pivot table. However, if you want to display geographical data with a map, Excel's Data Map feature lets you easily create a data map, as explained in the next section.

Microsoft Excel - Ch20 Task.xls

A1 = Average of Cost

	A	B	C	D	E
1	Average of Cost	Company			
2	Date	ABC Toy Company	Beach Blanket Bar	Fun in the Sun	Ocean Park In
3	12/12/97				
4	1/15/98	$56.00			
5	1/30/98				
6	2/7/98		$95.00		
7	2/14/98				
8	2/20/98			$95.00	
9	Grand Total	$56.00	$95.00	$95.00	

Sheet1 / Back Orders / Jagged Shovel / Sales Territories

Ready NUM

Figure 20.6 The PivotTable in the Sheet1 worksheet.

Using A Data Map

Excel's data map feature lets you create a geographical map from columns of data. One column must contain geographic data. You can add labels, text formats, and data to the map.

Task 4 illustrates how to create a data map.

Task 4 Creating data maps.

1. Click the Sales Territories sheet tab, and select the range B1:C8.

If your data contains ZIP codes, be sure they are formatted as text, not as numbers. Formatting ZIP codes as text prevents Excel from removing zeros that might be part of a ZIP code number.

2. Click the Map button on the Standard toolbar.
3. Drag a rectangle from cell E1 to cell H10 in the worksheet. This tells Excel the size and shape of the map you want.
4. In the Multiple Maps Available dialog box, select United States In North America, then click OK.

Note: If you have not installed the Data Map feature, the Multiple Maps Available dialog box will appear. To get Data Map to work properly, run the Microsoft Office Setup program, and install the Data Map feature.

HOLD That Skill!

Think about these guidelines when setting up data to create a map:

- Organize the information in columns on a worksheet. One column must contain geographic data, such as the names of states or countries.
- Your worksheet can contain additional data for each map feature, such as sales figures for each state. Include that data in the cells you select to create the map.
- If your worksheet has column headings, be sure to include those headings when you select the data to create the map.
- There are six types of data formats you can display in a map: Value Shading, Category Shading, Dot Density, Graduated Symbol, Pie Chart, and Column Chart.

Excel places the map in the rectangle you drew. The Microsoft Map Control dialog box should appear.

5. Click any cell in the worksheet to deselect the map and close the Microsoft Map Control dialog box.
6. Click the map, and drag the bottom-middle selection handle to Row 14. This makes the map taller.
7. Click any cell outside of the map to deselect the map.

Your map should look similar to the map and legend shown in Figure 20.7.

If you want to validate your data and prevent invalid data from being entered in a worksheet, you can use Excel's Data Validation feature to do this. In the next section, you'll see how to validate Excel data.

Using Data Validation

You can perform data validation on entries by using the Data Validation command to set up *data validation rules*. You can define data that is acceptable for any given cell or range of cells, and input messages or error alerts that display whenever a validated cell is selected. Error alerts can display whenever a validated cell is selected or when a user tries to enter an invalid value. If there is any invalid data on your worksheet, you can identify that data by using the Circle

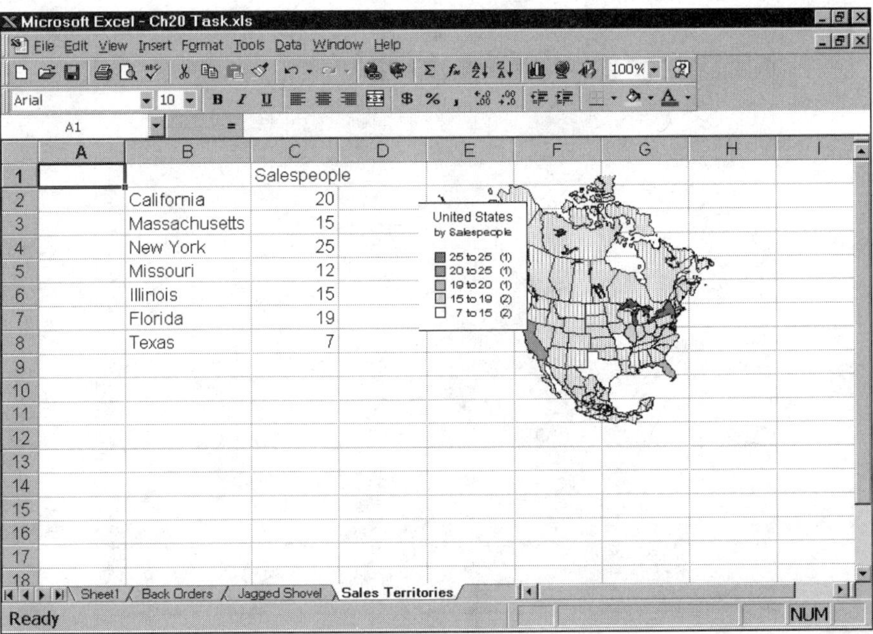

Figure 20.7 A data map with legend.

Invalid Data feature. You need to display the Auditing toolbar to use the feature. Excel identifies invalid data by marking the data with a red circle. You can correct the invalid data by typing over the data in the cells that contain a red circle.

Task 5 shows the steps required to validate data in a worksheet. Task 6 demonstrates how Excel finds invalid data and circles the data with a red circle. Then, you correct the invalid data on the worksheet.

Task 5 Validating data.

1. Click the Back Orders sheet tab.
2. Select cells C4:C11. This tells Excel what data you want to validate in the worksheet.
3. Choose Data|Validation. Excel should display the Data Validation dialog box, as shown in Figure 20.8.
4. In the Settings tab, click the Allow drop-down arrow, and choose Whole Number.
5. In the Data list, ensure that Between is selected.
6. In the Minimum box, type "1".
7. In the Maximum box, type "5".
8. Click the Input Message tab.

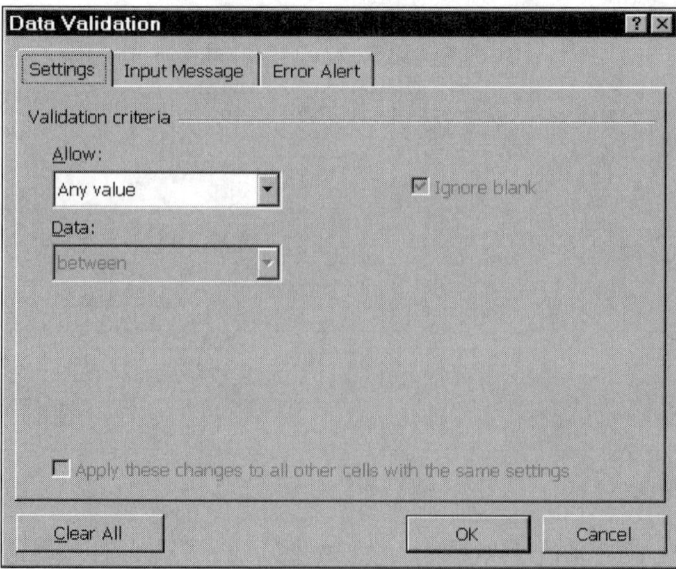

Figure 20.8 The Data Validation dialog box.

9. In the Input Message box, type "Any whole number from 1 to 5".
10. Click the Error Alert tab.
11. In the Error message box, type "Quantity is less than 1 or greater than 5".
12. Click OK.

Excel shows a text box next to cell C4 that reads *Any whole number from 1 to 5*, as shown in Figure 20.9.

Be sure you know how to validate numbers on a worksheet given the type of value you can allow, such as a whole number, the data (value), and the minimum number. You're also expected to enter an input message. You won't need an input title, so leave that box blank. You also should know how to enter an error message. You can leave the error title box empty.

The next task shows you how to circle invalid data, correct the data, and clear validation circles.

Task 6 Circling invalid data.

1. Click any cell in the Back Orders sheet.
2. Choose Tools|Show Auditing Toolbar. Excel should display the Auditing toolbar.

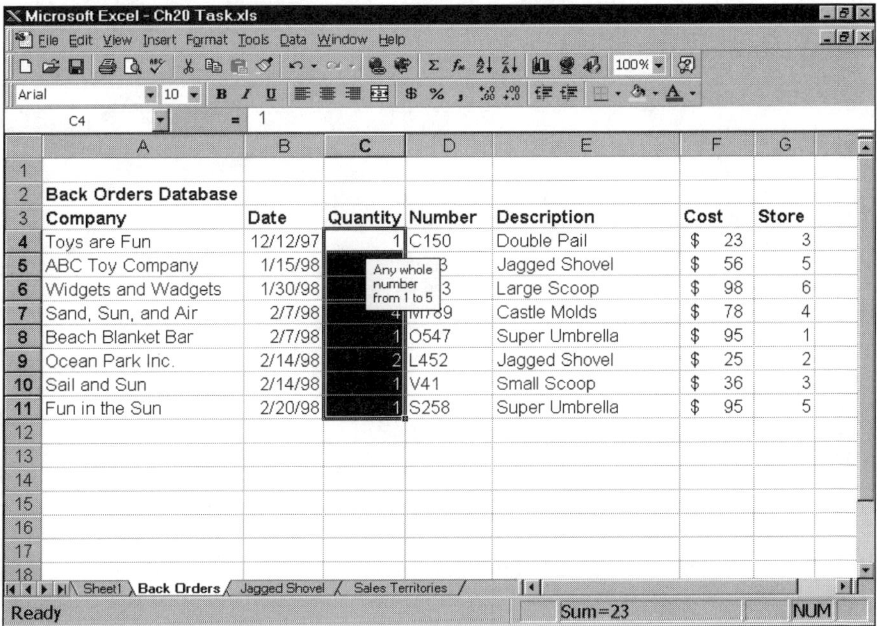

Figure 20.9 Validated data in the worksheet.

3. Click the Circle Invalid Data button on the Auditing toolbar. You should see a red circle around the Quantity column heading and the data in cell C6, as shown in Figure 20.10. The number 10 in cell C6 is greater than 5, and a number in the Quantity column must be between 1 and 5. Therefore the data is invalid.
4. Click cell C6, and type "5".
5. If a red circle still shows in cell C5, then click the Clear Validation Circles button on the Auditing toolbar.
6. Click the Close (X) button on the Auditing toolbar to close the toolbar.

It's essential that you know how to circle invalid data using the Auditing toolbar and to change the invalid numbers to the correct values.

In the next section, you'll use conditional formatting to change the text color of values that meet specific conditions.

Using Conditional Formatting

With Excel's Conditional Formatting command, you can perform conditional cell formatting. This command enables you to easily apply special formatting

Microsoft Excel - Ch20 Task.xls

	A	B	C	D	E	F	G
1							
2	Back Orders Database						
3	Company	Date	Quantity	Number	De		e
4	Toys are Fun	12/12/97	1	C150	Double Pail	$ 23	3
5	ABC Toy Company	1/15/98	10	Z123	Jagged Shovel	$ 56	5
6	Widgets and Wadgets	1/30/98	3	D563	Large Scoop	$ 98	6
7	Sand, Sun, and Air	2/7/98	4	M789	Castle Molds	$ 78	4
8	Beach Blanket Bar	2/7/98	1	O547	Super Umbrella	$ 95	1
9	Ocean Park Inc.	2/14/98	2	L452	Jagged Shovel	$ 25	2
10	Sail and Sun	2/14/98	1	V41	Small Scoop	$ 36	3
11	Fun in the Sun	2/20/98	1	S258	Super Umbrella	$ 95	5

Sheet1 | Back Orders | Jagged Shovel | Sales Territories

Figure 20.10 Invalid data circled in the worksheet.

settings that take effect when the contents of a cell meet specified conditions. For example, if the values fall below a specific number, you can show those values in bold blue, and, if the values are greater than a specific number, you can display those values in bold green.

Task 7 shows you how to set up conditional formatting, indicating that two sets of values should appear in different colors on the worksheet.

Task 7 Setting up conditional formatting.

1. In the Back Orders sheet, select cells F4:F11. This tells Excel where you want to place conditional formatting.
2. Choose Format|Conditional Formatting. Excel should display the Conditional Formatting dialog box (see Figure 20.11).

   Note: When the Office Assistant asks you if you want help with conditional formatting, choose No, Don't Provide Help Now.

3. In the Condition 1 area, accept the Cell Value Is option. Choose Less Than in the next text box, and type "50" in the last box.
4. Click the Format button. The Format Cells dialog box should appear.
5. In the Font Style list, choose Bold, and select the Rose color patch in the Color section.
6. Click OK.
7. Click the Add button.
8. In the Condition 2 area, accept the Cell Value Is option. Choose Greater Than, and type "75" in the last box.
9. Click the Format button. The Format Cells dialog box should appear.
10. Choose Bold, and select the Sky Blue color patch.

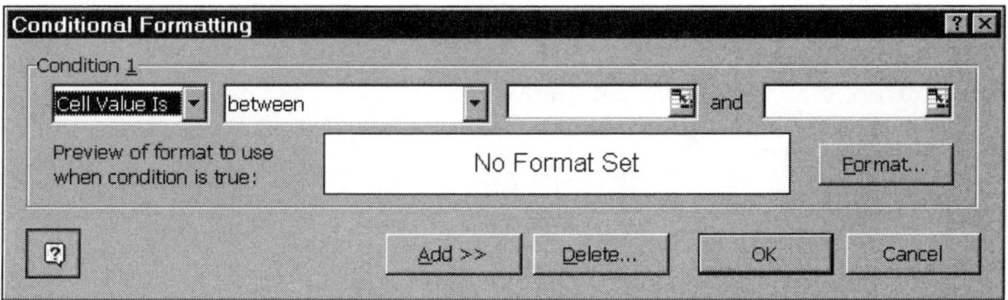

Figure 20.11 Conditional Formatting dialog box.

11. Click OK, click OK again, then click any cell outside of the selected range.

Excel displays numbers less than 50 in bold Rose and numbers greater than 75 in bold Sky Blue.

To answer the conditional formatting test question on the exam, be sure you know how to set up conditional formatting. You'll be asked to place conditional formatting in a field column so that the field column values below a specific number are shown in one bold color and the values greater than a specific number appear in a different bold color.

The next section shows you how to set up a logical formula that tests whether a condition is true or false, based on particular data in the worksheet.

Creating Logical Formulas

In Chapter 5, you learned how to use several statistical functions. Let's talk about another type of function called the *logical function*. Logical functions are formulas that you can use to create logical tests. A test enables a formula to make a decision based on particular data. A test might determine if a value is greater than 50, and the formula administering the test can perform one function if true and another if false.

The most common and useful logical function is the **IF** function, which allows you to develop several tests based on the operators you use in the test statement. The **IF** function looks like this: **IF (condition, value if true, value if false)**. For example, **IF(A3<=100,"Must be less than 100", A3*2)**. This logical formula uses the "Must be less than 100" condition to test the value in cell A3. The condition answer is either true or false. In the example, if the condition proves true, the first part of the function is calculated **(A3<=100)** and the text **"Must be less than 100"** is the answer. If the condition proves false, the second part of the function is calculated **(A3>100)**, and A3 is multiplied by 2.

The **IF** function tests a condition that is true or false. If the condition proves true, one value is returned. If the condition proves false, another value is returned. Proving a condition as true or false requires a relational operator. Relational operators include the following:

- > Greater than
- < Less than
- = Equal to
- >= Greater than or equal to

- <= Less than or equal to
- <> Not equal to

In the next task, you'll build a logical formula to test a condition and show results with the words *Yes* and *No*. Then, you'll copy the formula to a column to test the condition for all the sales data. The results in the last column will show either the word *Yes* or *No* in each cell that contains a logical formula.

Task 8 Building logical formulas (IF).

1. Click the Sales Territories sheet tab, and click cell D2. This is where you want the logical formula to appear.
2. Type "=IF(".
3. Click cell C2.
4. Type "=15,"Yes","No")".
5. Press Enter.
6. Click cell D2, and point to the fill handle.
7. Drag the fill handle to copy the logical formula down to cell D8.
8. Click any cell to deselect the range.

Excel shows the word *Yes* or *No* in each cell that contains a logical formula, as shown in Figure 20.12.

You'll need to know how to create a logical formula (using the **IF** command) to test a specific condition.

Looking Up A Value

Until now you've used statistical functions and the logical function. Another kind of function is the *lookup function*. Lookup functions are formulas that you can use to search for values within tables or lists. For instance, you can use a lookup function to find a tax amount in a tax table or the price of merchandise in a price table.

Excel's Lookup Wizard can step you through the process of searching for values in tables based on a lookup value, the value you are trying to find. As an example, if you have a price table that contains prices for merchandise based on item numbers, price is the lookup value. Suppose you want to search that table for item number 50. The Lookup Wizard searches vertically in a column of

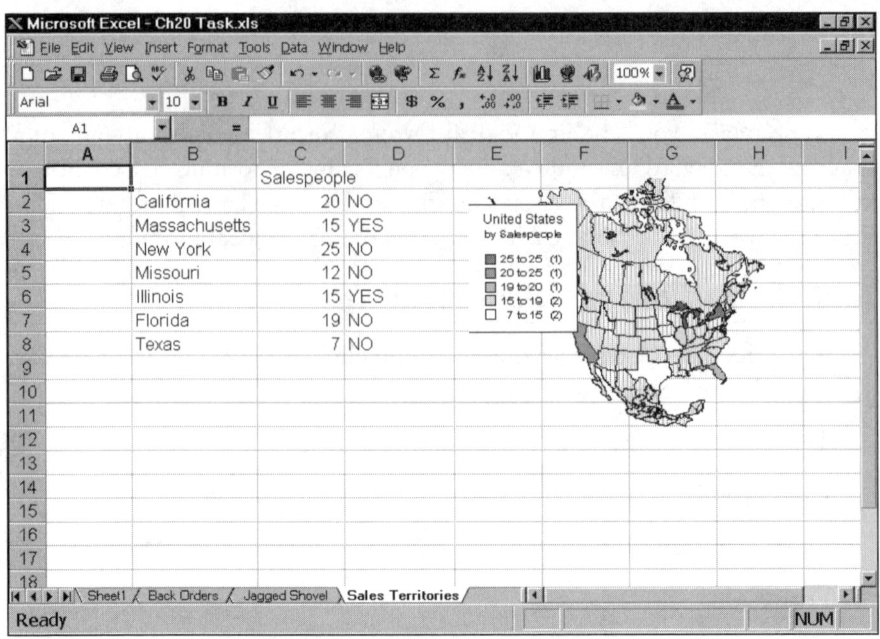

Figure 20.12 Logical formula results.

values and horizontally in a row of values, finds the value at the intersection of the column and row, and then returns that value from the table. For example, the price of item number 50 is returned and copied into a cell on the worksheet.

Excel can copy the results in two ways: It can copy just the lookup formula with its result into a cell or copy the lookup formula with its lookup parameters (the column label, the row label, and the formula with its result).

In Task 9, you'll use the Lookup Wizard to find an item number.

Task 9 Looking up a value with the Lookup Wizard.

1. Click the Back Orders sheet tab. Select A3:G11. This selects the range you want to search.

   Note: Be sure to include the column and row headings in the range you select. The Lookup Wizard refers to column headings as column labels and row headings as row labels.

2. Choose Tools|Wizard|Lookup. The Lookup Wizard—Step 1 Of 4 dialog box should appear, as shown in Figure 20.13. You should see the selected range $A$3:$G$11 in the dialog box. This is the range you want.

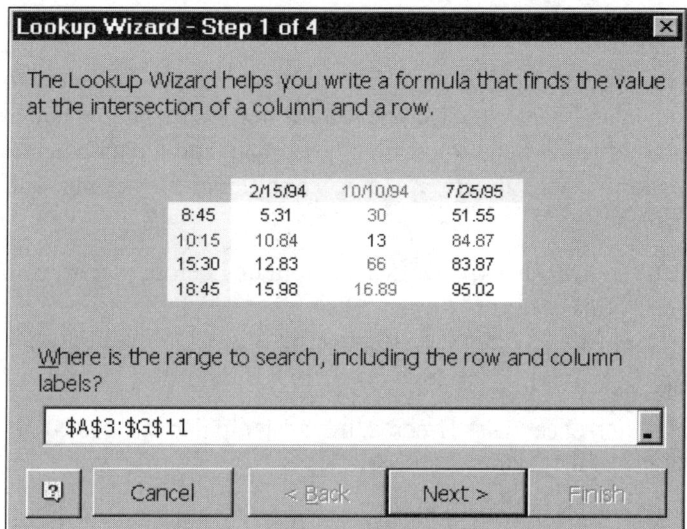

Figure 20.13 The Lookup Wizard—Step 1 Of 4 dialog box.

3. Click the Next button. The Lookup Wizard—Step 2 Of 4 dialog box should appear.
4. In the Which column contains the value to find box, choose Number. This selects the column label.
5. In the Which row contains the value to find box, choose Ocean Park Inc. This selects the row label.
6. Click the Next button. The Lookup Wizard—Step 3 Of 4 dialog box should appear. The Copy just the formula to a single cell option should be selected. This is the option you want. You should also see the return value of L452, which is the item number that the Lookup Wizard found.
7. Click the Next button. The Lookup Wizard—Step 4 Of 4 dialog box should appear.
8. Click cell A15. This tells Excel where to copy the formula.
9. Click the Finish button. Excel shows the result L452 in cell A15.
10. Close the workbook without saving the changes.

You'll need to know how to use the Lookup Wizard to search for a value in a particular column and row and copy the value to a single cell on the worksheet.

Practice Exercise

The sales manager at Sandy Shores Company has requested a query to retrieve specific data in an Excel list. Also, the records need to be filtered and extracted. You decide that you'll need to create a pivot table and a data map. You'll also have to perform data validation, set up conditional formatting, and build a logical formula.

Figure 20.14 shows what the worksheet contains before you go through the instructions in this exercise.

1. Open the Ch20 Prac Ex workbook file stored on your companion disk.
2. In the worksheet Sales Records, use a filter to find the record that meets the following criteria:
   - Product = Surfboard Wax
   - Price = $75

   Ensure that this is the only entry showing, and then redisplay all the worksheet data.

Sales Records				
Date	Customer Name	Invoice No.	Product	Price
2/7/98	Sunbrella	12058	Medium Umbrella	$ 50
2/8/98	Sail Away	12059	Jib	$ 63
2/9/98	Ocean Breeze	12061	Surfboard wax	$ 75
3/1/98	Beach Toys	12063	Shovels	$ 32
3/15/98	Waves Inc.	12068	Flip Flops	$ 28
3/12/98	Surfs Up	12061	Surfboard wax	$ 20

Figure 20.14 The Practice Exercise before you begin.

3. In the worksheet Sales Records, filter out the record that meets the following criteria:

   - Product = Surfboard Wax
   - Price = $20

   Ensure that this is the only entry showing. Then, extract the filtered data, and place it starting in cell B2 in the worksheet Surfboard Wax. Turn off the AutoFilter feature.

4. In the Sales Records worksheet, create a pivot table based on sales record data. The data is Price, the column heading is Product, and the row heading is Customer Name. Place the pivot table on a new worksheet.

5. In the Territories worksheet, create a data map starting in cell E2 and ending in I15 that shows the territories and sales data on a United States In North America map.

6. In the Sales Records worksheet, validate the invoice numbers with the following information:

   - Allow whole numbers from 12060 through 12070
   - Input the message "Any whole numbers between 12060 and 12070"
   - Make the Error Message *Whole numbers less than 12060 and greater than 12070*

7. In the Sales Records worksheet, circle the invalid data. Correct the invalid data with 12060 and 12065.

8. In the Sales Records worksheet, place conditional formatting on the Price column so that Price field column values below 30 are shown in one bold color and Price values greater than 50 are shown in a different bold color.

9. In the Territories worksheet, in the benefits column, create a logical (**IF**) formula to test a condition. If sales are less than or equal to 500, then a Yes answer should appear in the Benefits column, and, if sales are greater than 500, a No answer should appear in the Benefits column.

10. Use the Lookup Wizard to find Shovels.

11. Save the workbook with the same name.

12. Close the workbook.

Answers To Practice Exercise

1. Click the Open tool on the Standard toolbar, and double-click the file name Ch20 Prac Ex.
2. Select any cell in the list. This selects a cell within the list you want to filter. Select Data|Filter, and choose AutoFilter. You should see drop-down arrows next to each column heading in the list. Click the drop-down list for the Product column. The drop-down list shows the unique values for the column. Select Surfboard Wax. Click the drop-down list for the Price column. The drop-down list shows the unique values for the column. Select $75. This is the criterion you want to display. You should see one record, and the rest of the records should be hidden. Select Data|Filter, and choose AutoFilter. This removes the drop-down arrows from the column headings in the list and turns off the AutoFilter feature for this list.
3. Select any cell within the list you want to filter. Select Data|Filter, and choose AutoFilter. You should see drop-down arrows next to each column heading in the list. Click the drop-down list for the Product column. The drop-down list shows the unique values for the column. Select Surfboard Wax. Click the drop-down list for the Price column. The drop-down list shows the unique values for the column. Select $20. This is the criterion you want to display. You should see one record, and the rest of the records should be hidden. Select all the filtered data in the range, including the column headings. Click the Copy tool on the Standard toolbar. Click the Surfboard Wax sheet tab. Click cell B2. This is the cell that will be the top-left corner of the new list. Click the Paste tool on the Standard toolbar. This extracts the filtered data and displays it in the worksheet Surfboard Wax. Click any cell to deselect the data. Return to the Sales Records sheet, click in any cell outside of the selected data, press Esc to remove the copy marquee, then select Data|Filter|AutoFilter.
4. Click any cell in the Excel database. Choose Data|PivotTable Report. The PivotTable Wizard—Step 1 Of 4 dialog box opens. In the What Is The Data That You Want To Analyze? area, choose Microsoft Excel List Or Database, if it's not already selected. This tells Excel the source of the tabular data. Click the Next button to continue. The PivotTable Wizard—Step 2 Of 4 dialog box appears. In the Range box, the range should be $A$3:$E$9. This defines the data range you want to change. Click the Next button. The PivotTable Wizard—Step 3 Of 4 dialog box appears. The fields appear on buttons to the right in the dialog box. Drag the Price button to the DATA area. Drag the Customer button to the

ROW area. Drag the Product button into the COLUMN area. Double-click on the Sum of Price button in the DATA area. The PivotTable Field dialog box should open. Choose Average. Then, click the Number button. Choose Currency, and click OK. Click OK again. Click the Next button. The PivotTable Wizard—Step 4 Of 4 dialog box opens. Choose New worksheet. This specifies where you want the PivotTable to appear in the workbook. Click the Finish button. The PivotTable Wizard places the table in Sheet1 in the Ch20 Task workbook.

5. Click the Territories sheet tab. Select the range B1:C5. Click the Map button on the Standard toolbar. Drag a rectangle from cell E2 to cell I15 on the worksheet. This tells Excel the size and shape of the map you want to create. In the Multiple Maps Available dialog box, select United States In North America, and click OK. Excel places the map in the rectangle you drew. Click any cell in the worksheet.
6. Click the Sales Records sheet tab. Select cells C4:C9. Choose Data|Validation. Excel displays the Data Validation dialog box. In the Settings tab, choose Whole Number, type "12060" in the Minimum box, and type "12070" in the Maximum box. Click the Input Message tab. In the Input Message box, type "Any whole numbers between 12060 and 12070". Click the Error Alert tab. In the Error message box, type "Whole numbers less than 12060 and greater than 12070". Click OK. This validates the invoice numbers by displaying a text box with either the input message or error message, whichever applies.
7. Click any cell in the Sales Records sheet. Choose Tools|Show Auditing Toolbar. Excel should display the Auditing toolbar. Click the Circle Invalid Data button on the Auditing toolbar. You should see a red circle around the Invoice No. column heading and the data in cells C4 and C5. The invoice numbers in these cells are 12058 and 12059, but must be between 12060 and 12070 to be valid data. Therefore, the data is invalid. Click cell C4, type 12060, press Enter, and type 12065. If a red circle still shows in cell C3, then click the Clear Validation Circles button on the Auditing toolbar. Click the Close (X) button on the Auditing toolbar to close the toolbar.
8. Select cells E4:E9. Choose Format|Conditional Formatting. Excel shows you the Conditional Formatting dialog box. In the Condition 1 area, accept the Cell Value Is option, choose Less Than, and type "30" in the last box. Click the Format button. The Format Cells dialog box appears. Choose Bold, and select any color patch. Click OK. Click the Add button. In the Condition 2

area, accept the Cell Value Is option, choose Greater Than, and type "50" in the last box. Click the Format button. The Format Cells dialog box appears. Choose Bold, and select any different color patch. Click OK, click OK again, then click in any cell outside of the selected range. Excel displays the numbers in the Price column that are less than 30 in a bold color and the values greater than 50 in a different bold color.

9. Display the Territories worksheet. Click cell D2. This is where you want the logical formula to appear. Type "=IF(". Click cell C2. Type "<=500,"Yes","No")". *Note:* Be sure to enclose the words Yes and No in quotes. Press Enter. Click cell D2. Point to the fill handle, and drag it to copy the logical formula down to cell D5. Excel shows the word *Yes* or *No* in the cells that contain a logical formula.

10. Click the Sales Records sheet tab. Select A3:E9. This selects the range you want to search. Choose Tools|Wizard|Lookup. The Lookup Wizard—Step 1 of 4 dialog box should appear. You should see the selected range $A$3:$E$9 in the dialog box. This is the range you want. Click the Next button. The Lookup Wizard—Step 2 of 4 dialog box should appear. In the Which column contains the value to find box, choose Product. This selects the column label. In the Which row contains the value to find box, choose 3/1/98. This selects the row label. Click the Next button. The Lookup Wizard—Step 3 of 4 dialog box should appear. The Copy just the formula to a single cell option should be selected. This is the option you want. You should also see the return value of Shovels, which is the product that the Lookup Wizard found. Click the Next button. The Lookup Wizard—Step 4 of 4 dialog box should appear. Click cell A14. This tells Excel where to copy the formula. Click the Finish button. Excel shows the result Shovels in cell A14.

11. Click the Save tool on the Standard toolbar to save the workbook.

    When you finish the Practice Exercise, the PivotTable in Sheet1 should look like the one in Figure 20.15. Your Sales Records worksheet should look like the one in Figure 20.16. The Surfboard Wax worksheet should correspond to the one in Figure 20.17, and the Territories worksheet should look like the one shown in Figure 20.18.

12. Click the Close (X) button in the upper-right corner of the document window. This closes the workbook.

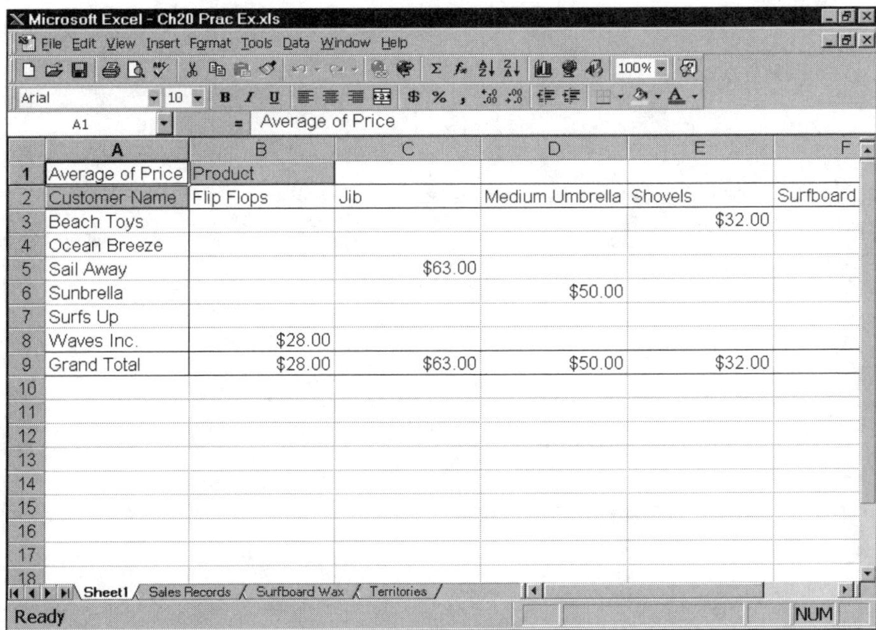

Average of Price	Product				
Customer Name	Flip Flops	Jib	Medium Umbrella	Shovels	Surfboard
Beach Toys				$32.00	
Ocean Breeze					
Sail Away		$63.00			
Sunbrella			$50.00		
Surfs Up					
Waves Inc.	$28.00				
Grand Total	$28.00	$63.00	$50.00	$32.00	

Figure 20.15 The completed Sheet1 worksheet.

Sales Records

Date	Customer Name	Invoice No.	Product	Price
2/7/98	Sunbrella	12060	Medium Umbrella	$ 50
2/8/98	Sail Away	12065	Jib	$ 63
2/9/98	Ocean Breeze	12061	Surfboard wax	$ 75
3/1/98	Beach Toys	12063	Shovels	$ 32
3/15/98	Waves Inc.	12068	Flip Flops	$ 28
3/12/98	Surfs Up	12061	Surfboard wax	$ 20

Shovels

Figure 20.16 The completed Sales Records worksheet.

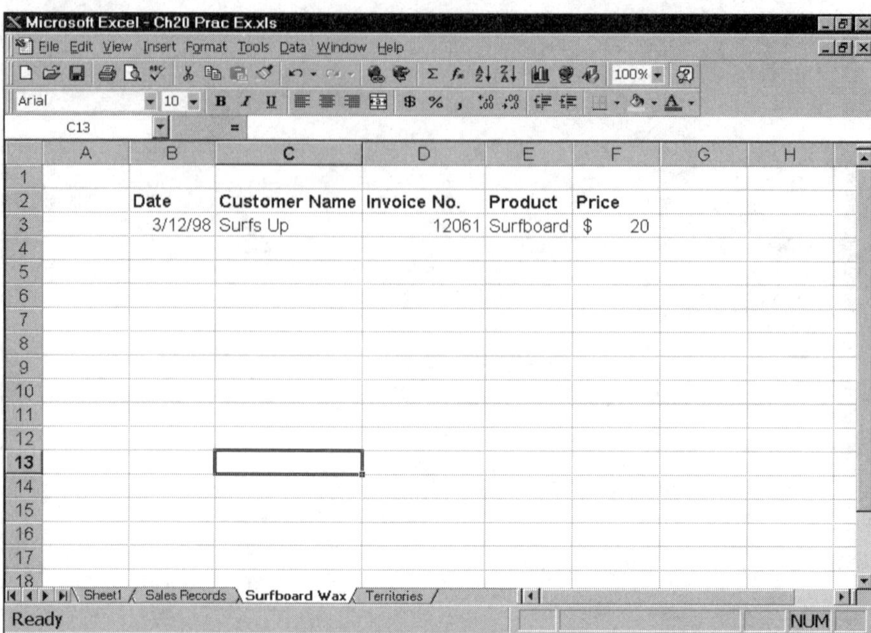

Figure 20.17 The completed Surfboard Wax worksheet.

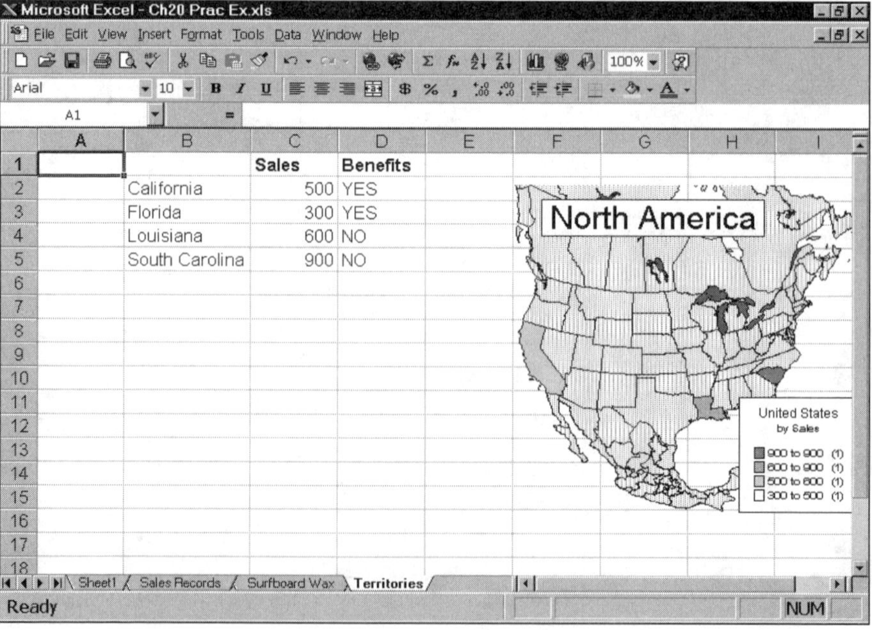

Figure 20.18 The completed Territories worksheet.

Need To Know More?

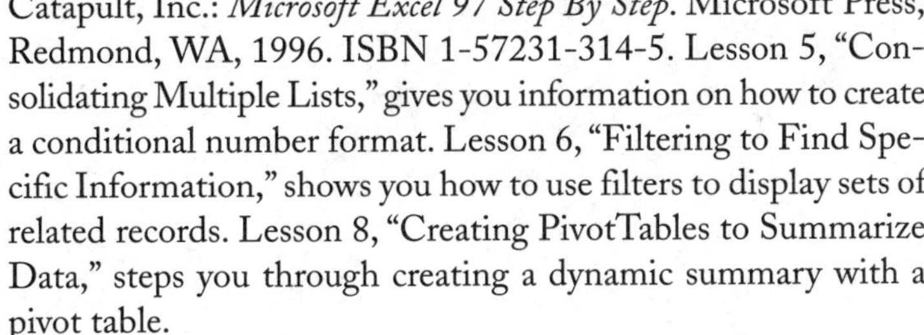

Catapult, Inc.: *Microsoft Excel 97 Step By Step*. Microsoft Press, Redmond, WA, 1996. ISBN 1-57231-314-5. Lesson 5, "Consolidating Multiple Lists," gives you information on how to create a conditional number format. Lesson 6, "Filtering to Find Specific Information," shows you how to use filters to display sets of related records. Lesson 8, "Creating PivotTables to Summarize Data," steps you through creating a dynamic summary with a pivot table.

Craig, Deborah: *How to Use Microsoft Excel 97 for Windows*. Que, Indianapolis, IN, 1996. ISBN 1-56276-469-1. Chapter 14, "Working with Lists of Data," shows you how to sort, search, and find records in an Excel list. Chapter 16, "More Advanced Functions," gives a nice explanation of and demonstrates the Lookup function.

Harvey, Greg: *Excel 97 for Windows for Dummies*. IDG Books Worldwide, Inc., Foster City, CA, 1996. ISBN 0-7645-0049-X. Chapter 9, "How to Face a Database," explains how to query data in Excel lists.

Neibauer, Alan: *Excel One Step at a Time*. IDG Books Worldwide, Inc., Foster City, CA, 1997. ISBN 0-7645-3139-5. Lesson 7, "Preventing and Correcting Worksheet Errors," explains how to validate cell entries and audit your worksheets.

Nicholson, John R. and Sean R. Nicholson: *Discover Excel 97*. IDG Books Worldwide, Inc., Foster City, CA, 1997. ISBN 1-7645-3047-X. Chapter 11, "Numbers Do Lie: Checking Your Worksheet," shows you how to use data validation. Chapter 14, "Making a List: Excel's Database Features," gives you information on querying data in Excel lists. Chapter 17, "A Bug in Your Worksheet: Basic Troubleshooting," talks about validating data and using the auditing tools in Excel worksheets.

Nossiter, Josh: *Using Microsoft Excel 97*. Que, Indianapolis, IN, 1996. ISBN 0-7897-0955-4. Chapter 13, "Analyzing Data in Tables," talks about managing data in Excel lists. Chapter 14, "More Analyzing and Auditing, Too," discusses Excel lists and databases. Chapter 15, "Databases in a Nutshell," has an explanation of querying Excel lists. Chapter 16, "Taming Monster Lists," explains how to work with pivot tables. Chapter 18, "Data Maps and Templates for Data That Fits a Mold," shows you how to create data maps.

21

Building Macros

Terms you'll need to understand:

- √ Macro
- √ Shortcut key
- √ Record
- √ Run
- √ Macro module
- √ Macro sheet
- √ Visual Basic

Skills you'll need to master:

- √ Creating macros
- √ Recording macros
- √ Running macros
- √ Editing macros
- √ Deleting macros

Working With Macros

Macros are special instructions that control how Excel functions. By recording a series of macro instructions into a macro module or macro sheet in a workbook, you can instruct Excel to perform any series of commands or actions for you. A macro can take the place of any mouse or keyboard action that you can perform in Excel. That is, a macro can cause Excel to accomplish a task by itself. You simply record a macro that shows Excel what you want to accomplish. Then, Excel can repeat the task at any time.

Macros are useful for automating repetitive or complex tasks. Although a macro is a series of programming instructions, you do not need to know anything about programming to create one. Excel offers a macro recording feature that translates your actions into macro instructions. The tasks in this chapter show you how to automate Excel through macros. You'll learn how to create, record, run, edit, and delete macros.

Creating And Recording Macros

You can create a macro by recording your actions. The macro recorder translates your actions into macro instructions and places the instructions into a new macro module. If you can perform an action in Excel, you can create a macro that will perform the action for you.

The upcoming task shows you how to create and name a macro, and assign a macro to a shortcut key, Ctrl+a.

Task 1 Creating macros.

1. Open the Ch21 Task workbook file located on the companion disk. Click on any cell in the worksheet.
2. Select Tools|Macro, and choose Record New Macro. You should see the Record Macro dialog box, as shown in Figure 21.1. The default macro name Macro1 appears in the Macro name box.

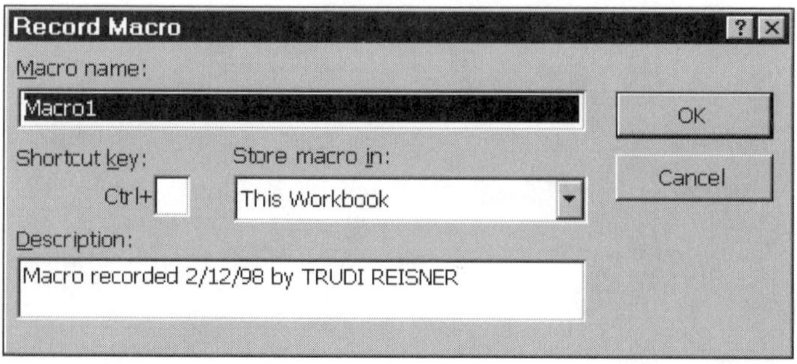

Figure 21.1 The Record Macro dialog box.

HOLD That Skill!

Here are some tips on creating and recording macros:

- A macro name can be up to 256 characters long with no spaces.
- A macro is recorded on a macro sheet in a workbook.
- You have the option to enter a description for a macro to explain its function. A description can be helpful for you and others who use the macro. The default description contains the date you created or last edited the macro and your user name.
- You can assign a *shortcut key* to a macro. A shortcut key is a key combination that executes the macro. Usually, a shortcut key consists of the Ctrl key plus another letter. For example, you could assign Ctrl+a to a macro. Then, you would press Ctrl+a to run the macro.

3. In the Macro Name box, type “font_chg”.
4. Press Tab.
5. In the Shortcut Key box, type “a”.

   ***Note:** When you run the macro, you'll press the appropriate letter key alone without pressing the Shift key, unless the Shift key is part of the shortcut key sequence. For example, Ctrl+Shift+A.*

6. Click OK.

The Recording mode indicator appears at the left end of the status bar at the bottom of the Excel window. This indicator means that any move you make from this point forward will be recorded by Excel until you stop the macro. The Stop Recording toolbar appears on screen. This toolbar contains two buttons: Stop Recording and Relative Reference. The Stop Recording button does just what it says—it stops the recording of a macro. The Relative Reference button allows you to switch between relative and absolute references. By default, Excel records absolute cell references unless you click the Relative Reference button on the Macro toolbar to specify that a cell or range of cells should be a relative reference. When you choose relative reference, the Relative Reference button appears depressed on the toolbar. Click the Relative Reference button again to switch back to absolute reference. The button no longer appears depressed.

Be prepared to create a new macro and name the macro. This macro will record entering data on the worksheet.

In the next task, you'll record your actions for formatting text with Times New Roman 12 point. Then, you'll stop recording the macro.

Task 2 Recording macros.

1. Select Format|Cells. The Format Cells dialog box should appear.
2. Click the Font tab, if necessary.
3. In the Font list, choose the Times New Roman font.
4. In the Font Size list, choose 12 point.
5. Click OK.
6. Click the Stop Recording button on the Macro toolbar.

The Recording mode indicator and the Stop Recording toolbar should disappear. You have now recorded a macro that contains instructions for formatting text with Times New Roman 12 point.

It's important that you know how to record and stop recording a macro.

After you have recorded a macro, you can run it at any time. In the next section, you'll run the macro you recorded in the preceding task.

Running Macros

Excel provides many ways to run macros. In this book, you'll learn how to run a macro using the Macro dialog box. Task 3 illustrates how to run a macro using the Macro dialog box.

Task 3 Running macros.

1. Select cell C1.
2. Select Tools|Macro, and choose Macros. You should see the Macro dialog box, as shown in Figure 21.2. Your font change macro should appear in the list of macros.
3. In the Macro name list, select font_chg, if necessary.
4. Click the Run button. The macro changes the font to 12 point Times New Roman in the selected cell.
5. Select cell C2.

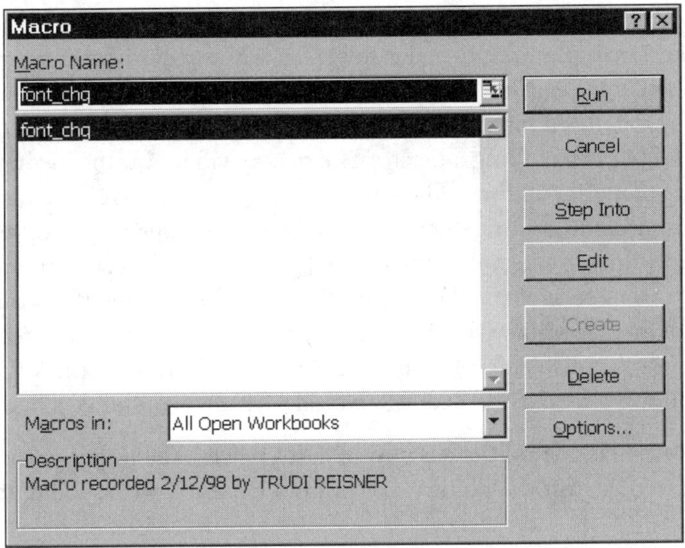

Figure 21.2 The Macro dialog box.

6. Press Ctrl+a.

   The macro applies the font changes to the text in cell C2.

In the Excel exam, you'll have to run a macro from the Macro dialog box.

After you create a macro, you might find that it needs additional commands or actions, or you might want to delete some commands or actions from the macro. What if you want to make changes to existing macro commands and actions or correct errors in a macro that doesn't run properly? No problem. You can make any of these changes to a macro by editing the macro, as you'll see in the next section on editing macros.

Editing Macros

Macro instructions are written in Visual Basic, a fairly easy-to-use programming language. With the macro sheet in view on screen, you can make changes to the Visual Basic instructions using Excel's editing commands. You can remove macro commands, edit the specific contents of a cell in the macro worksheet, or even insert new commands into the middle of a macro. Of course, making some changes will require knowledge of Visual Basic. Specific commands that relate to actions that you want are described in the Microsoft Excel manual that comes with the software.

Most likely, you'll want to clean up a recorded macro by removing stray commands. For example, if you make mistakes while recording a macro, those mistakes will appear in the macro and will be repeated each time you run the macro. Or, you might make an incorrect entry and then add another command to correct it while recording a macro. The macro will repeat the incorrect entry and the correction each time. The result will be fine, but there is no need to use system resources to continually repeat a mistake. In either scenario, you might want to edit the mistake out of the macro by removing the cells containing the incorrect macro commands. You'll probably have to examine the Visual Basic commands to determine where the mistake occurred. Remember to save the macro after you finish editing. You can use the Save button on the Visual Basic toolbar to save a macro, just like you would save any workbook.

The following task demonstrates how to edit a macro. You'll change the macro's font size setting from 12 point to 16 point Then, in Task 5, you'll delete the macro.

Task 4 Editing macros.

1. Select Tools|Macro, and choose Macros. You should see the Macro dialog box.
2. Select the font-chg macro, if necessary.
3. Click the Edit button. The Microsoft Visual Basic window should appear. You should see the Visual Basic toolbar and three window panes: Project—VBAProject, Properties—Module 1, and the Visual Basic Instructions (see Figure 21.3).

   You'll be working with the Visual Basic Instructions pane on the right. At the far-right end of the Visual Basic toolbar, you should see a line and column indicator: Ln *X*, Col *X*.
4. Click anywhere in Line 11 in the Visual Basic instructions, where it states **Size = 12**.
5. Click and drag over the number **12** to select it.
6. Type "16".
7. Click the Save button on the Visual Basic toolbar. This saves the changes you made to the macro.
8. Click the Close (X) button in the upper-right corner of the Microsoft Visual Basic window. This closes the window and returns you to the workbook.

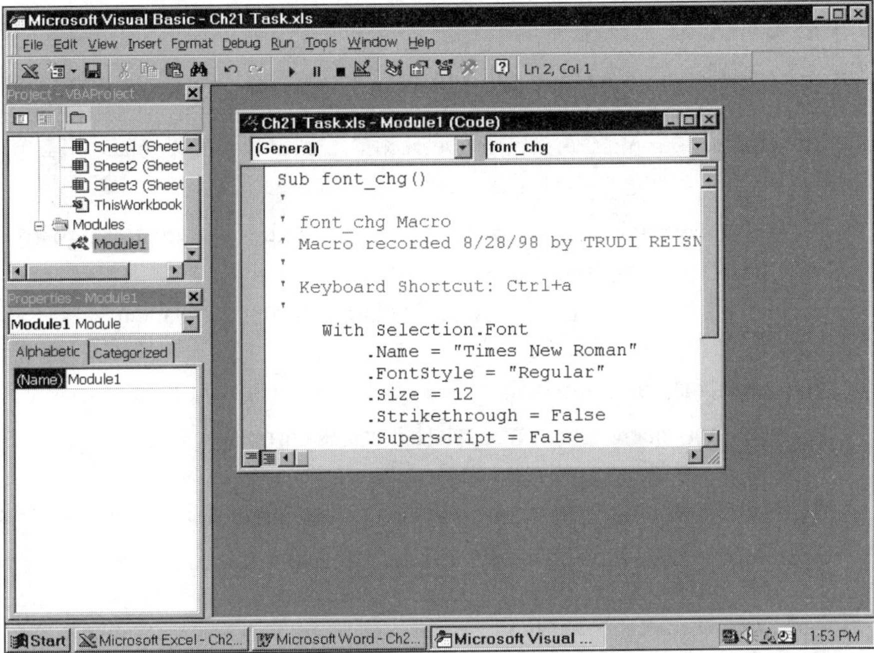

Figure 21.3 Macro sheet with Visual Basic instructions.

9. Click cell C1.
10. Press Ctrl+a.

    The macro applies the 16 point font to the text in the selected cell.

You'll be required to edit a macro. After you finish making the change, be sure that you don't click the Save button on the Visual Basic toolbar. Just close the Microsoft Visual Basic window. Excel saves the Visual Basic instructions automatically. Then, you'll run the macro you edited.

Task 5 Deleting macros.

1. Select Tools|Macro, and choose Macros. The Macro dialog box should appear.
2. Select the font_chg macro, if necessary.
3. Click the Delete button.
4. Choose Yes.

   Excel deletes the macro.
5. Close the Ch21 Task workbook file without saving changes.

Practice Exercise

The vice president of sales at Sandy Shores Company performs repetitive tasks in Excel worksheets. She would like to have a macro written to perform these repetitive tasks. Your mission is to create, record, run, and edit the macro. Then, you'll practice deleting a macro.

Figure 21.4 shows what the worksheet contains before you go through the instructions in this exercise.

1. Open the Ch21 Prac Ex workbook file stored on your companion disk.
2. Create a macro named Dollars, and use the shortcut key Ctrl+d.
3. Record the macro to format a selected cell as currency with zero decimal places.
4. Apply the macro to the numbers in the Current Salary column.
5. Edit the macro, and change the number of decimal places to two.

Note: Line 8 in the Visual Basic instructions contains the currency code $#,##0. At the end of the line, enter ".00".

Microsoft Excel - Ch21 Prac Ex.xls

	A	B	C	D
2		Sandy Shores		
3		Sales Team		
6		Starting Salary	% Increase	Current Salary
7	Blinder, Josh	50,000	5%	52,500
8	Fries, Cara	60,000	7%	63,000
9	Hunt, Neil	50,000	5%	52,500
10	Marston, Millie	70,000	10%	73,500
11	Zola, Lars	53,000	10%	55,650
12	Total			297,150

Figure 21.4 The Practice Exercise before you begin.

6. Save the macro.
7. Apply the macro to the numbers in the Current Salary column.
8. Delete the Dollars macro.
9. Save the workbook with the same name.
10. Close the workbook.

Answers To Practice Exercise

1. Click the Open tool on the Standard toolbar, and double-click the file name Ch21 Prac Ex.
2. Select Tools|Macro, and choose Record New Macro. The Record Macro dialog box appears. The default macro name Macro2 appears in the Macro name box. In the Macro Name box, type "Dollars". Press Tab. In the Shortcut Key box, type "d". Click OK. This creates a macro named Dollars and will use the shortcut key Ctrl+ d.
3. Select Format|Cells. The Format Cells dialog box opens. Click the Number tab. In the Category section, choose Currency. Click the down arrow next to Decimal Places until you see the number 0 (zero). Click OK. This records the Currency format setting with zero decimal places. Click the Stop Recording button on the Macro toolbar. This stops the recording of the macro.
4. Select the range D7:D12. Press Ctrl+ d. This applies the macro to the salary figures and displays dollar signs and zero decimal places. Click any cell to deselect the range.
5. Select Tools|Macro, and choose Macros. The Macro dialog box appears. Select the Dollars macro, if necessary. Click the Edit button. The Microsoft Visual Basic window appears. Click at the end of Line 8 in the Visual Basic instructions, where it states $#,##0. Type ".00", so the number format appears as $#,##0.00. The "00" you type must be inside the quotes at the end of Line 8. You have now edited the macro and changed the number of decimal places from zero to two.
6. Click the Save button on the Visual Basic toolbar. This saves the changes you made to the macro. Click the Close (X) button in the upper-right corner of the Microsoft Visual Basic window. This closes the window and returns you to the workbook.
7. Select the range D7:D12. Press Ctrl+d. This applies the macro to the salary figures and changes the number of decimal places to two.

8. Select Tools|Macro, and choose Macros. The Macro dialog box appears. Select the Dollars macro, if necessary. Click the Delete button. Choose Yes to confirm the deletion. Excel deletes the macro.
9. Click the Save tool on the Standard toolbar to save the workbook.

   When you finish the practice exercise, your worksheet should look like the one in Figure 21.5.
10. Click the Close (X) button in the upper-right corner of the document window. This closes the workbook.

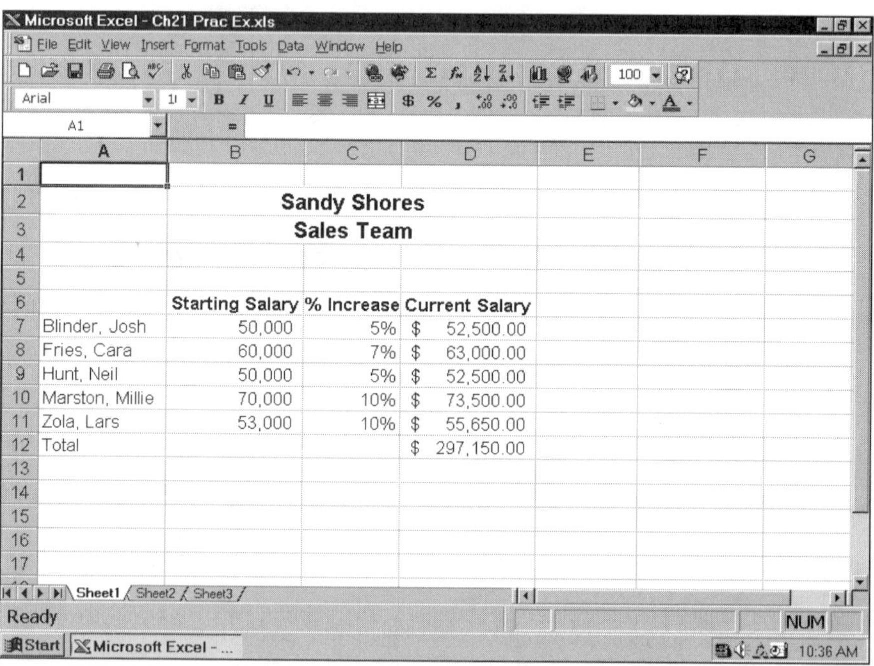

Figure 21.5 The completed Practice Exercise.

Need To Know More?

Craig, Deborah: *How to Use Microsoft Excel 97 for Windows*. Que, Indianapolis, IN, 1996. ISBN 1-56276-469-1. Chapter 17, "Automating Your Work with Macros and Templates," tells you how to create, record, run, and edit macros.

Harvey, Greg: *Excel 97 for Windows for Dummies*. IDG Books Worldwide, Inc., Foster City, CA, 1996. ISBN 0-7645-0049-X. Chapter 12, "Macros Like Your Mom Used to Make," explains how to create, record, run, and edit macros.

Nicholson, John R. and Sean R. Nicholson: *Discover Excel 97*. IDG Books Worldwide, Inc., Foster City, CA, 1997. ISBN 1-7645-3047-X. Chapter 13, "Macros and Templates and Style (Oh, My!)," gives you information on creating, recording, running, and editing macros.

Nossiter, Josh: *Using Microsoft Excel 97*. Que, Indianapolis, IN, 1996. ISBN 0-7897-0955-4. Chapter 19, "Introduction to Macros," talks about creating, recording, running, and editing macros.

Using Workgroup Functions

Terms you'll need to understand:

- ✓ Shared workbooks
- ✓ Accept
- ✓ Reject
- ✓ Track changes
- ✓ History
- ✓ Comments
- ✓ Conflicts
- ✓ Merge workbooks

Skills you'll need to master:

- ✓ Setting up shared workbooks
- ✓ Reviewing and changing shared workbooks
- ✓ Tracking changes and viewing a History list
- ✓ Using comments
- ✓ Resolving conflicts
- ✓ Merging workbooks

Sharing, Reviewing, And Merging Workbooks

Microsoft Excel users sometimes need to interact with associates who also use Excel. Excel users can easily work collaboratively and manage shared files effectively.

This chapter introduces you to the Excel 97 *shared workbooks* feature. Shared workbooks were called *shared lists* in Excel 95. In this chapter, you'll learn how to share Excel workbooks, track and display changes in workbooks, use comments, resolve conflicts, and merge workbooks.

Sharing Your Workbooks With Others

Excel's shared workbooks feature allows multiple users to modify a single workbook simultaneously. The shared workbook resides on a network so that users can make changes at the same time. Then, the shared workbook is updated to incorporate the changes. Each user can format the workbooks and make other choices, such as viewing and printing choices, that are used for their own filtered version of the workbook. Changes from multiple users are consolidated automatically at specified intervals, which is called *merging* workbooks.

HOLD That Skill!

In the Share Workbook dialog box, on the Editing tab, you can tell Excel that you want to allow simultaneous access to a workbook. After doing so, you can set further options on the Advanced tab. Here are the advanced share workbook options you'll need to set up:

- **Track Changes** Lets you control how long to track workbook changes. You need to enable the Keep Change History For option to see merged changes from other users.
- **Update Changes** Enables you to control how changes made by multiple users are consolidated into the main document. You can choose to see the changes whenever the file is saved or in minute-based intervals.
- **Conflicting Changes Between Users** Controls how conflicting changes are resolved. For example, when two users change the same cell to different values. Usually, this should always be set to the Ask Me Which Changes Win option.

When you share workbooks, you can track changes made by users over a number of days. Excel uses the History sheet to show a complete list of changes to the workbook. The History list includes the names of the users who made the changes, data that was deleted or replaced, and information about conflicting changes.

The following task steps through the process of setting up the shared workbooks feature so you can share workbooks with others.

Task 1 Setting up shared workbooks.

1. Open the Ch22 Task workbook file located on the companion disk.
2. Select Tools|Share Workbook. Excel should bring up the Share Workbook dialog box, as shown in Figure 22.1.
3. Choose Allow Changes By More Than One User At The Same Time option, if necessary.
4. Click the Advanced tab. Change the number of days to 45. This keeps the change history for 45 days.

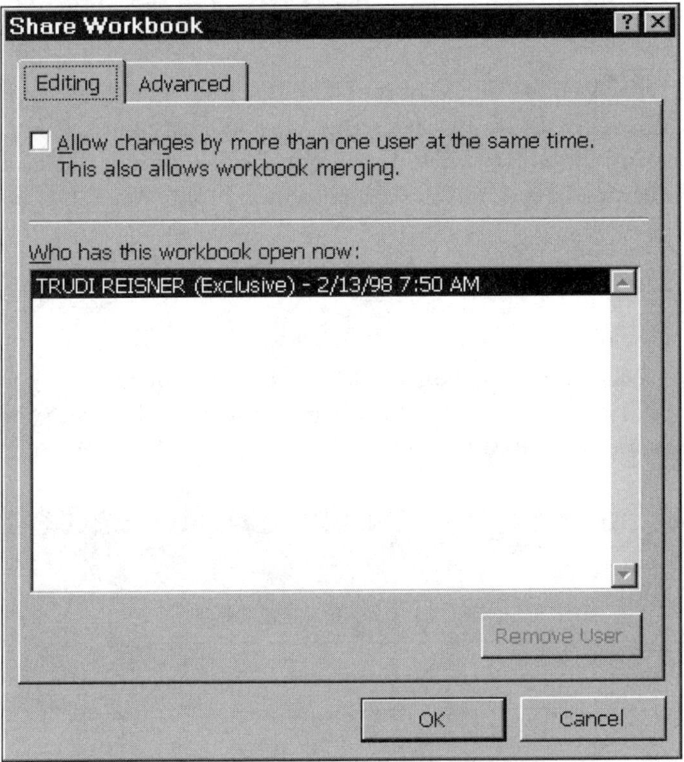

Figure 22.1 The Share Workbook dialog box.

5. Click OK. Excel should prompt you to save the workbook.
6. Click OK.

Excel should save the workbook on a network drive so that others can gain access to the shared workbook. You should see the workbook file name [Shared] in the Title bar, at the top of the Excel window.

It's important to know how to set up shared workbooks, allow changes by more than one user at a time, and specify the number of days you want to keep the change history.

Task 2 shows you how to review a shared workbook and make changes to it.

Task 2 Reviewing and changing shared workbooks.

1. In cell D5, type "9500", and press Enter.
2. Select Tools|Track Changes, and choose Accept Or Reject Changes. When prompted to save the workbook, click OK. Excel should open the Select Changes To Accept Or Reject dialog box, as shown in Figure 22.2.
3. Select the Who checkbox. In the Who box, you should see Everyone. The other options are Everyone But Me and a list of user names who are sharing the workbook with you. For the purposes of this task, leave the Everyone option and the default option in the When box.

   Note: If you want to review changes by all the users, clear the Who checkbox.

4. Select the Where checkbox. Click cell D5. This enters the cell reference in the Where box and indicates where you made a change to a value in a specific area on the worksheet.

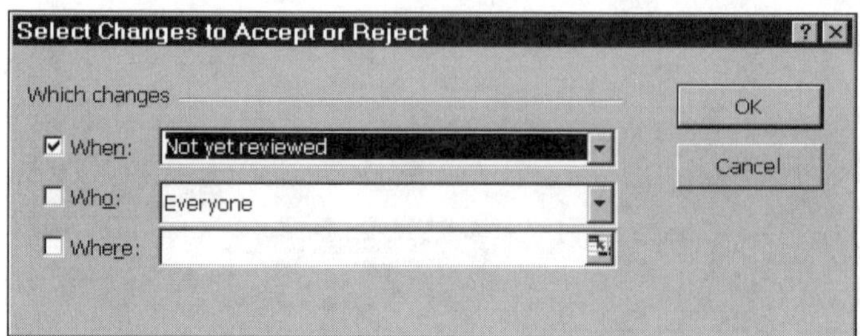

Figure 22.2 The Select Changes To Accept Or Reject dialog box.

Note: If you want to review changes to the entire workbook, clear the Where checkbox.

5. Click OK.

   In the Accept Or Reject Changes dialog box, read the information about the first change (see Figure 22.3). The information also contains any dependent changes that are affected by the action you take for this change. If necessary, use the scroll arrows to see all the information.

   To accept the change and clear its marquee, click the Accept button. To undo the change, click the Reject button. If Excel prompts you to select a value for a cell, click the value you want, and then click the Accept button.

   For each change, click the Accept or Reject button, or click the Accept All button or the Reject All button to accept or reject the rest of the changes.

   For the purposes of this task, click the Accept button.

Note: You must accept or reject a change before you can advance to the next change.

Be prepared to accept and reject changes using the Accept or Reject Changes dialog box.

When two people work on a shared workbook, if Person 1 makes a change to a cell and saves the workbook, and then Person 2 also saves his or her copy of the workbook, Person 2 will see any changes that Person 1 has made. The changes will be highlighted with a comment indicator in the workbook that

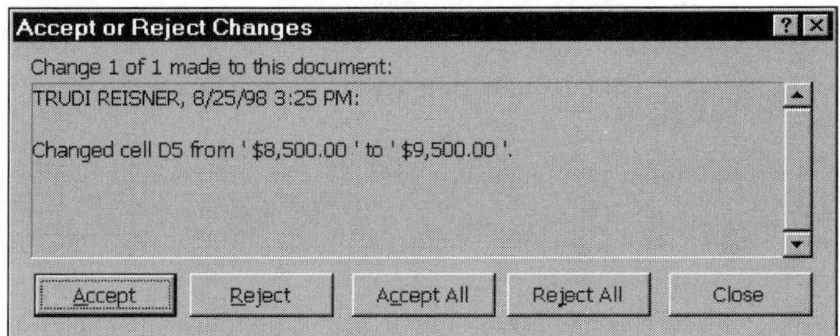

Figure 22.3 The Accept Or Reject Changes dialog box.

shows Person 2 the changes that Person 1 made, and the changes will be accepted as a matter of course.

Excel provides some features to help manage shared workbooks. Namely, Excel enables you to view who is using a file and supplies you with the History sheet. In Task 3, you'll check out who has the file open, and then you'll track the changes in a shared workbook by showing a history of changes. When you check the History list, Excel inserts a new sheet called the History sheet to show the changes.

Task 3 Tracking changes and viewing a History list.

1. Select Tools|Share Workbook. You should see the Share Workbook dialog box.
2. In the Editing tab, view the Who Has The Workbook Open Now list. You might see one or more names, accompanied by the date and time each user opened the workbook.
3. Click OK.
4. Select Tools|Track Changes, and choose Highlight Changes. The Highlight Changes dialog box should open (see Figure 22.4).
5. In the When drop-down list, you can choose any of the following:
   - Since I Last Saved
   - All

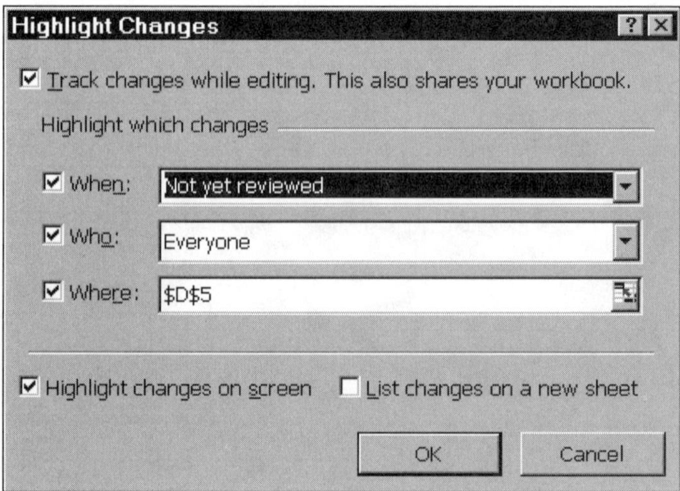

Figure 22.4 The Highlight Changes dialog box.

- Not Yet Reviewed
- Since Date

In this task, you want to show a history of all the changes, so click the When checkbox to clear it.

6. In the Who drop-down list, you can choose from
   - Everyone
   - Everyone But Me
   - Each User's Name Individually

   Click the Who checkbox to clear it.
7. In the Where drop-down list, select the cells that will be shown. If you leave this blank, it causes all cells to be included. Let's leave it blank in order to show a history of the changes. Click in the Where checkbox to clear it.
8. Choose List Changes On A New Sheet. This controls where changes are displayed.
9. Click OK. Excel should highlight the changes on the screen and show comments where the changes were made. Also, Excel should insert a History sheet in the workbook to show a history of the changes made, as shown in Figure 22.5.

Excel inserts a new sheet called History into your workbook. It shows you a detailed record of changes made to a sheet. The History sheet shows only the changes that fit the criteria selected in the Highlight Changes dialog box.

Be sure you know how to track changes made by everyone in a worksheet and display a History sheet.

When you select the Highlight The Changes On The Screen option in the Highlight Changes dialog box, Excel inserts a comment next to the cells where you make changes. In the next task, you'll view a comment for the change you made in the worksheet.

Task 4 Using comments.

1. Click the Sheet1 tab.
2. Point to cell D5.

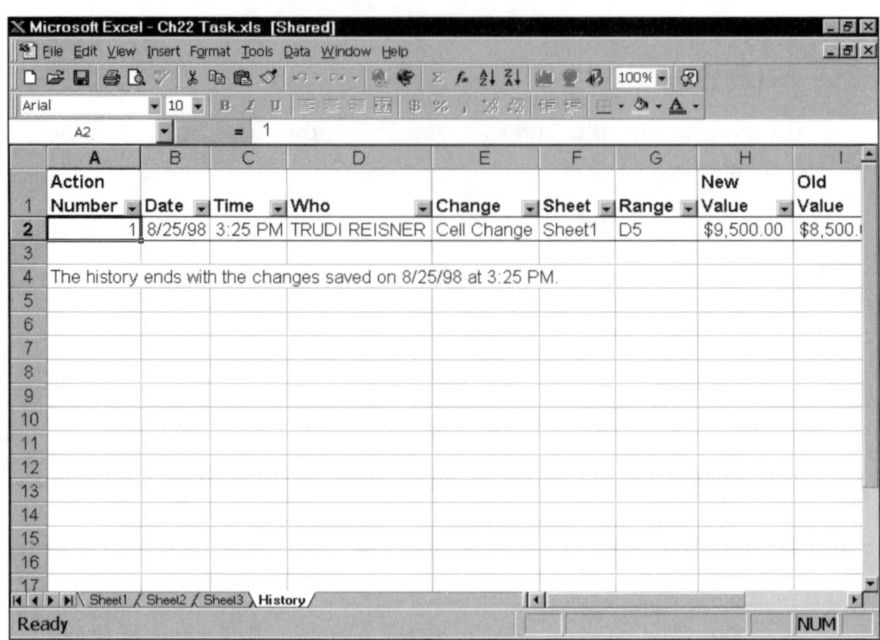

Figure 22.5 The History sheet, showing a history of changes.

You should see a comment in a light yellow text box with an arrow pointing to the cell where the change was made (see Figure 22.6). The comment includes the name of the person who inserted the comment, the date and time the change was made, and a description of the change.

> *Note: If more than one user adds a comment to the same cell in a shared workbook, the text of all saved comments for the cells appears when each user saves the shared workbook.*

If Person 1 and Person 2 both change the same cell to different values, a conflict arises. When an entry conflicts, the second person to save the workbook will see the Resolve Conflicts dialog box. They will need to resolve the conflict by using this dialog box before their version of the workbook can be saved. In the Resolve Conflicts dialog box, you select the conflicts you want to resolve and review them individually. To review them, click the Accept Mine or Accept Other button. If there are many changes that you want to accept from the same editor, click the Accept All Mine button or the Accept All Others button. The Resolve Conflict dialog box disappears when you resolve the conflict(s).

> *Note: If you reject another person's changes in favor of your own, that person will see your changes when he or she saves the workbook. At that*

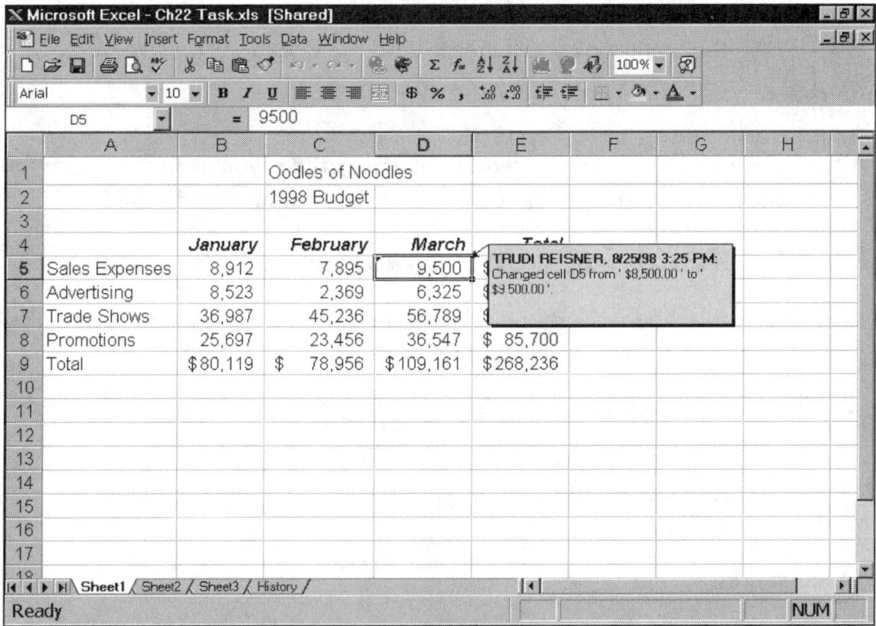

Figure 22.6 A comment on the shared worksheet.

point, no conflict will arise for this person. Your changes will simply be updated into his or her copy of the workbook, along with the change comment. If you click the Cancel button, Excel cancels your save of the document. You cannot save your version until you resolve the conflicts.

You'll be required to resolve a conflict on the exam.

When you have multiple copies of the same workbook that contain changes from various users, you can merge those changes into one workbook. To do so, you can select Tools|Merge Workbooks. Then, you save the shared workbook, if asked by Excel. The Select Files To Merge Into Current Workbook dialog box should appear. Select a copy of the shared workbook that has changes you want to merge. Click OK. Repeat these steps until all copies of the shared workbook are merged.

To merge several copies of a shared workbook at once, select more than one workbook by holding down the Ctrl or Shift key and then clicking on the file names.

Be ready to merge two workbooks. You'll be given the name of the workbook you'll merge with the workbook on screen.

When you're finished sharing a workbook with others, you need to remove the workbook from shared use. The next task shows you how to do this.

Task 5 Removing workbooks from shared use.

1. Select Tools|Share Workbook. Excel should open the Share Workbook dialog box, as shown earlier in Figure 22.1.
2. Click the Allow Changes By More Than One User At The Same Time checkbox. This should clear the checkbox.
3. Click OK. Excel should prompt you to confirm removing the workbook from shared use.
4. Click Yes.
5. Close the Ch22 Task workbook. After you remove the file from the shared list, Excel removes the History worksheet from the workbook.

Practice Exercise

The sales director and human resources manager at Sandy Shores Company would like to collaborate on revising the sales rep salaries. They need to share a workbook that contains the salary information. In this Practice Exercise, you'll set up a workbook for shared use, make a change to a sales rep's salary, and accept the change. Next, you'll track the changes by asking Excel to highlight the change in the worksheet, as well as display a History sheet to show the change. Then, you'll view a comment, and, finally, you'll merge workbooks.

Figure 22.7 shows what the worksheet contains before you complete the instructions in this exercise.

1. Open the Ch22 Prac Ex workbook file stored on your companion disk.
2. Set up the workbook so that it can be shared with others. Keep the change history for 50 days.
3. Change Neil Hunter's salary to $55,000.
4. Review and accept the change you made to the shared workbook.
5. Track the changes by showing the changes on the worksheet and a History sheet.

Microsoft Excel - Ch22 Prac Ex.xls

Sandy Shores
Sales Team

	Starting Salary	% Increase	Current Salary
Blinder, Josh	50,000	5%	52,500
Fries, Cara	60,000	7%	63,000
Hunt, Neil	50,000	5%	52,500
Marston, Millie	70,000	10%	73,500
Zola, Lars	53,000	10%	55,650
Total			297,150

Figure 22.7 The Practice Exercise before you begin.

6. View the comment.
7. Remove the workbook from shared use.
8. Save the workbook.
9. Close the workbook.

Answers To Practice Exercise

1. Click the Open tool on the Standard toolbar, and double-click on the file name Ch22 Prac Ex.
2. Select Tools|Share Workbook. Excel brings up the Share Workbook dialog box. Choose the Allow Changes By More Than One User At The Same Time option.Click the Advanced tab. Change the number of days to 50. This keeps the change history for 50 days. Click OK. Excel prompts you to save the workbook. Click OK. This sets up the workbook so that it can be shared with others.
3. Click cell B9, and type "55000", then press Enter. This changes Neil Hunter's salary to $55,000.
4. Select Tools|Track Changes, and choose Accept Or Reject Changes. When prompted to save the workbook, click OK. Excel opens the Select Changes To Accept Or Reject dialog box. Click in the Who checkbox, and leave the Everyone option. Click in the Where checkbox, click in the Where box, and then click cell B9. This enters the cell reference in the Where box. Click OK. In the Accept Or Reject Changes dialog box, read the information about the change. Click the Accept button. You have now reviewed and accepted the change you made to the shared workbook.
5. Select Tools|Track Changes, and choose Highlight Changes. The Highlight Changes dialog box opens. Click the When checkbox, the Who checkbox, and Where checkbox to clear all of them. Choose List Changes On A New Sheet. Click OK. Excel inserts a History sheet in the workbook to show a history of the changes. On Sheet1, Excel highlights the change on the screen and shows a comment where the change was made.
6. Click the Sheet1 tab. Point to cell B9. This displays the comment.

   Your worksheet should look like the one in Figure 22.8.
7. Select Tools|Share Workbook. Excel brings up the Share Workbook dialog box. Choose the Allow Changes By More Than One User At The Same Time option. This should clear the checkbox. Click OK. Excel prompts you to confirm removing the workbook from shared use. Click Yes. This removes the workbook from shared use.

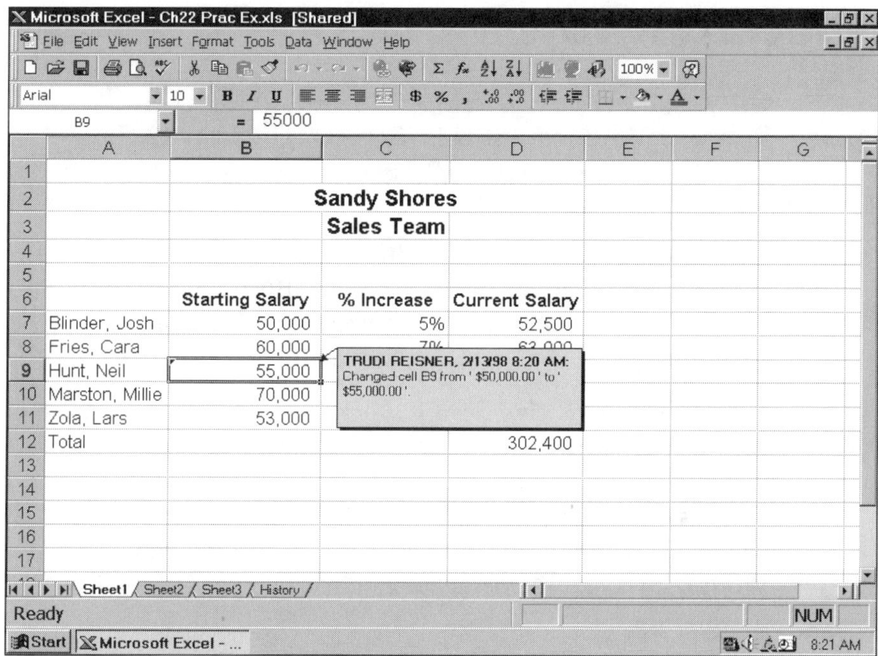

Figure 22.8 The completed Practice Exercise.

8. Click the Save tool on the Standard toolbar to save the workbook.
9. Click the Close (X) button in the upper-right corner of the workbook window to close the workbook.

Need To Know More?

Catapult, Inc.: *Microsoft Excel 97 Step By Step*. Microsoft Press, Redmond, WA, 1996. ISBN 1-57231-314-5. Lesson 12, "Sharing a Workbook with Others," discusses sharing workbooks and reviewing changes in workbooks.

Harvey, Greg: *Excel 97 for Windows for Dummies*. IDG Books Worldwide, Inc., Foster City, CA, 1996. ISBN 0-7645-0049-X. Chapter 6, "Oh, What a Tangled Worksheet We Weave," explains how to use comments in a worksheet.

Nicholson, John R. and Sean R. Nicholson: *Discover Excel 97*. IDG Books Worldwide, Inc., Foster City, CA, 1997. ISBN 1-7645-3047-X. Chapter 15, "Sharing the Workload: Group Projects," gives you information on combining files, sharing workbooks, and tracking changes. Chapter 17, "A Bug in Your Worksheet: Basic Troubleshooting," discusses resolving conflicts in worksheets.

Nossiter, Josh: *Using Microsoft Excel 97*. Que, Indianapolis, IN, 1996. ISBN 0-7897-0955-4. Chapter 17, "Linking Workbooks, Sharing Workbooks," talks about sharing workbooks.

Expert Printing

Terms you'll need to understand:

- √ Preview
- √ Print range
- √ Page setup
- √ Print area
- √ Print titles

Skills you'll need to master:

- √ Previewing worksheets
- √ Previewing portions of worksheets
- √ Setting print titles
- √ Printing a range of pages
- √ Printing entire workbooks

Printing Your Workbooks

Excel's Print command lets you print an entire workbook or a selected portion of a workbook. Excel's Print Preview feature enables you to see exactly how your workbook, worksheet, or selected data will print before you print it. This chapter shows you how to preview worksheets, preview specific cells on worksheets, print specific pages of a workbook, and print an entire workbook. You'll also see how you can set up *print titles* to print information on the left side of every page in a worksheet.

Previewing And Printing Workbooks

With the Print Preview command, you can display how selected cells or pages in a sheet will look when printed, including print titles (print titles are column and/or row headings that repeat on every printed page). In order to preview selected cells, you have to display Excel's Print dialog box.

You can print only the pages you specify or an entire workbook. To print Excel data, you have to display the Print dialog box. You can print the column and row headings that appear on the top and left sides of your worksheet on every page of a printout. Printed column and row headings are called print titles. To include print titles in your printout, you need to use the Page Setup dialog box.

In the upcoming tasks, you'll preview a worksheet and selected cells in a worksheet using the Print dialog box. Next, you'll specify print titles using the Page Setup dialog box, and, finally, you'll print a range of pages and the entire workbook.

Task 1 Previewing worksheets using the Print dialog box.

1. Open the Ch23 Task workbook located on the companion disk.
2. Press Ctrl+P. The Print dialog box should appear.
3. Click the Preview button in the Print dialog box. You should see the document in the Preview window (see Figure 23.1).
4. Click the Close button on the Print Preview toolbar.

Your document window should be displayed.

It's essential that you know how to preview a worksheet using the Print dialog box before you take the exam.

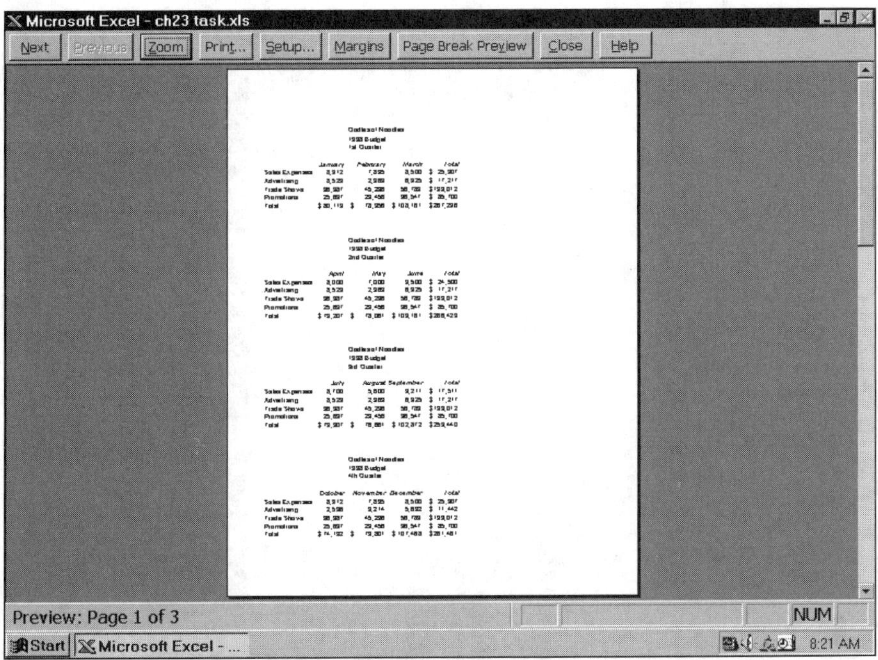

Figure 23.1 The Print Preview window.

Task 2 Previewing selected cells in worksheets.

1. Select cell B6. Hold down Ctrl, and select cell D6.
2. Press Ctrl+P. The Print dialog box should appear.
3. In the Print What area, choose Selection.
4. Click the Preview button in the Print dialog box. You should see the first cell in the Preview window (see Figure 23.2).
5. Click the Next button on the Print Preview toolbar. You should see the second selected cell in the Preview window.
6. Click the Close button on the Print Preview toolbar.
7. Click any cell to deselect the range.

When you take the exam, be prepared to select noncontiguous cells on a worksheet and preview them using the Print dialog box. Be sure to choose Selection in the Print What section of the Print dialog box so that you can preview the selected cells.

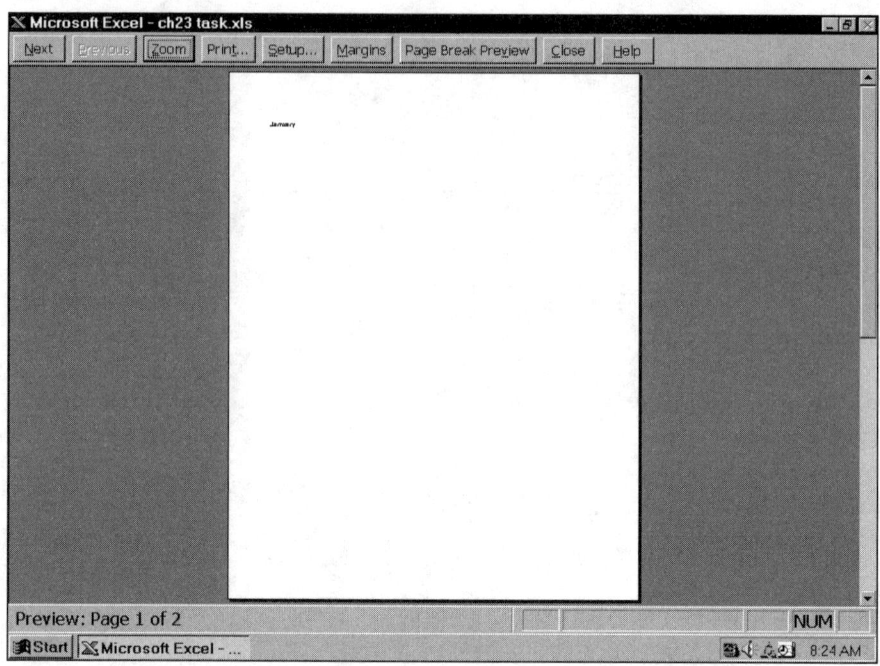

Figure 23.2 A selected cell in the Print Preview window.

Task 3 Setting print titles to print row headings in worksheets.

1. Select the range B6:D11.
2. Select File|Print Area|Set Print Area.
3. Select File|Page Setup. The Page Setup dialog box should open.
4. Click the Sheet tab.
5. In the Print Titles area, click the Columns To Repeat At Left box.
6. Drag the Page Setup dialog box out of the way, and click any cell in Column A (see Figure 23.3).

   This selects the row headings in Column A that you want to repeat on every printed page.
7. Click OK.

   Excel displays a border around the print area.
8. Click any cell to deselect the range.
9. Select File|Print Preview. The selected area displays with print titles.

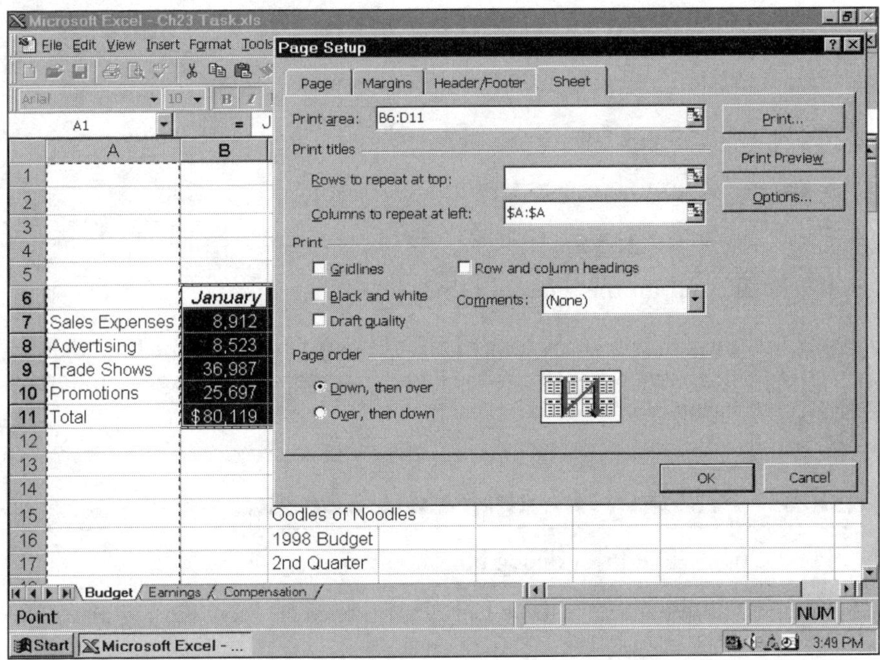

Figure 23.3 The Sheet tab in the Page Setup dialog box.

10. In the Print Preview window, click the Close button. This closes the Print Preview window.
11. Click File|Print Area|Clear Print Area. The print area range is cleared. Notice the selected range no longer displays with a border.
12. Select File|Page Setup. The Page Setup dialog box should open.
13. Click the Sheet tab, if necessary.
14. In the Print Titles area, click the Columns To Repeat At Left box, highlight AA, and press Delete. The print titles are removed from the page setup specifications.
15. Click OK to close the Page Setup dialog box.

It's important that you know how to set up print titles.

The next two tasks show you how to print selected pages (pages 1 and 2), and then print the entire workbook.

Task 4 Printing selected pages in the worksheet.

1. Press Ctrl+P. The Print dialog box should open.
2. In the Print Range area, choose Page(s).
3. Click in the From box, and type "1".
4. Press Tab. In the To box, type "2" (see Figure 23.4).
5. Click OK to print the selected pages.

Be sure you know how to print selected pages. In the Print dialog box, remember to choose Page(s), and enter the page numbers in the From and To boxes.

Task 5 Printing the entire workbook.

1. Press Ctrl+P. The Print dialog box should open.
2. In the Print What area, choose Entire Workbook, as shown in Figure 23.5.
3. Click OK to print the whole workbook.
4. Close the workbook without saving changes.

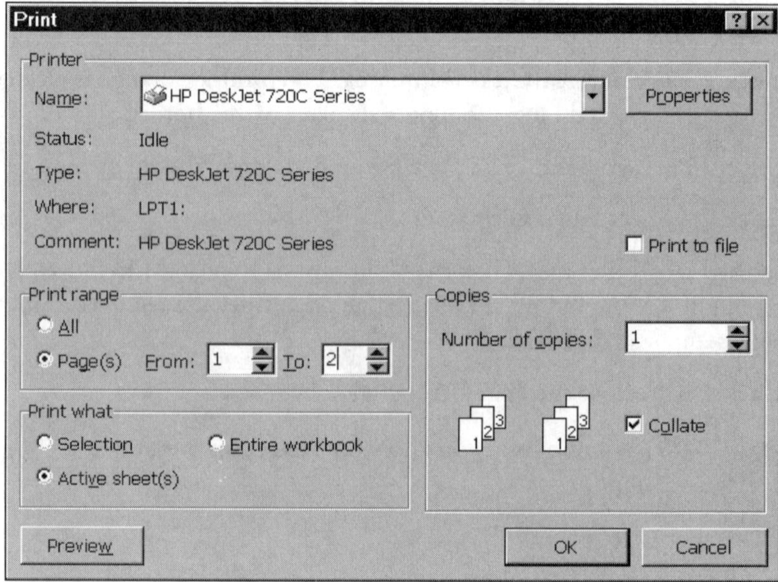

Figure 23.4 The Page option in the Print dialog box.

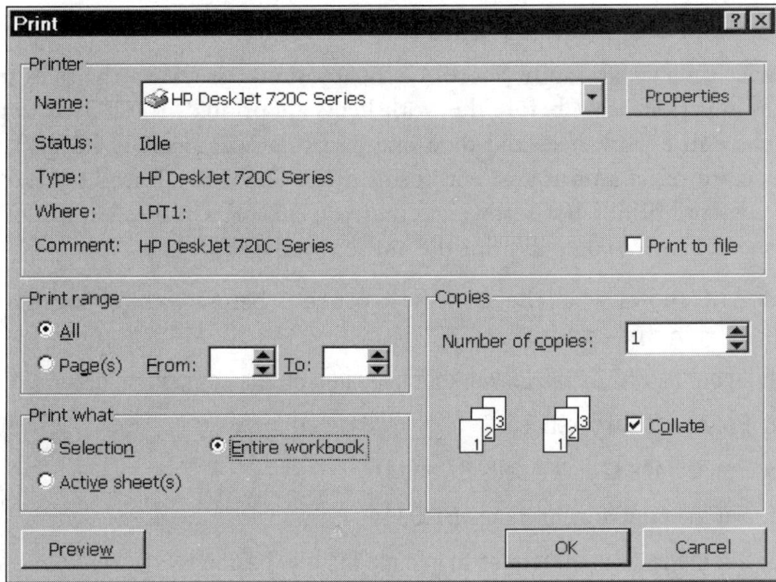

Figure 23.5 The Entire Workbook option in the Print dialog box.

Be prepared to print an entire workbook. Be sure to choose Entire Workbook in the Print What area of the Print dialog box.

Practice Exercise

The sales director at Sandy Shores Company wants to review the sales team salaries in various ways before the worksheets are printed. You'll need to preview the entire worksheet and then one particular salesperson's salary. You'll also need to select a print area with print titles. Then, you'll need to clear the print area and print titles settings so that you can print pages 2 and 3 of the worksheet. Finally, you will print the entire workbook.

Figure 23.6 shows what the worksheet contains before you go through the instructions in this exercise.

1. Open the Ch23 Prac Ex workbook located on the companion disk.
2. Preview the worksheet.
3. Preview the selected cells B7 and D7.
4. Set the print area for range B7:D11.
5. Set the column print titles to include the row headings.
6. Remove the print area range selection and print titles setup option.
7. Print only pages 2 and 3.
8. Print the workbook.

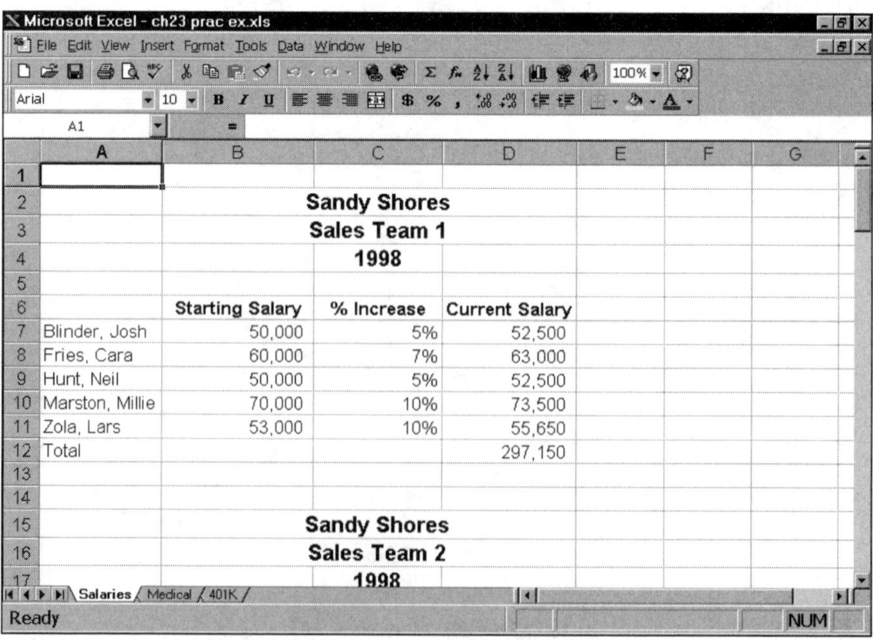

Figure 23.6 The Practice Exercise before you begin.

9. Save the workbook with the same name.
10. Close the workbook.

Answers To Practice Exercise

1. Click the Open button on the Standard toolbar, and double-click the file name Ch23 Prac Ex.
2. Press Ctrl+P. The Print dialog box appears. Click the Preview button in the Print dialog box. Excel displays the worksheet in Print Preview. Click the Close button on the Print Preview toolbar. This closes Print Preview.
3. Select cell B7. Hold down Ctrl, and select cell D7. Press Ctrl+P. The Print dialog box appears. In the Print What area, choose Selection. Click the Preview button in the Print dialog box. Excel displays the first selected cell in Print Preview. Click the Next button on the Print Preview toolbar. You should see the second selected cell in Print Preview. Click the Close button on the Print Preview toolbar. This closes Print Preview. Click any cell to deselect the cells.
4. Select the range B7:D11. Select File|Print Area|Set Print Area. Excel displays a border surrounding the print area.
5. Select File|Page Setup. Click the Sheet tab, if necessary. In the Print Titles area, click the Columns To Repeat At Left box. Drag the Page Setup dialog box out of the way, and click any cell in Column A. Click OK.
6. Select File|Print Area|Clear Print Area. Then, select File|Page Setup. In the Print Titles area, click the Columns To Repeat At Left box, highlight AA, press Delete, and then click OK.
7. Press Ctrl+P. The Print dialog box appears. In the Print Range area, choose Page(s). Click in the From box, and type "2". Press Tab. In the To box, type "3". Click OK. Excel prints pages 2 and 3.
8. Press Ctrl+P. The Print dialog box appears. In the Print What area, choose Entire Workbook. Click OK. Excel prints the entire workbook. Your worksheet should look the same as when you started the Practice Exercise, as shown in Figure 23.6.
9. Click the Save button on the Standard toolbar to save the workbook.
10. Click the Close (X) button in the upper-right corner of the document window. This closes the workbook.

Need To Know More?

Catapult, Inc.: *Microsoft Excel 97 Step By Step*. Microsoft Press, Redmond, WA, 1996. ISBN 1-57231-314-5. Lesson 10, "Printing Reports to Distribute Information Offline," covers the details of previewing and printing a worksheet.

Craig, Deborah: *How to Use Microsoft Excel 97 for Windows*. Que, Indianapolis, IN, 1996. ISBN 1-56276-469-1. Chapter 5, "Printing," gives you all the information you need about previewing and printing a worksheet.

Harvey, Greg: *Excel 97 for Windows for Dummies*. IDG Books Worldwide, Inc., Foster City, CA, 1996. ISBN 0-7645-0049-X. Chapter 5, "Printing the Masterpiece," explains how to preview and print worksheets.

Neibauer, Alan: *Excel One Step at a Time*. IDG Books Worldwide, Inc., Foster City, CA, 1997. ISBN 0-7645-3139-5. Lesson 4, "Rearranging and Previewing Worksheets," explains how to preview worksheets. Lesson 10, "Arranging and Printing Worksheets," discusses previewing and printing worksheets.

Nicholson, John R. and Sean R. Nicholson: *Discover Excel 97*. IDG Books Worldwide, Inc., Foster City, CA, 1997. ISBN 1-7645-3047-X. Chapter 9, "Get Ready, Get Set! Go to Page Setup," explains print titles. Chapter 10, "Out with the New: Printing Worksheets," covers previewing and printing worksheets.

Nossiter, Josh: *Using Microsoft Excel 97*. Que, Indianapolis, IN, 1996. ISBN 0-7897-0955-4. Chapter 5, "Putting It All on Paper: Printing Worksheets and Workbooks," has a nice discussion of previewing and printing worksheets.

Reisner, Trudi: *Easy Microsoft Office*. Que, Indianapolis, IN, 1997. ISBN 0-7897-1078-1. In Part VIII, "Formatting the Worksheet," refer to Task 54, "Previewing and Printing the Worksheet," which explains previewing and printing worksheets.

24

Sample Expert Level Test

Congratulations. You've almost finished the Expert test chapters, and you're just about ready for the test. Now, wouldn't you like to walk into the testing center and ace the exam? Go for it—you can do it! This chapter tells you what to expect, what to memorize, how to prepare, and it even provides a sample test that you can run through. You can look up the answers for the sample test in the following chapter.

What You Need To Know About The Excel Expert Exam

There are approximately 40 tasks on the MOUS Expert Excel exam. When you start the test, Excel opens, and the first task appears in a window. The time limit of the exam is 60 minutes. It's a good idea to answer as many questions as you know on the entire exam. When the time is up, Excel closes, the task window closes, and you can no longer answer questions. A progression bar appears while the MOUS exam software checks your test answers. After your test answers are checked, the exam software calculates your score. The scoring information is given to the test administrator.

Working Within The Framework

Each task is unrelated to the next task. If you can't answer something, look up the feature in Help. If you still can't perform the task, then proceed to the next task.

Deciding What To Memorize

Often, there is more than one way to accomplish a task. You should use shortcuts, such as shortcut menus and toolbar buttons to perform tasks in the fastest way possible. The exam does require you to perform specific steps to accomplish each goal.

Scoring Information

Immediately after you finish the test, the MOUS exam software calculates your score. The scoring information process takes about an hour. After the results are in, your test administrator will notify you as to whether you passed or failed. If you pass, an MOUS Certification certificate will be mailed to you within two weeks of the test date. If you fail, you can always retest again until you pass the exam.

Preparing For The Test

The first step you should take to prepare for an MOUS Excel exam is to carefully read the appropriate chapters in this book. Read Chapters 14 through 25 to prepare for the MOUS Expert Excel exam. In each chapter, be sure to step through each task and Practice Exercise, and read all the exam alerts, tips, and notes. Make sure you go through the test exercises, too. The next step you should take is to study and practice the information provided in the books and CDs referenced in the "Need To Know More?" section at the end of each chapter in this book. Another way to prepare for the test is to take Excel classes or get one-on-one Excel tutoring from an MOUS certified Excel trainer. If you do some or all of these things, you will be well-prepared for the test.

Taking The Test

When you take an MOUS Excel exam, the test administrator will give you two wipe-off boards (laminated paper) with several marker pens. You can use these boards for a scratch pad. The test administrator will instruct you as to when you can begin taking the test. The test administrator will be available for any questions you might have while you're taking the test. When the test is over, the test administrator will give you your test results.

Test Exercises

There are three test exercises in this chapter. Each test exercise starts with a scenario and is similar to the Practice Exercises presented in earlier chapters. Read each test exercise's scenario first. A figure showing the original worksheet is provided. You'll be working on three worksheets—a different one for each exercise. You should familiarize yourself with the worksheet before you proceed to the test tasks. A set of tasks are provided for each exercise. Carefully read the test tasks before you start working in Excel. In order to answer the test tasks, you need to perform Excel tasks. Chapter 25 provides the answers to the test exercises contained in this chapter.

Exercise 1

The Sales department at the Crunchy Granola Company tracks orders in an Excel workbook. Your job is to work on the sales report and complete it so that the Sales Manager can make some management decisions based on the figures in the report.

Figure 24.1 shows what the worksheet contains before you work through the instructions in this exercise.

1. Open the Expert Test Exercise 1 workbook located on the companion disk.
2. In the Sales 96 worksheet, place conditional formatting on the Quantity field column so that the Quantity field column values below 150 are shown in bold Violet and Quantity values greater than 200 in bold Lime.
3. In the Sales 97 worksheet, sort data by Employee in ascending order followed by Quantity in descending order.
4. In the Sales 98 worksheet, create a pivot table based on sales data. The data is Quantity, the column heading is Employee, and the row heading is Date. Place the pivot table on the same worksheet in cell A15.

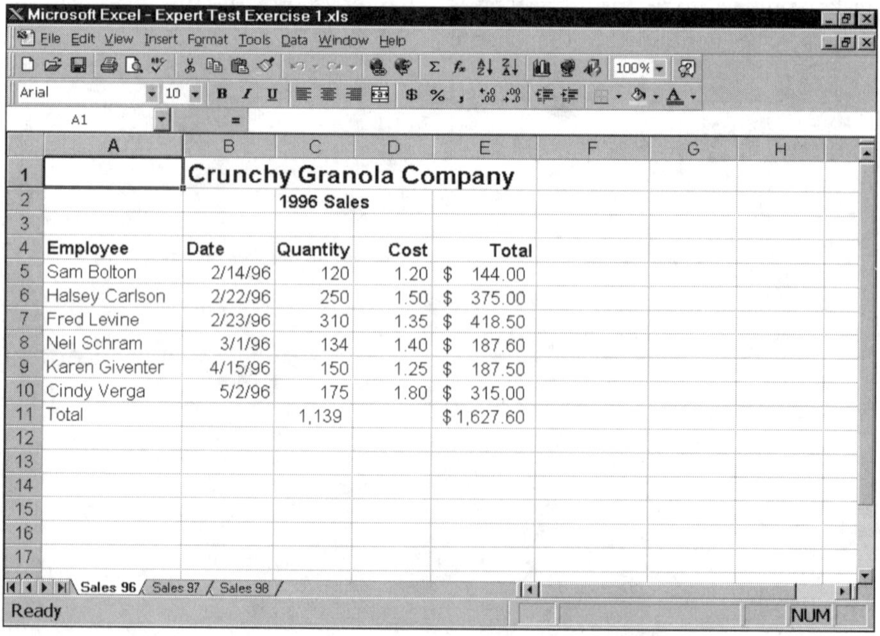

Microsoft Excel - Expert Test Exercise 1.xls

	A	B	C	D	E
1		Crunchy Granola Company			
2			1996 Sales		
3					
4	Employee	Date	Quantity	Cost	Total
5	Sam Bolton	2/14/96	120	1.20	$ 144.00
6	Halsey Carlson	2/22/96	250	1.50	$ 375.00
7	Fred Levine	2/23/96	310	1.35	$ 418.50
8	Neil Schram	3/1/96	134	1.40	$ 187.60
9	Karen Giventer	4/15/96	150	1.25	$ 187.50
10	Cindy Verga	5/2/96	175	1.80	$ 315.00
11	Total		1,139		$ 1,627.60

Sales 96 / Sales 97 / Sales 98

Figure 24.1 Test Exercise 1 before you begin.

5. In the Sales 96 worksheet, create a new query that imports data from the Microsoft Access 97 database Sales 94.mdb. (*Note:* Create a new data source.) Name the data source Sales 94. Select all the fields for the EMPLOYEES table. Do not filter or sort the fields. Save the query as Sales 96 Query. Place the imported information in cell A15 on the Sales 96 worksheet.
6. Export the Sales 96 worksheet as a tab-delimited text file with the name Sales 1996.TXT into the My Documents directory.
7. Widen column A and column E.
8. In the Sales 96 worksheet, filter out the record that meets the following criteria: DATE = 2/23/96. Ensure that this is the only entry showing.
9. Save the file with the same name.
10. Close the workbook.

Exercise 2

The principal at the Happy Dale High School monitors student attendance using an Excel worksheet. Your mission is to create a macro that enhances the worksheet, insert comments for the assistant principal to view when working with the attendance sheet, validate attendance numbers on the worksheet, and preview and print the worksheet in various ways. Then, the principal and assistant principal can look at the trends in the data and present the information at the next faculty meeting.

Figure 24.2 shows what the worksheet contains before you work through the instructions in this exercise.

1. Open the Expert Test Exercise 2 workbook located on the companion disk.
2. Create a macro that edits a selected cell to 16 point, Impact font. Use the shortcut key Ctrl+A. Apply the macro to cells D1 and D2.
3. Insert a comment into cell D6.
4. Validate the numbers in the Totals column on the worksheet with the following information:
   - Allow whole numbers between 3 and 5.
   - Show the input message *Any whole number between 3 and 5.*
   - Show the error message *Whole number is less than 3 or greater than 5.*
5. Change the data in cell F9 to 0. Circle the invalid data on the worksheet. Change the data in cell C9 to 1.

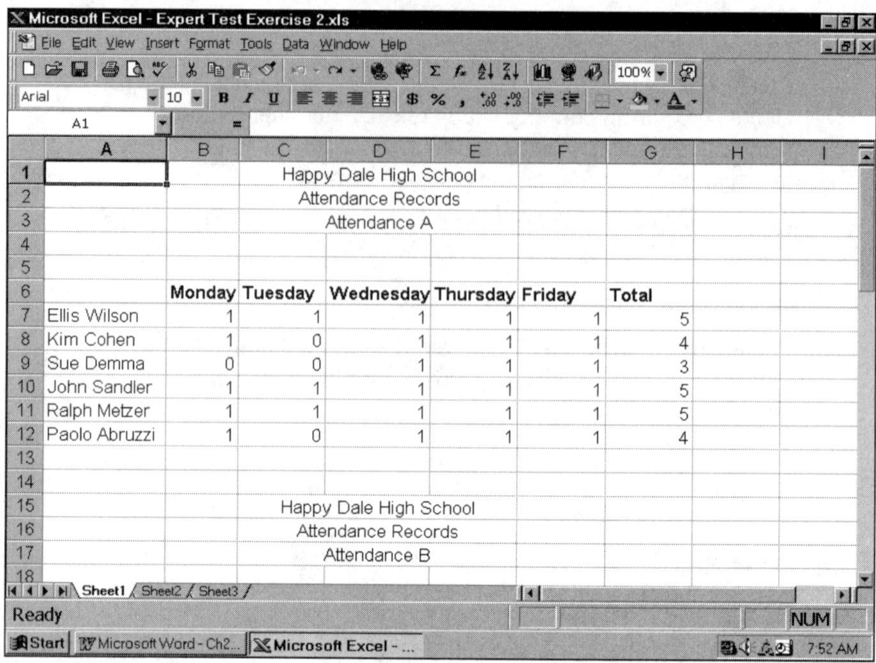

Figure 24.2 Test Exercise 2 before you begin.

6. Preview the worksheet.
7. Select cells A7 and G7. Preview the selected cells on the worksheet.
8. Print pages 2 and 3.
9. Use the Lookup Wizard to find the value for John Sandler on Wednesday. Copy the value to cell H10.
10. Save the workbook with the same name.
11. Close the workbook.

Exercise 3

The sales department at the Educational Toy Company uses two Excel worksheets to track the toy sales on a quarterly basis. Your role is to link the two sheets to calculate total toy sales for two quarters. Then, you'll need to test whether a territory has met the sales quota. Next, you'll enhance the entire worksheet to make it more attractive, so you can share the workbook with others who will review and make changes to the worksheet. Finally, after you format the worksheet, you'll save it as a template.

Figure 24.3 shows what the worksheet contains before you work through the instructions in this exercise.

1. Open the Expert Test Exercise 3 workbook located on the companion disk.
2. In cell D11 of the 1st Qtr worksheet, link the 1st Qtr sheet and the 2nd Qtr sheet to total the toy sales for both quarters.
3. Create a logical formula (**IF**) to test the condition whether a toy has met the sales quota of $150,000.
4. Use the Classic 3 style AutoFormat to format the 1st Qtr worksheet.
5. Widen column D.
6. Track the changes in the worksheet. Change the data in cell C6 to 39,000. Accept the change, highlight the change, and create a history sheet. Then, remove the workbook from the shared list.
7. Create a template from the worksheet.
8. Close the template.

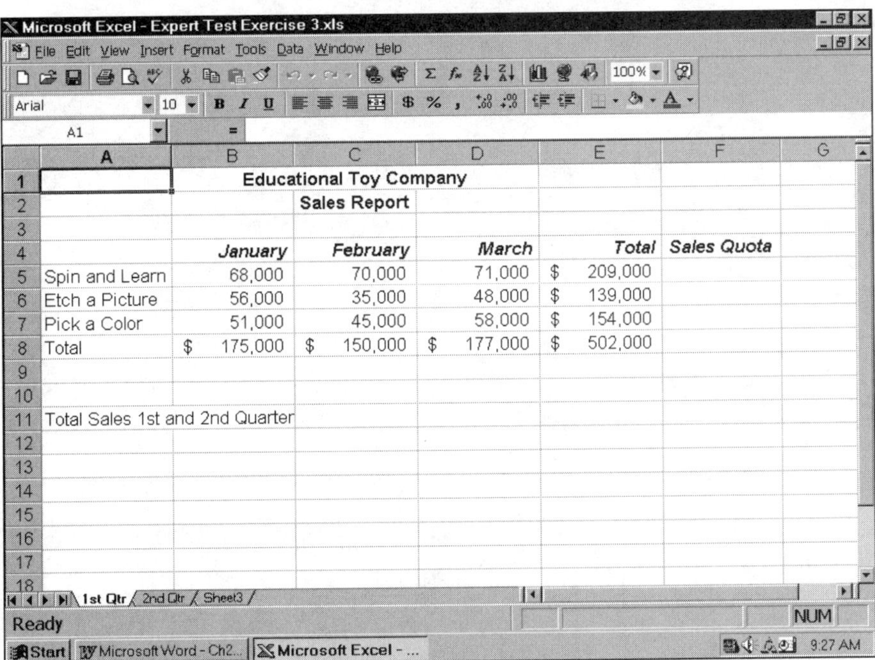

Figure 24.3 Test Exercise 3 before you begin.

25

Answers To Sample Expert Level Test

This chapter contains the answers to the Chapter 24 test exercises. Each set of answers contains step-by-step instructions. A figure shows the completed worksheet for each exercise, demonstrating what your worksheet should look like after you perform the Excel tasks necessary to complete each exercise in Chapter 24.

Exercise 1

1. Click the Open tool on the Standard toolbar, and double-click the Expert Test Exercise 1 file. This opens the Expert Test Exercise 1 workbook.
2. In the Sales 96 worksheet, select cells C5:C10. This tells Excel where you want to place conditional formatting. Choose Format|Conditional Formatting. Excel shows you the Conditional Formatting dialog box. In the Condition 1 area, leave the Cell Value Is option. Choose Less Than, and type "150" in the last box. Click the Format button. The Format Cells dialog box appears. Choose Bold and the Violet color patch. Click OK. Click the Add button. In the Condition 2 area, leave the Cell Value Is option. Choose Greater Than, and type "200" in the last box. Click the Format button. The Format Cells dialog box appears. Choose Bold, and the Lime color patch. Click OK. Then, click OK again. Click in any cell to deselect the highlighted values. You should see the Quantity field column values below 150 in one bold color and Quantity values greater than 200 in a different bold color.
3. Click on the Sales 97 sheet tab. Select the range A5:E10. Select Data|Sort. The Sort dialog box appears. Click the Sort By drop-down arrow. Choose Employee. This is the name of the first field (primary sort field) by which you want to sort. Choose the Ascending option. Click the Then By drop-down arrow. Choose Quantity. This is the name of the secondary sort field by which you want to sort. Choose the Descending option. Click OK. In the Sales 97 worksheet, Excel should sort the data by Last Name in ascending order followed by Quantity in descending order.
4. Click on the Sales 98 sheet tab. Click any cell in the Excel database. This selects a cell in the database for which you want to create a pivot table. Choose Data|PivotTable Report. The PivotTable Wizard—Step 1 Of 4 dialog box opens. The Office Assistant asks you if you want help with pivot tables. Choose No Don't Provide Help Now. In the Where Is The Data That You Want To Analyze area, choose Microsoft Excel List Or Database, if it's not already selected. This tells Excel the source of the tabular data. Click the Next button to continue.

   The PivotTable Wizard—Step 2 Of 4 dialog box appears. The Range box should display "$A$4:$E$11". Click the Next button.

   The PivotTable Wizard—Step 3 Of 4 dialog box appears. The fields appear on buttons to the right in the dialog box. These currently are the column fields. There are four areas you can define to create your PivotTable: ROW, COLUMN, DATA, and PAGE. Drag the Quantity button to the DATA area. Drag the Date button to the ROW area. Drag the Employee button to the COLUMN area. Click the Next button.

The PivotTable Wizard—Step 4 Of 4 dialog box opens. Choose Existing Worksheet. Click cell A15. You should see 'Sales 98'!$A$15 in the box. This specifies the starting cell for the PivotTable, which is the upper-left cell of the table. Click the Finish button. The PivotTable Wizard places the table in cell A15 in the Sales 98 worksheet. If the PivotTable toolbar appears, click the Close (X) button on the toolbar to close it.

5. Click the Sales 96 sheet tab. Choose Data|Get External Data. Choose Create New Query. The Choose Data Source dialog box opens. You should see <New Data Source> selected in the Databases tab. Click OK. The Create New Data Source dialog box appears. Next to Step 1, type "Sales 94". This is the data file name you're going to use for the data source. In Step 2, choose Microsoft Access Driver. This is the driver that will be used to access the data. For Step 3, click the Connect button. You should see a dialog box that lets you further define the data source. Click the Select button, double-click on the SALES94.mdb file name, and click OK. Click OK again. This closes the Create New Data Source dialog box and returns you to the Choose Data Source dialog box. The Sales 94 file should be selected. Click OK. The Query Wizard appears. Select EMPLOYEES in the Tables and Columns list. Click the right arrow button to copy all the fields for the EMPLOYEES table into the box on the right. Click the Next button. Click the Next button again. Click the Save Query button to save the query. Type "Sales 96 Query" for the query name. Specify cell A15 on the Sales 96 worksheet. The Query Wizard places the imported data in cell A15 on the Sales 96 worksheet.

6. Choose File|Save As. You should see the Save As dialog box. Click the Save As Type drop-down arrow. You should see a list of file formats. Choose Text (Tab delimited) (*.txt). In the File Name box, type "Sales 1996". In the Save In box, choose the My Documents directory. Click Save. This exports the worksheet Sales 96 as a tab-delimited text file with the name Sales 1996.TXT into the My Documents directory.

7. Double-click on the column header border between Column A and Column B. This widens Column A to accommodate the long entries in the column. Double-click on the column header border between Column E and Column F. This widens Column E, and changes the # signs in cell E11 to the correct answer $1,627.60.

8. Click on the Sales 96 sheet tab. Select any cell within the list. Select Data|Filter, and choose AutoFilter. You should see drop-down arrows next to each column heading in the list. Click the drop-down list for the Date column. The drop-down list shows the unique values for the column. Select 2/23/96. This is the criterion you want to display. You should see one record and the rest of the records are hidden. A blue arrow on the filter button indicates the filtered data is based on criteria you selected in the Date column. Select Data|Filter, and choose AutoFilter. This removes the drop-down arrows from the column headings in the list and turns off the AutoFilter feature for this list.
9. Click the Save tool on the Standard toolbar to save the workbook with the same name.

   When you finish the test procedures in Expert Test Exercise 1, your Sales 96 worksheet should look like the one in Figure 25.1.
10. Click the Close (X) button in the upper-right corner of the workbook window. This closes the workbook.

Exercise 2

1. Click the Open tool on the Standard toolbar, and double-click the Expert Test Exercise 2 file. This opens the Expert Test Exercise 2 workbook.

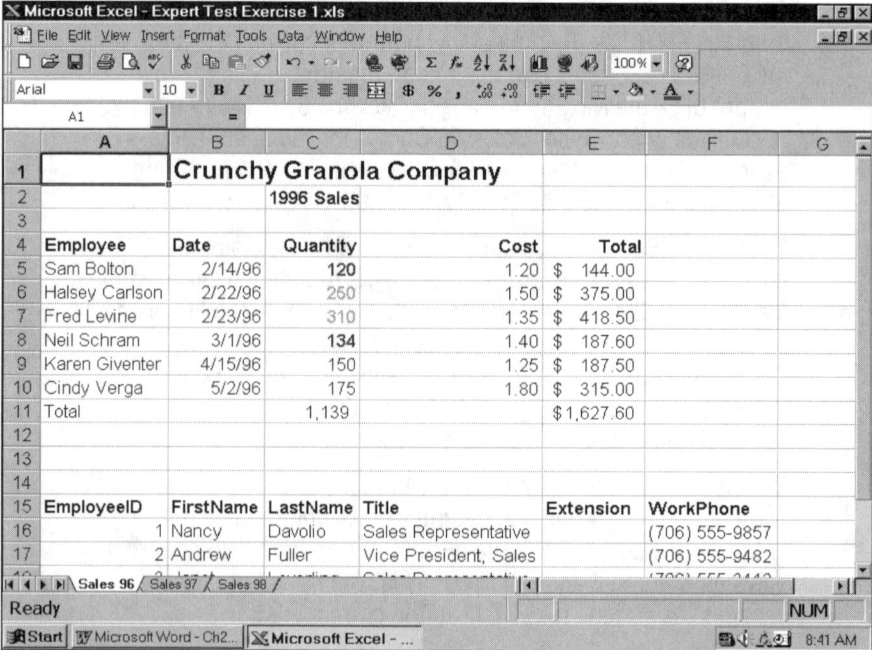

	A	B	C	D	E	F
1		Crunchy Granola Company				
2			1996 Sales			
3						
4	Employee	Date	Quantity	Cost	Total	
5	Sam Bolton	2/14/96	120	1.20	$ 144.00	
6	Halsey Carlson	2/22/96	250	1.50	$ 375.00	
7	Fred Levine	2/23/96	310	1.35	$ 418.50	
8	Neil Schram	3/1/96	134	1.40	$ 187.60	
9	Karen Giventer	4/15/96	150	1.25	$ 187.50	
10	Cindy Verga	5/2/96	175	1.80	$ 315.00	
11	Total		1,139		$1,627.60	
12						
13						
14						
15	EmployeeID	FirstName	LastName	Title	Extension	WorkPhone
16	1	Nancy	Davolio	Sales Representative		(706) 555-9857
17	2	Andrew	Fuller	Vice President, Sales		(706) 555-9482

Figure 25.1 The completed Test Exercise 1.

2. Select Tools|Macro, and choose Record New Macro. You should see the Record Macro dialog box. The default macro name, Macro1, appears in the Macro name box. In the Macro Name box, type "font". Press Tab. In the Shortcut Key box, type "a". Click OK. You should see the Recording mode indicator at the left end of the Status bar and the Stop Recording toolbar on screen. Select Format|Cells. The Format Cells dialog box opens. Click the Font tab, if necessary. In the Font list, choose Impact. In the Size list, choose 16. Click OK. Click the Stop Recording button on the Stop Recording toolbar. Select cells D1:D2. Press Ctrl+A. This applies the 16-point, Impact font to the title and subtitle.
3. Click cell D6. Choose Insert|Comment. Type a comment into the Comment box. Click any cell. Click cell E6. Choose Insert|Comment. Type a comment into the Comment box. Click any cell. This inserts a comment into cells D6 and E6.
4. Select cells G7:G12. This tells Excel which data you want to validate in the worksheet. Choose Data|Validation. Excel displays the Data Validation dialog box. In the Settings tab, click the Allow drop-down arrow, and choose Whole Number. In the Data list, make sure that Between is selected. In the Minimum box, type "3". In the Maximum box, type "5". Click the Input Message tab. In the Input Message box, type "Any whole number between 3 and 5". Click the Error Alert tab. In the Error message box, type "Any whole number less than 3 or greater than 5". Click OK. Excel shows a text box next to cell G7 that states *Any whole number between 3 and 5.*
5. Click cell F9. Type "0" and press Enter. Choose Tools|Auditing| Show Auditing Toolbar. Click the Circle Invalid Data button on the Auditing toolbar. You should see a red circle around the data in cell G9. Click cell C9. Type "1" and press Enter. Click the Circle Invalid Data button on the Auditing toolbar. The red circle should disappear in cell G9. Click the Close (X) button on the Auditing toolbar to close the toolbar.
6. Press Ctrl+P. The Print dialog box should open. Click the Preview button in the Print dialog box. You should see the worksheet in the Print Preview window. Click the vertical scroll arrow to scroll down through the worksheet. When you reach the bottom of the worksheet, click the Close button on the Preview toolbar to close the Print Preview window.
7. Click cell A7, hold down the Ctrl key, and click cell G7. This selects cells A7 and G7, two noncontiguous cells. Press Ctrl+P. The Print dialog box should open. In the Print What area, choose Selection. Click the Preview button in the Print dialog box. You

should see cell A7 in the Print Preview window. Click the Next button on the Preview toolbar. You should see cell G7 in the Print Preview window. You have now previewed selected cells on the worksheet. Click the Close button on the Preview toolbar to close the Print Preview window.

8. Press Ctrl+P. The Print dialog box should open. In the Print Range area, choose Page(s). Type "2" in the From box and type "3" in the To box. Click OK. This prints pages 2 and 3.
9. Click any cell in the Attendance A table. Choose Tools|Wizard|Lookup. The Lookup Wizard—Step 1 of 4 dialog box should open. The range $A$6:$G$12 should appear in the dialog box. This is the range you want to search, including column and row labels. Click the Next button. The Lookup Wizard—Step 2 of 4 dialog box should open. Select the Wednesday column label and the John Sandler row label. Click the Next button. The Lookup Wizard—Step 3 of 4 dialog box should open. The Copy just the formula to a single cell option should be selected. This is the option you want. Click the Next button. The Lookup Wizard—Step 4 of 4 dialog box should open. Click cell H10. Click the Finish button. Excel copies the value 1 to cell H10.
10. Click the Save tool on the Standard toolbar to save the workbook with the same name.

    When you finish the test procedures in Expert Test Exercise 2, your worksheet should look like the one in Figure 25.2.
11. Click the Close (X) button in the upper-right corner of the workbook window. This closes the workbook.

Exercise 3

1. Click the Open tool on the Standard toolbar, and double-click the Expert Test Exercise 3 file. This opens the Expert Test Exercise 3 workbook.
2. Click cell D11. This designates the cell that will contain the linking formula. Type "=". On the 1st Qtr worksheet, click cell E8. Type "+", click the 2nd Qtr sheet tab, and click cell E8. Press Enter. In cell D11, you should see the linking formula =E8+'2ndQtr'!E8, which links the data in the cell E8 on the 1st Qtr sheet to cell E8 on the 2nd Qtr sheet. This totals the toy sales on both sheets for the 1st and 2nd quarters.
3. Click cell F5. This is where you want the logical formula to appear. Type "=IF(". Click cell E5. Type ">150000,"Yes","No")". Be sure you enclose the words Yes and No in quotes in the formula. Press Enter. Click cell F5, and point to the fill handle.

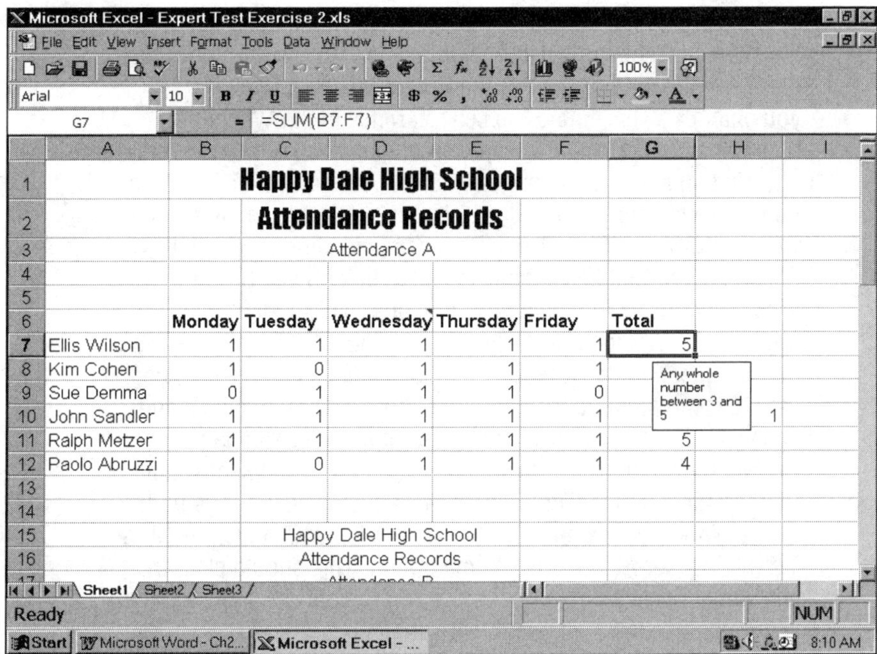

Figure 25.2 The completed Test Exercise 2.

Drag the fill handle to copy the logical formula down to cell F7. Click any cell to deselect the range. Excel shows the word Yes or No in each cell that contains a logic formula. This tests the condition whether a toy has met the sales quota.

4. Select A4:F8. These are the cells that contain the data you want to format. Choose Format|AutoFormat. The AutoFormat dialog box appears. In the Table Format list, choose Classic 3. When you select a format, Excel shows you what it will look like in the Sample area. Click OK. This formats the worksheet with the Classic 3 style AutoFormat to format the selected area of the 1st Qtr worksheet.

5. Double-click on the column header border between Column D and Column E. This widens Column D and changes the # signs in cell D11 to the correct answer $1,010,000.

6. Select Tools|Share Workbook. Excel brings up the Share Workbook dialog box. Choose the Allow Changes By More Than One User At The Same Time option. Click OK. Excel prompts you to save the workbook. Click OK. This sets up the workbook so that it can be shared with others. Click cell C9. Type 39000 and press Enter. Select Tools|Track Changes, and choose Accept Or Reject Changes. When prompted to save the workbook, click OK. Excel

opens the Select Changes To Accept Or Reject dialog box. Click the Who checkbox to select the option, and in the Who box, leave the Everyone option. Click in the Where text box. Click the cell you changed. This enters the cell reference in the Where box. Click OK. In the Accept Or Reject Changes dialog box, read the information about the change. Click the Accept button. You have now reviewed and accepted the change you made to the shared workbook. Select Tools|Track Changes, and choose Highlight Changes. The Highlight Changes dialog box opens. Click the When box, the Who box, and Where box to clear all of them. Choose List Changes On A New Sheet. Click OK. Excel inserts a History sheet in the workbook to show a history of the changes. Also, Excel highlights the change on the 1st Qtr worksheet and shows a comment where the change was made. You have now tracked the changes by showing them on the worksheet and a History sheet. Select Tools|Share Workbook. Excel brings up the Share Workbook dialog box. Choose the Allow Changes By More Than One User At The Same Time option. This should clear the checkbox. Click OK. Excel prompts you to confirm removing the workbook from shared use. Click Yes. This removes the workbook from shared use and deletes the History worksheet.

7. Select File|Save As. The Save As dialog box appears. Type a name for the template in the File Name text box. Select Template from the Save As Type drop-down list box. Click Save. This creates a template from the worksheet.

   When you finish the procedures in Test Exercise 3, your worksheet should look like the one in Figure 25.3.

8. Click the Close (X) button in the upper-right corner of the workbook window. This closes the workbook.

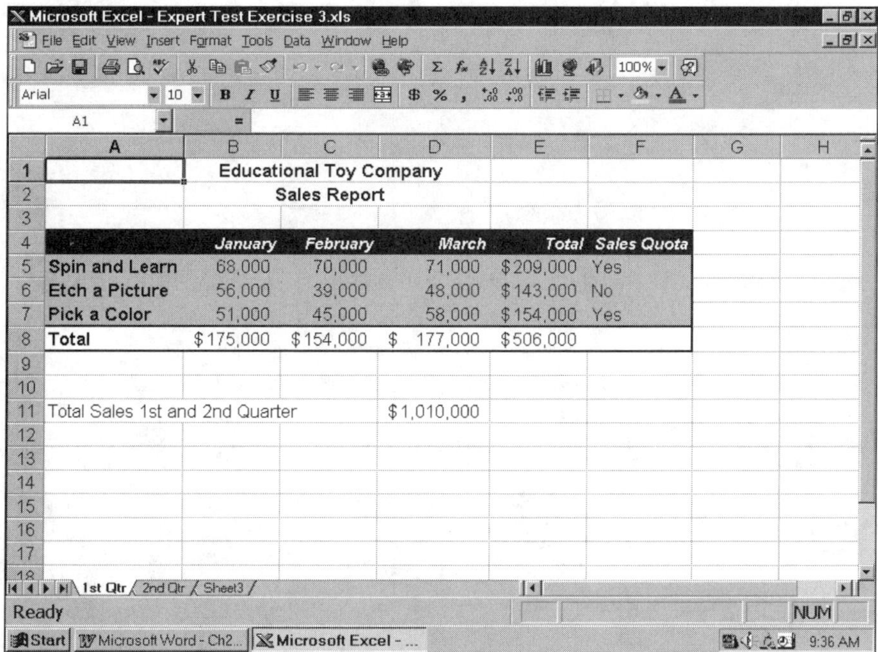

Figure 25.3 The completed Test Exercise 3.

Glossary

absolute reference—A cell reference in a formula that does not change when copied to a new location.

Access—The database management application that comes with Microsoft Office Professional Edition. Access can also be purchased independently. This book discusses Microsoft Access 97.

alignment—How data lines up in a cell. *See also* horizontal alignment and vertical alignment.

American Standard Code for Information Exchange (ASCII)—A way to code that translates letters, numbers, and symbols into a digital format.

application—A software program that you purchase and install on your computer to help with certain types of work. For example, you use a spreadsheet application to help with calculating and doing what-if analysis.

ascending order—A sort procedure in which Excel data is arranged from first to last, such as A to Z, or smallest to largest, such as 1 to 10.

AutoFormat—Predefined table formats used to enhance the appearance of a worksheet.

AutoSum—A tool on the Standard toolbar that creates a sum function by guessing what cells you want summed, based on the currently selected cell.

axis—One side of a chart. A two-dimensional chart has an X-axis (horizontal) and Y-axis (vertical). The X-axis contains all the data series and categories in the chart.

border—Line that can appear above, below, or to the left or right of a cell or range of cells.

browser—Software program, such as Internet Explorer, Netscape, CompuServe, or America Online, that can read and navigate HTML documents online.

categories—Reflect the number of elements in a data series in a chart. Normally, categories correspond to the columns that you have in your chart data, with the category labels coming from the column headings.

cell—Rectangular area in a worksheet that can hold data and represents the intersection of one row and one column. A specific cell can be identified by its row and column number, counting from the upper-left corner. For example, column A, row 4.

cell address—A specific cell can be identified by its row and column number, counting from the upper-left corner. For example, the cell located at the intersection of column A and row 4 has the cell address A4.

chart—A graphical representation that shows the relationship of numerical data, such as line charts, bar charts, and pie charts.

Chart Wizard—A series of dialog boxes that step you through the process of creating a chart on a worksheet.

clip art—Small drawings and cartoons that come with Excel 97. You can add clip art to your worksheets to add some pizzazz.

clipboard—Temporary memory storage area that holds selections of text or graphics after a cut or copy operation.

close—To shut down a workbook window or an application, most likely because you're not using it at the moment. A workbook or an application can be closed using the X close button located in the upper-right corner of the workbook or application window.

column—Vertical set of adjacent cells in a worksheet.

column heading—The name across the top of a column that describes the column's content, also known as the field name. *See also* field name.

comment—Provides detailed information about data used in a worksheet. A comment is indicated by a red triangle in the upper-right corner of the cell. The comment text is displayed in a box near the cell that contains the comment.

conditional formatting—Special formatting settings that take effect when the contents of the cell meet specified conditions.

context-sensitive help—Help feature that presents information relevant to a selected command or option.

copy—To replicate selected data onto the clipboard. Then, you can paste the data to another location.

criteria—To identify information in any field, such as the last name Anderson, so that you can locate an Excel record. (*See also* filter)

data series—The bar, pie wedges, lines, or other elements that represent plotted values in a chart. Often, data series correspond to rows of data in a worksheet.

database—A collection of data that is stored in files that allows you to retrieve, manipulate, and update the data that you store in it.

default—A standard setting that a program uses unless you specify a different setting.

descending order—A sort procedure in which Excel data is arranged from last to first, such as Z to A, or largest to smallest, such as 10 to 1.

directory—A section of a disk where files are stored, sort of like a drawer in a file cabinet. Also referred to as a folder.

drag and drop—A method used for quickly cutting and pasting data with the mouse.

export—To convert and save Excel workbook data as a different file type. (*See also* import)

field—A single piece of information in an Excel list or database, such as First Name, Last Name, Company, or Phone Number. A field can be a column item in a worksheet.

field name—The name given to a field, also known as a column heading, that helps you identify the field's contents. *See also* column heading.

file—A collection of related data that is organized in records and stored on disk with a unique name, such as an Excel worksheet, Excel list, Excel database, or Access database.

File Transfer Protocol (FTP)—The way files are sent and received over the Internet. Typically, a user needs an account on the remote system unless it allows anonymous FTP access.

fill—Copies an existing entry into any surrounding cells.

fill handle—Located in the lower-right corner of the selected cell. Used to copy an existing entry and highlight the cells into which you want to copy the entry.

filter—A feature that lets you specify criteria to display certain records in an Excel list and hide the others.

font—A collection of letters, punctuation marks, numbers, and special characters in a given typeface, weight, and size, such as Arial Bold 10-point.

font style—Changing text attributes to enhance the appearance of text, such as adding bold, italic, or underline.

footer—Special block of text that appears at the bottom of every page in a workbook.

format—Appearance of text and numbers in a worksheet. The format of any data selection or an entire workbook can easily be modified in Excel.

Format Painter—Quickly copies and pastes formats that are already used in a workbook to selected cells.

formula—Performs calculations on the data in the spreadsheet and displays the resulting value.

function—Stored formulas that perform common calculations. For example, you can add a range of cells by using the **SUM** function.

graphic object—Any element in your worksheet that isn't data, including line art, text boxes, charts, clip art, and WordArt.

hard page break—Marker within a workbook that forces the following text to start on a new page.

header—Special block of text that appears at the top of every page in a workbook.

horizontal alignment—Aligns data left, right, or center in a cell in relation to the left and right side of the cell.

hyperlink—Codes inserted in a workbook that allow you to jump from that location to another place in that workbook, another workbook, another location on the network, or the Internet.

Hypertext Markup Language (HTML)—The language that is used to define and describe the page layout of documents displayed in a World Wide Web browser.

icon—Graphic symbol or shape that can be clicked to activate an operation or program.

import—To convert and load a file that you created in one program into a different program. *See also* export.

insertion point—Blinking vertical bar in a cell or the formula bar that indicates where typed-in characters or inserted graphics will appear. The insertion point's location can be reset to the mouse pointer's position with a single click.

Internet—The global network of computers that enable some or all of the following: exchange of email messages, files, Usenet newsgroups, and World Wide Web pages. Also known as the Net.

intranet—An internal private network at a company that uses the same protocols and standards as the Internet network.

key—One or more fields used for criteria by which you sort data in an Excel list.

label—Text in a spreadsheet that identifies the data and helps document the worksheet. For example, column headings and row headings.

legend—Defines the separate elements of a chart. For example, the legend for an area chart shows what each area represents.

list box—Scrollable list (often drop-down) of options that you can choose from. List boxes appear in the Standard and Formatting toolbars and many dialog boxes.

lookup function—A formula that searches for values within tables or lists.

macro—Special instructions that perform any series of commands or actions for you in Excel.

map—A geographical representation of data in an Excel worksheet.

menu—List of related commands. Each name in the menu bar represents a different menu that drops down when its name is clicked.

menu bar—Horizontal bar near the top of a window, just below the title bar, that contains one or more menu names.

mode indicator—Information about the current activity in the Status bar along the bottom edge of the program window. For example, Ready mode indicates that Excel is ready for you to enter data or perform a command, and Recording indicates that a macro recorder is turned on.

move—To transfer a selection of data in one location and place it somewhere else.

Net—Another term for the Internet. *See also* Internet.

noncontiguous range—Multiple selected cells or ranges that aren't next to each other.

Normal—Name of the global template in Excel. Also the name of a default style for data.

Office Assistant—Excel 97's help program, which replaces Excel 95's Answer Wizard.

operator—A character (or characters) used to perform an operation or comparison. For example, + is the operator used for addition.

orientation alignment—Flips data sideways or prints it from top to bottom rather than left to right. Also rotates data to a specified number of degrees.

page break—Determines where one page begins and another ends, based on the paper size, margins, and selected print area.

page break preview—Displays how a document will print with the current page breaks.

points—Measure of type size based on the height of capital letters. One inch equals 72 points. Abbreviation is pt or pts.

preview—Displays how a page will appear when printed.

query—The capability to retrieve database information in a report, based on criteria you specify.

Query Wizard—Steps you through a series of dialog boxes to perform sort operations and simple queries in an Excel list and an external database.

range—A group of contiguous connected cells that can all be in a column, row, or any combination of columns and rows.

range name—A name assigned to a range. Naming a cell range makes it easier to reference cells in formulas, as well as cut, copy, move, and print data.

record—Group of information (fields) about one item or person. For instance, a record might include a person's name, address, city, state, and ZIP code.

relative reference—A cell reference in a formula that is adjusted when the formula is copied to a new location.

row—Horizontal set of adjacent cells in a table.

selection—Designated portion of a worksheet, from a single cell to an entire worksheet, that is to be modified by a subsequent operation. Generally, a selection is displayed in highlighted or reverse color.

selection handle—One of eight small black squares around the edge of a graphic. Resizing is accomplished by dragging any of these handles.

shading—An overall color and/or a pattern to lay on top of the color for selected cells that add a simple but dramatic effect to a worksheet.

sheet tabs—Tabs attached to the bottom of each worksheet. You use sheet tabs to move among worksheets in a workbook. By default, sheet tabs identify each worksheet with the name Sheet# and are numbered starting with the number 1. You can rename sheet tabs.

soft page break—Marker inserted into a worksheet by the program to indicate where a full page ends and a new page begins. The locations of the soft page breaks are automatically adjusted when data is added to or deleted from a worksheet.

sorting—A feature that arranges the data alphabetically and numerically in ascending or descending order, making it easy to locate the data you want.

split bar—Splits the sheet tabs from the horizontal scroll bar that displays more or fewer sheet tabs in a workbook.

status bar—Row of miscellaneous information along the bottom edge of the program window. This information includes the location of the insertion point and the status of certain operations, such as Extend Selection or Recording that appear only during the operations.

style—Defined and named set of formatting attributes that can be applied to any range of cells in one step. Each style must be given a unique name.

template—Generic, model workbook that can consist of basic formatting, styles, text, numbers, and/or graphics. Each newly created workbook must be based on a template. When a new workbook is created, Excel bases it on the default template called NORMAL.DOT.

text box—Dialog box area where a user types input.

title bar—Horizontal band along the top of a window, containing the window's name. Dragging the title bar moves the entire window.

toolbar—Usually located near the top, bottom, or side of a program window. This band of icons allows quick access to Excel operations.

Uniform Resource Locator (URL)—Standardized way in which any resource is identified within a Web document or to a Web browser. Most URLs consist of the service, host name, and directory path. For example, **http://www.amazon.com**.

validation—Comparing data entered against a predefined format in an Excel list or database.

value—A number in a spreadsheet.

vertical alignment—Aligns data up, down, or centered in a cell in relation to the top and bottom of the cell.

Web—*See* World Wide Web.

window—An area on your desktop that includes a variety of controls, informational displays, and work space for a program or document.

workbook—Organized set of data, charts, macros, or graphic elements that is identified by a single name. Each workbook consists of three sheets. The electronic form of a workbook stored on disk is called a file.

worksheet—Arrangement of alphabetic and/or numeric information, organized into rows, columns, and cells within a workbook.

World Wide Web—A program that organizes millions of documents, thousands of sites, and hundreds of indexes on the Internet. The Web is a fluid and often surprising collection of information and activity. Also called WWW.

wrap text—Continues data entry to the next line within a cell without changing the width of the cell.

WWW—*See* World Wide Web.

X close button—A button with an X on it in the upper-right corner of most Windows applications and every Excel 97 window. Click the X close button to close the program, file, or dialog box.

Index

B

C

D

E

F

G

H

I

K

L

M

P

Q

R

S

T

U

V

W

X

Y

Z

GET ON THE ROAD TO CERTIFICATION SUCCESS

LEARN IT!

EXAM PREPS are comprehensive and interactive (book and CD) study guides specifically designed to work with our popular *Exam Crams*. Our interactive study system goes one step further than other study guides by providing complete exam simulations that really work, plus thought-provoking case projects so that you can apply what you know.

ISBN: 1-57610-263-7 • $44.99 U.S., $62.99 CAN • Available Now

PASS IT!

EXAM CRAMS are 100% focused on what you need to know to pass an exam. Professionals, around the world, rate *Exam Cram* as the #1 exam guide.

> "I just finished writing and passing my Networking Essentials exam (70-058). I really couldn't have done it without the aid of the Exam Cram Networking Essentials book. I actually failed my first attempt at this exam about ten days ago, and based on the area where I did poorly, I studied this area in the book. Not only did I pass that part of the test on the second exam, I got 100%!!!! I will definitely be purchasing the whole line of books for my future MSCE exams."
>
> —*Ken Campbell*, Consultant

ISBN: 1-57610-229-7 • $29.99 U.S., $41.99 CAN • Available Now

From the Publisher of the bestselling Exam Cram Guides!
ON SITE
The Ultimate On-the-Job Solution Finder
Microsoft EXCHANGE SERVER 5.5
PLANNING DEPLOYMENT CONFIGURATION TROUBLESHOOTING
CD-ROM features deployment tools and utilities
Shannon R. Turlington and Kevin Schuler
Certification Insider Press

DO IT!

ON SITE books guide you through real-world, on-the-job planning, deployment, configuration, and troubleshooting challenges. This "in-the-thick-of-it-all" approach helps you move flawlessly through system setup, snafus, hiccups, and flare-ups. You'll find unique editorial features including decision trees, special contents pages, troubleshooting sections, and design and implementation checklists that will help you solve critical problems.

ISBN: 1-57610-258-0 • $39.99 U.S., $55.99 CAN • Available Now

We offer a complete line of best-selling guides for MCSE and MCSD Certification Professionals available at bookstores and computer stores nationwide.

Telephone 800.410.0192 • International callers 602.483.0192

www.coriolis.com

"Taking an exam without an Exam Cram book is worse than going to work without my trousers!"
– Christian, U.K.
ISBN: 1-57610-251-3
$29.99 U.S.
Available Now
ISBN: 1-57610-241-6
$59.99 U.S.
Available Now
"Thank you for writing and making available the valuable Exam Cram series of books. I not only passed the NT Server 4 in the Enterprise exam but also scored very high. I give credit to the very readable and understandable Exam Cram books."
—Richard Peppel
"I just wanted to thank you for writing the Exam Cram series of books. I have used them solely for studying for my tests (five in all.) I find that Exam Cram makes for a passing grade."
—Jack R. Watson
"The Exam Crams are by far the best studying companions! Since discovering your study guides, I have been able to cut my study time in half. Thank you!"
—Michael Dominguez, MCSE
EXAM CRAM
EXAM PREP
Certification Insider™ Press
CORIOLIS™

What's On The Companion Disk?

The companion disk contains the Excel documents needed to perform all tasks, practice exercises, and practice tests discussed in the book. These files are compressed in a zip format.

See the readme file located on the disk for more information about using these files.

Software Requirements:

- Excel 97
- Access 97
- WinZip or other file compression program

Hardware Requirements:

- Platform—Intel and compatible 486/66.
- Microsoft Windows 95, Windows 98, or Windows NT
- RAM: 8MB of memory minimum (16MB recommended)